W9-CCE-042

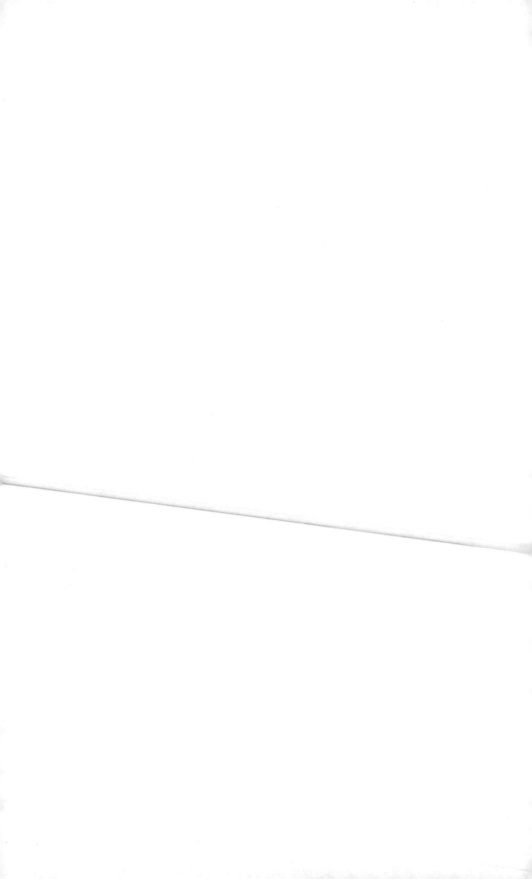

U.S. LAND AND NATURAL RESOURCES POLICY

U.S. LAND AND NATURAL RESOURCES POLICY

A Public Issues Handbook

Gary C. Bryner

GREENWOOD PRESS
Westport, Connecticut • London

Library of Congress Cataloging-in-Publication Data

Bryner, Gary C., 1951–
    U.S. land and natural resources policy : a public issues handbook
    Gary C. Bryner.
      p. cm.
    Includes bibliographical references and index.
    ISBN 0–313–29688–X (alk. paper)
    I. Public lands—Government policy—United States. 2. Natural
resources—Government policy—United States. 3. Public lands—
United States—Management. 4. Natural resources—United States—
Management. 5. Land use—Government policy—United States.
I. Title. II. Title: US land and resource policy management.
HD216.B79 1998
333.1'0973—DC21   97–16716

British Library Cataloguing in Publication Data is available.

Copyright © 1998 by Gary C. Bryner

All rights reserved. No portion of this book may be
reproduced, by any process or technique, without the
express written consent of the publisher.

Library of Congress Catalog Card Number: 97–16716
ISBN: 0–313–29688–X

First published in 1998

Greenwood Press, 88 Post Road West, Westport, CT 06881
An imprint of Greenwood Publishing Group, Inc.

Printed in the United States of America

The paper used in this book complies with the
Permanent Paper Standard issued by the National
Information Standards Organization (Z39.48–1984).

10 9 8 7 6 5 4 3 2 1

ain
HD
216
B79
1998

To Jonathan

Contents

Tables

Preface

Public lands are tremendously important to the economic, cultural, and personal lives of Americans. These lands are a primary source of the nation's natural resource wealth and a major contributor to economic activity. Just as important, they provide opportunities for recreation, reflection, spiritual renewal, and escape from the pressures of life. Because they play such a prominent position in our lives, the debate over how they should be used has engendered considerable controversy. There is great tension between demands for preservation and consumption, local control and national policies, and private property and public purposes.

Public lands issues are particularly controversial in the West because so much of the land is owned by the federal government. For several years, westerners have organized "sagebrush rebellions"—political campaigns and litigation strategies aimed at increasing local control over federal lands in their states. The growing interest in protection of private property rights affected by environmental regulations has heightened concern over the future of public lands policy. The loss of pristine lands, the decline of biodiversity, and the declining supply of natural resources also heighten the stakes surrounding public lands policy. The election of Bill Clinton in 1992 and the selection of Bruce Babbitt as Secretary of Interior in 1993 led to a flurry of legislative and administrative proposals to change public lands policy. Promises to change grazing, mining, timber, water, and wilderness policy were met with tremendous opposition, and little new legislation was enacted during the first term of the Clinton administration. These issues continue to occupy a major place on the policy agenda as the century draws to a close.

The purpose of this book is to bring together the relevant data and to outline the major issues that are at the heart of the debate over public lands. The book seeks to contribute to the debate and to improved policy making in general by providing a comprehensive and systematic assessment of the issues—the environmental conditions, problems, and trends; the major laws and regulations; the policy-making structure; and the broader political context in which this debate takes place. I hope readers will find in the book the data and analyses of issues that will help them understand the debate over public lands, the policy options confronting us, and the strengths and weaknesses of alternative positions and that will encourage them to enter the debate and, in so doing, help reinvigorate the role of public participation in the policy-making process. While I offer my own conclusions, I hope the book will be useful to those who take different positions.

The chapters outline information about the laws and policies currently in place and then discuss different ways of assessing how well the current policies are working and what alternatives are being considered. The debate over policy options surrounding public lands and natural resource policy poses daunting challenges for policy analysis, particularly because these policies implicate strongly held normative values. The traditional model of policy analysis centers on one key question, Does the policy at issue accomplish the objectives established for it?[1] Policy analysis here is understood as part of a rational enterprise of identifying a problem, formulating remedial goals, identifying possible consequences and assigning a value to each, and selecting the optimal alternative. Analysis focuses on the extent to which policy interventions have caused or will cause the desired outcome.[2] The policy itself may specify the criteria by which the policy is to be assessed or external criteria such as cost-benefit analysis, cost-effectiveness, comparative cost-efficiency, or other measures may be applied.

A second analytic approach places the policy effort in a broader context and asks to what extent the policy goal is relevant to the problem at which it is aimed. Will the promised policy actually solve the problem? How appropriate are the goals, given the nature of the problems? Policies may accomplish their goals rather efficiently and effectively, but if the goals are misdirected or fail to center on the problems to be solved, the policy effort will ultimately fail. This approach also focuses attention on the conflicting policy objectives we pursue and how efforts aimed at one set of goals may conflict with others.[3] For public lands and natural resources, ecological principles and imperatives provide the relevant context: how sound are the policies and their underlying assumptions, given the goal of preserving a healthy ecosystem for current and future generations?

Part of this broader analysis of policy goals also focuses on the political feasibility of the policy goals and their implementation. The more consonant policies are with the interests of political interests and institutions, the more likely there will be support for their effective implementation. Conversely, policies that challenge powerful or entrenched interests may still successfully achieve their goals, but policymakers and advocates need to be aware of the challenges they face in implementing these policies. Part of the inquiry is the consequences of specific policy efforts for the long-term capacity of politics and government. The cumulative impact of public policies shapes the prospects for future policy efforts and the long-term ability of government to accomplish the important purposes we have for collective action.[4]

Policy goals must also be assessed in terms of the impact of the policy effort on the broader society. To what extent do policy goals affect or contribute to important societal values? Are the policy goals consistent with fundamental societal commitments to free markets, equality, justice, fairness, individual rights, and other essential commitments of the polity? However, there may be little agreement over core public values or at least how they come together in assessing public policies. Since these fundamental social commitments are themselves to some extent inconsistent, successful policies will require a careful balancing of competing public concerns.[5]

Public lands and natural resource policies in place, as well as proposed policies, can all be assessed from this framework of evaluating the achievement of policy goals, the appropriateness of the goals themselves, the political implications, and the impacts on broad societal values. Using a combination of analytic approaches permits the analysis to examine normative and empirical issues, to go beyond a narrow technical discourse to a much broader examination of public policy. Using a common framework can also help aggregate the analysis of the different chapters in this book as well as compare the analysis here with other studies.

The outline of the book is as follows. Chapter 1 provides an overview of the politics of public lands and focuses in particular on the controversies in the West over land use, the tremendous challenge on public lands posed by the growing demand for recreational opportunities, the growing movement to protect private property from government regulation, the public lands reform agenda of the Clinton administration, and the tension between preservation and consumptive use of public lands and natural resources.

Chapter 2 traces the history and evolution of public lands and highlights the underlying values and concerns that have been reflected in major legislation and other policy developments.

Chapter 3 reviews the major provisions of federal public lands and natural resources laws and explores their interaction with environmental pollution, laws, property law, state and local policies and the interaction of federal land use and state law, and other relevant legal issues. It also includes a description of the federal departments, agencies, and bureaus responsible for public lands policies.

Chapters 4 through 9 focus on the key issues in public lands policy. Each chapter begins with a brief review of the goals and provisions of the current public lands policies and then turns to an assessment of how well those goals are achieved, how appropriate the goals are, and what alternative policy actions and goals should be considered. The specific topics for each chapter are as follows:

Chapter 4: biodiversity and endangered species

Chapter 5: forests and logging

Chapter 6: grazing

Chapter 7: mining and energy

Chapter 8: water resources

Chapter 9: wilderness, national parks, recreation areas

Chapter 10 summarizes the analyses in Chapters 4 through 9 and explores the values underlying the debate over public lands and natural resource policy.

NOTES

1. The framework outlined here is based on Frank Fischer, *Evaluating Public Policy* (Chicago: Nelson Hall, 1995).

2. For a discussion of these and related issues, see Edith Stokey and Richard Zeckhauser, *A Primer for Policy Analysis* (New York: W. W. Norton, 1978).

3. For a useful examination of assessing the impact of policies, see Lawrence B. Mohr, *Impact Analysis for Program Evaluation* (Pacific Grove, CA: Brooks Cole, 1988).

4. See Helen Ingram and Steven Rathgeb Smith, eds., *Public Policy for Democracy* (Washington, DC: Brookings Institution, 1993).

5. See Robert A. Heineman, William T. Bluhm, Steven A. Peterson, and Edward N. Kearny, *The World of the Policy Analyst: Rationality, Values, and Politics* (Chatham, NJ: Chatham House, 1990), for a study of how philosophical and ethical issues might be addressed in policy analysis.

Acknowledgments

I benefitted greatly from a great deal of help in writing this book. Two research assistants at Brigham Young University, Tyler Rushforth and Margaret Woolley, helped compile much of the information. Research support from the College of Family, Home, and Social Sciences at BYU was indispensable. I have had the great fortune to teach a course on natural resource policy with Professor Sam Rushforth, a botanist, and I am greatly indebted to him for all I have learned from him. I completed the project while I was a visiting scholar at the Natural Resources Law Center at the University of Colorado School of Law, and those delightful surroundings provided a wonderful setting in which to work. Several officials in the Department of the Interior and other federal agencies and on congressional committee staffs were most helpful in locating materials. The endnotes represent the great debt I owe to scholars and policy makers who have written about public lands and natural resource policy. Mildred Vasan, Nita H. Romer, Matt Christianson, Susan B. Prusak and others at Greenwood Press were a pleasure to work with. My family, as always, contributed to this book in ways they are not aware. I am particularly grateful for my son Jonathan's interest in nature and his sensitivity to the world around us, and I dedicate this book to him.

1

The Debate Over Public Lands and Natural Resource Policy

The primary focus of federal public lands and natural resource policy is on the eleven states in the western United States that contain 370 million acres of federal land, lands rich in minerals and timber; vast expanses of plains and grasslands, towering mountains, a rich array of plant and animal life, and some of the most wild, inaccessible lands on earth. Throughout most of the nineteenth century, Congress encouraged resource development in the West and provided free access to public lands. Westerners helped fulfill the young nation's manifest destiny as well as made their own fortune as they pushed cities, railroads, and settlements westward.

By 1872, however, the era of unrestrained growth and expansion began to draw to a close when Congress withdrew some lands from development and created the first national park. The creation of national forests and other protected areas followed as conservationists warned of threats to natural treasures. Not everyone accepted the idea that the resources of the West were finite. Those who saw in the plains, plateaus, and peaks of the West limitless resources rebelled against the idea of preserving the lands for development and robbing the nation of their wealth. One hundred and twenty-five years later, the debate continues: should some lands be set aside, untouched by the great reaping of resources? If so, which ones? Or should the land continue to provide the raw materials to fuel the American economy? Two issues help provide the context for the policy discussions that follow. First, the West is in the middle of a major transformation that began several decades ago and has important implications for public lands and natural resource policy. Some observers argue that there really are two Wests, the old and the new, and they represent incompatible views about what the West should become. Second, public lands policy clashes with the individualism and libertarian values Americans hold dear. The idea of preserving public lands for the needs of current and future generations is a tenuous one in American public philosophy and its commitment to the pursuit of self-interest. Both issues are explored later and provide the context for a review of the history and evolution of public lands policy, the subject of Chapter 2, as well as the specific issues discussed in subsequent chapters.

THE CHANGING AMERICAN WEST

The American West has been undergoing dramatic change over the past three decades, but national policymakers have been slow to respond. The election of Bill Clinton in 1992 and the confirmation of Bruce Babbitt as secretary of the interior in 1993 signaled the beginning of a major effort to revise public lands policies that have been in place for decades and longer; some policies have remained in place for more than a century. These policies have largely been insulated from change because of the confluence of strong interests: miners, ranchers, grazers, and loggers wanted access to raw materials and government subsidies to facilitate their harvesting, and the rest of the country wanted the natural resources at the lowest prices possible. However, that relationship began to unravel by the late 1960s and 1970s as more and more Americans began to be concerned about the loss of undeveloped lands, pristine areas, opportunities for outdoor recreation, protection of biodiversity, and preservation of natural resources.

Until that time, there was little disagreement among the dominant political interests: resource extraction, not preservation, was the primary purpose of public lands and natural resource policy. Preservationists were small in number and influence, and while they won some important victories, their efforts were overwhelmed by the clout of extractive industries and general public support for resource extraction, or at least indifference. Westerners demanded and got broad discretion to use public lands in pursuit of wealth. Resource development was the primary goal, and preservation was only a weak secondary concern. But the West is no longer dominated by those interests. An entire generation of preservationists, recreationists, environmentalists, and others now competes with the developers for control over the western public lands. Even nonwesterners have become passionate advocates for preservation. The economic, social, and environmental changes that led to the demand for these reforms will only accelerate during the next decades, and the issues will remain difficult and contentious. Some matters will become even more difficult to resolve as population pressures increase, and development continues to take its toll on natural resources. The demand for preservation and recreation will continue to grow. Decisions made during the next few years are critical for the future of the West. These decisions will determine whether the West is transformed in ways that ensure that natural resource use and development are environmentally sustainable or whether short-term profiteers will irreparably damage public lands, antigovernment sentiment will degenerate into increased violence, and conflict will make compromise impossible between local residents who have lived on public lands for generations and have long-standing expectations concerning their access to these lands against others who believe these lands are priceless national and international endowments that must be preserved for current and future generations at almost any cost.

Until the last few decades, people came to the West primarily for the natural resources that the lands contained. They left the urban comforts, refinements, and amenities for the pursuit of wealth and independence. Migrants to the late twentieth-century West now come to escape urban crime, pollution, and decay and seek solitude and recreation. The clashes in values could not be more striking. Neither the newcomers nor the longtime residents are monolithic. Some immigrants are as fearful of a strong federal government as are those who have worked public lands for generations. Some preservationists have been working to protect wild lands from development for decades, joined by others who have recently moved to the West.

Since the 1970s, the Great Basin states have grown faster than the rest of the country. Between 1980 and 1990 nonagricultural jobs increased by 56.1 percent in Nevada, 41.2 percent in Arizona, 31.0 percent in Utah, and 26.2 percent in New Mexico; in the United States as a whole, jobs grew by 22.0 percent. Population grew during the same decade by 50.7 percent in Nevada, 35.3 percent in Arizona, 18.3 percent in Utah, 16.8 percent in New Mexico, and 9.8 percent in the entire nation. High levels of growth present the typical challenges of traffic and air pollution, limited supplies of water, rising costs of housing, and increasing taxes. The natural beauty of spectacular national parks in Utah and Arizona, gambling in Nevada, a mild climate, a rural lifestyle, relatively low taxes, and other factors all draw people to the Southwest, and communications technologies makes it possible to live far from commercial centers.[1] Growth has been faster in areas containing public lands than in other regions: western counties that contain federal wilderness lands grew two to three times faster than all other counties during the 1970s and early 1980s.[2]

Previous economic booms in the West have been fueled by the development of energy and other natural resources. Growth in the 1980s and 1990s has been led by high-tech, service, and recreation industries. A study of the economic trends affecting the Colorado Plateau done for the Grand Canyon Trust documented the dramatic shift in the West during the past thirty years from resource-based to service industries such as tourism: "Open air, scenic beauty, pristine air and water, and premier parks and wilderness areas, all are pillars of much new economic activity on, and demographic migration to, the plateau." These trends are expected to accelerate during the next twenty years at a much faster rate than during the past two decades.[3] Earnings from service-based industries have increased over the past twenty-five years, as resource industries have become comparatively less important.[4]

Year	Resource-based earnings, $ billions	Manufacturing-based earnings, $ billions	Service-based earnings, $ billions
1970	15.9	7.2	76.4
1980	20.3	6.4	72.3
1990	11.3	6.4	80.3
1992	10.3	6.4	82.3

For westerners, service industries are a much more important source of employment and earnings than resource industries:[5]

Sector	% of total employment	% of total income
Farm employment	3.5	2.6
Service industries supporting agriculture	1.0	0.6
Mining	3.2	7.2
Manufacturing	5.4	6.4
Service-based industries	86.1	83.2

Policy Challenges

As the West undergoes a transition from resource extraction to recreation, tourism, species protection, and preservation, many laws are outdated and must be revised to reflect the new realities of urbanization and environmentalism. Urban sprawl and the resultant problems of air pollution, transportation gridlock, and loss of farmlands and open spaces are common problems across the West. A higher percentage of Utahns live in urban areas than do people in many eastern states. New suburbs are being built in Las Vegas without securing an adequate water supply. Some subdivisions in the Denver area are expected to run out of water within ten years. Arizona has averaged paving or otherwise developing the equivalent of one acre of land an hour for the past several years. Phoenix has more canals than Venice. Communities throughout the West vow not to become another California, yet they encourage urban sprawl by building new roads, offering cheap land, and imposing low taxes and minimal planning.[6]

The Colorado Plateau is part of a natural, economic, and social region, but policy making is difficult because political authority is so fragmented, divided among four states, thirty-one counties, numerous federal agencies, Native American tribes, and more than 200 communities. A major challenge is to overcome this fragmentation and develop new institutions, relationships, channels of communication, common goals, shared vision, increased cooperation, and creative new solutions to old problems.[7]

Political leaders are caught in the middle of the debate between the old and new West. Senator Harry Reid (D-NV) observed: ''The new West doesn't sweep the old West under the rug, but the new West recognizes that there is more to the states of Nevada and Idaho and Montana and Colorado than grazing cattle. No one wants to take away a person's livelihood, but we recognize that Nevada has changed. The whole West has changed." Representative Gerry E. Studds (D-MA), former chair of the House Merchant Marine and Fisheries Committee, argued: "The western interests are used to people at the Interior Department who view their role as to sell the nation's resources at the cheapest possible price, rather than to be their steward. Now they have a real steward, and they're understandably concerned."[8] Senator Max Baucus (D-MT) noted that 95 percent of Montana's economy is based on the extraction of natural resources: "It's true that values are changing in the West. But in Montana, it's timber, it's mining, it's agriculture, it's livestock. That's the economy." Senator Ben Nighthorse Campbell (R-CO), responding to Secretary of Interior Babbitt's initiatives, argued, "He's not supposed to be advocating the destruction of all these western jobs any more than [Reagan administration interior secretary] Jim Watt should have been advocating the destruction of the environment."[9]

There seems to be little room for compromise. In a typical case, for example, policymakers have been caught between those who sought to protect the largest remaining forest wilderness area in the Nez Perce National Forest and those who depended on the forest for logging jobs.[10] Interior Secretary Babbitt defended himself against the charge that he is insensitive to the jobs lost by the timber industry: "The forest plan for the Pacific Northwest is going to protect the jobs of 50,000 salmon fishermen whose jobs were being driven to extinction by the cut-and-run timber practices of the logging companies. These are small businessmen who were there a long time before anybody else." But industry representatives disagree. Michael J. Brown, lobbyist for the Gold Institute, said: "The public lands are used to employ large sections of the population. I don't hear the Interior Department talk about jobs a lot. They don't see that part of their agenda." William G. Myers of the National Cattlemen's Association said that Babbitt's proposals "are scaring the daylights out of the folks that have to make a living day in and day out."[11]

New Democrats were expected to make strong inroads in the West as young professionals who were fiscal conservatives, social liberals, and environmentalists moved into the area. Clinton carried some states in 1992, but there was some backlash in the 1994 election, and much of the blame was focused on Secretary of Interior Bruce Babbitt for pushing too far too fast and giving environmentalists too much say in developing policy reforms.[12] After 1994, it appeared that the West was moving clearly toward the Republicans. However, in 1996, Democrats gained back some of the ground they had lost in the previous elections: Clinton was the first Democrat since Harry S Truman to win Arizona in a presidential election. He also won in California, by thirteen percentage points; Nevada, but by only one point; New Mexico by eight points; Oregon by ten; and Washington by fifteen (he lost Colorado, Idaho, Montana, and Utah). But Republicans continue to dominate the Senate in western states. Republicans were elected or reelected to the Senate in Alaska, Colorado, Idaho, New Mexico, Oregon, and Wyoming. Democrats won only in Montana and South Dakota.[13] Democrats regained the majority in the California legislature and increased the number of state legislative chambers nationwide under their control from forty-six to forty-nine, while the Republican-controlled chambers fell from fifty to forty-four.[14] The Republicans and Democrats split the 1996 election in the West, and it is difficult to predict in what political direction, if any, the region will move.

One prediction seems safe but very disconcerting: western politics will become more contentious.[15] Conflicts between local residents and environmental activists occur throughout the West. Some have resulted in violence; most are ripe with tension. The standoff between Earth First! and logging interests in Dixie, Idaho, for example, had all the drama of monkey wrenching—sabotaging a D-8 Caterpillar tractor, spiking trees, burying activists up to their chests in a logging road to block traffic, and local residents who threatened to lasso activists walking along Main Street and sported T-shirts imprinted with the silhouette of a logger and the phrase, "Earth First! We'll log the other planets later." County commissioners in Catron County, New Mexico, passed an ordinance stating that federal officials did not have authority over grazing permits on federal lands and one requiring that "every head of household . . . is required [to have] a firearm of their choice, together with ammunition." One activist warned that if federal officials reduced his grazing rights, "there will be 100 people out there with guns to meet you."[16]

Tensions grew in 1995 as violent acts were aimed at Forest Service officials. In March, a small bomb blew out the windows in a district office in Carson City, Nevada. Activists threatened to respond violently when a Forest Service ranger cited a rancher for illegally piping water from the national forest to his land. Ranchers argued they were "fighting for their survival." Said one Nevadan: "We don't know what to do but to fight. If we can't use the land, we can't exist."[17] The militia movement promoted antigovernment sentiment in the West. Many are hostile toward government and heavily armed, have served in the military, and are unemployed or struggling financially.[18] In response, the Bureau of Land Management issued a "County Supremacy Safety Ordinance" for employees that required they keep in radio contact, notify supervisors of their destination, and avoid areas of known conflict.[19]

Other activists threatened, "When the hour strikes, there will be public officials dead in the street," or "We have a militia of 10,000 and if we can't beat you at the ballot box, we'll beat you with a bullet." Federal officials who try to enforce laws are met with armed resistance. Much of the anger is aimed at the endangered species act. Wrote one wise use activist to a Fish and Wildlife official: "There are literally thousands of groups in our land who, like the Reserve (New Mexico) group, could join in a common cause to rid themselves of the curse of the Endangered Species Act. I repeat that legislation must either be modified or repealed in its entirety. If not, you will be faced with rioting, bloodshed, rebellion and conflict that could make the Serbia-Bosnia affair look like a Sunday picnic.''[20]

A few public lands activists have also merged with Christian Patriots and other antigovernment groups. These groups center on federal public lands agents but challenge the entire federal government as well as the United Nations and international bankers. They charge that a proposed international park along the United States–Canada border is designed to become a staging area for a United Nations invasion of the United States.[21] They warn local officials not to sit in front of their living room windows. They threaten that their rebellion "will go to the end. It's going to be civil war if things don't change."

Some employees of federal agencies and others have complained that the federal response has been too timid in responding to threats of violence. Jeff DeBonis, director of the Public Employees for Environmental Responsibility, charged that the Clinton administration failed to take firm action to quell the rebellion and seek criminal penalties or civil monetary damages against county officials who threatened federal employees. Numerous criminal referrals in the Interior Department for damaging natural resources have not been prosecuted. Agency officials have taken a defensive mode rather than defending their employees against unlawful aggression.[22]

The tensions surrounding public lands and natural resources are particularly poignant, as people are struggling to hold on to a frontier lifestyle that seems destined for extinction. The movement taps into a much broader frustration with the federal government that includes unpopular policies such as unfunded mandates that impose environmental and other requirements on states and counties without providing the funds for compliance. The antifederal government sentiment encompasses Ross Perot's presidential campaigns, to the bombing of the Oklahoma City federal building. Democratic governor Ben Nelson of Nebraska, then chair of the Western Governors Association, argued that even moderates like himself are frustrated: "When you're a Governor, and you see what this does to your communities, you really do want to strike your desk and say, 'No more!' ''[23] The first generation of laws and regulations triggered a backlash against the federal government. The effectiveness of these laws and regulations as well as the additional ones that are needed will depend to a great extent on how well policy makers are able to respond to the issues raised by opponents of federal public lands policies and balance these concerns with the imperatives of effective policy making. Increased preservationist policies are essential and, in my view, inevitable, but their implementation requires a general acceptance of their legitimacy and need, and the arguments of opponents need to be understood and addressed even as they ultimately must give way to a broader view of the public interest.

PUBLIC LANDS AND PUBLIC VALUES

The differences between those who want to continue to harvest natural resources on public lands and those who seek preservation are rooted in fundamental values and commitments. Observers of the American policy such as Seymour Martin Lipset argue that the United States must be understood in terms of its commitment to a creed of "liberty, egalitarianism, individualism, populism, and laissez-faire."[24] America has a unique class structure that emphasizes "egalitarian social relations," a "stress on meritocracy," and "equal opportunity for all to rise economically and socially."[25] What is particularly important in understanding America's public philosophy is that its negative traits are intertwined with its positive attributes: the problems confronting the nation. America's commitment to individual rights, liberty, and protection of citizens against the abuse of power is naturally associated with the most commonly cited problems:

The lack of respect for authority, anti-elitism, and populism contribute to higher crime rates, school indiscipline, and low electoral turnouts. . . . Concern for the legal rights of accused persons and civil liberties in general is tied to opposition to gun control and difficulty in applying crime-control measures. The stress on individualism both weakens social control mechanisms, which rely on strong ties to groups, and facilitates diverse forms of deviant behavior.[26]

Unlike Europeans, Lipset argues, whose disagreements seem to reflect competing interests, in the United States conflicts are rooted in fundamental moral commitments. Americans are highly contentious, not because they disagree over core values but because they "quarrel sharply about how to apply the basic principles of Americanism they purport to agree about."[27]

Public Lands and Local Government

The idea of public lands, areas held in common by all Americans, conflicts with the idea of individualism and opportunity that in the past compelled these lands to be free for the taking. Until the passage of environmental laws in the late 1960s and early 1970s, federal land officials saw their role as facilitating resource development; as protective policies were instituted, westerners began to chafe at the restraints. The Sagebrush Rebellion began in the 1970s as an effort led by wealthy ranchers and others in the West to gain control of public lands. The movement had proponents in government in the 1980s, particularly Interior Secretary James Watt. The movement was reinvigorated in the early 1990s as the Wise Use and County Supremacy movements garnered attention. Between 1991 and 1995, fifty-nine western counties passed ordinances that claim authority to supersede federal environmental and land use laws and regulations. Organizations like the Mountain States Legal Foundation and the Individual Rights Foundation have led the legal fight against federal lands. By 1995, thirty-four counties in Nevada, California, Idaho, New Mexico, and Oregon had passed ordinances challenging federal control of local lands.[28]

The rebellion is symbolized by the actions of individuals like Richard L.

Carver, the vice chairman of Nevada's Nye County Commission. In 1994, Carver took a bulldozer and repaired a road in the Toiyabe National Forest that had been washed out in a storm and left unrepaired after forest officials ordered him not to proceed. When Carver threatened to run over national forest officials who blocked his efforts to reopen with a bulldozer a road that had been closed, he was joined by 200 county supremacists, many of whom bore weapons. Carver then sued a forest official for obstructing the work. The Nye County district attorney refused to prosecute the case and was subsequently voted out of office. Carver argued that when Nevada became a state, Congress never intended that the federal government would keep control of the vast majority of the state and that federal lands actually belong to the state and should be managed by the county. Proponents claimed that the ordinance was prompted by an "out of control Federal Government that is making life miserable for Westerners, particularly rural Westerners."[29] The war over control of public lands escalated in 1995, when the Justice Department filed a suit against Nye County, challenging two county resolutions that gave the county control over national forests and other federal lands and gave ownership to the county of the road through those lands. The resolutions declared that federal land in the county actually belonged to the state, and the county alone has authority to manage it. Although the resolutions are not technically law, local officials were enforcing them as though they were. The Justice Department challenged the ordinances as illegal and sought an injunction to ban their enforcement.

Nye County is viewed by many residents as nothing more than a U.S. colony, largely owned by the federal government and site of the proposed Yucca Mountain high-level radioactive waste dump. Some 93 percent of Nye County is owned by the federal government and includes an air force base and nuclear energy test sites. Local residents do not dispute those federal facilities but bristle against federal control of grazing and mining activities. One of the paradoxes is that independent-minded people are attracted to such counties; Nye County covers more than 18,000 square miles—the size of Vermont and New Hampshire—but has only 20,000 inhabitants. People are drawn to the West's openness, freedom, low taxes, and minimal zoning but are confronted by an unsympathetic federal landlord. Even little restraints are perceived as snubs and offenses that contribute to the tension. Every discussion of the federal government seems to degenerate into references to Waco and Ruby Ridge. Relations were cordial until the mid-1970s, when federal approval for grazing permits was virtually automatic and offered at bargain prices. Ranchers were permitted to lease their federal allotments to other ranchers, at several times the price they originally paid. But by the 1980s, public land management had become much more oriented to protection of lands, and the tension grew. Citizens are particularly frustrated with the impact of bureaucratic decisions on their livelihood.[30] Part of the problem is that many ranchers are small-business people who are barely solvent. A small change in policy such as the number of cattle that can be grazed can mean the difference between getting by and going out of business.

Another suit was filed on behalf of New Mexico residents challenging control of lands in Otero County, where nearly 90 percent of the land is federally owned. Until a decade ago, local residents were quite content with federal policy. In the late 1980s, federal agencies began restricting grazing and logging in order to protect sensitive lands and threatened species. Loggers and ranchers pushed the county to pass ordinances in 1992 and 1993 that gave county officials control over certain federal lands. The suit proposes that western states were denied the "equal footing" guaranteed by the Constitution when they were admitted to the union, because of the vast amount of federal lands within their borders. John Howard, the attorney representing counties in these cases, argues: "Because of how these lands have been managed, there has been a fundamental breaking of trust across the West. People at the local level are eager to claim more authority to determine what's best for them. For the last 10 years, the Federal Government has been giving these people the back of its hand." Proponents said that the case "was all about power. It's a struggle to re-establish the rights of people to live their lives and conduct their business with much less interference from environmentalists and the Government." Conservationists argued that the motivation for this rebellion was all about money, financed by "a few people who see an opportunity to make a lot of money if the laws change." But distrust of the federal government runs deep in this part of New Mexico, where, fifty years ago, residents were shaken out of their beds by the first atomic tests but were told by federal officials that the blast was the accidental explosion of an ammunitions dump.[31]

The Justice Department estimated in 1995 that at least thirty-five counties had declared authority over federal lands. The National Federal Lands Conference, a Utah-based group advocating county sovereignty, claimed that more than 300 counties had asserted some sovereignty over federal lands and that the idea had spread beyond the West to eastern states. Violence has already occurred, including shots fired at a Forest Service biologist in California and bombings in Arizona and Nevada.[32]

The county supremacy movement has stimulated a state supremacy drive. A 1995 Idaho petition drive, for example, urged the governor to declare state ownership of the federal lands within its borders. Members of Congress have proposed that some national forestlands be transferred to state control as a way to increase timber output. Republicans in Congress proposed a number of sales of public lands in order to reduce the federal deficit.[33] As new states came into the union, the federal government was given ownership of much of their land in exchange for statehood. Westerners argue that the issue is equity: eastern states were not required to sign over much of their territory when they became states, and it was unfair to make such demands on western states. Environmentalists counter that western control would be damaging to public lands since states will let parochial interests supersede national interests. Perhaps nothing raises the ire of westerners more than such charges: "There's a fear that we're going to rape and ruin the land, that we're going to rip it off, pave it, develop it," complained Jim Souby, executive director of the Western Governors Association. "[Easterners] immediately assume that because a proposal comes from somebody out West, it would create some nightmare. However, that isn't the climate you find in Las Vegas or Phoenix or anywhere else in the West."[34]

The county and state supremacy movements rely on historical and constitutional arguments far removed from reality. The states never owned these federal lands. The federal government had purchased or captured them before any state had been formed. When states were formed, they had no claim on any lands except those given to them by Congress. The federal government tried for decades to give away as much land as it could, but much of the West remained in federal hands. Nevertheless, those who have come to depend on the use of public lands for their livelihood have rooted their lives in strongly held expectations that the land would always be essentially under their control. These expectations are no longer tenable, but they represent formidable barriers to preservation and must be acknowledged and understood as the transition is made to more ecologically sustainable economic activity.

Public Lands and Private Property

No issue has been more contentious than the interaction of private property rights and preservation of public lands, natural resources, and wildlife, and few issues have energized westerners more than fears of loss of private property rights.[35] Private property takings provisions were attached to numerous environmental bills during the past two (103d and 104th) Congresses, although they failed to attract sufficient support for passage. When the House passed a bill to create the National Biological Survey in 1993, for example, private property provisions were added. They have been added to bills reauthorizing the Clean Water and Endangered Species Acts. The House Republican Contract with America's "Job Creation and Wage Enhancement Act" required that any regulation limiting the lawful use of land or water rights and affecting market value by at least 10 percent must provide compensation to the landowner.[36] The House passed a takings bill in March 1995, by a 277 to 148 vote, that would have required federal agencies issuing regulations aimed at protecting wetlands or endangered species that caused a decline in property values of 20 percent or more to compensate landowners for their loss.[37] In the Senate, Senators Bob Dole and Phil Gramm, both running for the Republican presidential nomination in 1995 and 1996, introduced takings legislation. The furthest the issue proceeded in the Senate in 1995 was passage of a bill by the Senate Judiciary Committee in December. The Senate proposal would require compensation when the actions of federal agencies decrease property values by 33 percent or more. The definition of takings would be expanded to include regulations that interfere with rents, water rights, maximization of profits, contractual rights, or any other interest that has been traditionally viewed by law as property.[38]

There is little agreement over the likely costs of takings legislation since it is not clear what level of regulation agencies will undertake if a takings provision is imposed. The Congressional Budget Office projected in 1996 that the cost of implementing the Senate bill would have been around $30 to $40 million, and might have been even lower as agencies avoid issuing regulations for which they would have to offer compensation. The Office of Management and Budget projected the cost of implementation to be several times higher than the $28 billion it estimated for the cost of implementing the House takings bill.[39]

Proponents of takings legislation charge that there is a "war" over property rights and that environmental regulation unacceptably undermines private property. Both sides agree that takings bills would have a dramatic impact on government regulation, making it too expensive to pursue many protective efforts. Critics of the proposals fear that agencies will be required to perform takings assessments that will consume scarce agency resources. Instead of a case-by-case determination and balancing of public and private interests, blanket rules about compensation would be imposed on agencies. Takings laws may also threaten private property as it becomes more difficult for governments to regulate the behavior of some property owners that affects their neighbors.[40]

Critics argue that the current system of private property protection is inadequate. The Fifth Amendment of the Constitution requires that "private property" not be "taken for public use without just compensation." When governments actually appropriate private property, they must provide fair compensation. When government regulation impacts the use of land, courts often intervene to settle differences. There is no clear, unambiguous standard; takings are determined on a case-by-case basis by examining the purpose of the action, the economic impact, and other factors. The Fifth Amendment limits only the federal government from taking private property; the Supreme Court has, by incorporation, included this right against state government action as part of the due process protection required by the Fourteenth Amendment. But the Court has not provided clear guidelines for determining when a taking has occurred and when compensation is due. There is little question that when governments actually take possession of land, fair compensation must be awarded the previous owner; the problem comes when government regulation places some limit on how property owners can use their land.

The decisions of the Supreme Court send mixed signals concerning the difference between a compensable taking and a regulation that must be complied with by property owners. The unpredictability and uncertainty of the law have contributed to the demand for statutory action. In some cases, if the government requires a physical intrusion, the Court has required compensation. The Court has assessed the economic impact of a regulation in determining whether it crosses the line to become a taking. But the justices have been unable to decide on enduring principles. They have devised some criteria for assessing government actions, but the weight given each factor and their overall balance vary from case to case. Many decisions appear to be the result of a judgment about whether the Court concludes that a regulation serves an important public purpose and is valid, or whether it is unjustifiably meddling in the affairs of landowners and is a taking.[41]

One view, represented in a 1915 Supreme Court case, recognizes broad discretion on the part of governments to write ordinances that limit the kinds of development that can occur within city boundaries. The principle offered by the Court appears to be that the impact of a regulation on private landowners is irrelevant if the action is within the legitimate police power of government. In *Hadacheck v. Sebastian*, for example, the Court upheld an ordinance of the city of Los Angeles that prohibited the operation of a brickyard within certain areas of the city. The owner of a brickyard who had purchased the land when it was outside city limits argued that the regulation caused the value of his property to fall from $800,000, when used for brick making, to $60,000. The Court found that regulation of development was one of the essential powers of government, and as long as it was not exercised arbitrarily, private interests must give way to progress and the good of the community.[42]

A second position offered by the Court is that if the burden of the regulation falls too heavily on one property owner, if the diminution of property value reaches a certain point, then compensation is required. The Court did not define that certain point with any precision, arguing that it depended on the particular facts of each case, and great weight should be given to legislative judgment. In *Pennsylvania Coal Co. v. Mahon*, a 1922 case, the property owners were bound by a covenant to the coal company that had sold them the surface rights of their land to permit the removal of coal without liability for any damage to the landowners. Pennsylvania subsequently enacted a law that prohibited coal companies from causing any damage to public or private buildings through mining operations, and the coal company brought suit against the law as an unconstitutional taking of its rights. The Court found that the law represented a taking of the coal company property since it made mining commercially impracticable in some areas and had virtually the same effect as appropriating or destroying the property.[43]

However, in *Keystone Bituminous Coal Association v. DeBenedictis*, 1987, the Court upheld a law aimed at protecting property from damage caused by mining. The Court found that protection of surface property was a valid public purpose, and the law did not interfere with the company's ability to earn a fair return on its property since it required only a small percentage of coal remain in the ground.[44] The Court eventually devised a balancing test for determining whether a taking had occurred in a 1978 case, *Penn Central Transportation Co. v. New York*. First, if government physically invades the private property, a taking has likely occurred. Second, the restriction is upheld if it is reasonably related to a policy that is likely to produce widespread benefits to the public and applies to all similarly situated property. Third, a taking has occurred if the regulation effectively prevents the landowner from receiving a reasonable return on the property. In *Penn Central*, the Court upheld a New York historic preservation law that authorized a commission to designate buildings as historic landmarks and required the commission's approval before exterior changes could be made. The Grand Central Terminal, owned by Penn Central, had been designated as a landmark, necessitating commercial approval for a plan to build an office building above the terminal. The commission rejected the proposal, Penn Central sued, and the Supreme Court ruled that the law was constitutional since it was expected to produce a widespread benefit, applied to all similarly situated property, and did not deprive the landowner of all of its value.[45]

Other cases add options to takings policy. In *Andrus v. Allard*, 1979, the Court ruled that a loss of future profits was not sufficient to invoke a takings claim in upholding a law that prohibited commercial transactions involving eagle feathers and other artifacts. The plaintiffs had owned the feathers before the law was passed and were prosecuted for selling them after enactment. The Court found that the feathers could still be possessed, exhibited, or donated.[46] In a 1986 case, *First English Evangelical Lutheran Church of Glendale v. County of Los Angeles*, the Court ruled that governments can be liable for damages imposed on landowners if regulations become sufficiently burdensome to be classified as a taking. The decision expanded the remedies available to property owners when "overregulation" has occurred to include injunctions against enforcement of the law and damages resulting from the restriction on development.[47] In *Nollan v. California Coastal Commission*, 1987, the Court found that while the commission had the power to forbid construction of a home on the beachfront, any conditions it placed on construction must be "reasonably related" to the problems created by the construction. The commission had required the landowner to provide an easement that would give the public access to the beach in order to get a building permit to construct a house on his property.[48] In *Dolan v. City of Tigurd*, a 1994 decision, the Court rejected an Oregon city's requirement that in order to obtain a construction permit to expand a plumbing supply business, the landowner give to the city 7,000 square feet for pedestrian and bike paths and for storm water management. The Court found the city's demand out of proportion with the impact caused by the expansion of the business. Chief Justice William Rehnquist argued for the following underlying principle: "One of the principal purposes of the Takings Clause is to bar government from forcing some people alone to bear public burdens, which in all fairness and justice, should be borne by the public as a whole."[49]

There are some limitations on takings. Governments can determine that some economic interests are not property rights. Under the Public Trust doctrine, governments can be recognized as the titleholders of land. The Supreme Court, for example, has ruled that states own the lands under navigable waters such as Lake Michigan.[50] Lower courts have applied the public trust doctrine expansively in order to preserve lands so they can serve as locales for ecological research and habitats for birds and animals and contribute to scenery and climate.[51] Federal law also permits the federal government to exercise control over navigable waters, including the power to change the course of a river in ways that affect the access to the water by riparian owners or adversely impact the value of their property.[52] Under section 404 of the Clean Water Act, a permit is required for fill or dredging that affects wetlands. The Supreme Court has recognized that the Army Corps of Engineers, the agency responsible for administering the law, has broad power to require permits for any area that is flooded or saturated enough to support vegetation that typically grows in saturated soil conditions.[53]

Proponents of takings laws argue that the current case law failed to provide adequate protection for landowners: "There are millions of people who feel that they are oppressed by the federal government and we have to face this problem," claimed Judiciary Committee chair Orrin G. Hatch (R-UT).[54] Hatch argued that government regulation is wildly out of control; regulations limiting land use or lowering potential profits are all takings of private property. Hatch said that "if the federal government continues to persecute and oppress people whatever the costs are, they're going to have to pay for it."[55] Groups like the Defenders of Property Rights have called for a complete overhaul of regulations so that there is minimal impact on private property rights. The Endangered Species and Clean Water Acts dealing with wetlands are the primary focus of attention, but some proponents of takings legislation would apply them to all agencies and all programs. Some Republicans opposed the bill, fearing it might undermine public health regulation, kindle litigation, and increase costs. Other opponents argued that government should not be required to compensate landowners every time a regulation that contributes to the public good reduces the value of property. Senator Joe Biden (D-DE) argued that the bill "would require us to pay people to obey legitimate environmental laws."[56]

The failure of the 104th Congress to enact private property legislation has fueled state and local efforts. According to one estimate, there are more than 500 property rights advocacy groups in the United States. They have introduced some one hundred bills in forty-four states and several bills in Congress. Thirteen states had passed property rights laws by the end of 1994; the fourteenth state, Arizona, was the first to pass a stand-alone property rights bill requiring state agencies to identify takings before acting, in 1992. However, opponents mounted a campaign against the bill and repealed it through a referendum vote in 1994.[57] By January 1996, eighteen states had enacted property rights laws.

Property rights proposals have taken one of two forms. One proposal, called "look before you leap," requires governments to assess the takings implications of laws, regulations, and other governmental actions. Nine of the takings bills passed by states were of this type. "Look before you leap" laws seek to deter governments from taking actions that would require compensation, thus saving government money. However, since there is no widely accepted definition of what constitutes a taking, the standards to be used are unsettled. The other kind of laws, takings compensation, specifies at what point the reduction in property values requires payment to the landowner. Compensation bills had been introduced in nineteen states by the end of 1994, but none has been enacted as of 1997. The typical bill defines takings as a property value loss of 50 percent or more. Takings proposals usually include one or both of the following requirements: (1) assessments of proposed regulations include an examination of the impact on property values, and (2) when property values decline beyond a certain point, the agency responsible must either exempt the landowner from compliance or offer compensation. Many require state agencies to perform a "takings impact analysis" before pursuing any action that might result in a loss of property value. Louisiana and Mississippi statutes require compensation for losses caused by state agriculture and timber regulations. Florida allows compensation in cases where a regulation imposes an "inordinate burden." Texas law exempts landowners from complying with regulations that would diminish their property value by more than 25 percent.

However, when takings proposals are made in popular referendums, they have largely failed. Sixty percent of Arizona voters rejected mandatory impact assessments. Washington voters similarly rejected an initiative that would have required elaborate assessments and compensation for any landowner whose property value declined as a result of state or local regulations. Opposition to these proposals is mainly a result of their projected costs and the likelihood that they will result in higher taxes. Opponents fear that regulation will become a "nightmare of dueling appraisers and dueling lawyers" who will argue over every analysis and every assessment. Takings could become an expensive new entitlement program and would have a chilling effect on reasonable environmental regulation. Some advocates of private property rights believe that regulation is essential for protecting property values: "We all live downstream, downwind or next door to property where pollution and other harmful activities have been restrained to protect *all* of our property values and our collective interest in safe, healthy and enjoyable communities."[58]

Proponents of state property rights legislation argue that their purpose is to prevent government from imposing on individual landowners the cost of providing public goods. They cite regulations such as those that limit logging in order to protect endangered species, restrictions on development that would adversely affect wetlands, and exactions that require landowners to dedicate land for highways or parks in order to have projects approved by local authorities. Such actions require property owners "to shoulder burdens that properly belong to society as a whole" and should be paid for by the public. They also emphasize that their proposals are not aimed at "most traditional environmental regulations [that] reflect the police power of government. . . . The government does not have to compensate the person who causes a nuisance because the individual has no right to create a nuisance to begin with. Most pollution regulations fall under this rule."[59]

Opponents fear that takings legislation, because they can apply to all regulations, may affect civil rights and other policy areas. They may discourage governments from pursuing environmental, public health, and other regulations and will be chilled by the threat of having to pay for them. Takings may interfere with community zoning efforts.[60] Proponents argue that environmental regulations issued under the police power or nuisance law are not affected by property rights. Opponents suggest that takings are balanced by government actions that enhance property values—"givings." But that overall balancing is too imprecise: the constitutional standard focuses on individual property owners whose property is taken.

The key question, then, is, What kinds of regulations should be considered a takings? One option is to expressly limit them to actual use of property in ways that do not pose a threat to public health or property values of others. Wetlands and endangered species are two such examples, although one can argue that the impact on ecological systems from loss of species or wetlands is a real loss imposed on others by the landowner, and no compensation should be required. Advocates of property rights argue that if government has to compensate regulated parties, rather than simply impose regulations on them, that will create a clear incentive for smaller, more focused, more careful government. But government is constantly redistributing wealth as it raises taxes and then spends the money. Which laws involve good redistribution, and which promote unsustainable redistribution?[61]

Some advocates of private property rights argue that they can replace most environmental and natural resource regulations. Richard Epstein, for example, has argued, "The *only* correct position is to recognize that *all* forms of regulation are subject to scrutiny under the takings clause." For Epstein, the rule is simple: "Any form of regulation thus requires compensation in cash for the losses inflicted (1) unless the regulation is necessary to prevent the kinds of losses that neighbors could enjoin under ordinary tort law principles . . . or (2) unless some compensation *in kind* is furnished to the party whose property is taken."[62] Epstein argues that there is still some role for traditional government regulation: "Damages and injunctions are routinely awarded in private lawsuits to control common law nuisances. In this setting, state action may be appropriate, especially where the diffuse nature of a potential harm places many people in a position [of harm]." If landowners could enjoin a polluter's actions without compensation, "the state may do so as well when acting as their agent. The state power allows intervention (by taxation and police protection) where the coordination problems for the innocent individuals preclude any system of effective private suit or self-help." Although there is still the threat that the state will exaggerate harms and overprotect, the possibility of error cannot be totally eliminated but only minimized. But the problem with the current regulatory regime is that "the most fanciful connections between an individual act and some ordinary harm may limit the use of private property."[63]

Epstein argues that while pollution may cause physical harm, that does not necessarily mean that a legal wrong has occurred. If the damage is done to the property itself, and not to that of neighbors, then there is no legal harm. This approach also helps defuse the conflict over environmental regulation, between those who favor preservation, even at the expense of production, and those who believe natural resources should be exploited for human consumption. The ordinary rules of evidence can be used to deal with claims of damage to another person or property: "The interconnectedness of what goes on in one place and what goes on in another cannot be presumed on some dubious theory of necessary physical linkage for all events."[64]

According to Epstein, there are several reasons that the more value government takes, the more it should pay. If compensation is not provided unless 100 percent of the property's value is lost, then government will never take actions that impose a total loss of value but will stop short. Governments will be more cautious if they have to foot the bill for the requirements they impose on others than if they can deflect those costs to others. The same rule should apply to regulation of property as applies to occupation. No private party could restrict the use of property that did not constitute a tort such as a trespass or nuisance. "Why," Epstein asks, "should the government be vested with a set of powers to restrict private behavior that it cannot derive from the powers vested in its individual citizens?"[65]

Others are even more ambitious in proposing free market principles and institutions for protecting natural resources. The use of market-based incentives in environmental regulation dates from writings in the 1930s.[66] Terry L. Anderson and Donald R. Leal argue that traditional public lands and natural resource policies—timber, grazing, energy production, and so on—are fundamentally flawed: "In government agencies, bureaucrats have incentives to provide constituents with the products and services they want at little or no cost to them. Entrepreneurs in the arena are rewarded with larger staffs, more authority, and larger budgets, but they do not face the reality check of profitability."[67] The role of government is to enforce property rights. "It is when rights are unclear and not well enforced that over-exploitation occurs":

At the heart of free market environmentalism is a system of well-specified property rights to natural resources. Whether these rights are held by individuals, corporations, nonprofit environmental groups, or communal groups, a discipline is imposed on resource users because the wealth of the owner of the property right is at stake if bad decisions are made.[68]

Information is costly to obtain. Environmental policy needs to take into account the incentives and the cost of information. Prices are critical in making good decisions and in getting the right incentives. Property rights, proponents believe, are the solution to problems of water allocation, protection of groundwater, and maintenance of fisheries. The problem of solid waste can be addressed through property rights and the enforcement of rules of liability and bonding. Air pollution, although more challenging, can be similarly regulated through property rights.

But the faith of free market environmentalists, critics charge, is misplaced. The public interest is not simply the accumulation of private interests but includes values and perspectives that go beyond the expression of economic self-interest. It cannot be reduced to measurements of willingness to pay. Such approaches reinforce the existing distribution of power and wealth and give greatly disproportionate power to the wealthy. They assume preferences do not change. The values and concerns of those besides property owners must be taken into account in determining questions of environmental quality and natural resource preservation and use. A reliance on markets is misplaced since existing markets fail to include all the costs of production in transactions but permit companies to externalize pollution. Existing markets fail to ensure that individuals have adequate information before making decisions and fail to remedy the inequities in the existing distribution of resources. Markets fail to reflect collective values about the environment since many of these values cannot be accurately represented through prices. They fail to provide for public goods: developers have little incentive to provide for public goods such as clean air, clean water, and clear vistas since they can be enjoyed by all.

Markets require enforcement, but the costs of enforcement of common law remedies such as nuisance are high. The enduring problems of causation, burden of proof, and remedy in the common law severely limit the effectiveness of the traditional approach. We have already tried the common law: the failure of the common law regulatory scheme, the problems of inadequate information, and inadequately functioning markets led to the development of new forms of regulation. The transaction costs in a reliance on a common law approach are significant. There is also less fostering of common responsibility and shared values as regulation is reduced to protection of individual interest. Even a move to strict liability, as Anderson and Leal propose, does not avoid problems of proving causality where there are multiple sources or provide prospective protection from harm. Courts give protection to "the average person of ordinary sensibilities" rather than groups of individuals who are particularly sensitive to pollution such as children and elderly persons with respiratory diseases.[69] Judges are not better suited than elected officials to strike the difficult balances between economic, social, and environmental trade-offs. These choices about values cannot be made through market transactions but require a broader political effort.

Nevertheless, given the importance of personal liberty as a fundamental American value, free market environmentalism wins lots of admirers. The freedom to produce pollution or use land in any way owners please expands their liberty, but those who are exposed to pollution and other damage have their liberty reduced. Individual freedom is a primary public goal but must be balanced with fairness, due process, equality, justice, public participation, precaution and risk minimization, and compensation for past damages. Markets give the illusion that subjective values can be reduced to dollar values and then compared. Many legitimate social goals are not given a high dollar value in the marketplace, such as clean air or protection of biodiversity. But critics of regulation have an important message to environmental policymakers: as more and more people, particularly small businesses, farmers, and others, fall within the regulatory reach of government, regulation must become more efficient, involve fewer administrative and transactional costs, and create more effective incentives for compliance.[70]

Many environmentalists argue that the existing understanding of private property must give way to a new understanding that recognizes the need to protect private lands from erosion and exhaustion and to preserve biodiversity on those lands. Our view of private property, they argue, must change from the traditional notion that owners can use and even destroy the property at will, to a new view that balances personal ownership and privacy with fostering healthy ecosystems. Farmers' choices about what crops to plant and what methods to use must be balanced with collective obligations to minimize erosion, enrich the soil by planting cover crops, and reduce water pollution from pesticide and fertilizer use. Private property is a legal, social construct that must be adapted to new challenges and needs.[71]

The World Wildlife Fund and others have supported "Homeowner's Protection Acts." These acts might include the following kinds of provisions:

- Improve the permit notification process by requiring legal notification to neighbors of proposed activities that generate pollutants or other adverse impacts with the potential to reduce the value of homes in the vicinity;
- Require compensation from any individual or corporation whose violation of the law, regulation, or permit has significantly contributed to a loss of the home's value;
- Set up a Homeowners Assistance Program that would require agencies to advise homeowners on regulatory requirements, including alternative solutions, compliance obligations, and how to pursue judicial claims for just compensation;
- Establish judicial procedures to promptly resolve takings claims brought by homeowners or other small landowners that would include agency participation in minitrials or other alternative dispute resolution procedures; and/or
- Allow compensation within a stewardship or Conservation Reserve Program to any family farmer who would be prohibited from farming because of changes in regulations after they purchased their farm.[72]

Private Rights and Public Regulation

A system of protecting environmental quality through private property rights is costly to create and enforce: it requires institutions to identify, distribute, oversee buying and selling, and enforce rights. It must also ensure that sufficient information is available to participants and that there are no externalities. In contrast, a system of common property is easier and less expensive to form: all parties have equal opportunity to use the collective resources, and there are no transaction costs. But commons, as Garrett Hardin and others have often reminded us, are susceptible to overuse and pollution. Rational beings will maximize their gain and, in so doing, inevitably lead to the destruction of the common resources.[73] Hardin proposes "mutual coercion, mutually agreed upon." But how do people agree to such a cooperative effort? If they could agree on a coercive scheme, perhaps they could agree on specific restraints. Cooperation is essential, but the problem is that members of the community are unable to organize themselves. How can a society plagued by noncooperation learn to cooperate?

Both a system of private rights and public regulation require coordination costs. The key question is, What are the comparative costs and benefits of private rights and regulation? What is the optimal mix? An active system of markets requires government intervention to ensure competition and other prerequisites. But government sometimes suffers from inadequate information, self-interested bureaucrats, domination by self-serving interest groups, and wastefulness that comes from a failure to bear the costs of actions taken. How can the government, required to make markets work, avoid the problems that plague governments? Does government suffer from fewer shortcomings when it enforces markets than when it designs and enforces regulations? When would the market-based approach likely work, and when would it not?[74] How will contamination of lands, erosion caused by clear-cutting, loss of biodiversity, and other problems be cured through property rights? How will property rights be distributed? Anderson and Leal argue that environmentalists will be able to join in the purchase of rights: the thirteen largest groups have together annual revenues of $400 million. But just two oil companies, Exxon and Mobil, receive that much revenue every day![75]

Are courts likely to be able to efficiently and effectively administer a private property-based approach to environmental regulation? The shift from a bureaucratic to a judicial scheme for protecting the environment will require courts, lawyers, legal instruments, and private landowners as litigants to play roles they have not been able to do in the past. Property rights in air, land, and water will have to be devised. These rights will be bought and sold, and the transactional costs of so many exchanges will be considerable. Litigation will greatly expand as all property owners are expected to regularly sue to protect their rights. There are numerous roadblocks to environmental suits brought by property owners. The high costs of litigation will discourage effective enforcement of private rights. Many violations will likely cause only modest damage, and litigation might cost more than the remedies to be gained. Enforcement may require a group of altruistic landowners whose suits to enforce rights will cost them more than they will gain. Resolution of causation issues will be complex, time-consuming, and expensive. Courts will differ in terms of the level of certainty required before legal causality is demonstrated. The cost of discovery, expert witnesses, and other elements of the process will be daunting for all but the largest cases. The costs of demonstrating injury will also be high in many cases; there will be little opportunity for economies of scale in determining injury and causality; each new case will require a new round of investigation.[76] In some cases where the injury is great, there will be a clear economic incentive to enforce private rights. But personal injury, toxic tort, and other kinds of cases have been widely criticized for producing inconsistent judgments and inequitable results. There is often little compensation to victims after legal bills are paid. A few large settlements or judgments may cause offending parties to go bankrupt so that subsequent victims are uncompensated.[77]

If regulation cannot be replaced by a system of private property rights, how can natural resource policy be made more consonant with the fundamental values that Americans hold so strongly? Preservationist policies are required to protect the landscape, habitats, and resources that make the West unique in the world. If such policies are not successful, the West will lose the very characteristics that have made it such a desirable place to live and work. But the transition to a more ecologically sustainable West has and will continue to be painful to many. While some residents of the West will always resist change, policies will need to balance economic development with preservation and provide for transitions from resource exploitation to protection. Ensuring that prices reflect true costs is essential. An open, public debate that acknowledges these profound differences in values and makes a compelling case for the choices that are required to preserve the natural wonders of the West is essential.

Public Lands and Public Values

Public lands arouse tremendously powerful emotions and demands. The West's boom and bust cycles are intertwined with public land and natural resource policies. The allure of past natural resource booms in uranium, oil, coal, timber, and other riches causes contemporary westerners to resist preservation for fear of locking up future wealth. But natural resource booms are not sustainable, economically or environmentally: booms followed by bust have failed to ensure the long-term cleanup of wastes and have left communities economically decimated. Some interests want to return to the pre-1970s, when resource extraction was unfettered, through cutbacks in environmental regulation or privatization of public lands. One of the major challenges in the West has been to develop a stable, sustainable economy that resists the allure of striking it rich on public lands and public policies that reinforce that goal. Some call for a comprehensive restructuring of public lands law and policy that would protect entire ecosystems. Others propose incremental reform within the existing legal structure that would give more discretion to communities and bring a wider range of interests together to set policy and more flexibility to tailor policies to local priorities, conditions, and concerns. Two questions are central as policymakers and concerned citizens explore options as the West moves into the twenty-first century, and public lands become even more important: how can we balance national concerns with local needs? How can we make the transition to ecologically sustainable economic activity?

One set of stories we tell depicts the land as an economic resource. Ranchers, loggers, miners, and others may even love the land they work and care for it. They have enormously strong attachments to it. But the land is to be used; wealth is to be taken from it. Another narrative is public land as wilderness, places of solitude, spiritual renewal, and sensual experience. Writes Terry Tempest Williams: "The open expanse of sky makes me realize how necessary it is to live without words, to be satisfied without answers, to simply be in a world where there is no wind, no drama. To find a place of rest and safety, no matter how fleeting it may be, no matter how illusory, to regain composure and locate bearings."[78] These competing stories about the history of the West frame the issues that face policymakers and the public as they chart its future.

Wallace Stegner wrote that the West is a land of hope and opportunity, but that has often translated into environmental pillage: "Too often the Western states have been prosperous, at the expense of their fragile environment, and their civilization has too often mined and degraded the natural scene while drawing most of its quality from it. . . . There are varieties and degrees of hope, and the wrong kinds, in excessive amounts, go with human failure and environmental damage as boom goes with bust." Stegner faults "uninformed, unrealistic, greedy, expectation" about the resources that could be taken from the land that has resulted in exploitation of resources and collapse of communities. Nowhere are the carelessness and self-deception clearer, for Stegner, than in the lack of water in the desert lands. Water is used up or poisoned by fertilizers and pesticides. Yet he remained until his death optimistic that westerners will be able to "work out some sort of compromise between what must be done to earn a living and what must be done to restore health to the earth, air and water."[79]

What are the prospects for such a compromise? The shift from public policies that are not rooted in the ecological realities of the West to those that are more likely to secure sustainability will be contentious, because the traditional values are so strongly held. But as the requirements of an ecologically sustainable future become better understood, as protected lands become more scarce and valuable, and as more people become convinced of the threats unbridled growth and development poses to the quality of life of the West, the prospects for more preservation seem promising. The chapters that follow focus on the ecological considerations that ought to guide policy making for public lands and natural resources. These policies will be informed and reinforced by the articulation of stories that illustrate the possibilities for a future that is centered on preserving wild lands, open spaces, wildlife habitats, and natural resources so they can contribute to overall ecological health and quality of life for current and future generations and preserve the characteristics that represent the enduring allure of the West.

NOTES

1. Dirk Johnson, "Far from an Arid Economy, Desert States Thrive," *New York Times* (May 13, 1991).

2. William E. Riebsame, "Ending the Range Wars," *Environment* (May 1996): 4–9, 27–29.

3. Walter E. Hecox and Bradley L. Ack, "Charting the Colorado Plateau: An Economic and Demographic Exploration" (Flagstaff, AZ: The Grand Canyon Trust, 1996).

4. Ibid.

5. Ibid.

6. Timothy Egan, "Urban Sprawl Strains Western States," *New York Times* (December 29, 1996): A1.

7. Hecox and Ack, "Charting the Colorado Plateau." See also Riebsame, "Ending the Range Wars": 28.

8. Margaret Kriz, "Quick Draw," *National Journal* (November 13, 1993): 2711–16; quotes at 2713.

9. Ibid.

10. Vaughn Roche, "At Loggerheads in the Wilderness," *Washington Post* (September 4, 1993).

11. Kriz, "Quick Draw"; quotes at 2714.

12. *Greenwire* (March 14, 1995): No. 4.

13. Keith Bradsher et al., "The 1996 Elections: The States," *New York Times* (November 7, 1996): B11.

14. James Brooke, "The 1996 Elections: The States—The Legislatures; G.O.P.'s Recent Momentum at the State Level Is Halted," *New York Times* (November 7, 1996): B8.

15. See Jacqueline Switzer with Gary Bryner, *Environmental Politics*, 2d. ed. (New York: St. Martin's Press, 1997): Chapter 4.

16. Vince Bielski, "Armed and Dangerous," *Sierra* (September/October 1995): 33–34; quote at 34.

17. *Greenwire* (April 3, 1995): No. 13.

18. Jerry Kammer, "Taking Aim," *Deseret News* (April 30, 1995): V1.

19. Paul Rauber, "National Yard Sale," *Sierra* (September/October 1995): 28–33.

20. Fund-raising letter from Jeff DeBonis, founder and executive director, PEER, "Inciting Violence" (1996).

21. Bielski, "Armed and Dangerous."

22. Jeff DeBonis, "Buffaloed by the Land-Use Bullies," *New York Times* (July 7, 1995).

23. Erik Larson, "Unrest in the West," *Time* (October 23, 1995): 52–66, at 55.

24. Seymour Martin Lipset, *American Exceptionalism: A Double-Edge Sword* (New York: W. W. Norton, 1996): 19.

25. Ibid.: 53.

26. Ibid.: 290.

27. Ibid.: 26.

28. Keith Schneider, "A County's Bid for U.S. Land Draws Lawsuit," *New York Times* (March 9, 1995): A1. For an overview of the issues raised by the county and state supremacy movements and challenges to federal regulatory power, see R. McGreggor Cawley, *Federal Land Western Anger: The Sagebrush Rebellion and Environmental Politics* (Lawrence, KS: University Press of Kansas, 1993) and Jacqueline Vaughn Switzer, *Green Backlash: The History and Politics of Environmental Opposition in the U.S.* (Boulder, CO: Lynne Reinner Publishers, Inc., 1997).

29. Ibid.

30. Larson, "Unrest in the West," at 65–66.

31. Keith Schneider, "Bold Plan Seeks to Wrest Control of Federal Lands," *New York Times* (April 8, 1995).

32. Larson, "Unrest in the West."

33. Rauber, "National Yard Sale."

34. Margaret Kriz, "Land Wars," *National Journal* (September 2, 1995): 2146–51; quote at 2150.

35. Keith Schneider, "When the Bad Guy Is Seen as the One in the Green Hat," *New York Times* (February 16, 1992).

36. 104th Congress, H.R. 1, Title IX.

37. 104th Congress, H.R. 925.

38. 104th Congress, S. 605, "Omnibus Property Rights Act of 1995."

39. Global Action and Information Network, "Dole and 'Takings' Bill" (January 10, 1996).

40. Suellen Lowry, "Cloaked in the Constitution, Property Rights Movement Targets Environmental Laws," *Wildlife Advocate* (Summer 1994): 3.

41. For a discussion of these issues, see Roger W. Findley and Daniel A. Farber, *Environmental Law* (St. Paul: West, 1992): 279–92.

42. 239 U.S. 394 (1915).

43. 260 U.S. 393 (1922).

44. 480 U.S. 470.

45. 438 U.S. 104.

46. 444 U.S. 51.

47. 482 U.S. 304.

48. 483 U.S. 825.

49. 114 S. Ct. 2886 (1994), at 2316.

50. *Illinois Central Railroad Co. v. Illinois*, 146 U.S. 387 (1892).

51. See Findley and Farber, *Environmental Law*: 294–96.

52. *United States v. Rands*, 389 U.S. 121 (1967). However, if the waterway in dispute is a pond that was converted to use as a private marina, the government may not be required by others to ensure public access to the marina. See *Kaiser Aetna v. United States*, 444 U.S. 164 (1979).

53. *United States v. Riverside Bayview Homes*, 474 U.S. 121 (1985).

54. "Senate Panel Begins Debate on Property Rights Bill," *Congressional Quarterly Weekly Report* (December 16, 1995): 3805.

55. Global Action and Information Network, "Dole and 'Takings' Bill."

56. Ibid.

57. Hertha L. Lund, "Property Rights Legislation in the States: A Review" (PERC Policy Series, Issue No. PS-1 (January 1995).

58. Neal R. Peirce, "Takings—The Comings and Goings," *National Journal* 28 (January 6, 1996): 37.

59. Lund, "Property Rights Legislation in the States": 3.

60. But see *Village of Euclid v. Amber Realty Co.*, 272 U.S. 365 (1926) and *Agins v. City of Tiburon*, 447 U.S. 255 (1980): normal zoning is not considered by the courts to be takings.

61. Jonathan Rauch, *Demosclerosis: The Silent Killer of American Government* (New York: Times Books, 1994): 161–62.

62. Richard Epstein, *Simple Rules* (Cambridge: Harvard University Press, 1995): 132.

63. Ibid.: 133.

64. Ibid.: 278.

65. Ibid.: 132.

66. James E. Krier, "The Tragedy of the Commons, Part Two," *Harvard Journal of Law and Public Policy* 15 (Spring 1992): 325–47, at 325–26.

67. Terry L. Anderson and Donald R. Leal, *Free Market Environmentalism* (Boulder, CO: Westview Press, 1991): 58–59.

68. Ibid.: 3.

69. Michael C. Blumm, "The Fallacies of Free Market Environmentalism," *Harvard Journal of Law and Public Policy* 15 (Spring 1992): 371, 387.

70. Ibid., at 371–73; Krier, "The Tragedy of the Commons, Part Two."

71. Eric T. Freyfogle, "Problems with Plowshares," *New York Times* (January 31, 1992).

72. National Wildlife Federation, "Contract with America: Private Property Rights" (n.d.).

73. Garrett Hardin, "The Tragedy of the Commons,"*Science* 162 (1968): 1243.

74. Krier, "The Tragedy of the Commons, Part Two," at 340–43.

75. William Funk, "Free Market Environmentalism: Wonder Drug or Snake Oil?" *Harvard Journal of Law and Public Policy* 15 (Spring 1992): 511–16, at 514.

76. Edward Brunet, "Debunking Wholesale Private Enforcement of Environmental Rights," *Harvard Journal of Law and Public Policy* 15 (Spring 1992): 311–24.

77. Ibid.: 313–15.

78. See Terry Tempest Williams and Mary Frank, *Desert Quartet* (New York: Pantheon Books, 1995): 12.

79. Wallace Stegner, excerpts from the introduction to *Where the Bluebird Sings to the Lemonade Springs* (New York: Penguin Books, 1992) reprinted in *New York Times* (March 29, 1992).

2

The Evolution of Public Lands Policy

Throughout much of American history, public lands have been largely viewed as vessels of natural resources. They have had little value except what could be harvested and sold. But there has also been for more than a century a competing expectation, that public lands should be preserved for their inherent value. The first view has clearly dominated policy making; the second continues to struggle for acceptance. The public lands as natural resources perspective itself has engendered a debate. Some interests, motivated by the promise of immediate profits, have argued that the maximum harvesting of resources is in the national interest: we should use the resources while they are available and in demand. Conservationists have also recognized the importance of resource production but call for sustainable yield and careful control over harvesting to ensure that resources are not depleted faster than nature can regenerate them. Preservationists, in contrast, often see the value of public lands much greater if protected against commercial development and reserved for ecological, aesthetic, and even spiritual purposes. These competing interests have risen and fallen over time, and the debate continues. This chapter charts the evolution of these competing expectations for public lands.

PUBLIC LANDS AS NATURAL RESOURCES

When the nation was formed, the term "public lands" referred to all lands west of the original colonies, and the U.S. government was anxious to sell or give these lands away to settlers as quickly as possible. As new lands were gained by conquest and purchase, their distribution to private parties accelerated.

Table 2.1
Acquisition of the Federal Public Domain, 1781–1991 (In Millions of Acres)

Year and Acquisition	Total	Land	In-land water
Aggregate	1,837.8	1,804.7	33.1
1781-1802 (State Cessions)	236.8	233.4	3.4
1803, Louisiana Purchase[1]	529.9	523.4	6.5
1819, Cession from Spain	46.1	43.3	2.8
Red River Basin[2]	29.6	29.1	0.5
1846, Oregon Compromise	183.4	180.6	2.7
1848, Mexican Cession[1]	338.7	334.5	4.2
1850, Purchase from Texas	78.9	78.8	0.1
1853, Gadsden Purchase	19.0	19.0	(Z)
1867, Alaska Purchase	375.3	362.5	12.8

Notes: Areas of acquisitions are as computed in 1912. Excludes outlying areas of the United States amounting to 645,949 acres in 1978.
Z: Less than 50,000.
[1]Data for Louisiana Purchase exclude areas eliminated by Treaty of 1819 with Spain. Such areas are included in figures for Mexican Cession.
[2]Represents drainage basin of Red River of the North, south of 49th parallel. Authorities differ as to method and date of its acquisition. Some hold it as part of the Louisiana Purchase; others, as acquired from Great Britain.
Source: U.S. Department of Commerce, Statistical Abstract of the United States, 1995 (Washington, DC: U.S. Government Printing Office, 1995): 227.

Table 2.1 charts the growth of the nation's lands. Table 2.2 outlines their disposition to states and private interests.

The Ordinance of 1785 authorized the sale of land, at least 640 acres in size and with a minimum price of one dollar an acre, to the highest bidder. Between 1785 and 1934, when the sale of public lands ended, more than a billion acres of public land were transferred to private landowners. Congress was intimately involved in public lands policy; according to one account, between 1789 and 1834, Congress passed 375 land laws that dealt with the size of lots for sale, the selling price, provisions or credit sales, and preemptions rights. But lands were not always made available to homesteaders: the system was corrupted by speculators who procured the land for timber, mining, grazing, railroad, and other interests.[1] Public land policy was also shaped by local residents, Spanish and American ranchers in the 1800s who sought to manage conflicts over access to the broad expanses of land. Until 1841, cattle ranchers could graze on whatever lands they chose, and contention over land often resulted. In 1841, Congress passed the Pre-Emption Act, which provided for the settlement of lands made available by forcing Native Americans onto reservations. The 1862 Homestead Act encouraged settlement of the West by giving immigrants the right to homestead on up to 160 acres of land. Cattle owners continued to graze cattle on the open range, but after bad weather decimated the open-range cattle industry in 1885 and 1886, the federal government expanded homesteading to encourage settlement of the West.[2]

John Wesley Powell, a geologist and Civil War major who explored the Colorado River and other areas west of the hundredth meridian in the 1870s, was

Table 2.2
Disposition of Public Lands, 1781–1993

Type of Disposition	Acres
Disposition by methods not elsewhere	303,500,000
Granted or sold to homesteaders[b]	287,500,000
Total unclassified and homestead dispositions	591,000,000
Granted to states for:	
Support of common schools	77,630,000
Reclamation of swampland	64,920,000
Construction of railroads	37,130,000
Support of miscellaneous institutions[c]	21,700,000
Purposes not elsewhere classified[d]	117,600,000
Canals and rivers	6,100,000
Construction of wagon roads	3,400,000
Total granted to States	328,480,000
Granted to railroad corporations	94,400,000
Granted to veterans as military bounties	61,000,000
Confirmed as private land claims[e]	34,000,000
Sold under timber and stone law[f]	13,900,000
Granted or sold under timber culture law[g]	10,900,000
Sold under desert land law[h]	10,700,000
Total miscellaneous dispositions	224,900,000
Grand Total	1,144,380,000

[a]Chiefly public, private, and preemption sales, but includes mineral entries, scrip locations, and sales of townsites and townlots.
[b]The homestead laws generally provide for the granting of lands to homesteaders who settle upon and improve vacant agricultural public lands. Payment for the land is sometimes permitted, or required, under certain conditions.
[c]Universities, hospitals, asylums, etc.
[d]For construction of various public improvements (individual items not specified in the granting acts), reclamation of desert lands, construction of water reservoirs, etc.
[e]The Government has confirmed title to lands claimed under valid grants made by foreign governments prior to the acquisition of the public domain by the United States.
[f]The timber and stone laws provided for the sale of lands valuable for timber or stone and unfit for cultivation.
[g]The timber culture laws provided for the granting of public lands to settlers on condition that they plant and cultivate trees on the lands granted. Payments for the lands were permitted under certain conditions.
[h]The desert land laws provide for sale of arid agricultural public lands to settlers who irrigate them and bring them under cultivation.
Source: U.S. Department of the Interior, Bureau of Land Management, *Public Lands Statistics 1996* (March 1997): 5.

one of the first to raise questions about the sustainability of development in the West, the "Lands of the Arid Region," as he called them. He urged that mapping of the western river basins be completed before further development was encouraged, and he was convinced that growth in the West should be limited. Perhaps most notable, he celebrated the uniqueness and beauty of the desert and saw it as much more than a source of gold and other minerals.[3] But few others saw caution and planning as concepts relevant to the vast expanse of lands in the West. The first federal lands preservation efforts did not begin until 1872, when Yellowstone National Park was established. In 1891, forest preserves, the forerunners of national forests, were established. Preserves also included the first formal public lands grazing system, where lands were leased to ranchers. But the vast majority of western lands remained unregulated open range, dominated by a few large cattle owners, who increasingly fought competition from sheepherders as well as from farmers and homesteading and opposed the creation and enlargement of forest preserves.

The western states were treated much differently than their eastern counterparts when they joined the union. As part of the price of admission, many western states were required to give large portions of their land to the federal government. Table 2.3 shows the great disparity among states in the amount of federal lands they include.

Dissatisfaction with federal management of public lands in the 1920s led to the first calls for ceding the lands to states. Droughts in the 1930s exacerbated the effects of decades of overgrazing and led to passage of the Taylor Grazing Act of 1934, which replaced open range grazing with a federal permitting program that formalized the informal grazing patterns. A new Grazing Service in the Interior Department was created to oversee the system. The 1946 Anderson–Mansfield Act created a new public lands system and authorized millions of dollars of federal funds for range improvements. The Grazing Service and the General Land Office were consolidated to form the Bureau of Land Management.[4] But by then much of the public estate had been damaged through unsustainable use.

Other laws passed by Congress facilitated the harvesting of what were believed to be endless resources. The 1872 Mining Law, still in effect in 1997, opened up public lands to mining; all prospectors had to do was to stake out their claim by marking its boundaries, filing a written record at a local office, and spending at least $100 a year in mining activity; once these minimal requirements are satisfied, prospectors can buy the lands for $2.50 to $5.00 an acre. As long as mining efforts continue, these lands can be sold, transferred, and mortgaged. The federal government does not charge royalties on minerals harvested in these lands and has not raised the price of buying lands since 1872. In contrast, coal miners must pay a modest royalty on the value of the coal they harvest from public lands. Timber cutting and grazing on public lands have taken place for more than a century at rates far below what is paid for harvesting resources on private lands. Throughout the nineteenth and early twentieth centuries, scandals about land deals regularly rocked the federal and state governments. The Teapot Dome scandal, for example, implicated many of President Harding's cabinet members in a scheme of private profiteering of public lands. Industrialists unashamedly preached a religion of consumption and profiteering.

Although the Forest Reserve Act of 1891 set aside forestlands for preservation, it was not until several years later that President Grover Cleveland actually ordered lands to be protected, because few states were willing to let any of their forests be protected from logging. During the presidencies of Theodore Roosevelt, Taft, and Wilson, new national forests were created by Congress, and it passed laws to protect historical sites and migratory birds and created the National Park Service in 1918. The primary concern of the conservationists who supported these laws was the efficient use of land, trees, and minerals. They abhorred the waste of natural resources, recognizing that they were limited. Conservation efforts were tempered, however, by World War I and the demand for resources to support the war effort.

By the 1930s, preservationists, those who sought to preserve lands and not just manage their efficient use, began to have some political success, culminating in the creation of the first wilderness lands in 1939. Once again a world war overwhelmed preservation efforts, however, and it was not until 1964 that Congress passed the Wilderness Act, an important milestone in recognizing the importance of protecting public lands. The 1969 National Environmental Policy Act required federal agencies to conduct environmental assessments of major actions, and that act eventually had a significant impact on the process of making decisions about the management of public lands. However, the dominant approach to public lands was the idea of multiple use. Throughout the 1960s and 1970s, Congress enacted a host of laws to protect natural resources but also to ensure their commercial development. The Multiple Use Sustained Yield Act of 1960 and the Classification and Multiple Use Act of 1964 gave explicit recognition to the idea that public lands need not only be seen as places for timber and grazing. The Federal Land Policy and Management Act of 1976 sought to broaden the interests involved in the management of public lands but continued to favor resource development (See Chapter 3). Table 2.4 charts the changes in the revenues to the federal government from the harvesting of public lands and the resources they contain. Table 2.5 shows how federal revenues from federal lands and resources were shared with states in 1993. Table 2.6 outlines how revenues are distributed in different federal funds.

The Public Lands Reformers

In the 1980s, a number of members of Congress began to try to reform public lands policies by increasing the charges placed on public lands' users and increasing environmental protections. Senator Dale Bumpers (D-AR) began sponsoring legislation in the late 1980s to overhaul the mining law but failed to get his bill out of the Energy and Natural Resource Committee. The House debated

Table 2.3

Comparison of Federally Owned Land with Total Acreage of States, Fiscal Year 1994

State	Acreage owned by Federal Government	Total State Acreage[a]	% owned by government[a]
Alabama	1,081,371.5	32,678,400	3.31
Alaska	242,795,767.9	365,481,600	66.43
Arizona	32,488,417.9	72,688,000	44.70
Arkansas	2,932,563.1	33,599,360	8.73
California	46,956,437.6	100,206,720	46.86
Colorado	24,140,220.4	66,485,760	36.31
Connecticut	12,358.7	33,135,360	0.39
Delaware	241,642.0	1,265,920	19.10
District of Columbia	9,151.9	39,040	23.44
Florida	2,719,390.1	34,721,280	7.83
Georgia	1,676,945.3	37,295,360	4.50
Hawaii	688,139.5	4,105,600	16.76
Idaho	32,946,170.9	52,933,120	62.24
Illinois	1,078,210.7	35,795,200	3.01
Indiana	470,098.6	23,158,400	2.03
Iowa	417,634.0	35,860,480	1.17
Kansas	376,699.5	52,510,720	0.72
Kentucky	1,073,673.8	25,512,320	4.21
Louisiana	1,011,232.7	28,867,840	3.50
Maine	329,478.8	19,847,680	1.66
Maryland	529,977.7	6,319,360	8.39
Massachusetts	201,947.6	5,034,880	4.01
Michigan	4,713,346.4	36,492,160	12.92
Minnesota	7,303,590.6	51,205,760	14.26
Mississippi	1,358,177.9	30,222,720	4.49
Missouri	2,107,879.7	44,248,320	4.76
Montana	25,959,402.3	93,271,040	27.83
Nebraska	700,446.8	49,031,680	1.43
Nevada	58,264,528.6	70,264,320	82.92

State	Acreage owned by Federal Government	Total State Acreage[a]	% owned by government[a]
New Hampshire	762,667.3	5,768,960	13.22
New Jersey	638,192.0	4,813,440	13.26
New Mexico	26,549,504.6	77,766,400	34.14
New York	423,120.7	30,680,960	1.38
North Carolina	2,447,946.7	31,402,880	7.80
North Dakota	1,848,925.6	44,452,480	4.16
Ohio	349,725.6	26,222,080	1.33
Oklahoma	769,790.8	44,087,680	1.75
Oregon	36,939,181.5	61,598,720	59.97
Pennsylvania	725,499.2	28,804,480	2.52
Rhode Island	17,658.9	677,120	2.61
South Carolina	791,436.9	19,374,080	4.09
South Dakota	2,697,618.3	48,881,920	5.52
Tennessee	1,563,946.3	26,727,680	5.85
Texas	2,356,223.0	168,217,600	1.40
Utah	33,660,506.3	52,696,960	63.88
Vermont	432,370.5	5,936,640	7.28
Virginia	3,018,082.6	25,496,320	11.84
Washington	11,456,307.5	42,693,760	26.83
West Virginia	1,092,265.2	15,410,560	7.09
Wisconsin	2,917,079.9	35,011,200	8.37
Wyoming	31,024,073.9	62,343,040	49.76
Total	657,256,773.2	2,271,343,360	28.94

Note: This table represents the most current data available from the General Services Administration. Data do not include inland water

[a]Source: U.S. Census of Population.

[b]Excludes trust properties.

Source: U.S. Department of the Interior, Bureau of Land Management, *Public Lands Statistics 1996* (March 1997): 6-7.

Table 2.4
Receipts from the Disposition of Public Lands and Resources, 1785 through Fiscal Year 1996

Fiscal year[a]	Sales of public land and materials	Sales of timber	Fees and commissions	Mineral leases[b]	Outer Continental Shelf leases[c]	Miscellaneous[d]	Total
1785-1880	-	-	-	-	-	$208,059,657	$208,059,657
1881-1890	$76,923,581	-	$13,471,437	-	-	8,873,661	99,268,679
1891-1900	21,312,029	-	9,152,920	-	-	3,027,577	33,492,526
1901-1910	64,777,706	-	16,074,789	-	-	13,242,241	94,094,736
1911-1920	27,940,144	$767,589	14,734,586	-	-	23,580,948	67,023,267
1921-1930	6,734,345	7,537,400	7,173,853	$76,371,588	-	6,636,922	104,454,108
1931-1940	1,334,320	4,289,226	1,944,753	44,602,550	-	5,813,130	57,983,979
1941-1950	2,197,428	24,711,054	1,228,873	146,207,799	-	25,548,418	199,893,572
1951-1960	23,462,798	208,631,073	9,075,890	615,668,922	$434,731,179	107,926,288	1,399,496,150
1961-1970	28,799,311	478,508,666	36,265,491	1,093,760,046	2,917,726,546	214,394,232	4,769,454,292
1971-1980	56,763,803	1,557,613,025	199,418,739	3,086,894,984	30,444,943,752	509,994,006	35,855,628,309
1981-1990	112,271,638	1,744,202,105	65,496,865	2,806,020,807	16,387,602,279	1,046,408,043	22,162,001,737
1991	18,521,150	167,963,621	1,802,858	[e]1,188,470	NA	41,111,425	230,587,524
1992	9,735,550	204,711,350	1,313,752	837,624	NA	40,181,430	256,779,706
1993	11,543,079	150,697,815	1,334,164	1,043,948	NA	79,728,932	244,347,938
1994	8,656,641	70,713,911	1,272,205	2,304,296	NA	42,381,980	125,329,033
1995	14,182,861	45,523,649	1,155,225	3,629,381	NA	39,155,208	103,646,324
1996	12,648,767	92,854,210	939,027	2,396,996	NA	38,248,488	147,087,488
Total	497,805,151	4,758,724,694	381,855,427	7,884,302,047	50,185,003,756	2,412,884,978	66,120,576,053

[a]As of June 30 through 1976; thereafter, as of September 30. [b]Act of February 25, 1920 (41 Stat. 437; 20 U.S.C. 181 seq.). Collection and distribution responsibilities for receipts under this act were transferred to the Minerals Management Service as of October 1, 1983. As of fiscal year 1984, includes only oil and gas pipeline right-of-way rentals. [e]1991 amount is amended from 2,227,063 to 1,188,470. [c]Before 1880, includes all receipts from sale or lease of public lands and resources. After 1880, includes sales of Indian lands, revenues from grazing, rental of land, mineral leasing under special laws, and revenues from other miscellaneous sources. NA.--Not available. Offshore region transferred from Bureau of Land Management to Minerals Management Service jurisdiction effective May 10, 1982.

Source: U.S. Department of the Interior, Bureau of Land Management, *Public Lands Statistics 1996* (March 1997): 105.

34

Table 2.5

Allocation of Receipts to States and Local Governments by Program, Fiscal Year 1996

States	Sales of public lands and materials	Mineral leases and permits	Taylor Grazing Act		Other	Total
			Section 3 permits	Section 15 leases		
Alabama	$275	-	-	-	-	$275
Alaska	1,082	ª$1,001	-	-	-	2,083
Arizona	38,790	24,054	$65,903	$85,853	-	214,600
California	89,308	37,259	26,489	73,166	-	226,222
Colorado	32,726	103,412	75,201	31,872	-	243,211
Idaho	55,930	15,482	210,719	20,712	-	302,843
Minnesota	8					8
Montana	46,346	227,949	132,117	111,866	ᵇ$137,511	655,789
Nebraska	112			411		622
Nevada	ᶜ349,100	8,868	268,738	11,609	-	638,315
New Mexico	22,146	283,303	209,398	141,827	ᵇ7,681	664,355
North Dakota	17	191	-	8,256	-	8,464
Oklahoma	-	75	-	73	-	148
Oregon	409,803	3,534	143,072	27,510	ᵈ73,619,931	74,203,850
South Dakota	212	605	-	76,148	-	76,965
Utah	35,318	24,752	158,512	-	-	218,582
Washington	4,537	-	-	21,762	-	26,299
Wyoming	37,288	230,906	204,683	357,448	-	830,325
Total	1,123,500	961,391	1,494,832	968,513	73,765,123	78,313,359

ªNo receipts for Alaska National Petroleum Reserve lands in fiscal year 1996.

ᵇExecutive Order 10787, November 6, 1958, from nonmineral leasing.

ᶜIncludes Clark County land sales under the Santini-Burton Act of December 23, 1980.

ᵈFY 1996 special O&C payment and special CBWR payment as required by PL 103-66, as amended by PL 103-443 (108 Stat. 4631, 1994).

Source: U.S. Department of the Interior, Bureau of Land Management, *Public Lands Statistics 1996* (March 1997): 110.

Table 2.6
Allocation of Receipts by Source and Fund, Fiscal Year 1996

Source of receipts	Indian trust funds	Reclamation fund	States and counties	Other funds	Total
Mineral leases and permits[a]	$6,709	$584,210	$961,391	$844,686	$2,396,996
Sales of public land	-	4,149,597	310,978	1,630,606	6,091,181
Sales of public timber & materials	-	12,537,646	812,522	6,962,866	20,313,034
Fees and Commissions	-	-	-	939,027	939,027
O&C lands[b]	-	-	73,039,181	4,435,501	77,474,682
Coos Bay Wagon Road lands[c]	-	-	580,750	2,532,734	3,113,484
Grazing leases	-	-	968,513	968,512	1,937,025
Grazing district fees	-	-	1,494,832	10,463,824	11,958,656
Rights-of-way[c]	-	-	-	5,827,496	5,827,496
Miscellaneous leases and permits	-	-	145,192	1,160,203	1,305,395
Nonoperating revenue	-	-	-	11,298,426	11,298,426
Other[c]	-	-	-	4,432,086	4,432,086
Total	**6,709**	**17,271,453**	**78,313,359**	**51,495,967**	**147,087,488**

[a]Includes $864,040 from Bankhead-Jones lands and $1,532,956 from other lands.
[b]PL 103-66 dated August 10, as amended by PL 103-443, dated November 2, 1994, requires special payments to counties funded from the general fund of the U.S. Treasury.
[c]Excludes O&C, CBWR.
Source: U.S. Department of the Interior, Bureau of Land Management, Public Lands Statistics 1996 (March 1997): 111.

a new mining law in 1992, but sponsors could not bring the issue to a vote before the session ended. The House passed a bill in 1991 that would have increased the grazing fees by several times, but western senators also blocked that initiative. Representatives tried to add provisions to increase revenue from grazing, mining, and timber harvests on Interior Department appropriations bills, but the Senate always managed to block those efforts.[5]

The Clinton Administration

Western land issues have never played a major role in presidential politics, but they have had a marginal impact. The Carter administration's public lands reform proposals fueled the Sagebrush Rebellion, which helped to defeat Carter and elect Ronald Reagan in 1980. The election of the Clinton administration initially led to some optimism that economic and environmental goals could be more closely integrated. The appointments of Bruce Babbitt as interior secretary and Vice President Gore allies Carol M. Browner as Environmental Protection Agency (EPA) administrator and Kathleen McGinty as head of the newly created White House Office of Environmental Policy (later abolished, and McGinty was named chair of the Council on Environmental Quality) were key decisions in shifting the focus of environmental policy on the White House. The administration promised to lead the way in finding more cost-effective ways to address environmental problems. Congress promised to give more discretion to federal agencies to remedy problems with environmental laws and their implementation, something members were loath to do during the previous two Republican administrations. The buzzwords became, as one EPA official put it, "pollution prevention and market-based approaches and voluntary programs." But even though partisanship had been reduced, there were still institutional differences between Congress and the White House that posed challenges as Congress faced reauthorization of the Endangered Species Act, the Clean Water Act, and many other environmental laws, and the White House pursued administrative changes.[6]

Babbitt's appointment as interior secretary created tremendous expectations. The *Washington Post* wrote, "No department will make a bigger U-turn with the change of administrations than the one he is scheduled to inherit from his predecessors, James Watt, Donald Hodel, and Manuel Lujan." Babbitt himself had described the department as "a mess," with employees demoralized, the public lands suffering from neglect, and the "paranoid right," as Babbitt called them, challenging the whole idea of public lands. Environmentalists insisted that Babbitt be named interior secretary, and after an outpouring of support for Babbitt, he and the president agreed. His first days in office heightened those expectations as he began describing his new home the "Department of the Environment" and emphasized that the new West was no longer dominated by ranchers, miners, and loggers, but by urban dwellers who wanted to conserve public lands.[7]

Early in 1993, the Clinton administration proposed sweeping changes in public lands policies, including raising grazing fees, imposing hard-rock mining royalties, and below-cost timber sales in national forests, as part of a budget bill aimed at reducing the federal deficit. The proposals were immediately attacked by members of Congress from western states, many of whom were Democrats or represented states where Clinton had won in 1992. Western senators like Max Baucus (D-MT), for example, argued that while reforms were necessary, the proposed royalty of 12.5 percent for hard-rock mining was too high. However, opponents failed to remove the proposals from the Senate budget resolution. They then appealed to the president. After two weeks of meetings, the proposals were deleted from the budget initiative, as the White House sought to trade support for its budget proposals, Clinton's top priority, for retreat on public lands reforms. Administration officials pledged to pursue the policy changes through administrative actions; the secretary of agriculture has the authority to stop below-cost timber sales, and the secretary of the interior can raise grazing fees.

Environmentalists and their allies in Congress severely criticized the administration for caving in to the demands of western senators and failing to get commitments for support of other reforms in return.[8] Representative George Miller (D-CA) complained that the budget bill was the "first real chance we had for reform, and it was just given away." A Sierra Club official was more direct: "The signal [the administration] sent was that they tucked their tails between their legs when the western Senators barked."[9] The proposals for mining, grazing, and timber reform would have raised only $821 million, a tiny fraction of the $300 billion deficit, but were nevertheless championed by the administration as a way to move toward a balanced budget. Once the proposals were taken out of the package, Secretary Babbit began describing them as free-market economic reforms, aimed at conserving resources and allocating them more efficiently.[10]

In October 1993, the administration's initiative to add grazing fee hikes and new environmental safeguards for grazing lands to the Interior Department appropriations bill failed when the Senate was unsuccessful in ending a filibuster of the bill by Republicans and western Democrats. The proposals were eventually dropped from the bill, but not until after western senators blasted the administration for launching a "war on the West." However, while the Senate resisted changes, the media gave increasingly favorable attention to Secretary Babbitt's efforts to get welfare cowboys, as he called them, to pay fair prices for using public lands and to increase environmental protection. Babbitt's agenda of reorienting the Bureau of Reclamation away from dam building and toward water conservation, amending the Endangered Species Act to increase habitat preservation, and updating mining and logging policies raised tremendous opposition among some in the West, while encouraging many others who believed such changes were long overdue. Babbitt argued that public land policy should be guided by the idea of "dominant public use," requiring the preservation of ecosystems, rather than "multiple use," where logging, mining, and ranching interests dominate. Dominant public use requires policymakers to look at the needs for biodiversity, watershed protection, and landscape, as well as the opportunities for extractive industries, and set priorities.[11]

Some changes were pursued through administrative actions, such as the creation of the National Biological Survey, to inventory plant and animal life. However, when the administration eventually sought congressional support, the survey was limited by conservatives who feared it would lead to more regulation. Part of the criticism was rooted in the perception of some western members of Congress and governors that the Interior Department officials failed to include them in policy formation discussions or warn them of initiatives affecting their states.[12]

Administrative policy making satisfied no one, as criticism of agency officials came from both environmentalist and industry directions. Dale Robertson, chief of the Forest Service, was forced out of his job and moved to a position in the Agriculture Department because of criticism that he was too willing to acquiesce to timber industry demands, failed to end below-cost timber cuts, and was unable to deal with internal dissent. The associate chief was similarly removed from office. Critics of federal resource policy took particular aim at the Forest Service for sponsoring unsustainable levels of timber cutting that lost money as well as resulted in environmental damage to streams and wildlife habitat and for ignoring environmental preservation laws in making agency decisions. Jack Ward Thomas, a scientist who had designed the Clinton administration's plan to resolve the spotted owl conflict in the Northwest, replaced Robertson; Thomas resigned in 1996.[13] Jim Baca, head of the Bureau of Land Management, was also bumped up to the Interior Department in January 1994, because his aggressive stance toward revising mining and grazing policy had upset western officials.[14]

Public land reform was stymied by a combination of forces. Babbitt's expansive ambitions fueled opponents: the wise use movement saw him a "perfect Darth Vader," said one leader. The movement convinced a few western senators like Ben Nighthorse Campbell (R-CO) that the changes Babbitt promised would end development and end the traditional West, and they convinced the president. The president's decision to remove the grazing and mining reforms from the budget bill surprised even the cattle ranchers who were pushing for a reduction in proposed fees but "never thought the whole thing would be gone." Clinton continued to push Babbitt to soften his charge in order to protect jobs or do whatever was necessary to protect his political support in the few areas of the West where he won in 1992—Montana, Colorado, Nevada, New Mexico, and California. But Clinton's victories in these areas were due to urban support, not miners, grazers, and loggers, and the political retreat did little to win new converts to the president and only frustrated and alienated his supporters.[15]

Public lands conflicts were not limited to the West. In the Everglades National Park, phosphorus-laden water from sugarcane and vegetable farms threatened the park's wildlife. Farmers and federal officials agreed on a general plan in

July 1993 to reduce the amount of land in production in order to provide filtration marshes to absorb the phosphorus. The negotiations reached an impase when farmers demanded that they not be required to take additional conservation steps in the future, a state sugar tax be imposed to generate revenue for environmental restoration, and other provisions. The Interior Department sought broad discretion to devise a management plan to protect the entire ecosystem that might require further restrictions on farmlands.[16] In November 1996, Florida voters rejected a ballot initiative to impose a tax of one penny on each pound of raw sugar grown in the Everglades region. The money would have been used for conservation and protection programs.[17]

In 1994, Secretary of Interior Babbitt chose grazing policy as his major reform effort. "Rangeland Reform '94" put in place major policy changes aimed at giving greater protection to rangelands and giving the public greater opportunity to participate in decisions. The Interior Department began taking a more conciliatory stance, promising to give westerners more input into department policy proposals. Western senators' opposition to the department's grazing and other proposals forced some policy concessions. That, in turn, angered environmentalists and their congressional allies. The proposal for "multiple resource advisory councils," made up of ranchers and conservationists, to advise the department on rangeland matters, for example, was criticized by conservationists as politicizing rangeland policy. Existing grazing advisory boards were composed solely of ranchers; the new approach asked governors to nominate five members from timber, mining, and ranching interests; five from conservation and sportsmen groups; and five from state and local officials or others who use public lands and are not represented in the other groups. The secretary of the interior would make the formal appointment. The council would determine the number of head of cattle to be grazed on lands and how to spend the state's share of the grazing fees collected.[18]

Babbitt's conciliatory style and willingness to strike deals even when he was not being undercut by the president frustrated his allies, who saw in him a willingness to settle for too little protection. His compromises on timber cuts in the Northwest's old-growth forests, pollution of the Everglades by the sugar industry, endangered species in southern California, and grazing reform satisfied few stakeholders. Conservationists feared that so much development had already occurred that we cannot compromise on what remains. Jobs in the extractive industries rely on developing resources at existing levels and cutbacks were bitterly criticized. Babbitt promised to push administrative changes in grazing when the legislative package stalled, then abandoned that effort and delegated policy development to local interests, with broad federal guidelines. His multiple-resource advisory councils were supposed to be community-based opportunities for grazing and conservation interests to fashion compromise. But those efforts were swamped by the determined efforts of grazing interests and their allies to resist any real change.

The Interior Department, said Bruce Babbitt in a 1994 interview, "has been in the cross-fire—every day since it was established—between the forces who wanted to seize the public land base and exploit it and the [conservationists]. It has been a constant theme for 150 years."[19] Babbitt's promises of fundamental change and his reliance on compromise and conciliation proved to be quite problematic. His ambitious promises fueled the fear of the old West, and his willingness to compromise (and the abandonment of some positions ordered by the president) infuriated the new West. The wise use movement renewed its efforts to reduce federal control of public lands; the environmental movement felt betrayed.[20] However, as the 103d Congress ended in October 1994, the only major conservationist legislation enacted created two new national parks in California—Death Valley and Joshua Tree—and a third protected area, the Mojave Desert.

Why did Congress and the Clinton administration accomplish so little in 1993 and 1994, when the Democrats were in control of both the legislative and executive branches? Democrats failed to respond effectively to the problems raised by critics of environmental and natural resource policy. Members of Congress in the West were all too willing to distance themselves from the Clinton administration. The administration was remarkably unwilling to make any demands in exchange for compromises on public lands reform. By 1994, candidates in congressional races could openly run against environmental regulation, a dramatic shift from what had been a strong bipartisan issue.[21] The wise use movement, states' rights advocates, industry lobbyists, and trade associations all combined to form a powerful political partnership for Republicans.

The Republican Resurgence

In 1994, Republican candidates in a number of western states were successful in running against Babbitt and Clinton's western lands reforms and their "war on the West." The Republicans effectively integrated attacks on Democrats for launching a war on the West with antitax, anti-Washington, and antieastern sentiments. The migration of newcomers to the West was expected by many to bolster the conservation movement, but some immigrants were conservatives from areas like southern California who continued to vote Republican. The anti-Washington sentiment was strong and was bolstered by a number of developments: ranchers who had depended on public lands for generations and feared the Babbitt reforms, families that saw their children leave western states because no jobs were available, and residents who argued that many western states were basically colonies that exported their resource base. Since most of the resources were located on public lands, development, not conservation, demanded priority.[22]

Few issues were more politically potent for Republicans than threats to private property (see Chapter 1). Throughout the late 1980s and into the 1990s there were backlashes against environmental preservation efforts by property owners whose wealth had been threatened by cleanup of hazardous waste sites, protection of wetlands and endangered species, and other environmental regulations. The Sagebrush Rebellion found a powerful ally in the private property protection movement found throughout the nation. These groups helped prevent Congress from revisiting environmental laws in the early 1990s because of the fear that the conservative movement would force amendments to weaken the law.[23] But the failure of Congress to respond to the private property/wise use movements contributed to the Republican takeover of Congress in 1994. Once in office, members attached private property takings provisions to numerous environmental bills, including the reauthorization of the Clean Water and Endangered Species Acts.[24]

There was some green backlash to antigovernment, antipreservationist sentiment in the West. In New Mexico, for example, the green party fielded candidates in a number of races in 1994. Candidates ran for office under the green banner as they concluded that the Democratic Party had become too closely tied to big business and failed to deal with environmental problems.[25] But the antigovernment, antipreservation movement found strong allies in the Republican Party. The traditional extractive industries, private property protection advocates, and their congressional allies were able to resist a Democratic Congress and White House in 1993 and 1994. The tension between Washington and the West culminated in the 1994 congressional election: once the Republicans gained control of Congress in 1995, the prospects for environmental and budget reforms were dead.

The 1994 House Republican "Contract with America" promised to "roll back government regulations and create jobs."[26] One of its central pieces was the Job Creation and Wage Enhancement Act, introduced at the beginning of the 104th Congress. It did not mention the environment directly but included provisions designed to change administrative law and the rule-making process for major rules, increase opportunities for regulated industries to help shape the provisions, ensure that only relatively serious risks are regulated, require a demonstration that the benefits resulting from these regulations costs exceed the cost of compliance with them and that the regulation proposed is the most cost-effective option, create a regulatory moratorium on the issuance of new regulations until the regulatory reform agenda is enacted, establish a regulatory "budget" that places a cap on compliance costs to be imposed on industry, change the way federal programs are funded, so that unfunded federal mandates require additional votes by Congress, require federal agencies to compensate property owners for loss in property values resulting from environmental regulation, and increase procedural protections for those subject to regulatory inspections and enforcement such as a right to have counsel present during inspections and legal actions that can be taken against regulatory officials.

Other reforms that were proposed as part of Congress' regulatory agenda include delegating more autonomy and responsibility to states to formulate and implement policies; giving Congress the power to review and overturn proposed regulations by enacting a joint resolution of disapproval that would be subject to presidential veto; holding "correction days" to take up proposals for legislation to eliminate existing federal rules that are considered "obnoxious or burdensome to state or local governments" to be proposed by a congressional task force that would identify possible regulations, confer with the relevant committees, and (if there was broad support) bring them to the House floor for an up-or-down two-thirds majority vote; and creating a "regulatory burden commission" to propose legislation on an industry-by-industry basis.[27]

Frank Lutz, the Republican pollster who worked with Newt Gingrich (R-Ga.) in creating the Contract with America, told his clients that "Americans believe Washington has gone too far in regulating and they want to turn the clock and paperwork back." Party strategist William Kristol suggested Republicans immediately identify regulatory "excesses" and organized a meeting entitled "What to Kill First: Agencies to Dismantle, Programs to Eliminate, and Regulations to Stop." William Niskanen, head of the Cato Institute, called on Congress to "rein in what I call the 'Nanny State.' Stop telling states where to set speed limits. . . . Stop telling businesses about whether and when employees and customers may smoke."[28] Heritage Foundation analysts published "real life 'horror' stories of individuals who have lost their property or had their business harmed because of overzealous government regulators" and called on Congress to compensate property owners for regulatory takings.[29]

Western Republicans took over key committee and subcommittee chairs and took aim at the environmental and public lands laws, regulations, and agencies that they have been criticizing for years. Congressional Republican leaders laid out an ambitious environmental agenda. House Majority Leader Dick Armey (TX) promised: "If we don't close down the Environmental Protection Agency, we at least put a snaffle bit on them and ride the pony down. They're out of control." Senator Alan Simpson (WY) promised to restrain Secretary Babbitt and to "go through his little agency with a fine-toothed comb." The antiregulatory rhetoric had a populist ring as proponents challenged the ability of the federal government to enforce existing laws and promised to eventually rewrite the laws to ensure changes were long-lasting.[30] Environmentalists were slow to respond to the charges of the wise use movement and other critics of regulation and initially unable to effectively articulate the benefits of preservation efforts and the economic advantages of policy reform in areas such as national park concessions and mining law.[31]

The 104th Congress pursued its own idea of reform of natural resource policy along three tracks. First, it sought to restructure the process by which federal agencies issued regulations. Bills required cost-benefit analysis of regulations, new procedures that gave regulated industries more opportunities to challenge regulations, and more scientific, judicial, and congressional review of proposed regulations. Second, Congress proposed revisions to virtually every natural resource and environmental law. The House bill to reauthorize the Endangered Species Act would have no longer required recovery plans for all threatened and endangered species, prohibit only direct actions affecting endangered species but not affecting their habitat, and compensate landowners if regulations reduce their property values by 20 percent or more and require the federal government to buy their land if it is devalued by 50 percent or more. Other House bills would have permitted states to take responsibility for recovery plans for threatened and endangered species or would create tax and other incentives to encourage habitat protection; one would make the act itself a voluntary program in which landowners would be encouraged to participate. Senate bills ranged from proposals protecting only the species themselves rather than their habitat and weakening the protection given to imperiled species, to giving discretion to the secretary of commerce or interior to make decisions concerning protection of species.[32] Bills aimed at the U.S. Forest Service and timber policy would have opened up new areas for timber cuts and expedite procedures for awarding contracts.[33] Rangeland reform bills would have raised grazing fees modestly, extended the length of permits, reduced environmental controls over public lands, and reversed many of the reforms pursued through rule making by the Clinton administration.[34] Mining reform legislation would have required, for the first time, royalties for hard-rock mining on federal lands and would have replaced the current patent system with a fair market value requirement for purchasing federal lands, as a way to forestall more fundamental changes in mining law.[35] Bills in both houses would establish a voluntary program of transferring Bureau of Land Management lands to state control.[36]

The third approach pursued by Congress was to use the budget process to reshape public lands policy. The battle between congressional Republicans and the Babbitt–Clinton team was particularly nasty during the summer of 1995. Congressional budget cuts, Babbitt charged, would force the Interior Department to close 200 small national parks and restrict access to Yellowstone, Grand Canyon, and other major parks. Babbitt's National Heritage Tour went from town to town, warning citizens of the impending threat to their beloved national parks. In response, the chair of the House Appropriations Committee, Bob Livingston (R-LA), proposed that the Interior Department's public affairs budget be cut by two-thirds. The committee also voted to cut spending on construction in parks by 40 percent and virtually defund the Park Service's acquisition fund. That proposal would permit the service to complete only a small amount of the $4.5 billion in needed projects. The biggest conflicts focused on the following proposals:

- allowing states to take control of Bureau of Land Management (BLM) lands within their borders and expand mining, logging, and grazing;

- allowing states to take over national parks and other protected areas;

- appointing a commission to determine which parks should be transferred to states, transferred to private parties, or closed;

- permitting counties to enact ordinances providing that they, not federal agencies, have authority to manage federal lands;

- continuing the salvage logging provision that suspended environmental laws in national forests; and

- cutting funds for administering the new Mojave National Reserve in California and return control of the land to the BLM.[37]

The Concurrent Resolution on the Budget for fiscal year (FY) 1996, for example, which set overall tax and spending guidelines for the Appropriations Committees, was passed by the House and Senate in June 1995 (as a resolution, it is not legally binding and is not submitted to the president, although it does bind the House and Senate to the figures for total spending and revenues). The resolution outlined how Congress planned to achieve a balanced budget by the year 2002 and called for a 13 percent spending reduction in the natural resources and environment category.[38] The budget resolution included a number of provisions aimed at reducing environmental regulation of air pollution and toxic wastes and assumed in estimating revenues the sale of public lands and opening the Arctic National Wildlife Refuge for oil development leases and reduced funding for acquisition of lands for conservation (these provisions had to be attached to regular bills that are enacted into law to be binding).

Rescissions bills revoke money already appropriated in a current year: the July 1995 Rescissions Act prohibited the EPA from implementing certain regulations, cut millions of dollars from global environmental and energy efficiency programs, exempted some logging from environmental controls and opened salvage logging to live and healthy trees as well as diseased ones, barred the Forest Service from creating Habitat Conservation Areas in the Tongass National Forest, prohibited the National Biological Survey from searching for the Alabama sturgeon in several Alabama waterways to ensure no protective actions are taken, and granted thousands of grazing permits and exempted others from environmental impact statement requirements.[39]

Supplemental appropriations provide for additional spending in a current year. A 1995 Defense Department supplemental spending bill eliminated air pollution regulations aimed at southern California and imposed a moratorium on new listings of threatened and endangered species.[40] Legislation to reform the National Park Service was defeated on the House floor, but the key provisions were resurrected in the House Resources Committee and included in the FY 1996 reconciliation bill.[41] The reconciliation bill that Congress passed in November 1995, omnibus legislation that amends revenue and spending authority to ensure compliance with the budget resolution, also included environment-related provisions, including opening the Arctic National Wildlife Refuge in Alaska in order to raise $1.3 billion in revenue to the federal government from oil leases. President Clinton vetoed the reconciliation bill in December 1995.

While riders have often been attached to appropriations bills, their use by members of the 104th Congress to prohibit enforcement of regulations and statutory provisions by the EPA, the Interior Department, and other agencies through appropriations riders was unprecedented.[42] The thirteen House appropriations bills for FY 1996 included eight riders aimed at implementation of the Endangered Species Act, eight affecting wilderness protection, six aimed at forests, six affecting research on renewable energy, five aimed at grazing, three affecting western water reform, and thirty-six aimed at clean air, clean water, and hazardous waste regulations.[43] The House appropriations bill for the EPA (and other agencies) included seventeen environmental riders.[44] The Senate appropriations bill included seven riders. Despite threats by the Clinton administration to veto any bill with riders and deep budget cuts, the bill reported by the conference committee included several riders and imposed major budget cuts.[45] The FY 1996 interior appropriations bill proposed by the House Appropriations Subcommittee included a $12 billion budget that would have cut spending by $1.5 billion from the 1995 level and $1.8 billion from the Clinton administration request and would have made the following additional policy changes: a moratorium on the listing of new species under the Endangered Species Act, an end to the moratorium imposed in the last Congress on new mining patents; replacing the more preservationist-oriented National Park Service with the Bureau of Land Management in managing the Mojave Preserve, which was created in the 1994 California desert protection act (the bill gave $1 for the National Park Service to manage the Mojave National Preserve in California, and the balance of the $600,000 went to the BLM); budget cuts for the National Biological Service, created to improve research on biodiversity, and shifting it to the U.S. Geological Survey; a ninety-day moratorium on the implementation of new grazing regulations that cattle and sheep ranchers oppose; and reducing efforts to study the ecology of the Columbia River Basin and the impact of protecting endangered fish on logging in the region.[46] Other provisions would have reduced Department of Energy conservation programs, prohibited issuance of new standards for consumer appliance energy efficiency, and increased timber harvesting in the Tongass National Forest.[47] The full committee proposed to eliminate the National Biological Survey.[48] President Clinton vetoed the appropriations bill in December 1995. In his veto message, he argued that the bill "would threaten public health and the environment" as well as end important social programs.[49] The bill was "unacceptable because it would unduly restrict our ability to protect America's natural resources and cultural heritage, promote the technology we need for long-term energy conservation and economic growth."[50]

By the end of 1995, Congress had passed, and the president had signed (or permitted to become law without his signature), six appropriations bills; the president had vetoed (and Congress had failed to override) four bills; and Congress had failed to pass three appropriations bills.[51] The debate over these appropriations bills, the continuing resolutions aimed at keeping the government open until the appropriations bills were passed, and the balanced budget or reconciliation bill consumed the congressional agenda and prevented consideration of most other legislation. While some budget cuts were not enacted into law, agency programs were affected by the reductions in spending that have been required in the continuing resolutions that were passed in the fall of 1995 and winter of 1996. The government shutdowns that occurred before continuing resolutions were passed and the uncertainty, in general, surrounding funding of these agencies have had a major impact on a number of environmental programs, such as the publication of the Toxic Release Inventory, which reports the release of toxic chemicals into the air and water and onto land.[52] There have also been reductions in pollution inspections, enforcement actions, studies of water pollution, and Superfund cleanups.[53] Table 2.7 provides an overview of the federal budget and traces changes in the share of the budget allocated to natural resources. Table 2.8 summarizes the Interior Department's FY 1997 budget.

The Revolution in Retreat

Environmental groups began to challenge the new Republican agenda in the spring of 1995. The largest environmental organizations proposed an Environmental Bill of Rights, signed by Americans throughout the nation and presented to Congress and the White House.[54] They painted the Republican leaders as antienvironmental extremists. But the Republicans deflected the criticism successfully for most of 1995. Why did the Republican juggernaut, which appeared so formidable during the first one hundred days, fail? The Senate, as by design, moved more slowly and declined to pass many of the bills that were pushed through the House. House and Senate Republicans were sometimes unable to broker differences that arose in conference committees when bills did get through the Senate. By the fall of 1995, the leadership was forced to halt virtually all other efforts to conduct the budget negotiations. Even within the House, the leadership failed to keep Republicans together after the first one hundred days. The coalition of libertarians, the Christian Right, fiscal conservatives, balance-the-budget-at-all-costs freshmen, and moderate Republicans in the House splintered once most of the bills that sprang from the Contract with America were voted on, and the agenda turned to more controversial issues. Moderate Republicans bolted and joined Democrats to defeat appropriations bills that were too heavily laden with riders aimed at preventing enforcement of environmental laws and other measures that dealt with sensitive social issues, such as abortion.[55]

The most important factor was President Clinton's decision to challenge the House Republicans' agenda, rather than cooperate with their legislative plans. The president found the most political success in confronting the Republicans over Medicare and, to a lesser extent, the environment. The president's favorability ratings vacillated around 45 percent throughout the first half of 1995 (except for a brief spurt after the Oklahoma City bombing) until November, when he turned Medicare and other budget differences into polarizing issues. Even his threat to veto the welfare reform bill, despite promises to sign a very similar version several months earlier, seemed to boost his political stature, and he finished 1995 with a 52 percent approval mark.[56]

Table 2.7
Federal Government Outlays for Natural Resources and Environment, Fiscal Years 1965–2002

Year	Water Resources	Conservation and land management	Recreational resources	Pollution control and abatement	Other natural resources	Total
1965	1,546	341	218	134	292	2,531
1970	1,514	376	363	384	428	3,065
1975	2,608	655	803	2,523	757	7,346
1980	4,223	1,043	1,677	5,510	1,405	13,858
1981	4,132	1,191	1,597	5,170	1,478	13,568
1982	3,948	1,084	1,435	5,012	1,519	12,998
1983	3,904	1,503	1,454	4,263	1,548	12,672
1984	4,070	1,302	1,581	4,044	1,595	12,593
1985	4,122	1,481	1,621	4,465	1,668	13,357
1986	4,041	1,388	1,513	4,831	1,866	13,639
1987	3,783	1,473	1,564	4,869	1,675	13,363
1988	4,034	2,189	1,673	4,832	1,878	14,606
1989	4,271	3,324	1,817	4,878	1,890	16,182
1990	4,401	3,553	1,876	5,170	2,080	17,080
1991	4,366	4,047	2,137	5,861	2,148	18,559
1992	4,559	4,581	2,378	6,075	2,432	20,025
1993	4,258	4,777	2,620	6,061	2,522	20,239
1994	4,528	5,161	2,619	6,050	2,706	21,064
1995	4,791	5,318	2,828	6,512	2,656	22,105
1996*	4,729	4,876	2,568	6,517	2,860	21,550

*estimate

48

Table 2.7 continued
Total Outlays for Grants to State and Local Governments 1960–2002 (in Millions of Dollars)

Year	Agriculture	Defense	Commerce	EPA	Interior	Other	Total
1960	44	-	-	40	24	-	108
1965	74	12	-	75	22	-	183
1970	104	19	-	194	91	2	411
1975	136	-	24	2,025	247	5	2,437
1980	111	-	110	4,603	531	8	5,363
1981	121	-	97	4,181	538	7	4,944
1982	199	-	83	4,079	510	-	4,872
1983	189	-	123	3,266	440	-	4,018
1984	204	-	140	2,921	513	-	3,779
1985	198	-	167	3,197	506	-	4,069
1986	212	-	139	3,419	486	-	4,255
1987	171	-	158	3,251	493	-	4,073
1988	176	-	140	2,895	537	-	3,747
1989	158	-	151	2,797	500	-	3,606
1990	197	-	93	2,874	580	-	3,745
1991	228	-	126	3,071	614	-	4,040
1992	214	-	55	3,038	621	-	3,929
1993	224	-	64	2,852	656	-	3,796
1994	269	-	62	2,700	733	-	3,765
1995	352	-	11	2,912	873	-	4,148
1996*	321	-	60	2,828	800	-	4,009

*estimate

Source: Executive Office of the President of the United States, Office of Management and Budget, Historical Tables: Fiscal Year 1997 (Washington, DC: U.S. Government Printing Office, 1996): 50–59, 201–39.

Table 2.8

Interior Department Spending, Fiscal Year 1997 (in Thousands of Dollars of New Budget Authority)

	Fiscal 1996 Appropriation	Fiscal 1997 Appropriation
Interior Department		
Bureau of Land Management		
Management of lands	$ 567,453	572,164
Fire protection, firefighting	235,924	252,042
Payment in lieu of taxes	113,500	113,500
Other	189,078	152,969
Subtotal	$ 1,105,955	$ 1,090,675
Fish and Wildlife Service		
Resource management	502,610	523,947
Construction	74,955	43,365
Land acquisition	35,900	44,479
Other	31,366	40,814
Subtotal	$ 645,831	$ 652,605
National Park Service		
Operations	1,082,481	1,152,311
Construction	129,225	163,444
Land acquisition, state aid	49,100	53,915
Other	43,861	44,588
Subtotal	$ 1,367,667	$ 1,414,258
Bureau of Indian Affairs		
Indian programs	1,384,934	1,436,902
Claim settlements, payment to Indians	80,645	69,241
Other	122,833	99,531
Subtotal	$ 1,588,412	$ 1,605,674
Geological Survey	732,163	738,913
Minerals Management Service	188,995	163,395
Bureau of Mines*	64,000	---
Surface Mining Reclamation	269,857	271,757
Territorial affairs	103,126	88,726
Department offices	133,116	151,294
Total, Interior Department	**$ 6,199,122**	**$ 6,177,297**
Forest Service (Agriculture Department)		
National forest system	1,283,657	1,274,781
Forest research	178,000	179,786
Fire protection, firefighting	385,485	530,016
Construction	224,400	174,974
Timber receipts (to Treasury)	*-44,548*	---
Other	291,631	201,402
Total, Forest Service	**$ 2,363,173**	**2,360,959**

Table 2.8 continued

	Fiscal 1996 Appropriation	Fiscal 1997 Appropriation
Energy Department		
Clean-coal technology	---	-123,000
Fossil energy research	417,018	364,704
Naval Petroleum Reserve	148,786	143,786
Energy conservation	537,189	569,762
Strategic Petroleum Reserve	---	---
Other	76,163	64,845
Total, Energy Department	**$ 1,179,156**	**$ 1,020,097**
Other Related Agencies		
Indian health	1,986,800	2,054,000
Indian education	52,500	61,000
Smithsonian Institution	376,092	370,407
National Endowment for the Arts	99,494	99,494
National Endowment for the Humanities	110,000	110,000
Other Agencies	173,555	893,616
Grand Total	**$ 12,539,892**	**$ 13,146,870**

* For termination of the agency and cleanup activities.
Source: PL 14-128; Allan Freedman, "After Interior's Smooth Ride, Some Issues Left Behind," Congressional Quarterly Weekly Report (October 5, 1996): 2859.

The House Republicans greatly contributed to public skepticism and cynicism through their unabashed pro-business initiatives. House Majority Whip Tom DeLay (Texas) kept a book in his office listing how much the 400 largest political action committees (PACs) gave to Republicans and Democrats during the past two years. House leaders have created their own PACs to funnel money to the reelection campaigns of loyal Republican members. Representative John Boehner, chair of the Republican Conference, coordinated efforts among interest groups to raise money in support of the provisions in the Contract with America.[57] In 1994, Democrats received about two-thirds of the contributions made by the largest PACs; in 1995, Republicans received nearly 60 percent.[58] The access given in return to lobbyists was remarkable, even by Washington standards. Lobbyists were invited to write bills and sit with committee members in hearings.[59] A Senate Banking Committee staff member drafted a bill long sought by the securities industry after he had accepted a job with a banking and securities firm. Other people who worked for securities firms were also involved in writing the bill.[60] Journalists described lobbyists ensconced in rooms next to the House Chamber, tapping out on their laptops talking points for Republican members to use in floor debates. Industry lobbyists helped write the House regulatory moratorium bill.[61]

Reports on the new congressional leaders regularly emphasized their close ties to business.[62] Senator Slade Gorton (R-WA) was singled out for having lobbyists draft a public lands bill and then having to ask the lobbyists to explain the provisions in the bill he was sponsoring: an aide wrote to him that the "coalitions delivered your [Endangered Species Act] bill to me on Friday. . . . I know that you are anxious to get the bill introduced, however, it is important that we have a better than adequate understanding of the bill prior to introduction."[63] Pressure groups were created to focus on specific issues. The Frontiers of Freedom think tank, created by former Wyoming Republican senator Malcolm Wallop, devised a Freedom Index to indicate congressional support for property rights and champion private property owners' rights to do whatever they want with their property.[64] The Fair Government Foundation lobbied against campaign finance reform and regulation of lobbyists. Project Relief was created by industries that favored regulatory reform.[65] These groups reinforced the belief that the Republicans were uninterested in changing the way in which Washington works but were quite content to keep the system in place and working for them. The free flow of campaign money created a fissure in the congressional Republican establishment. Some members, led by the House leadership, sought to raise as much money as possible to ensure the revolution continued. Other members feared that a continuation of business as usual threatened their future by making voters even more skeptical of all politicians.[66]

Republican-proposed spending cuts also contributed to the stalling of the revolution. Most cuts were aimed at Democratic constituents—the poor, mothers on welfare, recipients of Medicaid and Medicare—and failed to include programs of interest to Republicans, such as home mortgage deductions for second homes, subsidies to corporations, Social Security payments to wealthy citizens that represent several times the amount they contributed to the Social Security system, or the other $200 billion worth of grants and tax breaks that go to Americans who earn more than $50,000 a year.[67] The House Republican Medicare reform proposal was widely criticized for buying off doctors and other groups in exchange for their support. The tax cuts they proposed primarily benefited wealthy taxpayers; the taxes to be increased, through a reduction in the Earned Income Tax Credit, fell on the working poor.[68] Special tax breaks were aimed at the funeral industry, convenience store owners, research and experimentation tax credit for businesses, insurance companies, truckers, newspaper publishers, natural gas and water utilities, and other interests that had close ties to influential members or had given major campaign contributions.[69] But the failure of the Republican effort was ultimately due to the widespread public support for environmental, health, and safety regulation. This strong underlying support caused a split between Republicans and gave the Clinton administration the incentive to resist congressional relief efforts.

The fiscal year 1997 budget process was much less contentious. The House and Senate passed the conference report in June 1996, laying out Congress' plan to achieve a balanced budget by the year 2002.[70] The resolution called for a $3.8 billion cut in environmental and natural resource spending over the next six years, a 17 percent reduction from the Clinton administration proposal. The resolution also included instructions to open the Arctic National Wildlife Refuge to energy development.[71] The FY 1997 appropriations bill for the Veterans Administration (VA), the Department of Housing and Urban Development (HUD) and independent agencies (including the EPA) was passed with no controversial riders.[72] The FY 1997 Interior Department appropriations bill, which also funds the Forest Service, was passed in June 1996.[73] The $12 billion spending bill cut spending $500 million from 1996 spending. The White House threatened a veto of the bill because it provided $235 million less for energy conservation funding than the president had requested. There were some two dozen amendments considered by the House floor. Amendments were passed that (1) struck an exemption for 40,000 acres of private land in California from coverage under the Endangered Species Act and (2) eliminated an order to the Interior Department to sell $200 million in oil reserves from the Strategic Petroleum Reserve. Amendments that failed included (1) a repeal of the 1995 salvage timber bill (by a vote of 208 to 211) and (2) elimination of the Forest Service's budget to build new roads in national forests that would essentially stop logging in roadless areas (the amendment passed on June 19 by 211 to 210 and was called up the next day, when the amendment failed on a 211 to 211 vote as Democrats opposed to logging were joined by Republican deficit hawks who opposed the subsidy to the timber industry). The administration also threatened a veto because of spending cuts, particularly for energy efficiency programs. The House also dropped a proposal to sell oil from the Strategic Petroleum Reserve to raise $220 million in revenue; the oil was pumped into the reserve when oil was selling for $35/barrel but would be sold at less than $20/barrel. The bill generated opposition from conservative Republicans, who believed spending was too high, and from Democrats, who believed it was too low.[74] The Clinton administration also promised to veto the bill if it included an amendment that would have exempted 40,000 acres of private lands in California from the Endangered Species Act; the House dropped the proposal. The U.S. Fish and Wildlife Service designated in May 1996 about 700,000 acres of federal, state, and county land and a small fraction of private land as a critical habitat for the marbled murret. The House Appropriations Committee included a provision that would exempt the designation for most of the private land. On the House floor, proponents defended the vote as a referendum on private property rights and the right of private landowners to profitably use their land. But opponents were successful in portraying the proposal as a bailout for special interests, particularly for the Pacific Lumber Company, a firm that had greatly increased its logging rates in order to pay for junk bonds used to finance its takeover by Maaxam, Inc. The House voted 257 to 164 to strip the provision. Republicans who voted against the amendment apparently saw the exemption as too narrowly designed to benefit one company and believed the entire ESA should be reformed rather than pursuing piecemeal exemptions.[75]

The agencies funded in the bill included the following appropriations for 1997[76]:

Bureau of Land Management	$1.077 billion
National Park Service	1.322 billion
U.S. Forest Service	2.197 billion
Energy Department (selected programs in this bill)	1.072 billion
U.S. Geological Survey	.730 billion
Office of Surface Mining and Enforcement	.270 billion
U.S. Fish and Wildlife Services	.625 billion

The House passed on June 12 a $12.3 billion FY 1997 agriculture appropriations bill, which included funding for several new and existing land conservation programs.[77] The Environmental Quality Incentives Program provides technical assistance to farmers to manage soil and water resources. The Conservation Reserve Program pays farmers not to cultivate fragile farmlands. The Wetlands Reserve Program pays farmers not to cultivate wetlands. The Farmland Protection Program prevents farmlands from being converted to nonagricultural uses. The Conservation Farm Option pays farmers of certain crops (wheat, feed grains, upland cotton, and rice) for conservation efforts. No funding was provided for the Wildlife Habitat Incentives Program, which helps landowners improve wildlife habitat on private lands. The Clinton administration objected to the bill because it funded the program at levels below those authorized in the new farm bill.[78]

As the 104th Congress came to a close, members passed an omnibus parks bill that they had been considering for months, which included federal funds to help purchase the Sterling Forest on the border of New Jersey and New York, creation of a trust to preserve the Presidio in San Francisco, creation of a tallgrass prairie reserve in Kansas, a swap of lands in Utah for a ski resort, and dozens of other projects. The deal went through after the White House agreed to continue negotiations with Senator Frank Murkowski (R-AK) over the rights of an Alaskan logging company to continue timber cuts in the Tongass National Forest. The negotiations were aimed at permitting the company to close its pulp mill but continue to log for an additional two years and send the timber to other mills.[79] The parks bill, a 700-page package offering benefits to forty-one states, was held up by Murkowski's demand that it include an extension of the Ketchikan Pulp Company's fifty-year logging contract by an additional fifteen years. The White House threatened to veto the bill if the Alaska amendment remained. The House removed it, but Murkowski insisted on its inclusion in the Senate bill. Murkowski eventually lifted his hold on the bill (the courtesy senators allow each other to block consideration of a bill until questions are resolved) in exchange for a promise from the White House to agree that if the pulp mill closed, the Forest Service would allow the company to cut enough timber to operate its sawmills for two years. The failure of the Alaskan delegation in this and other issues on their agenda was striking, given the power that Murkowski and Young held as chairs of the resource committees in the Senate and House. Some argued that their failure to build coalitions and their aggressive criticism of environmental regulation helped fuel the backlash against the Republican Congress.[80]

The 104th Congress did enact three other major environmental laws, new safe drinking water, pesticide, and fisheries laws. Those measures enjoyed strong bipartisan support. The Safe Drinking Water Act revises the act's standard-setting process, creates a funding mechanism to help states improve their drinking water systems, and gives states more flexibility in how they must meet federal regulations.[81] The Magnuson fisheries reauthorization bill seeks to limit overfishing by changing the definition of optimum yield to mean "maximum sustainable yield . . . as reduced by any relevant social, economic or ecological factor" and put in place a four-year moratorium on implementation of new quota systems through September 2000.[82] The passage of the pesticide reform bill in August 1996 ended fifteen years of debate over how to amend the nation's two major pesticide laws: the Federal Insecticide, Fungicide and Rodenticide Act (FIFRA), which governs the registration of pesticides with the Environmental Protection Agency, and the Federal Food, Drug and Cosmetic Act (FFDCA), which directs EPA in setting pesticide safety levels in foods. The most significant change was the revision of the Delaney clause, which had prohibited the use of any food additive that had been shown to be carcinogenic. The new law requires the EPA to set a uniform pesticide tolerance for raw and processed foods that is "safe," defined as a "reasonable certainty of no harm," which is typically understood to agencies to pose no more than a one-in-a-million lifetime cancer risk.[83]

Aside from those bills, environmentalists believe it was the worst environmental Congress on record, while conservative Republicans argue the groundwork was laid for fundamental reforms in law and regulation. For Representative George Miller (D-CA), the 104th Congress was a "shameful, arrogant event that should not be repeated." For Representative Thomas J. Bliley Jr. (R-VA), "our work is not done, but the 104th Congress has taken giant steps to modernize our health and environmental programs." Congress did pass a great number of provisions that would have changed policy concerning grazing, mining, the Arctic National Wildlife Refuge, logging, and other areas, but these were largely attached to budget bills that were vetoed by the president. Business groups argue that at least Congress did not add new or more onerous regulations. Policy analysts pointed to the requirement of balancing costs and benefits of regulations under the new drinking water bill. Libertarians faulted Congress as "no enemy of big government." In comparison with the previous Congress, when the Democrats were in charge of both chambers and both branches of government, they passed only one major environmental bill, the California Desert Protection Act.

The consequences of the 1996 election are not particularly encouraging for the reform of public land, natural resource, and environmental policy. The Pacific West and the Northeast were Democratic strongholds, while the Republicans dominated most of the rest of the country. Republicans received one-third of 1 percent more votes nationwide than did the Democrats, the smallest margin the majority party has achieved since 1952. The Republicans got only 48.9 percent of the nationwide House vote in 1996, the smallest margin for the party winning a majority since 1938. The House is more closely divided between the parties than it has been for four decades.[84] Many of the moderates from both sides of the Senate aisle retired in 1996, raising fears that the Senate has become more polarized. The rancor raised by ethics investigations of the Republican Speaker and Democratic president in 1996 and 1997 also increased tension. The prospects are not promising for new legislation that will find common ground among those who want to reform public lands and natural resource policy to reduce subsidies and increase preservation and those who want to do more to encourage resource development.

Unsettled Policy

During the first one hundred years of America, public values and private interests mutually reinforced each other in encouraging the development of the West. The pursuit of self-interest that led settlers westward to make homes and find riches was also the collective, national interest. Americans had a national duty to help tame the West and push the nation's borders to the Pacific. After a hundred years, when resources no longer seemed infinite, Congress tried to change the rules. But no new consensus has emerged to replace the old one, and public lands and natural resource policy is quite unsettled.[85] Congress, the White House, the Interior Department and other agencies, and the courts have all launched policy-making forays, but no one view predominates. Compromises are needed for different policy areas, such as endangered species, grazing, timber, and minerals, and sometimes for different geographic areas, as resource plans are tailored to specific conditions. Over time, a new set of policies for the new West will emerge. The most important direction policies can take is to move toward ecosystem protection and preservation of land and resources for their ecological value. But for the immediate future, policymakers will struggle with a host of issues on a case-by-case basis, until a new consensus emerges. Chapters 4–9 provide a guide to the issues. But before turning to that discussion, Chapter 3 provides an overview of public lands and natural resource agencies and laws.

NOTES

1. The study was done by Patricia Limerick and cited in Bill Bradley, *Time Present, Time Past* (New York: Alfred A. Knopf, 1996): 218. For more on the evolution of natural resource policies, see Patricia Nelson, *The Legacy of Conquest: The Unbroken Past of the American West* (New York: W.W. Norton, 1987); Christopher McGrory Klyza, *Who*

Controls Public Lands? (Chapel Hill, NC: University of North Carolina Press, 1996); and Robert H. Nelson, *Public Lands and Private Rights: The Failure of Scientific Management* (Lanham, MD: Rowman and Littlefield Publishers, Inc., 1995).

2. William E. Riebsame, "Ending the Range Wars," *Environment* (May 1996): 6.

3. John Wesley Powell, *Exploration of the Colorado River and Its Canyons* (1895), excerpted in part in Joseph Holmes, *Canyons of the Colorado* (San Francisco: Chronicle Books, 1996).

4. Riebsame, "Ending the Range Wars."

5. Andrew Taylor, "President Will Not Use Budget to Rewrite Land-Use Laws," *Congressional Quarterly Weekly Report* (April 3, 1993): 833–34.

6. Jon Healey, "From Conflict to Coexistence: New Politics of Environment," *Congressional Quarterly Weekly Report* (February 13, 1993): 309–13; quote by EPA official Tom Roberts, at 313.

7. John Hamilton, "Babbitt's Retreat," *Sierra* (July/August 1994): 53–58, 73–77; quotes at 54–55.

8. Richard L. Berke, "Clinton Backs Off from Policy Shift on Federal Lands," *New York Times* (March 30, 1993).

9. Donald J. Hellman, legislative counsel, the Wilderness Society, quoted in Margaret Kriz, "Turf Wars," *National Journal* (May 22, 1993): 1232–35; quotes at 1232.

10. Kriz, "Turf Wars"; quote at 1233.

11. Margaret Kriz, "Quick Draw," *National Journal* (November 13, 1993): 2711–16; quote at 2713.

12. Ibid.

13. Tom Kenworthy, "Top 2 Forest Service Officials Shifted amid Criticism of Agency's Direction," *Washington Post* (October 29, 1993).

14. "BLM Head Offered New Position," *Washington Post* (January 27, 1994).

15. Hamilton, "Babbitt's Retreat."

16. John H. Cushman, "Everglades Cleanup Agreement Fails," *New York Times* (December 19, 1993): 17.

17. Robert Pear, "The 1996 Elections: The States—The Initiatives," *New York Times* (November 7, 1887): B7.

18. Catalina Camia, "Babbitt Offers Interest Groups More Input in Lands Policy," *Congressional Quarterly Weekly Report* (February 19, 1994): 430.

19. Quoted in Jack Anderson and Michael Binstein, "Babbitt's Battle for the Land," *Washington Post* (July 10, 1994).

20. Hamilton, "Babbitt's Retreat"; quote at 74.

21. Paul Larmer, "As Elections Near, Green Hopes Wilt," *High Country News* (October 17, 1994): 1.

22. Margaret Kriz, "Shoot-Out in the West," *National Journal* (October 15, 1994): 2388–92.

23. Keith Schneider, "When the Bad Guy Is Seen as the One in the Green Hat," *New York Times* (February 16, 1992).

24. Suellen Lowry, "Cloaked in the Constitution, Property Rights Movement Targets Environmental Laws," *Wildlife Advocate* (Summer 1994): 3.

25. Dirk Johnson, "Rebellion of Greens Is Brewing in the West," *New York Times* (July 24, 1994): 18.

26. See Ed Gillespie and Rob Schellhas, eds., *Contract with America* (New York: Times Books, 1994): 125–41.

27. Ibid.

28. Cindy Skrzycki, "Hill Republicans Promise a Regulatory Revolution," *Washington Post* (January 4, 1995): A1.

29. Craig E. Richardson and Geoff C. Ziebart, *Red Tape in America: Stories from the Front Lines* (Washington, DC: Heritage Foundation, 1995): v.

30. Quoted in Carl Pope, "Open Season on the Environment," *Sierra* (January/February 1995): 13–14.

31. Tom St. Hilaire, "Restoring the Green Agenda," *National Parks* (January/February 1995): 24–25.

32. 104th Congress, H.R. 2364, the Endangered Species Recovery Act; H.R. 2374, the Endangered Natural Legacy Protection Act; H.R. 2444, the Endangered Species Habitat Conservation Act; S. 768, Endangered Species Act reauthorization; and a draft reauthorization bill sponsored by Senator Dirk Kempthorne (R-ID).

33. 104th Congress, S. 391; S. 1054.

34. 104th Congress, S. 852, H.R. 1713, the Public Grazing Act of 1995.

35. 104th Congress, S. 506, H.R. 1580.

36. 104th Congress, H.R. 2032, S. 1031.

37. Margaret Kriz, "Land Wars," *National Journal* (September 2, 1995): 2146–51.

38. 104th Congress, H. Con. Res. 67. The resolution established the following budget authority and outlays for the Natural Resources and Environment budget category (300):

	Budget Authority	Outlays (in $billions)
FY 1996	$19.3	$20.2
FY 1997	19.1	19.9
FY 1998	17.2	17.8
FY 1999	18.6	19.1
FY 2000	17.7	17.8
FY 2001	17.9	18.2
FY 2002	17.8	18.1

Budget authority sets a ceiling on how much agencies can spend during each fiscal year; actual outlays may include funds spent in one year that were authorized in previous years. The budget resolution is enforced through congressional rules: in the Senate, for example, if an amendment to an appropriations bill violates a provision of the budget resolution, a point of order can be raised; the amendment fails unless at least three-fifths of the Senate votes to waive the Budget Act. Spending in the Natural Resources and the Environment category was $22 billion in 1995.

39. PL 104–19 (July 27, 1995), Emergency Supplemental Appropriations for Additional Disaster Assistance, for Anti-terrorism Initiatives, for Assistance in the Recovery from the Tragedy That Occurred at Oklahoma City, and the Rescissions Act, 1995. An earlier version of the act was vetoed by President Clinton because of some of the spending cuts and environmental riders it included.

40. 104th Congress, H.R. 889.

41. 104th Congress, H.R. 260 was defeated on the House floor; a similar bill, S. 1144, was considered by the Senate Resources Committee. S. 309 would reform the concessions policy of the National Park Service.

42. A note on the budget process. Under the Constitution, no money can be spent by the federal government unless it is appropriated by Congress in a bill that originates in the House of Representatives. The executive branch submits a budget to Congress in January. The Office of Management and Budget (OMB) sets guidelines, agencies submit specific proposals, and OMB compiles final budget. The Congressional budget process includes the following: (1) House and Senate Budget Committees propose a budget resolution that is expected to be passed by the House and Senate; (2) a reconciliation bill may be passed to reconcile permanent and annual appropriations and revenues with the budget resolution; (3) thirteen appropriations bills must be passed by September 30 of each year in order to fund federal agencies and programs for the fiscal year beginning October 1 (riders may be attached to appropriations bills that mandate or prohibit specific actions); (4) continuing resolutions keep the government operating until appropriations bills are passed; when these temporary stopgap provisions run out, agencies whose appropriations bills have not been enacted must shut down; and (5) rescissions may be passed to rescind appropriated funds and may include riders.

43. Natural Resources Defense Council, "Stealth Attack: Gutting Environmental Protection through the Budget Process" (Washington, DC: NRDC, August 1995).

44. When H.R. 2099 was considered on the House floor, an amendment proposed by Representatives Louis Stokes (D-OH) and Sherwood Boehlert (R-NY) that would have stripped the seventeen riders from the bill passed 212 to 206 on July 28. House leaders watched carefully for an opportune time when several members would be away and arranged for a revote on July 31; the amendment to remove the riders failed on a 210 to 210 vote (amendments receiving a tie vote fail to gain a majority of members and hence fail). Stokes announced plans to offer a nonbinding motion to instruct the conferees when they are named in the House on October 25 not to include the riders in the final appropriations bill.

45. The conference report includes many provisions that were riders in the House and Senate bills.

46. "Congress Slashes Interior Spending," *National Parks* (November/December 1995): 18–19.

47. 104th Congress, H.R. 1977; U.S. House of Representatives, Committee of Conference, *Making Appropriations for the Department of the Interior and Related Agencies for the Fiscal Year Ending September 30, 1996, and for Other Purposes.*

48. Bob Benenson, "Interior Measure Takes Aim at Democratic Spending," *Congressional Quarterly Weekly Report* (June 24, 1995): 1837.

49. William J. Clinton, message to Congress vetoing HR 2099, the fiscal year 1996 appropriations bill for the Departments of Housing and Urban Development and independent agencies, reprinted in *Congressional Quarterly Weekly Report* (December 23, 1995): 3903.

50. William J. Clinton, message to Congress vetoing HR 1977, the fiscal year 1996 appropriations bill for the Department of the Interior, reprinted in *Congressional Quarterly Weekly Report* (December 23, 1995): 3903.

51. The following fiscal year 1996 appropriations bills were passed: agriculture, defense, legislative branch, military construction, transportation, and treasury, postal service, general government.

The president had vetoed (and Congress had failed to override) the following appropriations bills: commerce, justice, state, judiciary, interior, veterans affairs, housing and urban development, and independent agencies.

Congress had failed to pass the following appropriations bills: District of Columbia, foreign operations, labor, health and human services, and education.

52. Cindy Shrzycki, "Deregulation by Default," *Washington Post National Weekly Edition* (March 4–10, 1996): 6–7.

53. Natural Resources Defense Council, "The Year of Living Dangerously" (Washington, DC: NRDC, 1995): 7.

54. B. J. Bergman, "Standing Up for the Planet," *Sierra* (March/April 1995): 79–80.

55. Katharine Q. Seelye, "House G.O.P. to Face the Divisive Issues," *New York Times* (March 27, 1995): A8; Robin Toner, "Rifts Emerge inside G.O.P. (March 16, 1995): A1.

56. Thomas B. Edsall, "It's Confrontation That's Paying Off for Bill Clinton," *Washington Post National Weekly Edition* (January 1–7, 1996): 12.

57. David Maraniss and Michael Weisskopf, "Cashing In: The GOP Revolutionaries Have a Sure-fire Way of Telling Friend from Foe," *Washington Post National Weekly Edition* (December 4–10, 1995): 6–7.

58. Nancy Gibbs and Karen Tumulty, "Master of the House," *Time* (December 25, 1995/January 1, 1996): 68.

59. Associated Press, "A Lobbyists' Perk Will Die," *New York Times* (May 25, 1995): A13.

60. Jane Fritsch, "Securities-Bill Staff Has Ties to the Industry," *New York Times* (May 25, 1995): A1.

61. Maraniss and Weisskopf, "Cashing In."

62. David Rogers, "Bliley's Pro-Business Reputation, Stock Portfolio Symbolize Postelection Strength of Corporations," *Wall Street Journal* (December 23, 1994): A14.

63. League of Conservation Voters, "The Anti-Environment Revolution: Let the Lobbyists Write the Laws" (n.d.).

64. Stephen Engelberg, "Business Leaves the Lobby and Sits at Congress's Table," *New York Times* (March 31, 1995): A1.

65. Timothy Noah, "New Single-Issue Pressure Groups Sprout Up on the Right to Support the Republican Agenda," *Wall Street Journal* (May 31, 1995).

66. Maraniss and Weisskopf, "Cashing In."

67. Matthew Miller, "It's Christmas: Let's Means-Test," *The New Republic* (January 8, 15, 1996): 28–30.

68. John F. Stacks, "Good Newt, Bad Newt," *Time* (December 25, 1995/January 1, 1996): 93.

69. Clay Chandler, "Something for Almost Everyone," *Washington Post National Weekly Edition* (January 1–7, 1996): 19.

70. H. Con. Res. 178, H. Rpt. 104–612 to the nonbinding FY 1997 budget resolution.

71. Environmental and Energy Policy Institute, *Monthly PULSE* (July 1996): 3.

72. 104th Congress, H.R. 3666, H. Rpt. 104–628 (1996).

73. 104th Congress, H.R. 3662, H. Rpt. 104–625 (1996).

74. Allan Freedman, "House Passes Interior Bill, but Difficulty Lies Ahead," *Congressional Quarterly Weekly Report* (June 22, 1996): 1748–50.

75. Ibid.

76. Environmental and Energy Policy Institute, *Monthly PULSE*: 6–7.

77. 104th Congress, H.R. 3603, H. Rpt. 104–613.

78. The Federal Agricultural Improvement and Reform Act, H.R. 2854, P.L. 104–127. See Environmental and Energy Policy Institute, *Monthly PULSE*: 7–8.

79. John H. Cushman Jr., "Senate Approves Parks Bill after Deal on Alaskan Forest," *New York Times* (October 3, 1996): A1.

80. Margaret Kriz, "The Alaska Three," *National Journal* (October 12, 1996): 2172–76.

81. P.L. 104–182.

82. 104th Congress, H.R. 39, S. 39; Environmental and Energy Study Institute, *Monthly PULSE* (October 1996): 14–15.

83. Environmental and Energy Study Institute, *Monthly PULSE* (October 1996): 20–21.

84. Rhodes Cook, "Thinnest of Margins Shows Country's Great Divide," *Congressional Quarterly Weekly Report* (February 15, 1997): 441–44.

85. Patricia Nelson Limerick, "A History of the Public Lands Debate," paper presented at the Natural Resources Law Center, "Challenging Federal Ownership and Management: Public Lands and Public Benefits," University of Colorado School of Law, Boulder, CO (October 11–13, 1995).

3

Public Lands and Natural Resource Policy

The federal government's public lands and natural resource policies, like many other policy areas, are diffuse and fragmented, involving a number of agencies and authorized by a mélange of laws. The push to develop resources, tame wilderness, and gain wealth has shaped these policies for nearly 200 years. During the past three decades, laws and policies have begun to reflect a shift in policy toward balancing resource development and preservation, and agencies and programs have begun a transformation to pursuing a more complicated set of objectives. The policy shifts pose difficult challenges to agencies as they re-create themselves in response to new demands. This chapter provides an overview of the programs, agencies, and laws that are involved in the management of public lands. The chapters that follow explore in more detail the issues that are part of these policy shifts as the old and new West collide.

PUBLIC LANDS AND PUBLIC AGENCIES

There are five major classifications of public lands. They roughly range from designations that primarily seek to foster resource development to those that prohibit development. Rangelands are open to livestock grazing, national forests are primarily reserved to provide a continuous supply of timber but also open to recreation and other uses, and national wildlife refuges provide habitat for migratory birds and animals; these three designations are typically called "multiple use." Two kinds of areas are limited to recreational and other nonconsumptive uses: national parks are primarily dedicated to recreational use and closed to development, and wilderness lands are protected as undeveloped areas.

The United States has set aside more lands as public than any other nation. About thirty percent of the nation's land, some 657 million acres, is managed by the federal government: most of it, 73 percent, is in Alaska; 22 percent is in the western states. Some lands are managed by the Bureau of Reclamation, the U.S. Army Corps of Engineers, and branches of the military. Other areas, designated as national memorials, heritage corridors, historic reserves, historic sites, international parks, and scientific reserves, are not part of the National Park System but receive financial and technical assistance from the Park Service.

The size of protected, restricted-use lands increased significantly between 1990 and 1995, primarily through the designation of lands in Alaska in 1980. During those years, the park system grew by 280 percent, the wildlife refuge system by 300 percent, and the wilderness system by 900 percent. The state's federal lands contain an estimated 54 percent of its grazing lands; 40 percent of the nation's commercially accessible timber; much of its energy resources, particularly shale oil, coal, geothermal energy, and uranium; and most of the asbestos, beryllium, copper, lead, molybdenum, phosphate, potash, and silver.[1]

More than half of public lands are managed by the U.S. Forest Service (USFS), located in the U.S. Department of Agriculture, responsible for 192 million acres, and the Bureau of Land Management (BLM), an agency in the U.S. Department of the Interior, responsible for 267 million acres. The other two principal land management agencies are also in the Interior Department: the Fish and Wildlife Service (FWS), which has jurisdiction over 87 million acres, and the National Park Service (NPS), which manages 77 million acres. These lands include national forests, national parks, Bureau of Land Management lands, national wildlife refuges, historic and cultural sites, wilderness areas, and other protected lands.

The national forest system includes 159 forests and nineteen grasslands in forty-four states, Puerto Rico, and the U.S. Virgin Islands, which are managed to ensure sustainable yield (harvested no faster than it is replaced) and multiple use (logging, mining, oil and gas exploration, grazing, farming, hunting, recreation, and conservation of plants and animals, soils, and watersheds), managed by the U.S. Forest Service. Logging is the chief economic use of the lands, although recreation is the greatest source of revenue. Some Forest Service lands have been set aside as wilderness areas.[2]

The BLM manages 41 percent of all federal lands, and owns an additional 300 million acres of subsurface minerals. Included in its acreage are 137 wilderness areas that make up 5.1 million acres. National resource lands include grasslands, prairies, deserts, scrub forests, and other areas managed for multiple use, primarily mining, grazing, oil and gas development, and logging.

The National Park Service has jurisdiction over 12 percent of all federal lands, including fifty-four national parks and 314 other units (national monuments, memorials, battlefields, parkways, lakeshores, seashores, recreation areas, preserves, wild and scenic river ways, and scenic trails). Some 43 percent of NPS lands are wilderness areas. Camping, sport fishing, hiking, and boating are permitted in parks, and recreation areas also permit sport hunting, mining, and oil and gas development. The National Park Services protects areas in forty-nine states, the District of Columbia, Puerto Rico, the Virgin Islands, Guam, Samoa, and the Northern Marianas.

The National Wilderness Preservation System includes 474 areas managed by the agencies previously listed, but where no development or roads are permitted, and use is limited to sport fishing, hiking, camping, nonmotorized boating, and, in some areas, sport hunting and horseback riding. Mining and energy development are permitted only if authorized before wilderness designation. Motor vehicles are permitted only for emergencies. In Alaska, wilderness areas are open to aircraft landing.

The U.S. Fish and Wildlife Service manages 504 wildlife refuges and thirty-two wetland management districts. Wetlands, islands, and coastal areas make up about half of the total FWS lands, and 84 percent of the lands are located in Alaska. The FWS administers 20.6 million acres of wilderness lands, 22 percent of its total lands.[3] Of the 87 million acres in the National Wildlife Refuge System, 76 million are in Alaska; 65 percent of the refuge that lie outside Alaska are west of the Mississippi River. The FWS seeks to conserve and protect fish and wildlife but permits hunting, fishing, and other recreational activities along with economic uses that are compatible with the purposes for which particular refuges were established, such as oil and gas development.

Table 3.1 provides a brief description of these agencies and their jurisdictions. Table 3.2 summarizes the amount of land each agency manages. Table 3.3 describes the distribution of public land agencies' holdings in the various states and demonstrates the tremendous variation in the percent of land in states that are federally managed. Table 3.4 provides an additional perspective by depicting the distribution of Native American lands across the states. While these lands are not classified as federal lands, they raise important issues about local control, development of resources, and other issues. Table 3.5 describes the source of lands that have come under the jurisdiction of federal land agencies. Finally, table 3.6 shows how the size of the federal estate has grown over time.

Public Lands Agencies

The Department of the Interior was created in 1849 by Congress.[4] Several offices—the General Land Office, the Office of Indian Affairs, the Pension Office, and the Patent Office—were eventually added to the department, and it became a kind of catchall for miscellaneous federal programs. In 1950, it was reorganized by the Truman administration and became primarily responsible as the custodian of national lands and resources. Interior Department documents describe its jurisdiction and mission this way: "As the nation's principal conservation agency, the Department of the Interior has responsibility for most of our nationally owned public lands and natural resources." This involves four main efforts:

Table 3.1
Federal Public Lands Agencies

Agency	Land in Acres	Number of Units	Management Goals	Permitted Activities
U.S. Forest Service	191.5 million located in 44 states, Puerto Rico, and the Virgin Islands	156 individual forests, 20 grassland units	To permit a variety of uses, including recreation, timber harvesting, fish and wildlife habitat and livestock grazing, under the multiple use and sustained yield standards.	Virtually all non-consumptive and economic uses. Logging is the chief economic use; recreation is far and away the largest dollar-valued output.
U.S. Fish and Wildlife Service (F&WS)	87.4 million acres, 76 million of which are in Alaska. 65 percent of the refuges outside of Alaska (476) are west of the Mississippi River.	504 refuges	To conserve and protect fish and wildlife.	Hunting, fishing and other recreational activities along with economic uses that are compatible with the purposes for which particular refuges were established. Oil & gas development and livestock grazing are among the economic uses allowed on lands in the refuge system. Millions visit refuges every year.
National Park Service (NPS)	About 77 million in 49 states, the District of Columbia, Puerto Rico, Virgin Islands, Guam, Samoa, and the Northern Marianas	368 including the newest park, Death Valley National Park in California	To protect parks from significant degradation so that future as well as current generations can enjoy them.	Hiking, camping and other recreational activities. Millions of visitors enjoy them each year.

Agency	Land in Acres	Number of Units	Management Goals	Permitted Activities
Bureau of Land Management (BLM)	About 268 million located chiefly in 11 contiguous western states and Alaska. Alaskan lands total 88.9 million acres. Odd lots are located in other states, like 589 acres in Wisconsin and 3962 acres in Louisiana. Acreage excludes Outer Continental Shelf lands as well as federal mineral resources where the surface is owned by state, local or private parties.	59 districts, subdivided into 137 resource areas	To permit a variety of uses, including recreation, livestock grazing, fish and wildlife habitat, mineral production and timber harvesting under the multiple use and sustained yield standard.	Virtually all nonconsumptive and economic uses under the multiple use and sustained yield standard. The most extensive economic activity is livestock grazing; millions of visitors enjoy recreational opportunities annually.

Source: Natural Resources Defense Council, *Statistics: A Fact Sheet on Public Lands*, in "Selling Our Heritage: Congressional Plans for America's Public Lands," (New York: NRDC, July 1995).

Table 3.2
Acres Managed by the Four Federal Agencies, Fiscal Years 1964 and 1994
(Number of Acres, in Millions)

Agency	# of Acres, 1964	# of Acres, 1994
Forest Service	186.3	191.6
Bureau of Land Management	464.3	267.1
Fish and Wildlife Service	22.7	87.5
National Park Service	27.5	76.6
Total	700.8	622.8

Source: U. S. General Accounting Office, "Land Ownership: Information on the Acreage, Management and Use of Federal and Other Lands" (Washington, DC: U.S. GAO, March 1996): 3.

- fostering sound use of our land and water resources;
- assessing and protecting our fish, wildlife, and biological diversity;
- preserving the environmental and cultural values of our national parks and historical places; and
- providing for the enjoyment of life through outdoor recreation.

The department also "assesses our mineral resources and works to ensure that their development is in the best interests of all our people by encouraging stewardship and citizen participation in their care." Finally, the department "has a major responsibility for American Indian reservation communities and for people who live in island territories under United States administration."[5]

The Interior Department is organized along the following lines. The Office of the Secretary is responsible for all activities of the department. The assistant secretary for policy, management, and budget is responsible for management and administrative functions. The assistant secretary for fish and wildlife and parks oversees conservation programs, coordination with other federal agencies, and the Fish and Wildlife Service, the National Biological Service, and the National Park Service. The assistant secretary for water and science has jurisdiction over programs that support the development of natural resources and oversees the Bureau of Reclamation, the U.S. Bureau of Mines, and the U.S. Geological Survey. The assistant secretary for land and minerals management is responsible for public land management, mining, energy and other resource development, and mining reclamation and oversees the Bureau of Land Management, the Minerals Management Service, and the Office of Surface Mining Reclamation and Enforcement. The assistant secretary for Indian affairs manages all activities related to Native Americans and oversees the Bureau of Indian Affairs. The assistant secretary for territorial and international affairs is responsible for U.S. insular areas (Guam, American Samoa, the Virgin Islands, the Commonwealth of the Northern Mariana Islands, and the Trust Territory of the Pacific Islands), the Freely Associated States (Republic of the Marshall Islands and Federal States of Micronesia), and all other international activities of the department.

Several offices provide support services. The solicitor is the principal legal adviser to the secretary. The office includes five divisions: Conservation and Wildlife, Energy and Resources, Indian Affairs, Surface Mining, and General Law. There are seven regional offices, each headed by a regional solicitor: Alaska, Northeast (the office is located in Massachusetts), Pacific Northwest (Oregon), Pacific Southwest (California), Rocky Mountain (Denver), Southeast (Georgia), and Southwest (New Mexico). The inspector general (IG) conducts audits and investigations of the department in order to encourage efficiency and identify fraud and abuse. There are five IG offices: Eastern (the office is located in Virginia), Central (Colorado), Western (Colorado and California), Caribbean (St. Thomas), and North Pacific (Guam). The Office of Hearings and Appeals includes administrative law judges and boards of appeals that hear cases concerning contract and lease disputes and appeals of administrative decisions and conduct rule-making hearings. Decisions of appeals board constitute final department decisions.

The following bureaus are located in the Interior Department:

• U.S. Fish and Wildlife Services

• National Biological Survey

• National Park Service

• Bureau of Reclamation

• Bureau of Land Management

• Minerals Management Service

• U.S. Geological Survey

• U.S. Bureau of Mines

• Office of Surface Mining Reclamation and Enforcement

• Bureau of Indian Affairs

The National Park Service. The objective of the Park Service is to provide for public access and recreation on public lands, while protecting the resources "unimpaired for the enjoyment of future generations." Proposals for new areas can come from Congress, state and local officials, or the public. In order for an area to be selected as a protected area by the NPS, it must

• possess nationally significant natural, cultural, or recreational resources;

• be a suitable and feasible addition to the system; and

• require direct NPS management instead of protection by some other governmental agency or by the private sector.

Table 3.3
Percentage of Each State's Acreage Managed by the Four Federal Agencies as of September 30, 1994

State	Total acres of state[a]	Total federal acres managed by the agencies	% by FS	% by BLM	% by FWS	% by NPS	The 4 federal agencies[b]
Alabama	33,431,680	801,611	1.98	0.33	0.05	0.03	2.40
Alaska	393,747,200	238,874,995	5.60	22.42	19.38	13.26	60.67
Arizona	72,963,840	29,874,028	15.42	19.54	2.29	3.69	40.94
Arkansas	34,036,480	3,246,065	7.49	0.86	0.88	0.30	9.54
California	101,676,160	43,013,642	20.29	17.02	0.24	4.76	42.30
Colorado	66,624,000	23,455,115	21.76	12.46	0.10	0.89	35.21
Connecticut	3,548,160	6,759	0[c]	0	0.01	0.18	0.19
Delaware	1,534,080	23,968	0	0	1.56	0	1.56
Florida	38,392,320	3,845,884	2.96	0.07	0.63	6.36	10.02
Georgia	37,745,280	1,393,406	2.29	0	1.25	0.15	3.69
Hawaii	4,133,760	544,462	0[c]	0	6.97	6.20	13.17
Idaho	53,487,360	32,439,588	38.23	22.15	0.09	0.19	60.65
Illinois	36,059,520[a]	342,631	0.76	0[c]	0.19	0[c]	0.95
Indiana	23,158,400[a]	214,176	0.83	0	0.03	0.06	0.92
Iowa	36,016,640	41,611	0	0[c]	0.11	0[c]	0.12
Kansas	52,660,480	137,426	0.21	0[c]	0.05	0[c]	0.26
Kentucky	25,863,040	780,705	2.65	0	0.01	0.36	3.02
Louisiana	31,776,000	1,368,834	1.90	0.97	1.40	0.04	4.31
Maine	21,594,240	169,216	0.25	0	0.21	0.33	0.78
Maryland	7,870,080	98,993	0	0	0.51	0.75	1.26
Massachusetts	5,914,240	65,580	0	0	0.21	0.90	1.11
Michigan	37,448,320[a]	3,731,491	7.62	0.20	0.30	1.84	9.96
Minnesota	54,014,080[a]	3,637,840	5.23	0.28	0.79	0.43	6.73
Mississippi	30,903,040	1,510,381	3.74	0.19	0.63	0.33	4.89
Missouri	44,613,760	1,605,889	3.34	0.01	0.11	0.15	3.60
Montana	94,109,440	26,773,255	17.92	8.58	0.65	1.30	28.45
Nebraska	49,522,560	528,145	0.71	0.02	0.33	0.01	1.07

State	Total acres of state[a]	Total federal acres managed by the agencies	% by FS	% by BLM	% by FWS	% by NPS	The 4 federal agencies[b]
Nevada	70,762,880	56,846,081	8.22	67.77	3.24	1.10	80.33
New Hampshire	5,941,120	735,995	12.17	0	0.05	0.16	12.39
New Jersey	5,257,600	104,222	0	0	1.06	0.92	1.98
New Mexico	77,822,720	22,927,727	11.98	16.56	0.42	0.49	29.46
New York	32,056,320[a]	86,663	0.04	0	0.07	0.15	0.27
North Carolina	33,710,080	2,011,072	3.68	0	1.19	1.09	5.97
North Dakota	45,250,560	1,699,378	2.44	0.14	1.02	0.16	3.76
Ohio	26,450,560[a]	254,371	0.83	0	0.03	0.10	0.96
Oklahoma	44,737,920	412,975	0.67	0.01	0.22	0.02	0.92
Oregon	62,139,520	32,113,362	25.20	25.31	0.85	0.31	51.68
Pennsylvania	28,806,400[a]	588,805	1.78	0	0.03	0.23	2.04
Rhode Island	787,840	1,499	0	0	0.19	0[c]	0.19
South Carolina	19,960,960	747,591	3.06	0	0.55	0.13	3.75
South Dakota	49,357,440	2,637,349	4.08	0.57	0.39	0.31	5.34
Tennessee	26,972,800	1,023,461	2.34	0	0.17	1.29	3.79
Texas	171,057,280	2,312,283	0.44	0	0.22	0.69	1.35
Utah	54,338,560	32,467,853	14.92	40.80	0.19	3.85	59.75
Vermont	6,153,600	370,453	5.76	0	0.10	0.16	6.02
Virginia	27,088,640	2,090,328	6.09	0	0.43	1.19	7.72
Washington	45,207,680	11,603,057	20.29	0.78	0.30	4.30	25.67
West Virginia	15,508,480	1,085,401	6.66	0	0.01	0.33	7.00
Wisconsin	35,932,800[a]	2,003,680	4.23	0.45	0.52	0.38	5.58
Wyoming	62,604,160	30,102,224	14.79	29.38	0.09	3.82	48.08
Total	**2,340,750,080**	**622,751,526**	**8.18**	**11.41**	**3.74**	**3.27**	**26.60**

[a] This information, provided by the Bureau of Census, Department of Commerce, reflects data from the 1990 Census. [b] Percentages may not add because of rounding. [c] Although the agency managed land in this state, the amount managed is less than 0.005 percent of the state's acreage. [d] The total acreage shown for this state does not include the Great Lakes water area.

Source: U. S. General Accounting Office, "Land Ownership: Information on the Acreage, Management, and Use of Federal and Other Lands" (Washington, DC: U.S. GAO, March 1996): 20-22.

Table 3.4

Acreage Held in Trust for Individual Indians and Indian Tribes, by State, in 1995

State	Number of acres
Alabama	1,683
Alaska	215,837
Arizona	18,843,819
California	548,738
Colorado	1,076,890
Connecticut	2,086
Florida	164,546
Idaho	836,758
Iowa	3,408
Kansas	30,327
Louisiana	2,279
Maine	219,053
Massachusetts	493
Michigan	21,248
Minnesota	763,444
Mississippi	20,528
Montana	5,286,101
Nebraska	65,890
Nevada	934,956
New Mexico	7,650,579
New York	52,918
North Carolina	56,736
North Dakota	854,332
Oklahoma	467,534
Oregon	785,740
Rhode Island	2,532
South Carolina	630
South Dakota	5,015,326
Texas	125
Utah	3,720,076
Washington	2,616,094
Wisconsin	214,193
Wyoming	1,812,611
Total	**52,287,510**

Notes: This acreage includes federal trust, tribal/restricted fee, and/or government lands. Federal trust lands are those whose title is held by the United States in trust for individual Indians or Indian tribes. Tribal/restricted fee lands are those whose title is held by individual Indians or tribes. Government lands consist of a small amount of acreage owned by the United States for special uses such as federal schools and hospitals for Native Americans and for administrative offices. The amount of acreage was provided as of November 7, 1995, for Alabama, Connecticut, Florida, Louisiana, Maine, Massachusetts, Mississippi, New York, North Carolina, Rhode Island, and South Carolina, and for other states as of September 15, 1995.

Source: U. S. General Accounting Office, "Land Ownership: Information on the Acreage, Management, and Use of Federal and Other Lands" (Washington, DC: U.S. GAO, March 1996): 38-39.

Table 3.5

Means by Which the Four Federal Agencies Acquired Acreage from Nonfederal Parties, 1964 to 1994

	Acres acquired				
Means used	Forest Service	Bureau of Land Management	Fish and Wildlife Service	National Park Service	Total
Purchase	1,479,348	297,080	1,998,247	1,303,292	5,077,967
Gift or donation	522,326	14,646	586,377	631,747	1,755,096
Exchange	2,179,643	724,402	256,576	90,708	3,251,329
Other*	105,138	35,822	34,976	601,279	777,215
Total	**4,286,455**	**1,071,950**	**2,876,176**	**2,627,026**	**10,861,607**

Note: Totals may not add because of rounding. * "Other" includes acreage acquired through condemnation and takings.
Source: U. S. General Accounting Office, "Land Ownership: Information on the Acreage, Management, and Use of Federal and Other Lands" (Washington, DC: U.S. GAO, March 1996): 27.

In order to be considered as nationally significant, an area must have all four of the following characteristics:

• serve as an outstanding example of a particular type of resource;

• possess exceptional value or quality in illustrating or interpreting the natural or cultural themes of our nation's heritage;

• offer superlative opportunities for recreation, for public use and enjoyment, or for scientific study; and

• retain a high degree of integrity as a true, accurate, and relatively unspoiled example of the resource.

The NPS considers a wide range of natural areas as suitable for park designation, such as a remnant of a once widespread but now rare landscape or biotic area, an uncommon landform or biotic area, an area that includes exceptional biodiversity or geologic characteristics, a site containing rare plants or animals, a critical habitat for the survival of a rare species, an area of unusual and extensive fossils, and an area where extensive scientific research has occurred.

Cultural areas, those that "possess exceptional value or quality in illustrating or interpreting our heritage and that possess a high degree of integrity of location, design, setting, materials, workmanship, feeling, and association," include sites associated with significant historical events and persons, associated with American ideas or ideals, representative of historical periods of architecture or style, illustrative of a way of life or culture, or likely to yield important information about cultures and ways of life in America.

Recreational areas include areas that provide for "recreational activities different from those available at the local or regional level," sites near major population centers that can provide "exceptional recreational opportunities" for visitors from throughout the nation and not just local residents, areas that include unique recreation areas that are "scarce and disappearing," and other sites that

Table 3.6
Area of the Federal Public Domain, 1781–1991 (in Millions of Acres)

Year	Land area total	Public domain	Acquired
1802	200.0	-	-
1850	1,200.0	-	-
1880	900.0	-	-
1912	600.0	-	-
1946	413.0	-	-
1950	412.0	-	-
1955	407.9	-	-
1959	768.6	-	-
1960	771.5	-	-
1965	765.8	-	-
1970	761.3	-	-
1975	760.4	-	-
1976	762.2	-	-
1977	741.5	-	-
1978	775.2	712.0	63.3
1979	744.1	684.3	59.8
1980	719.5	648.0	71.5
1981	730.8	668.7	62.2
1982	729.8	670.0	59.8
1983	732.0	672.4	59.6
1984	726.6	658.9	67.7
1985	726.7	656.2	70.5
1986	727.1	662.7	64.4
1987	724.3	661.0	63.3
1988	688.2	623.2	65.0
1989	662.2	597.9	64.3
1990	649.8	587.4	62.4
1991	649.3	587.6	61.8

[1]Owned by federal government. Compromises original public domain plus acquired lands. Estimated from imperfect data available for indicated years. Prior to 1959, excludes Alaska, and 1960, Hawaii.
Note: Areas of acquisitions are as computed in 1912. Excludes outlying areas of the United States amounting to 645,949 acres in 1978.
Source: U.S. Department of Commerce, Statistical Abstract of the United States, 1996 (Washington, DC: U.S. Government Printing Office, 1996): 228.

represent a "unique combination of natural, cultural, and recreational features that collectively offer outstanding opportunities for public use."

Sites that are nationally significant historical, cultural, and recreational areas must also be suitable for park designation. They must "represent a natural or cultural theme or type of recreational resource that is not already adequately represented in the National Park Service" or by some other federal agency. Finally, their inclusion in the system must be feasible: they must be of "sufficient size and appropriate configuration to ensure long-term protection of the resources and to accommodate public use." The NPS considers costs of acquisition of lands, access, threats to the land and facilities, and the required staffing and development.

The Park Service also works with others in protecting important sites through technical or financial assistance. Federal law provides for more than twenty different protective designations for public lands, such as a national landmark, national battlefield, national seashore, national lakeshore, national historic site, national wild and scenic river, national trail, biosphere reserve, wilderness, area of critical concern, national conservation area, national recreation area, marine or estuarine sanctuary, or national wildlife refuge. There is a presumption in favor of other designations: "additions to the National Park System will not usually be recommended if another arrangement can provide adequate protection and opportunity for public enjoyment." Congress has not always been consistent in the designation it uses, but national parks are traditionally used to protect "the most spectacular natural areas with a wide variety of features." National monuments are usually smaller areas, "established primarily to protect historic, scientific, or natural features containing fewer diverse resources or attractions than national parks." The president, under the 1906 Antiquities Act, can designate national monuments. The secretary of the interior can designate national natural landmarks and national historic landmarks. National parks typically preclude hunting and mining; other designations sometimes allow for grazing, hunting, and energy exploration and development. Congress or the secretary of the interior may designate rivers as part of the wild and scenic rivers system. Congress may designate new national scenic and national historic trails.

The Park Service may also develop shared management arrangements with state and local governments. Areas may be given special titles or designations but continue to be managed by state or local governments or private parties. The Park Service, through its National Register of Historic Places, lists cultural resources of significance. Congress may also authorize the NPS to work with state or local governments and private parties to protect nationally significant areas.

Parks are usually created through an act of Congress. The NPS plays a major role in evaluating the suitability of potential sites. Park Service staff first decide if an area has potential for designation. If so, they conduct a detailed study of management options; this sometimes requires additional funds authorized by Congress. Other federal, state, local, and tribal officials are consulted, and the staff provide public participation through workshops, hearings, and public comment periods on draft documents. Boundary studies are conducted to ensure that the designation includes significant features or opportunities for recreation and provisions to protect resources essential to the purposes for establishing the park. Park Service studies do not normally offer recommendations but are used by the secretary of the interior in making recommendations and by members of Congress in formulating legislation.

The Park Service develops and implements park management plans that provide for a variety of services to park visitors, such as concessions, campgrounds, and educational programs. The Park Service administers the state portion of the Land and Water Conservation Fund, the National Outdoor Recreation coordination and state comprehensive outdoor recreation planning, technical assistance for the National Wild and Scenic Rivers and the National Trails Systems, the National Register of Historic Places, national historic landmarks, historic preservation, Historic American Buildings Survey, Historic American Engineering

Record, and interagency archaeological services.[6] The National Park Service is divided into the following regions:

• Alaska Region
• Mid-Atlantic Region: Delaware, Maryland, Pennsylvania, Virginia, and West Virginia
• Midwest Region: Illinois, Indiana, Iowa, Kansas, Michigan, Minnesota, Missouri, Nebraska, Ohio, and Wisconsin
• National Capital Region: Metropolitan Washington, D.C. (includes units in Maryland, Virginia, and West Virginia)
• North Atlantic Region: Connecticut, Maine, Massachusetts, New Hampshire, New Jersey, New York, Rhode Island, and Vermont
• Pacific Northwest Region: Idaho, Oregon, and Washington
• Rocky Mountain Region: Colorado, Montana, North Dakota, South Dakota, Utah, and Wyoming
• Southeast Region: Alabama, Florida, Georgia, Kentucky, Mississippi, North Carolina, Puerto Rico, South Carolina, Tennessee, and the Virgin Islands
• Southwest Region: Arizona (northeast corner), Arkansas, Louisiana, New Mexico, Oklahoma, and Texas
• Western Region: Arizona (all but the northeast corner), California, Hawaii, and Nevada.[7]

National Biological Service. The National Biological Service (NBS) was created in 1993, when several functions from different bureaus in the Interior Department were transferred to the NBS in order to "provide the scientific understanding and technologies needed to support the sound management and conservation of our Nation's biological services."[8] The NBS provides scientific support and technical assistance concerning the protection of biological resources. The service headquarters are in Washington, D.C., and have four regional offices in Louisiana, Colorado, Washington, and West Virginia; sixteen science centers; eighty-eight field stations; and fifty-four cooperative research units at colleges and universities.[9] Congressional opposition to the NBS, as indicated in Chapter 2, resulted in the service being placed in the U.S. Geological Survey in 1996.

The Bureau of Land Management. The Bureau of Land Management was established in 1946 by consolidating the General Land Office (created in 1812) and the Grazing Service (created in 1934). The Federal Land Policy and Management Act of 1976 is the major source of its statutory authority. The bureau manages timber, hard-rock minerals, oil and gas, geothermal energy, wildlife habitat, endangered plant and animal species, rangeland vegetation, wild and scenic rivers, conservation and wilderness areas, watersheds, wild horses and burros, and open spaces under general principles of multiple use and sustained yield. It is responsible for overseeing and managing energy and mineral leases and ensuring compliance with relevant regulations and for surveying federal lands and maintaining records of mining claims. The BLM operates the following state offices (some offices within the state designation are actually located in adjacent states):

State	Number of Cities with Offices
Alaska	6
Arizona	7 (one office in Utah)
California	17
Colorado	13
Idaho	9
Montana	13 (one office in South Dakota, one in North Dakota)
Nevada	10
New Mexico	11 (two offices in Oklahoma)
Oregon	15 (two offices in Washington)
Utah	13
Wyoming	12

The eastern states office is located in Virginia; other offices are in Mississippi, Missouri, and Wisconsin.[10]

BLM's goal is to permit a variety of uses, including recreation, livestock grazing, fish and wildlife habitat, mineral production and timber harvesting, under the multiple use and sustained yield standards. The agency is divided into fifty-nine districts and subdivided into 137 resource areas, almost all of which are in the eleven contiguous western states and Alaska. The most extensive economic activity is livestock grazing, but millions of visitors each year pursue recreational opportunities on BLM lands.[11] The BLM also has an extensive volunteer program, which involves 15,000 volunteers in projects aimed at protecting fish and wildlife habitat, building and maintaining recreation trails, helping with recreational activities, planting trees and shrubs, making range improvements, working on geological surveys and fossil excavations, discovering and restoring archaeological sites and artifacts, protecting riparian zones, reducing erosion and pollution, conducting fire prevention activities, producing materials for public information, feeding and caring for animals, constructing and maintaining signs and facilities, surveying lands, and assisting with administrative functions.

Fish and Wildlife Service. The U.S. Fish and Wildlife Service has its roots in the Bureau of the Fisheries, created in 1871 as an independent agency, and eventually placed in the Department of Commerce. In 1885 the Bureau of Biological Survey was created in the Department of Agriculture. In 1939, both agencies were transferred to the Interior Department, and in 1940, they were consolidated into one agency.[12] In 1956, Congress created the U.S. Fish and Wildlife Service and divided it into two offices, the Bureau of Commercial Fisheries and the Bureau of Sport Fisheries and Wildlife.[13] In 1970, the commercial program was transferred to the Commerce Department.[14] In 1974, Congress renamed the sport fisheries and wildlife program the U.S. Fish and Wildlife Service.[15] The FWS includes headquarters in Washington, D.C., seven regional offices, numerous field facilities, a network of wildlife law enforcement agents, more than 500 wildlife refuges and 166 waterfowl production areas consisting of more than 92 million acres, and seventy-eight national fish hatcheries. The FWS' mission is to "conserve, protect, and enhance fish and wildlife and their habitats for the continuing benefit of the American people." The agency seeks to "foster an environmental stewardship ethic based on ecological principles and scientific knowledge of wildlife."[16] It is responsible for migratory birds, endangered species, some marine mammals, and inland sport fisheries. Its programs aimed at protecting land and water environments include the following:

• surveillance of pesticides, heavy metals, and other contaminants;
• studies of fish and wildlife populations;
• ecological studies;
• environmental impact assessment, including hydroelectric dams, nuclear power sites, stream channelization, and dredge-and-fill permits; and
• environmental impact statement review.

Programs aimed at protecting fish and wildlife resources and ensuring that recreational fishing occurs at sustainable levels include wildlife refuge management for migratory birds and mammals, production of fish at hatcheries, and surveys and research on species and habitat. The FWS is responsible for identifying, protecting, and restoring endangered species. It develops the Federal Endangered and Threatened Species List, prepares recovery plans, and coordinates local, national, and international enforcement efforts under the Endangered Species Act. The agency also operates a public information program and gives grants to state and local governments for conservation projects. The FWS has seven regional offices, located in the following cities: Albuquerque, New Mexico; Anchorage, Alaska; Atlanta, Georgia; Hadley, Massachusetts; Denver, Colorado; Portland, Oregon; and twin cities, Minnesota.

Bureau of Mines. The U.S. Bureau of Mines was established in 1910.[17] Its primary goal is to "help ensure that the Nation has adequate supplies of nonfuel minerals for security and other needs."[18] It conducts research on the extraction, processing, use, and recycling of nonfuel minerals and publishes studies on mining exploration, production, demand, prices, imports, exports, and other issues.

U.S. Geological Survey. The U.S. Geological Survey, established by Congress in 1879,[19] is responsible for the "classification of the public lands and the examination of the geological structure, mineral resources, and products of the national domain."[20] Activities include topographic and geologic mapping, chemical and physical research, assessing the nation's energy and water supplies, long-term monitoring of the global environment, and investigating natural hazards. The survey issues thousands of maps and reports each year.

Office of Surface Mining Reclamation and Enforcement. The Office of Surface Mining Reclamation and Enforcement (OSM) was established in 1977 under the Surface Mining Control and Reclamation Act.[21] The agency has regional coordinating offices in Pennsylvania, Illinois, and Colorado that are responsible for reviewing mining plans and permit applications for mining on federal lands. There are also thirteen field offices and eight area offices that provide assistance to states and tribal governments. OSM collects and disburses abandoned mine land fees, establishes standards for reclamation and enforcement, provides guidance and training for reclamation, and oversees states' mining regulation and mining reclamation activities. Most states have their own regulatory programs; in some states that have chosen not to create their own program, OSM has primary responsibility.[22]

Bureau of Indian Affairs. The Bureau of Indian Affairs was established as part of the War Department in 1824 and was transferred to the Interior Department when it was created in 1849.[23] The objectives of the bureau are to "encourage and assist Indian and Alaska Native people to manage their own affairs under the trust relationship to the Federal Government, to facilitate, with maximum involvement of Indian and Alaska Native people, full development of their human and natural resource potential, to mobilize all public and private aids to the advancement of Indian and Alaska Native people for use by them; and to promote self-determination by utilizing the skill and capabilities of Indian and Alaska Native people in the direction and management of programs for their benefit."[24] The bureau operates area offices in South Dakota, New Mexico, Oklahoma, Montana, Virginia, Alaska, Minnesota, Arizona, Oregon, and California.

Minerals Management Service. The Minerals Management Service was established in 1982.[25] The service has four primary responsibilities: assess the nature, extent, recoverability, and value of leasable minerals on the Outer Continental Shelf; ensure the orderly and timely inventory and development, as well as the efficient recovery, of mineral resources; encourage utilization of the best available and safest technology; and provide for fair, full, and accurate returns to the federal treasury for produced commodities and safeguard against fraud, waste, and abuse.[26] The service works with Congress, the twenty-three coastal states, local governments, environmental groups, industry, and others in granting and monitoring leases for the Outer Continental Shelf lands. It collects royalties from extraction of resources from onshore federal lands and the Outer Continental Shelf. The service is headquartered in Washington, D.C., with offices in Virginia and Colorado (the Royalty Management Program), three regional offices, and two administrative service centers.[27]

Bureau of Reclamation. The Bureau of Reclamation was originally established as the Reclamation Service in the U.S. Geological Survey, under the 1902 Reclamation Act. In 1907 the service was separated from the survey and was renamed the Bureau of Reclamation in 1923. The bureau's mission has been to help facilitate the development of the West by developing water storage and delivery and hydroelectric power facilities, protecting water quality, providing recreational fish and wildlife benefits, and controlling damaging floods. Its mission is currently more focused on conservation and protection of water and related resources, facilitating recreation, preserving environmental resources, and providing technical support to other agencies. Its major offices cover the following regions: Great Plains (office located in Montana); lower Colorado (Nevada); mid-Pacific (California); Pacific Northwest (Idaho); and upper Colorado (Utah).[28]

Department of Agriculture—U.S. Forest Service. The Department of Agriculture seeks to improve farm income, develop markets for farm products, curb hunger and malnutrition, protect the environment and natural resources, provide rural development and conservation programs, conduct research, and inspect and grade food quality and safety.[29] The Natural Resources and Environment area is one of nine major divisions in the department. The Forest Service falls under the jurisdiction of the undersecretary for this area. The Forest Service was formed when the Transfer Act of 1905[30] transferred forest reserves from the Interior Department to the Agriculture Department. Forest reserves were set aside for the first time in 1891 by the president under authority of the Creative Act of 1891.[31] The reserves were designated national forests in 1907. The Organic Act of 1897, as amended,[32] the Weeks Law of 1911, as amended,[33] the Multiple Use-Sustained Yield Act of 1960,[34] the Forest and Rangeland Renewable Resources Planning Act of 1974,[35] and the National Forest Management Act of 1976[36] all provide statutory authority for the service.

The service's broad mission is "to achieve quality land management under the sustainable, multiple-use management concept to meet the diverse needs of people." Specific objectives include:

- Advocating a conservation ethic in promoting the health, productivity, diversity, and beauty of forests and associated lands;

- Protecting and managing the national forests and grasslands to best demonstrate the sustainable, multiple-use management concept;

- Providing technical and financial assistance to state and private forest landowners, encouraging them toward active stewardship and quality land management in meeting their specific objectives;

- Providing technical and financial assistance to cities and communities to improve their natural environment by planting trees and caring for their forests;

- Developing and providing scientific and technical knowledge, improving our capability to protect, manage, and use forests and rangelands;

- Providing international technical assistance and scientific exchanges to sustain and enhance global resources and to encourage quality land management; and

• Assisting states and communities in using the forests wisely to promote rural economic development and a quality rural environment.[37]

The Forest Service seeks to balance the "Nation's tremendous need for wood and paper products" with "recreation and natural beauty, wildlife habitat, livestock forage, and water supplies." Forest Service activities include fighting fires and checking spread of disease and pests; building roads for logging; developing trails, campgrounds, water sport areas, and other recreational facilities; managing rangelands; and providing refuges for endangered birds, animals, and fish. The system includes about 35 million acres of wilderness and 175,000 acres of primitive areas where logging is prohibited. The Forest Service operates cooperative programs with state forestry officials and conducts basic and applied research on sustaining the nation's forests. It operates a network of eight forest experiment stations, a Forest Products Laboratory, the International Institute of Tropic Forestry (which conducts projects throughout the United States, Puerto Rico, and the Pacific Trust Islands), and cooperative research with state agricultural colleges. The service's International Forestry Division provides assistance to other countries in promoting sustainable development and global climate stability. The Forest Service also operates or participates in several employment programs, including the Youth Conservation Corps, Jobs Corps, the Senior Community Service Employment Program, and the Volunteers in the National Forest Program.[38] The Forest Service includes the following field offices: Northern (office in Missoula, Montana); Rocky Mountain (Lakewood, Colorado); Southwestern (Albuquerque, New Mexico); Intermountain (Ogden, Utah); Pacific Southwest (San Francisco); Pacific Northwest (Portland, Oregon); Southern (Atlanta, Georgia); Eastern (Milwaukee, Wisconsin); and Alaska (Juneau, Alaska).

Forest and Range Experiment Stations include the following: Intermountain (Ogden, Utah); North Central (St. Paul, Minnesota); Northeastern (Radnor, Pennsylvania); Pacific Northwest (Portland, Oregon); Pacific Southwest (Berkeley, California); Rocky Mountain (Fort Collins, Colorado); Southeastern (Asheville, North Carolina); Southern (New Orleans); Forest Products Laboratory (Madison, Wisconsin); and International Institute of Tropical Forestry (Rio Piedras, Puerto Rico).[39]

The Natural Resource Conservation Service (NRCS), formerly known as the Soil Conservation Service, is responsible for helping private landowners conserve and protect natural resources through voluntary programs in conservation technical assistance. The NRCS reports every five years on the state of natural resources on nonfederal lands; conducts surveys on soils; collects data on snowpack and seasonal water supplies; funds research on new plants that contribute to erosion reduction, wetland restoration, water quality improvement, coastal dune stabilization, carbon sequestration, and other needs; conducts analyses of floods and floodplains; fosters water quality, conservation, and fish and wildlife habitat; encourages voluntary watershed protection programs; conducts flood prevention projects; provides emergency assistance to protect watersheds; provides technical assistance and cost-sharing grants for voluntary programs to conserve the Great Plains; helps community groups to develop solutions to problems of resource use and conservation; helps protect people from abandoned mines; purchases easements from landowners who voluntarily agree to protect and restore wetlands; protects lands for migratory waterfowl; and operates programs to protect the water quality of the Colorado River Basin.[40]

OVERVIEW OF MAJOR PUBLIC LANDS AND NATURAL RESOURCE LAWS

Public Lands Laws

General Mining Law of 1872. The mining law was enacted in the Ulysses S. Grant administration to encourage western settlement and was the last of the homesteading acts. It was amended in 1920 to remove oil and gas so that the federal government could charge royalties for them. It applies to BLM and USFS lands (national parks, wilderness and wildlife refuge lands contain mining claims), and mining is considered highest use of the lands. Miners may patent or buy land at $2.50/acre for placer deposits, $5.00/acre for lodes; demonstrate a legitimate mineral discovery; spend $500.00 on "assessments" and $100.00/ year; and can sell or lease land and charge royalties. No royalties are required (coal mines pay 8 percent royalty; oil and gas industries pay 12.5 percent leasing fees; mining royalties on private lands are as high as 18 percent of gross proceeds).

Taylor Grazing Act of 1934. The act creates the authority given to federal agencies concerning management and protection of "vacant" federal lands; regulations by the Department of Interior govern the issuance of grazing permits, the determination of fees (measured as animal units per month or AUMs), and other regulations governing grazing. Both Congress and the Clinton administration have proposed changes to the law and how it is implemented.[41]

The Wilderness Act of 1964. The act defines wilderness as roadless areas of at least 5,000 acres that are free from human development and authorizes the creation of the national wilderness lands system; wilderness areas are to be created by Congress and managed by whatever federal agency had jurisdiction over the land before wilderness designation.[42]

Federal Land Policy Management Act (FLPMA) of 1976. FLPMA establishes overall public management and policy objectives for federal lands and requires resource management plans by the U.S. Forest Service and the Bureau of Land and Management; governs the sale and acquisition of public lands; provides for public participation in public lands policy making; authorizes the Interior Department to regulate grazing; and orders the BLM to identify wilderness study areas and make recommendations concerning creation of new wilderness areas.[43]

Public Range Lands Improvement Act (PRLIA) of 1978. PRLIA calls for protection and improvement of public rangelands. The Taylor Act established the grazing fee formula; PRLIA gave power to the president to set the formula by executive order; the interior or agriculture secretary can change it.

Multiple-Use Sustained-Yield Act (MUSYA) of 1960. MUSYA requires the U.S. Forest Service to manage forestlands in ways that "best meet the needs of the American people" and ensure "a high-level annual or regular periodic output of the various renewable resources of the national forest."[44]

Forest and Rangeland Renewable Resources Planning Act of 1974. FRRRPA requires the U.S. Forest Service to conduct assessments of renewable resources under its jurisdiction, develop land and resource management plans, conduct research, and establish extension programs; it also provides standards for Forest Service roads and timber sales; amended by the National Forest Management Act of 1976.[45]

Energy

Low-Level Radioactive Waste Policy Act of 1980, as amended. The 1980 law gave states six years to establish regional sites for the disposal of low-level radioactive wastes. In 1985, the deadline was extended to the end of 1992.

Atomic Energy Act of 1954. This act provides the basic framework for regulating atomic energy produced by private and government bodies, including the licensing of facilities by the Atomic Energy Commission and the limiting of liability of companies for nuclear accidents (the Price–Anderson Act of 1954). The Energy Reorganization Act of 1974 replaced the Atomic Energy Commission with the Nuclear Regulatory Commission.

Department of Energy Organization Act of 1974. The act created the Department of Energy, bringing programs from several agencies under one department.

Energy Policy and Conservation Act of 1975. The act ordered federal agencies to establish standards for labeling the energy consumption of household appliances, furnaces, and other devices.

Energy Conservation and Production Act of 1976. The act ordered the federal government to devise energy conservation standards for the construction of new buildings and provided funds to assist low-income homeowners to insulate their homes, study energy use in industrial facilities, and provide funds to state energy conservation offices and other state efforts to audit and make more energy-efficient hospitals and schools, and established the Corporate Average Fuel Efficiency standards for new motor vehicles.

Water

Clean Water Act (CWA) (1948), as amended. Under the CWA, all navigable water bodies are to be fishable and swimmable. Water quality standards are to be set by states that provide the basis for emissions from point sources; these sources must have permits issued as part of the National Pollution Discharge Elimination System. States regulate permits subject to EPA oversight. The law requires different standards of performance for existing and new sources and publicly owned treatments works (POTWs) and different standards for each regulated pollutant. Technology-based standards are required for existing sources (best practicable control technology currently available); conventional pollutants (best conventional control technology); toxic pollutants (best available technology economically); and new sources to achieve the greatest degree of effluent reduction achievable with the best available demonstrated control technology. States can enforce their ambient water quality standards to limit discharges into water. Federal water quality standards are based on the levels of effluent discharge that can be assimilated by receiving waters. Major spills of oil and hazardous substances must be reported to the National Response Center. The U.S. Army Corps of Engineers issues permits for discharge of dredged and fill material into navigable waters: EPA can object if a discharge will have an unacceptable, adverse impact on the environment.[46]

Safe Drinking Water Act (SDWA) (1974), as amended. The SDWA authorizes the EPA to issue national primary drinking water standards that set maximum levels of specified contaminants in drinking water; regulates underground injection through EPA standards; and provides technical assistance and grants. Congress reauthorized the Safe Drinking Water Act in 1996. The new law creates a $1 billion/year state revolving fund (SRF) for communities to improve drinking water facilities; up to 15 percent of a state's allocation can be used to protect source waters. Under the 1986 law, the EPA was required to issue standards for twenty-five contaminants every three years; the bill requires the EPA to issue, within eighteen months of passage and then every five years, a list of contaminants subject to regulation; the agency must issue a standard for at least five contaminants on the list within three and one-half years; the agency is to use cost-benefit analysis and risk assessments in formulating standards. States are given discretion in several areas: they can exempt on an interim basis water systems serving fewer than 10,000 people from monitoring requirements, for example, and grant variances and exemptions from federal requirements for systems serving fewer than 3,300 people.[47]

Coastal Zone Management Act (CZMA) of 1972. CZMA provides grants and other forms of assistance to states to protect coastal areas.[48]

The Marine Protection, Research, and Sanctuaries Act (MPRSA) of 1972. MPRSA, also known as the Ocean Dumping Act, requires permits from EPA for ocean dumping; some wastes, such as high-level radioactive and medical wastes, cannot be dumped.

Coastal Barrier Resources Act of 1982. In order to protect coastal barrier lands, the act prohibits federal agencies from giving flood insurance or other subsidies for construction of new or modification of existing structures on certain barrier islands. A 1990 reauthorization doubled the area of protected lands.

Deep Sea Bed Hard Minerals Resources Act of 1990. Authorizes the Department of Commerce's National Oceanic and Atmospheric Administration to regulate mining of hard mineral resources such as manganese, nickel, cobalt, and copper by American citizens in international waters.

Magnuson Fisheries Management and Conservation Act. Freshwater fishing in the United States is encouraged through federal and state policies that limit the length and time of fishing seasons and the size of fish catch. Agencies stock rivers and lakes, fertilize nutrient-deficient lakes, protect habitats from sediment buildup, limit pollution, and protect against predators, parasites, and disease.[49] The act authorizes agencies to manage fisheries from 3 to 200 miles off American coastlines as public resources. International law recognizes national control over each nation's 200-mile coastline: foreign fishers can take fish only with the permission of the relevant government. Federal agencies place quotas on the amount of certain kinds of fish taken. The law has been used to protect these fisheries from fishing by foreign fleets but has failed to prevent overfishing by U.S. companies. The federal government gives subsidies to companies to upgrade their boats and equipment. The regional fishing councils established under the law are dominated by representatives of the fishing industry. The industry pays no royalties on fish harvests.[50] In September 1996, Congress amended the Magnuson act to move toward more sustainable fishing of the nation's waters.

General Environmental Laws

National Environmental Policy Act (NEPA) of 1969, as amended. [51] NEPA requires all "major Federal actions significantly affecting the quality of the human environment" to include an environmental impact statement that identifies the environmental impact of the proposal and its alternatives. Council on Environmental Quality regulations[52] provide additional details on how environmental impact statements (EISs) are to be prepared. The law is primarily a public disclosure act, requiring agencies to provide information on the environmental consequences of projects they fund, authorize, or undertake themselves.

The Endangered Species Act of 1973. [53] The purpose of the ESA is to protect species of fish, wildlife, and plants that are of aesthetic, ecological, educational, historical, recreational, and scientific value and to ensure that the United States meets relevant international conservation commitments. Endangered species are defined as in "danger of extinction throughout all or a significant portion of its range"; threatened species are "likely to become an endangered species within the foreseeable future throughout all or a significant portion of its range." Interior and Commerce Department agencies are to determine which species should be listed; individuals may petition the agencies to have species designated. Fish and Wildlife Service (Interior Department) deals with land species; National Marine Fisheries Service (Commerce Department) deals with marine species. Agencies are to develop "conservation plans" for conservation and survival of endangered species. Federal agencies are to ensure that their authorizing, funding, or operations do not jeopardize endangered or threatened species or harm their critical habitats (section 7). The 1978 amendments created a cabinet-level Endangered Species Committee to balance protection of endangered species with value of construction projects; it can authorize projects to proceed even if they jeopardize the continued existence of a species if five of seven members decide that protection interferes with "human" needs. The 1988 reauthorization required the Fish and Wildlife Service and the National Marine Fisheries Service to spread recovery activities more evenly among all species listed; required each recovery plan to include a site-specific management agenda, criteria by which to judge success of the plan, and estimated time frame and expenses; double the penalties for violating the act; and established a $5 million/year fund to assist African nations in protecting elephant populations.

Solid Waste Disposal Act (1965), as amended by the Resources Conservation and Recovery Act (RCRA). [54] RCRA authorizes the EPA to establish "cradle to grave" regulation of hazardous wastes; operate a federal program in states that fail to develop their own; set regulations for state programs and oversee them; and provide grants and technical assistance to states. States have primary responsibility for enforcing these laws and implementing regulations, although the EPA can step in if states fail to take appropriate action. RCRA's provisions include criteria to be used by the EPA in determining which hazardous substances are to be regulated; mandates concerning the treatment, storage, and disposal of wastes; exemptions for household wastes and small generators that produce less than 100kg/month; a manifest system to keep track of hazardous waste shipments; prohibitions against the disposal of free hazardous liquids in landfills and other specified wastes; requirements for the labeling of wastes; and establishment of a permitting system for treatment, storage, and disposal (TSD). The law also created a special program for leaking underground storage tanks that involves the creation of a state inventory, testing tanks, establishing performance standards, and replacing leaking tanks and a program for tracking medical wastes that included demonstration projects in several eastern and midwestern states.

Comprehensive Environmental Response, Compensation, and Liability Act (CERCLA) of 1980 (Superfund), as amended. [55] CERCLA, or Superfund, provides for the cleanup of hazardous waste sites. It requires the EPA to arrange for remedial action for any hazardous substance when "necessary to protect the public health or welfare or the environment." The EPA is to conduct investigations, monitoring, surveys, and tests of hazardous waste sites and enter into a cooperative agreement with the state involved to ensure the site is cleaned up. CERCLA orders the EPA to prepare a National Contingency Plan, an outline of methods for discovering, assessing, ranking, and remediating hazardous waste problems, and to issue a National Priorities List of sites to be cleaned up that is to be updated no less often than annually. CERCLA gives priority to the protection of groundwater. Under CERCLA, the EPA is to identify potentially responsible parties (PRPs) who can be held legally responsible for cleanup of the waste sites and encourage settlements among them to finance the cleanup;

if no PRPs can be identified, the act authorizes the use of funds from the Hazardous Substance Superfund, comprising general appropriations and a tax on the production of selected industries. Treatment of waste is the most favored remedy, and transportation of wastes off-site is the least favored remediation option. Cleanup is to take place at a level that "assures protection of human health and the environment."

Emergency Planning and Community Right to Know Act (EPCRKTA) of 1984. [56] Section 313 of CERCLA, also called EPCRKTA or the Right-to-Know law, requires certain manufacturers to report to the states and EPA the volume of each of some 300 chemicals and twenty chemical categories they release each year into the environment. The inventory requirement applies only to manufacturing facilities with at least ten employees that manufacture more than 25,000 pounds or use more than 10,000 pounds of any chemical included in the inventory. The reporting requirements apply to chemicals that are either released into the environment or transported off-site for subsequent treatment, storage, or disposal. Facilities are also required to submit information concerning their efforts to reduce the production of wastes and recycle. The EPA publishes an annual Toxics Release Inventory based on the data. Other sections regulate accidental release of toxics and require plant and community emergency planning.

Air Pollution Control (Clean Air) Act (CAA) (1955), as amended. [57] The CAA authorizes the EPA to set National Ambient Air Quality Standards for ozone, carbon monoxide, PM_{10}, sulfur dioxide, nitrogen dioxide, and lead; states must develop State Implementation Plans to achieve these standards. States issue permits to major stationary sources for five years; sources must submit data showing they are in compliance with their permit conditions. EPA also sets emission standards for the construction of new stationary sources and for new sources in clean air areas (Prevention of Significant Deterioration program). EPA sets emission standards that mandate certain control technologies for 189 hazardous air pollutants; standards are enforced by state officials. EPA sets standards for motor vehicle emissions; state inspection and maintenance programs seek to ensure standards are maintained. EPA issues standards for reformulated gas and alternative fuels; some states must ensure that these fuels are used by certain users and during certain times. EPA also regulates acid rain emissions from power plants through an emissions trading program and limits Chlorofluorocarbon (CFC) use and emissions from industrial and commercial sources.

Pollution Prevention Act (PPA) of 1990. The PPA provides grants for states to encourage pollution prevention and recycling and data collection.[58]

ASSESSING PUBLIC LANDS AGENCIES AND POLICIES

As both Chapters 1 and 2 indicated, public lands agencies and the policies they pursue have been widely and vigorously criticized from all sides. Environmentalists believe the agencies have been too interested in facilitating the interests of the extractive industries; industries find the agencies too bogged down in red tape and reviews; fiscal conservatives find the programs too willing to subsidize private interests that use the lands; and farmers and other landowners find agencies too intrusive and threatening to private property rights. The literature on the implementation of public policies is quite pessimistic. The policies themselves, as expressed in statutes, are often vague and unclear. Adequate resources may not be provided; expectations created by statutes may overwhelm the political will to accomplish effectively the goals identified. In the United States, the separation of powers has made implementation difficult because the legislature may be of a different party than the executive branch officials who are responsible for implementation. Implementation is further complicated by federalism: most national policies are implemented by state officials who have their own political agenda and policy priorities or who may be interested in ensuring their state's autonomy and independence. Policy statements such as statutes often give little attention to the imperatives of implementation by administrative agencies or to the importance of creating effective incentives for compliance by regulated parties.[59]

The problems with implementation of environmental laws are not limited to shortcomings of federal agencies; they are ultimately rooted in the statutes they administer. Some laws include very specific and detailed mandates for implementing agencies. The specific problems with each major policy are addressed in the chapters that follow. Before moving to those discussions, however, it is important to review the broader criticisms of environmental, natural resource, and public lands policy as they provide the general context for assessments of specific programs, agencies, and laws.

The dominant criticism of environmental policy comes from economics. For two decades, studies, reports, books, and articles have argued that policies should be made more efficient through rigorous use of cost-benefit, cost-effectiveness, and other assessments and through the use of market-based policies that use economic incentives rather than traditional command and control regulations.[60] Inefficiency results from national standards imposed on all sources, regardless of local conditions and environmental needs. The Office of Management and Budget and other executive branch agencies, beginning in the Nixon administration, have focused on the costs of compliance with regulations and their impact on economic activity. Tension between the EPA and the White House has continued in both Democratic and Republican administrations.[61] Part of the problem is policies that encourage the selection of alternatives with lower initial costs, but with greater cleanup costs in the long run.[62] Other critics have focused on mismatches between regulatory efforts and the seriousness of some environmental risks: many problems that pose serious risks are given minimal attention, while other problems that are much less serious are given priority.[63]

Another criticism is rooted in federalism and blames federal laws for relying too heavily on centralized programs run by federal agencies. Much like the economic critique, policies that are run from Washington fail to reflect the diversity of problems and possible solutions and impose a "one size fits all" solution, rather than allowing state and local governments to tailor policies to their resources, priorities, and environmental conditions. Critics of regulation have also focused on bureaucratic, administrative problems that are characteristic of large, complex agencies. The implementation of environmental and natural resource laws is particularly problematic because of the breadth of agencies' jurisdiction, scientific uncertainties concerning the causes and consequences of pollution, the political and ideological conflict in which agencies have become intertwined, and the interaction of federal and state regulatory and management efforts.[64]

Advocates of private property rights argue that federal natural resource and environmental laws have failed to give sufficient protection to those rights and call for expansion of property rights and common-law protections as an alternative to traditional bureaucratic policy (see Chapter 1). Representatives of regulated industries regularly raise concerns with the inflexibility given them under regulatory requirements, the uncertainty that comes from a ponderous regulatory process, and the short timelines given them to comply with mandates. They often blame regulators (and congressional staff members) for failing to have some minimum manufacturing experience to help guide them as they impose restrictions on industrial activity. They seek more cooperative interaction with regulators so that environmental improvements can be achieved in ways that still permit firms to satisfy financial and other objectives.

Another problem is policy fragmentation. The vice president's National Performance Review, released in 1993, concluded that the federal government has failed to serve as a model of responsible environmental behavior but has contributed much to the nation's environmental problems. Environmental management is "divided among numerous federal agencies with inconsistent mandates and conflicting jurisdictions that follow bureaucratic, not ecological, boundaries." As a result, "the government spends far too little time focused on the health of whole ecosystems."[65] Bureaucratic barriers inhibit federal agencies from working together to protect the environment.[66] Elements of the environment are much more interconnected than is recognized. Reducing pollution in one form, such as air emissions, is likely to shift or produce it in another form, yet the statutory scheme creates separate programs with independent tasks and particular criteria for regulatory action. Such a fragmented approach threatens to result in transferring, rather than reducing, risks and subjects industry to competing and contradictory regulatory requirements. This is particularly true of toxic substances that cross frequently from one medium to another, unlike many of the traditional pollutants, which were more likely to remain within their medium. Since the costs of reducing pollution can be so great, expensive regulatory requirements that simply shift pollutants from one form or medium to another without reduction consume resources that should be employed elsewhere.

Other critics argue that federal agencies have failed to ensure an adequate

scientific basis for regulation, including shortcomings in basic ecological research as well as in policy-oriented research. Despite continual growth in the
regulatory tasks and the environmental problems under its jurisdiction, the EPA,
Department of Interior, and other agencies have suffered budget cuts, and appropriations fall woefully short of what is required to accomplish all the tasks
delegated to them. One study described environmental policy as a pathological
cycle of regulatory failure as it falls further and further behind in fulfilling the
overwhelming mandates it is to implement. It suffers from a lack of a coherent
regulatory mission, resulting from the lack of an organic statute and the differences and inconsistencies among the ten major laws it implements; a complicated and fragmented bureaucratic structure of programs or media, functional,
and regional offices; constant tension between itself, members of Congress, and
the White House over how laws are to be interpreted; lack of discretion in
program offices; and declining employee morale.[67]

Much of the responsibility for the successes and failures of environmental
policy ultimately lies in state enforcement efforts. But studies have criticized
state legislatures for failing to delegate sufficient authority to regulatory bodies
for them to effectively implement environmental law, inadequate staffing of state
regulatory agencies, and resistance to effective enforcement of environmental
laws by officials who fear that may discourage investment and development.
The level of compliance among regulated industries and state and local governments is often minimal, a result of ineffective implementation of federal laws
by state regulatory agencies as well as federal bureaucratic problems.[68]

Political theorists argue that the traditional approach to policy making has
focused on the protection of individual rights. Policies are ultimately justified
in terms of rights to clean air, clean water, access to wilderness areas, and other
individualistic values. But critics argue that liberalism cannot provide an effective basis for regulation, because individuals will always argue that their right
to use their property any way they wish or their right to engage in activities
that may produce pollution or resource damage will override concerns about the
impact of individual choice. A more effective approach to preservation of natural
resources lies in the development of collective, community-based approaches
that emphasize shared responsibility for natural resources and public lands.[69]

These and other criticisms of environmental, natural resource, and public
lands policies are all important in assessing these policies and in exploring alternatives. But the ultimate set of criteria by which these laws, programs, and
agencies must be assessed is the extent to which they ensure the ecological
sustainability of economic life. Policies ought to be efficient, consistent with
political values, rational and comprehensive, and politically viable and encourage priority setting, incentives for compliance and protective actions that go
beyond requirements, and so on. But if they ultimately do not remedy the problems at which they are aimed, they are failures. The Council on Environmental
Quality's (CEQ) 1990 report of the two decades of efforts since the first Earth
Day on April 22, 1970, found that modest progress was made in reducing air

pollution, primarily by phasing out lead in gasoline and reducing emissions of sulfur dioxide and particulates through modernization of industry and shift to cleaner-burning fuels. Emissions of other pollutants, such as carbon monoxide, nitrogen oxide, and volatile organic compounds, have not been reduced; but even here, there is some claim of victory, since emissions have been relatively constant in the face of tremendous increases in population, the number of vehicles on the road, and the number of miles traveled. However, the viability of wetlands, estuarine ecosystems, and coastlines has declined significantly during the past twenty years. Shellfish harvest has declined, the number of beaches closed for pollution has increased, oil spills continue to plague coastal areas, populations of waterfowl have fallen, and wetland acreage has declined. Water quality in many streams and rivers has improved, but global problems of carbon dioxide and CFC emissions have worsened.[70]

Optimists like Gregg Easterbrook believe that pollution in the Western world "will end within our lifetimes," that the "most feared environmental catastrophes, such as runaway global warming" are unlikely, that environmentalism, "which binds nations to a common concern, will be the best thing that's ever happened to international relations," and that "nearly all technical trends are toward new devices and modes of production that are more efficient, use fewer resources, produce less waste, and cause less ecological disruption than technology of the past."[71] Others find that "just about every important measure of human welfare shows improvement over the decades and centuries"—life expectancy, price of raw materials, price of food, cleanliness of the environment, population growth, extinction of species, and the quantity of farmland.[72]

Tom Tietenberg and other economists argue that we will never run out resources—the earth's air, water, and crust will serve earth dwellers for millions of years to come. The problem is not the existence of these resources "but whether we are willing to pay the price to extract and use those resources." However, some resources will become increasingly scarce in some localities, and rise in extraction costs will cause consumption of some resources to decline. The failure of markets to incorporate environmental costs, such as pollution, climate modification, and loss of genetic diversity, produces "falsely optimistic signals and the market makes choices that put society inefficiently at risk."[73]

The optimists may be right in claiming that human ingenuity can respond to these problems and reverse these troubling trends. While the trends in environmental damage, resource loss, and food production are all negative, they may be reversible. Such changes, however, pose a tremendous challenge to our ingenuity, our governments, and our collective and individual wills. "We may be smart enough to devise environmentally friendly solutions to scarcity," one scholar has written, but we must emphasize "early detection and prevention of scarcity, not adaptation to it." But if we are not as smart and as proactive as optimists claim we are, "we will have burned our bridges: the soils, waters, and forests will be irreversibly damaged, and our societies, especially the poorest ones, will be so riven with discord that even heroic efforts at social renovation will fail."[74] Conservation of lands—setting aside areas for protection or non-development—is not enough; human activity is pervasive, and there are only very limited opportunities for establishing wilderness, refuge, and other protected areas. Humans are an integral part of the earth's ecology, and the primary challenge is to find ways of meeting human needs and protecting natural resources move effectively.[75] The chapters that follow assess specific policies in terms of their ecological consequences but also consider their economic and political characteristics.

NOTES

1. National Resources Section, Environment and National Resources Policy Division, Congressional Research Service, "Natural Resource Issues in the 105th Congress" (January 31, 1997): 4; G. Tyler Miller Jr., *Living in the Environment* (Belmont, CA: Wadsworth, 1996): 610–12.

2. U.S. Department of the Interior, National Park Service, "Parks, etc." (n.d.).

3. Energy and Environment Study Institute, "Public Lands," *1996 Briefing Book on Environmental and Energy Legislation* (Washington, DC: EESI, 1996): 66–70, at 66.

4. 43 U.S.C. 1451.

5. Office of the Federal Register, National Archives and Records Administration, *The United States Government Manual 1995/96* (Washington, DC: U.S. Government Printing Office, July 1995): 319, 321.

6. Ibid.: 326.

7. U.S. Department of the Interior, National Park Service, "Criteria for Parklands" (n.d., no. p.).

8. Office of the Federal Register: *The United States Government Manual*, 327.

9. Ibid.

10. U.S. Department of the Interior, Bureau of Land Management, "Making a Difference in America's Public Lands" (n.d., n.p.).

11. Natural Resources Defense Council, "Selling Our Heritage" (Washington, DC: NRDC, July 1995).

12. Reorganization Plan III, 5 U.S.C. app.

13. Fish and Wildlife Act, 16 U.S.C. 742a.

14. Reorganization Plans 3 and 4, 5 U.S.C. app.

15. 16 U.S.C. 742b.

16. Office of the Federal Register, *The United States Government Manual*: 325.

17. Organic Act of 1910, 30 U.S.C. 1, 3, 5–7.

18. Office of the Federal Register, *The United States Government Manual*: 327.

19. 43 U.S.C. 31.

20. Office of the Federal Register, *The United States Government Manual*: 328.

21. 30 U.S.C. 1211.

22. Office of the Federal Register, *The United States Government Manual*: 328–29.

23. See the Snyder Act of 1921, 25 U.S.C. 13, the Indian Reorganization Act of 1934, 25 U.S.C. 461 et seq., the Indian Self-Determination and Education Assistance Act of 1975, as amended, 25 U.S.C. 450, Title XI of the Education Amendments of 1978, 20 U.S.C. 2701 note, and the Hawkins-Stafford Elementary and Secondary School Improvement Amendments of 1988, 20 U.S.C. 2701.

24. Office of the Federal Register, *The United States Government Manual*: 329.
25. Secretarial Order 3071 under the authority of section 2 of the Reorganization Plan No. 3 of 1950, 5 U.S.C. app.
26. Office of the Federal Register, *The United States Government Manual*: 330.
27. Ibid.
28. Ibid.: 332–33.
29. Ibid.: 112.
30. 16 U.S.C. 472.
31. 26 Stat. 1103.
32. 16 U.S.C 473–78.
33. 16 U.S.C. 480.
34. 16 U.S.C. 528–31.
35. 16 U.S.C. 1601–10.
36. 90 Stat. 2947.
37. Office of the Federal Register: *The United States Government Manual*, 139.
38. Ibid.: 140–41.
39. Ibid.: 141.
40. Ibid.: 141–43.
41. 43 U.S.C. 315.
42. 16 U.S.C. 1113.
43. 43 U.S.C. 1701–1784.
44. 16 U.S.C. 528–531.
45. Forest and Rangeland Renewable Resources Research Act of 1978; Renewable Resources Extension Act of 1978; Wood Residue Utilization Act of 1980.
46. Water Pollution Control Act Amendment of 1956; Federal Water Pollution Control Act Amendments of 1961; Water Quality Act of 1965; Clean Water Restoration Act of 1966; Water Quality Improvement Act of 1970; Federal Water Pollution Control Act Amendments of 1972; Clean Water Act of 1977; Federal Water Pollution Control Act Amendments of 1983; and Water Quality Act of 1987; 33 USC 1251–1387.
47. Safe Drinking Water Amendments of 1977, 1979, 1980, 1986, 1996; Lead Contamination Control Act of 1988; 42 U.S.C. 300f to 300j–26.
48. 16 U.S.C. 1451–64.
49. Miller, *Living in the Environment*: 658.
50. Ibid.
51. 42 U.S.C. 4321–4347.
52. 40 *CFR* 1500.
53. 16 USC 1531–44.
54. Resource Recovery Act of 1970; Resource Conservation and Recovery Act of 1976; Quiet Communities Act of 1978; Used Oil Recycling Act of 1980; Solid Waste Disposal Act Amendments of 1980; Hazardous and Solid Waste Amendments (1984); Medical Waste Tracking Act of 1988; 42 USC 6901–6992k.
55. Superfund Amendments and Reauthorization Act (1986); Superfund Revenue Act of 1986; Superfund extension (1990); Superfund surety bond liability (1990); 42 USC 9601–9675 and 26 USC 4611, 4612, 4661, 4662, 4681, 4682.
56. 42 U.S.C. 11001–11050.
57. Clean Air Act amendments (1963); Motor Vehicle Air Pollution Control Act (1965); Clean Air Act Amendments of 1966; Air Quality Act of 1967; National Emission

Standards Act (1967); Clean Air Amendments of 1970, 1977, and 1990; 42 USC 7401–7671.

58. 42 U.S.C. 13101–09.

59. See, generally, Eugene Bardach, *The Implementation Game* (Cambridge: MIT Press, 1977); Andrew Dunsire, *Implementation in a Bureaucracy* (Oxford: Martin Robinson, 1978); Malcolm Goggin, Ann Bowman, James P. Lester, and Peter O'Toole Jr., *Implementation Theory and Practice* (Glenview, IL: Scott Foresman/Little, Brown, 1990); Daniel Mazmanian and Paul Sabatier, eds., *Effective Policy Implementation* (Lexington, MA.: Lexington Books, 1981); Robert T. Nakamura and Frank Smallwood, *The Politics of Policy Implementation* (New York: St. Martin's Press, 1980).

60. Council on Environmental Quality, *Environmental Quality* (Washington, DC: U.S. Government Printing Office, 1975): 494–96.

61. Council on Environmental Quality, *Environmental Quality* (Washington, DC: U.S. Government Printing Office, 1991): 47–78.

62. National Performance Review, *Creating a Government That Works Better and Costs Less: Reinventing Environmental Management* (September 1993): 1–2.

63. U.S. General Accounting Office, Transition Series, "Environmental Protection Agency" (December 1992): 8–9.

64. Council on Environmental Quality (Washington, DC: U.S. Government Printing Office, 1981): 19.

65. National Performance Review, *Creating a Government*, at 2.

66. Ibid., at 3.

67. Walter A. Rosenbaum, "The Clenched Fist and the Open Hand: Into the 1990s at EPA," in Norman J. Vig and Michael E. Kraft, eds., *Environmental Policy in the 1990s*, 2d ed. (Washington, DC: Congressional Quarterly Press, 1994): 125–35.

68. Barry Commoner, *Making Peace with the Planet* (New York: Pantheon, 1990); Robert W. Crandall and Lester B. Lave, *The Scientific Basis of Health and Safety Regulation* (Washington, DC: Brookings Institution, 1981); John D. Graham, Laura C. Green, and Marc J. Roberts, *In Search of Safety: Chemicals and Cancer Risk* (Cambridge: Harvard University Press, 1988).

69. See Michael Sandel, *Democracy's Discontent* (Cambridge: Harvard University Press, 1995).

70. Executive Office of the President, Council on Environmental Quality, *Environmental Quality: Twentieth Annual Report* (1990): 8–13.

71. Gregg Easterbrook, *A Moment on the Earth: The Coming Age of Environmental Optimism* (New York: Viking Penguin, 1995): xvi.

72. Julian Simon, "Pre-Debate Statement," in Norman Myers and Julian L. Simon, *Scarcity or Abundance? A Debate on the Environment* (New York: W. W. Norton, 1994): 5–22.

73. Tom Tietenberg, *Environmental and Natural Resource Economics*, 3d ed. (New York: HarperCollins, 1992): 356–57.

74. Thomas F. Homer-Dixon, quoted in William K. Stevens, "Feeding a Booming Population without Destroying the Planet," *New York Times* (April 5, 1994).

75. Anne E. Platt, "It's about More than Sea Cucumbers," *World Watch* (May/June 1995): 2.

4

Biodiversity and the Preservation of Endangered Species

THE POLICY FRAMEWORK

The first American laws affecting wildlife were based on English laws that limited the taking of game to the wealthy. In the mid-nineteenth century, states began taking responsibility for wildlife protection and began to regulate fishing within their waters in the 1860s. The primary focus of state law was on conserving wildlife as a food source. The federal government's role throughout the century was limited to an 1868 statute that prohibited the hunting of furbearing animals in Alaska and prohibited hunting in Yellowstone National Park in 1894. By 1900, concern for wildlife broadened beyond food and hunting, and Congress passed the Lacey Act, which prohibited interstate commerce of wildlife products that had been banned by states and importing birds or animals determined by the federal government to be injurious to agriculture or horticulture. The act was the first attempt to manage wildlife, authorizing the secretary of agriculture to take actions necessary to preserve and restore game and wild birds.[1]

Legislation enacted in the twentieth century focused on four issues: migratory and game birds, wild horses and burros, marine mammals, and endangered species. The 1918 Migratory Bird Act limited hunting and prohibited the taking of nests or eggs. The law was bolstered by conventions signed with Mexico in 1936 and with Japan in 1972. The 1940 Bald Eagle Protection Act protected the national symbol in response to fears it was becoming extinct and was amended in 1962 to protect young eagles and in 1972 to protect eagles from predator control efforts. The 1971 Wild Free-Roaming Horses and Burros Act protected burros and horses on public lands and when they wandered onto private lands. The 1972 Marine Mammal Protection Act (MMPA) prohibited the taking of marine mammals, except for scientific research and use by native peoples of the Arctic and Pacific Coasts. The MMPA was a compromise between the demands of commercial fishing interests that believed marine resources should be viewed as an important food resource with commercial value, environmentalists who sought protection for marine ecosystems, and general public support for protecting whales and dolphins. Some protection had been given to marine mammals under the Endangered Species Act and numerous state laws, but the laws were inadequate to protect all the species that were threatened with extinction or might be so in the future.[2]

In 1966, Congress responded to concerns raised in the Interior Department that native invertebrates were in danger of extinction by enacting the Endangered Species Preservation Act, which required the secretary of the interior to develop a plan to conserve, protect, restore, and propagate selected species of native fish and wildlife that the secretary found were "threatened with extinction." The law suffered from a number of shortcomings: it included only native vertebrates, species were to be preserved only when it was considered "practicable and consistent" with the "primary purposes of the federal agencies," wildlife refuge areas were narrowly defined, and Congress provided inadequate funding. Congress amended the law in 1969; the Endangered Species Conservation Act added protection to new species, including those threatened with worldwide extinction; broadened protection beyond fish and wildlife; prohibited the importation of those species into the United States; and mandated procedures for identifying new species that were "threatened with worldwide extinction."[3] The Nixon administration argued that these two laws were insufficient to protect threatened species and lobbied Congress for a more powerful law. The Endangered Species Act (ESA) of 1973 made important policy shifts by requiring all federal agencies to conserve endangered species, expanding conservation measures beyond protection of habitat, and broadening coverage to any member of the animal kingdom.

The Endangered Species Act

The purpose of the Endangered Species Act is to protect species of fish, wildlife, and plants that are of aesthetic, ecological, educational, historical, recreational, and scientific value and to ensure that the United States meets relevant international conservation commitments. Endangered species are defined as in "danger of extinction throughout all or a significant portion of its range"; threatened species are "likely to become an endangered species within the foreseeable future throughout all or a significant portion of its range." Interior and Commerce Department agencies are to determine which species should be listed; individuals may petition the agencies to have species designated. The Fish and Wildlife Service, in the Interior Department, deals with land species; the National Marine Fisheries Service, located in the Commerce Department, has jurisdiction over marine species.

Any "interested person" may petition the interior secretary to list a species as either endangered or threatened. The secretary then has ninety days to determine whether or not the petition has presented sufficient scientific and commercial evidence to initiate action. The secretary may decide whether or not to actually list the species or decide that more information is needed. In practice, the relevant agencies take five major steps. First, the FWS and the NMFS review petitions for species protection submitted by the public. Second, they determine whether or not species should be placed on their list of species that are facing possible extinction and whether or not habitat critical to the species' protection should be designated. Third, they consult with federal agencies proposing activities that may affect listed species. Fourth, they develop plans to aid in the recovery of listed species. Fifth, they review conservation plans and associated applications from private individuals permitting them to proceed with activities that may incidentally harm listed species.[4]

When a species is listed, the interior secretary must designate the relevant critical habitat based on the best scientific and commercial data available, while also considering any economic or other impacts of the designation. Section 7 provides guidelines for federal agencies to follow in protecting listed species. Species can be listed for any of the following reasons: (1) present or threatened destruction of habitat; (2) overutilization for commercial, recreational, scientific, or educational purposes; (3) losses due to disease or predation; (4) the inadequacy of existing laws and regulations to protect the organism in question; and (5) other natural or man-made factors affecting its continued existence.[5]

The ESA is one of the strongest environmental laws ever enacted. In order to protect the remaining species, section 9 of the ESA prohibits any government or private entities from "taking" any protected species. "Taking" is defined in the law to mean to "harass, harm, pursue, hunt, shoot, wound, kill, trap, capture, or collect, or attempt to engage in any such conduct." Section 7 prohibits federal agencies from allowing actions that are "likely to jeopardize the continued existence of any endangered species or threatened species or result in the destruction or adverse modification of habitat of such species."[6] In *Tennessee Valley Authority v. Hill*,[7] a 1978 case, the Supreme Court ruled that section 7 of the Endangered Species Act required a nearly completed federal dam not to open because it would threaten the snail darter, a three-inch tannish-colored fish. The Court found that the plain intent of Congress in enacting the ESA was that "all Federal departments and agencies shall seek to conserve endangered species and threatened species," and this goals was to be pursued whatever the cost.[8]

In response to the Court's ruling, the 1978 amendments to the ESA created a cabinet-level committee to resolve conflicts between species protection and federal projects—labeled the "God Squad" or the "Extinction Committee."[9] The committee can authorize projects to proceed even if they jeopardize the continued existence of a species if five of seven members decide that protection interferes with ''human'' needs. The specific criteria to be used in exempting actions from the act include (1) there are no reasonable or prudent alternatives to the agency action, (2) the benefits of the agency action clearly outweigh the benefits of alternative courses of action that would preserve the critical habitat of the species, (3) the action is in the public interest and of regional or national significance, (4) neither the agency nor the exemption applicant has made irreversible or irretrievable commitments of resources, and (5) the agency establishes reasonable mitigation and enhancement measures, including habitat acquisition and improvement, to minimize the adverse effects of the action on the species' critical habitat.

In 1979, the review committee ruled that the Tennessee Valley Authority (TVA) project should be halted in favor of protecting the snail darter, but Congress then intervened later that year and exempted the Tellico Dam from the ESA. Other populations of snail darter were discovered, and the tiny perch was eventually removed from the endangered list. The committee reviewed one other case, a dam project in Wyoming that threatened whooping cranes. In 1991 it was convened to consider whether forty-four proposed timber sales on BLM lands in Oregon should proceed despite their adverse impact on the spotted owl. The Forest Service first began taking the spotted owl into account in the late 1970s as it made timber management plans. The Forest Service proposed to create islands of uncut timber around nesting sites. Environmentalists challenged a number of Forest Service timber sales for failing to protect the owl, and timber groups also challenged Forest Service and BLM regulations aimed at protecting it. The Forest Service was enjoined in 1992 from further timber sales, prompting efforts by the Clinton administration to resolve the issue (see Chapter 5). The committee voted in 1992 to grant an exception from the ESA for only one-fourth of the sales, thus preventing cutting in the other areas.[10]

The 1988 reauthorization required the FWS and NMFS to spread recovery activities more evenly among all species listed; required each recovery plan to include a site-specific management agenda, criteria by which to judge success of the plan, and estimated time frame and expenses; doubled the penalties for violating the act; and established a $5 million/year fund to assist African nations in protecting elephant populations. Critical habitat was defined in the law to mean ''the specific areas within the geographical area occupied by the species, at the time it is listed . . . on which are found those physical or biological features (I) essential to the conservation of the species and (II) which may require special management considerations or protection; and specific areas outside the geographical area occupied by the species at the time it is listed . . . upon a determination by the Secretary that such areas are essential for the conservation of the species.''[11] The law also requires the secretary of the interior to establish recovery plans for the conservation of species, to include ''such site-specific management actions as may be necessary to achieve the plan's goal for the conservation and survival of the species.''[12] It is a federal offense to buy, sell, possess, export, or import any species listed as endangered or threatened or any product made therefrom.

Implementing the ESA

The Bureau of Biological Survey in the Department of Agriculture originally had jurisdiction over wildlife, except for marine fisheries which were regulated by the Bureau of Fisheries in the Department of Commerce. Both agencies were added to the Department of the Interior and then formed the U.S. Fish and Wildlife Service in 1940. In 1956, the Fish and Wildlife Act created a Bureau of Sports Fisheries and Wildlife and a Bureau of Commercial Fisheries; in 1970 the Bureau of Commercial Fisheries was transferred to the National Oceanic and Atmospheric Administration in the Commerce Department, and the agency became the National Marine Fisheries Service. The Bureau of Sports Fisheries and Wildlife was renamed the Fish and Wildlife Service in 1974. The jurisdictions of the two agencies overlap. Under the Marine Mammals Protection Act, for example, the National Marine Fisheries Service is responsible for protection of whales, porpoises, and seals; the Fish and Wildlife Service is responsible for all other marine mammals, such as manatees, dugongs, polar bears, sea otters, sea turtles (on land), and walruses. The two agencies must also work with the Marine Mammal Commission, an independent body created by the act, which is, in turn, supported by the scientific community through the Committee of Scientific Advisors on Marine Mammals. Various congressional committees and subcommittees have jurisdiction over different types of animals and habitats. The 104th Congress eliminated the Merchant Marine and Fisheries Committee, which had been functioning for more than a century, and divided its responsibilities among other committees, making the protection of the oceans and sea life more fragmented.[13]

Courts have played a major role in the implementation of the law, primarily as a result of citizen suit provisions, included in many environmental laws, which authorize individuals and groups to sue federal agencies for failing to implement nondiscretionary provisions of the law. One of the most successful strategies used by interest groups is the citizen suit, common to most environmental legislation. Such suits have forced agencies to give protection to species and habitats that they otherwise did not plan to do. Property owners have used the Constitution itself as the basis for lawsuits charging federal agencies with actions that cause economic losses or property takings, primarily landowners whose land has been declared critical habitat for listed species. The act itself prohibits the "taking" or killing or harming of a listed species. The U.S. Fish and Wildlife Service expanded that prohibition in 1975 to include the destruction of critical habitat, and the Supreme Court upheld that interpretation of the law in 1995.[14] Environmental organizations championed the decision as favoring the protection of entire ecosystems, not just individual species, but opposing groups used the decision to focus pressure on Congress to revise the law. Other lawsuits challenge agency actions that adversely affect property owners, such as limits on the distribution of irrigation water by federal agencies in order to preserve instream flows for endangered fish, and argue that the law should be limited when it poses a serious economic hardship.[15] Tables 4.1, 4.2, and 4.3 show the distribution of threatened and endangered species and their habitat by state.

International Law and Biodiversity

Since one of the purposes of the Endangered Species Act is to ensure that the United States meets its global commitments to preserve biodiversity, a brief review of these international environmental agreements is needed.[16] A great number of treaties to protect threatened and endangered species has been signed and ratified, including the Convention for the Preservation and Protection of Fur Seals, 1911; the Washington Convention on Nature Protection and Wild Life Preservation in the Western Hemisphere–Organization of American States, 1940; the International Convention for the Regulation of Whaling, 1946; the Paris International Convention for the Protection of Birds, 1950; the International Plant Protection Convention, 1951; and the Antarctic Treaty, 1959. The Convention on the Conservation of Migratory Species of Wild Animals (CMS), adopted in Bonn in 1979 and entered into force in 1983, seeks to conserve species of wild animals that migrate across or outside national boundaries by restricting harvests, conserving habitat, and controlling other adverse factors. The Convention on International Trade in Endangered Species of Wild Fauna and Flora (CITES), adopted in 1973 in Washington, D.C., and entered into force in 1975, places limits on international trade in threatened and endangered species of wild fauna and flora. The Convention on Wetlands of International Importance Especially as Waterfowl Habitat (Ramsar Convention), adopted in 1971 in Ramsar, Iran, and entered into force in 1975, seeks to limit the loss of wetlands. The United Nations (UN) Food and Agricultural Organization (FAO) International Undertaking on Plant Genetic Resources, adopted in Rome in 1983 and entered into force in 1984, seeks to ensure that plant genetic resources are conserved and are accessible for plant breeding, for the benefit of present and future generations; it protects cultivated varieties of plants, plants or varieties that have been in cultivation in the past, primitive versions of cultivated plants, wild relatives of such plants, and certain special genetic stocks.

The most recent and most ambitious global accord is the Framework Convention on Biological Diversity, adopted in Rio de Janeiro in 1992 and entered into force in 1993. It has two goals: (1) to conserve biodiversity, defined as the "variability among living organisms from all sources . . . and the ecological complexes of which they are part" and (2) to ensure the "fair and equitable sharing of the benefits arising out of the utilization of genetic resources." The heart of the convention is a set of actions each party promises to pursue:

• monitor the components of biological diversity . . . paying particular attention to those requiring urgent conservation measures;

Table 4.1
Types of Wildlife Habitats on Public Lands, Fiscal Year 1996

State	Lakes Acres	Reservoirs Acres	Fishable Streams Miles	Riparian/ Wetlands[a] Acres	Big game Acres	Small game Acres	Waterfowl Acres
Alaska	1,872,547	-	176,708	22,200,679	62,243,000	58,522,000	19,839,000
Arizona	1,164	10,160	1,146	51,027	13,426,985	13,460,585	32,225
California	129	65	1,071	62,393	1,719,500	2,130,250	9,455
Colorado	561	18,149	2,934	42,705	8,225,014	8,582,671	55,330
Eastern States	-	-	-	-	1,557	1,600	3,157
Idaho	687	36,924	3,350	46,983	9,226,816	11,310,336	80,780
Montana	3,500	34,000	1,234	76,871	7,483,000	5,632,098	308,000
Nevada	24,570	11,300	2,381	51,340	20,877,867	58,264,529	44,776
New Mexico	1,620	131	329	19,616	10,206,000	10,038,000	26,700
Oregon	59,355	14,146	10,949	252,000	9,451,851	81,302,005	91,780
Utah	2,906	24,828	2,644	154,064	19,221,912	15,788,040	91,524
Wyoming	4,552	32,821	2,752	92,256	16,935,886	16,585,980	94,566
Total	1,971,591	181,524	205,498	23,049,934	179,029,388	208,446,289	20,677,293

[a]The riparian land and wetlands acres have been combined in one heading "riparian/wetland acres."
Source: U.S. Department of the Interior, Bureau of Land Management, Public Lands Statistics 1996 (March 1997): 38.

Table 4.2
Federally Listed Threatened or Endangered and Candidate Plant Species, Fiscal Year 1996

Administrative State	Threatened or endangered (T/E) plants[a] Number	Candidate plant species[a] Number	Estimated habitat Acres	Recovery plans[b] Number
Alaska	-	15	15,019,000	-
Arizona	10	46	5,407,000	7
California	-	-	-	-
Colorado	10	6	200,000	6
Eastern States	131	3	-	-
Idaho	3	1	10 524	3
Montana	-	7	55,000	-
Nevada	9	4	103,500	1
New Mexico	-	-	-	-
Oregon	8	7	1,000	3
Utah	-	-	-	-
Wyoming	1	52	69,600	-
Total	-	-	20,874,624	-

[a]Total number of species cannot be directly obtained by adding the various State totals because many species occur in more than one State. [b]Recovery plans that have been prepared, approved, and are in the process of being implemented. The total number of recovery plans cannot be obtained by adding State totals as a plan may cover more than one state.
Note: Changes in number of T/E or candidate species and estimated habitat is based on current Federal Register Listings and further verification of a species' presence on public land. Some states did not submit data to the Department of the Interior.
Source: U.S. Department of the Interior, Bureau of Land Management, *Public Lands Statistics 1996* (March 1997): 133.

- identify processes and categories of activities which have or are likely to have significant adverse impacts on the conservation and sustainable use of biological diversity;
- establish a system of protected areas or areas where special measures need to be taken to conserve biological diversity;
- regulate or manage biological resources important for the conservation of biological diversity;
- rehabilitate and restore degraded ecosystems and promote the recovery of threatened species;
- establish or maintain means to regulate, manage, or control the risks associated with the use and release of living modified organisms resulting from biotechnology which are likely to have adverse environmental impacts;
- subject to national legislation, respect, preserve and maintain knowledge, innovations, and practices of indigenous and local communities embodying traditional lifestyles relevant for the conservation and sustainable use of biological diversity;
- cooperate in providing financial and other support for in-situ conservation . . . particularly to developing countries;
- adopt measures for the ex-situ conservation of components of biological diversity, preferably in the country of origin of such components; and

Table 4.3
Federally Listed Threatened or Endangered and Candidate Animal Species, Fiscal Year 1996

Administrative State	Federally listed threatened or endangered (T/E) species						Candidate animal species Number	Estimated habitat[a]		Recovery plans[b] Number
	Mammal Number	Birds Number	Fish Number	Amphibians Number	Reptiles Number	Invertebrates Number		Acres	Miles	
Alaska	-	3	-	-	-	-	8	NA	NA	3
Arizona	6	7	10	-	2	1	103	13,573,094	434	20
California	-	-	-	-	-	-	-	-	-	-
Colorado	-	8	6	-	-	1	2	100,000	-	-
Eastern States	24	15	34	3	16	92	32	6,000	-	-
Idaho	7	13	6	-	-	15	8	1,667,877	1,144	14
Montana	3	6	1	-	-	1	27	4,913,553	750	7
Nevada	-	3	16	-	1	1	3	100,000	100	12
New Mexico	-	-	-	-	-	-	-	-	-	-
Oregon	3	7	11	-	-	1	3	500	90	24
Utah	-	-	-	-	-	-	-	-	-	6
Wyoming	3	4	5	1	-	-	44	30,418,883	100	19
Total	-	-	-	-	-	-	-	23,402,387	35,543	-

[a]Terrestrial, wetland, and riparian habitat are measured in acres; aquatic habitat is measured in miles.
[b]Recovery plans that have been prepared, approved, and in the process of being implemented. The total number of plans cannot be directly obtained by adding the state totals as one plan may cover more than one state.
Note: Total numbers of species cannot be directly obtained by adding the various State totals because many species occur in more than one State. Changes in values over the previous year are attributed to better data based on recent investigations, verification efforts, and clearance activities for rights-of-way, oil and gas leases, mining permits, etc. Some states did not submit data to the Department of the Interior.
Source: U.S. Department of the Interior, Bureau of Land Management, *Public Lands Statistics 1996* (March 1997): 134.

• promote and cooperate in the use of scientific advances in biological diversity research in developing methods for conservation and sustainable use of biological resources.

The most controversial proposal dealt with the rights of states over their own natural resources and their development by external powers. Parties agreed that "the authority to determine access to genetic resources rests with the national governments." Access to these resources "shall be on mutually agreed terms and . . . subject to prior informed consent of the Contracting Party providing such resources, unless otherwise determined by that Party." Parties agreed to transfer "technologies that are relevant to the conservation and sustainable use of biological diversity . . . under fair and most favourable terms, including on concessional and preferential terms." Protection was also given to patents and other intellectual property rights.[17] Parties agreed to facilitate the exchange of information, promote technical and scientific cooperation, and ensure that all parties share in the benefits of research and product development. Each party promised to take "all practicable measures" to promote and advance "priority access on a fair and equitable basis" by contracting parties, especially developing countries, to the results and benefits arising from biotechnologies based on the genetic resources provided by contracting parties, and to channel resources to the developing world.[18] President Clinton signed the treaty in 1993, but, as of the end of 1997, the U.S. Senate had not ratified it. Table 4.4 lists threatened and endangered species in the United States and elsewhere.

THE DEBATE OVER PROTECTING ENDANGERED SPECIES

Endangered and threatened species can be found throughout much of the nation; approximately 90 percent of the 2,450 counties in the continental United States are home to these species. The United States contains more biodiversity than all but a few tropical countries, and most of its biodiversity is found in its forests.[19] Between 1985 and 1991, 492 plants and animals were either listed or proposed to be listed as an endangered species. Plants made up 68 percent of these species, while vertebrate animals made up 19 percent, and invertebrates 13 percent. Twenty percent were subspecies or populations (18 percent and 2 percent, respectively). The majority of those that were not full species were either mammals or birds. Seventy percent of the mammals and 80 percent of the birds that were listed or proposed to be listed were either subspecies or populations.[20]

A growing number of species are showing signs of population decline. A Nature Conservancy study found that one-third of the 20,500 species studied are of concern because of population levels and habitat conditions.[21] Another study found that more than half of the species currently listed as threatened and endangered are connected with forests. Some ten forest ecosystems have been identified as hot spots of species endangerment because of logging, agriculture, grazing, water pollution, commercial and residential development, and the

Table 4.4
Threatened and Endangered Wildlife and Plant Species, November 1994

Item	Mammals	Birds	Rep-tiles	Amphib-ians	Fishes	Snails	Clams	Crusta-ceans	Insects	Arach-nids	Plants
Total Listings	**335**	**274**	**112**	**21**	**116**	**23**	**59**	**17**	**33**	**5**	**496**
Endangered species, total	307	252	79	15	76	16	53	14	24	5	406
U.S. only[1]	55	74	14	7	65	15	51	14	20	5	406
Foreign only[1]	252	178	65	8	11	1	2	-	4	-	1
Threatened species, total	28	22	33	6	40	7	6	3	9	-	90
U.S. only[1]	9	16	19	5	40	7	6	3	9	-	90
Foreign only[1]	19	6	14	-	-	-	-	-	-	-	-

- Represents zero.

[1] Species outside United States and outlying areas as determined by Fish and Wildlife Service.

Note: Endangered species are defined as one in danger of becoming extinct throughout all or a significant part of its natural range. Threatened species: One likely to become endangered in the foreseeable future.

Source: U.S. Department of Commerce, *Statistical Abstract of the United States, 1996* (Washington, DC: U.S. Government Printing Office, 1996): 240.

spread of exotic species.[22] While only fewer than 2 million species have been identified, estimates of the earth's biodiversity range from 7 million to 200 million species. UN studies have found that current extinction rates are some one hundred times greater than natural background extinction rates.

The federal government has established 503 units in the National Wildlife Refuge System; more than 75 percent are wetlands aimed at protecting migratory waterflow. Most of the species recognized as endangered live in these refuge systems. Some 85 percent of these lands are in Alaska, and the Arctic National Wildlife Refuge on Alaska's North Slope is one of the prime areas of the system. Like other public lands, refuges are threatened by development and pollution. Private organizations have stepped in to preserve private lands. The Nature Conservancy, for example, has protected nearly 11,000 square miles of sensitive lands.

Opponents of the ESA, such as timber and mining interests, as well as large and small landowners/farmers, argue that the law should be fundamentally changed since it hinders economic development. Supporters, on the other hand, argue that ESA has rarely conflicted with important development projects and that "its inherent flexibility strikes an effective balance between legitimate ecological and economic needs."[23] Some environmentalists argue that hunting should be regulated to ensure it contributes to biological diversity. But hunting and other groups support sport hunting as a major recreational activity. Sales of fishing and hunting licenses are important sources of funding to purchase, restore, and protect wildlife habitat. The debate, of course, is much more complex.

The U.S. General Accounting Office (GAO) completed a study in 1992 of the implementation of ESA by the relevant agencies. The GAO found that only 20 percent of the listed species have had critical habitat designated for them. The agencies claim that this is because there is a widespread belief that defining such habitat does not necessarily increase the chances for species survival and is thus low on the task list compared to other ESA requirements. The GAO also discovered that between 1987 and 1991, when other federal agencies requested FWS or NMFS to consider the effects of particular actions (such as commercial development) on a listed species, the agencies found that such actions would not put the relevant species in jeopardy in over 90 percent of the cases. In the other 10 percent of the cases, the agencies offered alternative plans so that the projects could still proceed 90 percent of the time.[24] Fewer than two-thirds of the listed species have approved recovery plans. There are now over 650 species listed as endangered or threatened, but the agencies recognize 600 candidate species as being either endangered or threatened. Unfortunately, it is projected that all of these will not be put on the list until 2006. In addition, the agencies estimate that there could be up to 3,000 more species that are endangered or threatened.[25]

Another GAO study found that of the 781 total listed species, 712 (90 percent) have the major part of their habitat on nonfederal lands, and 517 have over 60 percent of their habitat on nonfederal lands. FWS and NMFS address conflicts over nonfederal lands through two channels. First, any activity that requires federal approval or uses federal funds must go through the consultation process of the ESA's section 7. Federal agencies are required to consult with FWS/ NMFS to determine whether or not the intended project/activity will "jeopardize" the continued existence of the respective protected species. If there is a possibility that damage could be done, the FWS/NMFS will require the party to implement a program to minimize the harmful effects.[26] Second, the habitat conservation planning process stated in section 10 addresses all projects/activities that do not require federal funding or federal approval. Landowners whose activity is found to be in conflict with the protection of a listed species must be granted a permit to allow some incidental takings of the species. In order to receive such a permit, the landowner must devise a habitat conservation plan, which is "a formal plan that specifies the effects that landowners' activities are likely to have on listed species, the measures that will be taken to minimize and mitigate these effects, the alternatives that the applicant considered and reasons why such alternatives were not implemented, and any other measures the Service may require."[27]

When such conflicts arise, agencies have taken legal action to enforce the law's prohibition against the taking of listed species and to stop or delay activities on nonfederal lands that represented a threat to listed species. In response, private citizens claimed that these actions have deprived them of their property without compensation in violation of the Fifth Amendment to the Constitution.[28] From 1988 to 1993, 4,230 ESA violations were adjudicated. Most involved the importing or exporting of protected species or products made from these species: 126 cases involved illegal takings of protected species, eighty-six involved criminal charges, and the remaining forty were civil cases. Of the eighty-six criminal charges, seventy-one resulted in convictions that included heavy fines, short-term jail sentences, or a combination of both.[29]

Assessing the ESA

Perhaps no federal law has been more criticized by regulated industries, developers, land owners, and others than the Endangered Species Act. An analysis by the Center for the Study of American Business (CSAB), for example, criticized virtually every provision of the act and its implementation by federal agencies. First is ESA's failure to recognize economic and social costs when implementing species protection; there are no provisions in the act that allow such costs to be considered when devising protection plans. The costs that are associated with protecting listed species are often substantial. For instance, the Interior Department's inspector general estimated in 1990 that the total cost of protecting all species would run around $4.6 billion, and this figure is considered a very low estimate.[30] CSAB also charges the ESA with a failure to save the species it protects. From 1966 to 1994, 1,354 species have been listed as either endangered or threatened. Of these, only nineteen, as of 1994, had been delisted.

Seven of the nineteen species were delisted because they became extinct, while eight more were listed in error, as more populations were discovered elsewhere. The CSAB report also challenged the success stories that ESA has produced. For example, the bald eagle, the brown pelican, and the peregrine falcon have all made progress toward recovery not because of any particular action taken under the ESA but because in 1972, the pesticide DDT was banned, the major cause of the birds' dwindling populations.[31] The CSAB report also criticized the ESA's land-use regulations as a taking of private property because it deprives landowners of some or all of its value. ESA also has a "perverse" incentive structure because of the regulatory taking of private property. Landowners often will avoid reporting listed species on their land and instead simply drive the species off their land or even destroy them in order to prevent regulations from taking effect.

Industry groups have proposed several changes to the law. First, the CSAB report recommended that ESA be amended to require agencies to calculate the costs and benefits of protecting a species. Such a provision should also require the government to pay for the habitat necessary to protect the species. This would encourage federal agencies to carefully consider the costs of implementing protection procedures. CSAB also recommended that the ESA change its incentive structure. Instead of encouraging landowners to drive a species off their land to avoid federal regulations, the policymakers should remove the ESA's threat of regulatory takings. In addition, the ESA should provide positive incentives for landowners to retain and protect listed species that exist on their land. For example, in an attempt to save wolves, the Defenders of Wildlife created its own private preservation incentive by offering landowners $5,000 if wolves bred and had pups on their land. Third, the ESA should rely more on objective taxonomy, which really refers to limiting protection to just species, instead of subspecies and populations, since those categories are more nebulous to determine. Such a provision would prevent political abuse of the act as well as "insure that biological diversity is maximized by channeling resources to the most genetically distinct groups of endangered species." Finally, CSAB recommended that the ESA encourage private sector involvement. Currently, many listed species have no recovery plan devised for them because the FWS and NMFS simply do not have the time or resources necessary to create such a plan. CSAB suggests competitive bidding by individuals and private wildlife management organizations for wildlife recovery jobs as a way to improve the efficiency of preservation efforts.[32]

In contrast, other studies suggest that the protection offered by the ESA is coming much too late to effectively protect species and their habitats.[33] Much of the ESA current policy debate centers around the discrepancy between legal definitions and biological realities. The ESA has two relevant definitions: first, the ESA extends different levels of protection to different kinds of animals: vertebrates (which include fish, amphibians, reptiles, birds, and mammals), invertebrates, and plants. Second, the ESA "defines populations and species without highlighting the subtleties of their distinctions or the difficulty of their determination.''[34] Protecting the different types of species unequally is not consistent with biological realities, some argue. Lynne Corn has compared the biological food chain with a house. The plants make up the foundation, the invertebrates are the walls, and the vertebrates are the roof. Although the walls and foundation do not need the roof, the roof cannot survive without the foundation and walls. Thus, it does not make much sense to protect the vertebrates the most and the plants the very least. This is one reason many conservation biologists are beginning to argue for whole ecosystem protection, instead of just focusing on individual species. However, argues Corn, ''ecosystems are even more difficult to describe and categorize than populations, subspecies, and species.'' Even though the ESA supposes that species, subspecies, and populations are completely distinct categories, biologists view the differences as much blurrier. ''Populations, subspecies, and species are not static, but change with the ongoing processes of habitat modification and evolution.''[35]

When populations of two kinds occur together without interbreeding, they are considered different species. When the populations do not occur together, the judgement of whether they belong to different species or are just geographic varieties of the same species can be arbitrary to the members in aggregate of a group of populations that interbreed or potentially interbreed with each other under natural condition; a complex concept.[36]

One reason the concept of species is so unclear is that very few have actually been studied in nature. Moreover, when they are studied, the lines between species, subspecies, and populations are still nebulous. For example, African elephants have not, under any circumstance, bred with any other species. But many ducks that would not normally be classified as the same species will, in captivity, breed with other species of ducks.[37]

One of the more controversial aspects of the ESA is its inclusion of populations and subspecies in the definition of ''species.'' Opponents argue that protecting such ''subspecies'' is not necessary to retain biodiversity and that such inclusion inhibits economic development even more. Supporters, on the other hand, argue that by ''[u]sing distinct population and subspecies listings, the ESA can be selectively enforced to protect a species in one area but not another. Including subspecies and populations on the protected species list thus makes the act more, rather than less, flexible.''[38] Another debate centers on whether the act protects species that are not truly endangered but actually exist in sufficient numbers in enough regions to allay any fears of likely extinction.

While some complain that the ESA has far too much power and does not leave room for economic development, most environmentalists laud it as ''the most comprehensive legislation for the preservation of endangered species ever enacted by any nation.'' The ESA ''stands as the final barrier against the relentless increase in species depletion and extinction.'' The primary goal of the ESA was to ''elevate regard for threatened and endangered species over that of the economic and political forces'' that for so long have dominated. In fact, most advocates of the ESA are pushing to make the act stronger, not weaker, or more ''balanced'' toward economic interests that developers would like to see. ESA advocates argue that developers are already getting away with far too much destruction of species and habitat.[39]

One of the biggest challenges with the ESA is how to protect endangered plants and animals on private lands. A 1996 report by the Environmental Defense Fund found that, overall, less than 10 percent of the endangered and threatened species protected by the U.S. Fish and Wildlife Service are improving in status, and nearly 40 percent are declining. On private lands, the trends are worse: nearly ten species are declining for every one that is improving. The report argued that there are insufficient incentives to encourage private landowners to conserve species, ineffective mitigation efforts when habitats are destroyed through development because of vague standards concerning what is required, and few guidelines for what landowners can and cannot do under the law. The FWS is also slow to take action: by the time most species are added to the endangered list, their numbers are so low that recovery becomes nearly impossible. Perhaps most important, critics argue that the law fails to provide a mechanism for protecting and restoring entire ecosystems but is limited to addressing individual species and their habitats.[40]

Reforming the ESA in the Clinton Administration

The Clinton administration has tried a number of actions to address criticisms of the act. In March 1993, Interior Secretary Bruce Babbitt proposed a plan for the threatened California gnatcatcher (a rare bird) that he offered as a precedent to help avert ''the environmental and economic train wrecks we've seen in the last decade.''[41] Developers in the valuable California property will be exempt from any laws against harming the habitat of the gnatcatcher if they agree to at least preserve enough of the bird's habitat, or relevant ecosystem, in order for it to survive. In April 1993, the Clinton administration reached an accord with Georgia Pacific Corporation, the largest timber company in the country. Georgia Pacific agreed to restrict its logging activities on 50,000 acres throughout Arkansas, the Carolinas, Louisiana, and Mississippi. In return, the administration agreed it will not invoke any further ESA restrictions on the company's logging. Such a voluntary plan is symbolic of the new approach used by the timber industry to try to avoid legal and political problems associated with the ESA and other environmental legislation and was championed by Interior Secretary Babbitt as a precedent for future disputes between industry and environmental interests.

In June 1994, Secretary Babbitt announced new policies aimed at reducing conflict in the implementation of the ESA. They included minimizing the social and economic impact of recovery planning under the act; conducting independent scientific peer review of listing and recovery decisions; requiring agencies to identify quickly and clearly activities on private lands that may be affected by a listing decision; creating cooperative, ecosystem-based approaches to conserve species before crises arise; ensuring that decisions made under the act represent the best available scientific information; and providing for a closer relationship between federal and state officials.[42] In August 1994, Secretary Babbitt announced that when a landowner makes an agreement with the government regarding the protection of listed species, the government will not make further demands, so landowners will not have to worry about future problems or conflicts with ESA policy. Such an agreement "will be the deal, and the regulatory agency will not be back . . . making any additional demands for land or money," said Babbitt.[43] In 1996, Babbitt negotiated an agreement with southern California's largest developer. The Irvine Company agreed to set aside 21,000 acres of prime land for a nature reserve. Local governments and the Nature Conservancy agreed to add an additional 18,000 acres. The agreement protects threatened coastal sage scrubland and forty-two species of plants and animals and was a key step in an effort to establish a regionwide network of natural habitat preserves from the Mexican border to the edge of Los Angeles. In exchange, the company was promised it could build housing tracts, shopping malls, and industrial parks elsewhere without further ESA challenges.[44]

These agreements were part of a broader effort to protect endangered species through ecosystem preservation. The White House Office on Environmental Policy created an Interagency Ecosystem Management Task Force in 1993 to implement an ecosystem approach to environmental management. This task force established an interagency work group to study major issues that contribute to the effectiveness of ecosystem management and prepared the "Ecosystem Management Initiative Overview," which summarizes agencies' efforts to define and clarify goals, put principles into practice, and learn lessons from ongoing ecosystem management. The Clinton administration announced a plan in 1994 to focus on three already established federal restoration projects that include the Pacific Northwest's old growth forests, the Everglades and Florida Bay in south Florida, and the Anacostia River's urban watershed in Maryland and Washington, D.C. The ecosystem management initiative sought (1) to manage lands along ecological boundaries; (2) ensure cooperation and coordination among federal agencies and with state, local, and tribal governments, the public, and Congress; (3) use monitoring, assessment, and the best science available; and (4) consider all human and natural components and their interactions.[45] This new kind of approach "recognizes that plant and animal communities are interdependent and interact with their physical environment (soil, water, and air) to form distinct ecological units called ecosystems that span federal and non-federal lands."[46]

The initiative has raised a number of questions. A U.S. General Accounting Office's study of the ecosystem management proposal focused on three congressional concerns: (1) the status of federal initiatives to implement ecosystem management, (2) additional actions required to implement this approach, and

(3) barriers to government-wide implementation.[47] The "Ecosystem Management Initiative Overview," according to the GAO, failed to "identif[y] the priority to be given to the health of ecosystems relative to human activities when the two conflict." Currently, BLM's and FWS' definitions favor a minimum level of ecosystem integrity over nonsustainable economic development. The GAO recommended:

The practical starting point for ecosystem management will have to be to maintain or restore the minimum level of ecosystem health necessary to meet existing legal requirements. As the understanding of ecosystems increases through the experience gained from ecosystem management initiatives, including the four pilot projects, needed changes to existing legislative requirements can be sought to better define and achieve the minimum required level of ecosystem integrity and functioning.[48]

The administration also needs to take practical steps that will precisely identify what needs to be done and who should be involved. The GAO recommended the following steps: (1) delineating, on the basis of reasonable ecological and management criteria, the boundaries of the geographic areas to be managed as ecosystems, (2) understanding their ecologies (including their current conditions and trends, the minimum level of integrity and functioning needed to maintain or restore their health, and the effects of human activities on them), (3) making management choices about desired future ecological conditions, about the types, levels, and mixes of activities over time among the various land units within the ecosystems, and (4) adapting management on the basis of continually researching, monitoring, and assessing ecological conditions.[49]

The GAO study emphasized other barriers to ecosystem management. First, understanding the complete science behind an ecosystem will require gathering and connecting massive volumes of scientific data. Information concerning socioeconomic factors and potential impact will also have to be gathered and analyzed in order to determine key relationships between ecological conditions/trends and human activities in order to make the most efficient and acceptable trade-offs. Unfortunately, these types of data are either not available or are extremely difficult to find. Currently, there are large gaps in our data bank. In addition, the way ecosystems actually function is still fairly nebulous, even to the scientific world. Such uncertainty allows for much heated debate over the interpretation of data.

Second, coordination and cooperation among different federal agencies whose environmental jurisdictions overlap will be "hampered by disparate missions and separate, lengthy planning requirements—both of which are rooted in the existing federal land management framework." Finally, "[collaboration and consensus-building] with state, local, and tribal governments; the public; and Congress will be constrained by incentives, authorities, interests, and limitations embedded in the larger national land and resource use framework, many of which are beyond the ability of the federal land management to control or affect.''[50]

Some developers have supported the ecosystem management approach because it allows them to plan ahead for the future, instead of being caught unguarded with an announcement that an endangered species is on their property. Developers can "pay up front . . . look at all the habitat and all the populations, set aside enough land and say the species is protected and then say none of the other populations are important to the protection of the species."[51] Opponents of the ecosystem management idea fear that the approach would be a new threat to property rights and prompt new clashes between landowners and preservationists.[52] One skeptic argued that "the key ecosystem concept, while quite useful within the realm of science from which it was borrowed, is inappropriate for use as a geographic guide for public policies. Instead of introducing science into public policy, use of the ecosystem concept interjects uncertainty, imprecision, and arbitrariness." Ecosystem management, would, in effect, greatly increase federal control of private lands and minimize any economic activity on public lands and is "predicated on a number of dubious assumptions that promise to cripple the application of the concept in public policy."[53]

One of the major components of the Ecosystem Management Initiative is the creation of the National Biological Survey (NBS), which would be responsible for studying and compiling all information about all species that live in the United States. The survey is designed to provide the necessary information to identify biological trends before they turn into crises and map out the nation's ecosystems. The entire United States would be subject to the NBS' studies and ecosystem protection, even the 70 percent of U.S. territory that is privately owned. Such a federal undertaking as the NBS is an enormous task. Peter Raven, director of the Missouri Botanical Garden, estimates that 250,000 species exist in the United States, of which only 150,000 have actually been identified. In addition, the physical boundaries of ecosystems themselves are very nebulous to even the best of scientists.

Critics argue that the ecosystem management concept is based on several assumptions: ecosystems and the environment in general are in terrible shape and in grave danger of becoming completely annihilated; "general federal management and protection of ecosystems offer the necessary new approach to ensure proper protection of the environment," and the ecosystem concept is a clear and sound basis upon which to base environmental policy; the NBS will indeed provide the necessary and complete map of our nation's ecosystems to help avoid potential "train wrecks," and additional information is really what is needed to avoid these conflicts.[54] Critics challenge each of those assumptions. America's environmental condition, is they argue, actually improving as pollution levels fall each year. Rangeland condition is also improving. According to the BLM, in 1992, 39 percent of BLM rangeland is in "good" or "excellent" condition, while only 17 percent was classified as such in 1975. About 75 percent of our nation's total land is forests, marshes, rangelands, grasslands, wilderness, parks, and deserts that are available for species' use; 20 percent is devoted to cropland; and only 5 percent is currently used for human construction.[55] The "ecosystem concept is geographically amorphous—a useful attribute in the realm of research but a fatal flaw in the world of people, property, policy and regulation" since there are no widely agreed-upon classification system for ecosystems or ecosystem attributes, little agreement over how to sample and measure data, and inadequate knowledge about which species and which interactions are essential to ecosystems. Ecosystem boundaries are arbitrary, imprecise, and variable over time; they can vary in size from a backyard to the drainage basin of the Mississippi River and are little more than geographic guesses; there are no criteria for choosing one ecosystem pattern as the "best" in federal policy making; and any given area may simultaneously be in many different ecosystems.[56]

Other criticisms focus on the challenges in making ecosystem maps: "[I]ntegrating the sheer volume of ecological data that proponents of the NBS wish to map as a coherent whole is a cartographic impossibility."[57] More important, the NBS will not prevent environmental-economic train wrecks "as long as the policy playing field remains tilted against fulfillment of legitimate societal aspirations tied to economic growth and private-property rights whenever there is a conflict with environmental goals." The case of the spotted owl well illustrates the challenge. Even if we knew where every owl was at all times, what each one ate, and how healthy it was, that would still not have prevented the conflict in the Pacific Northwest.[58]

Congressional Reform Efforts

When the Republicans gained control of Congress in the 1994 election, amending the Endangered Species Act in response to the criticisms of landowners, industries, and developers was their top environmental policy goal. House leaders established an Endangered Species Task Force, which held hearings throughout May 1995. Representatives Don Young (R-AK) and Richard Pombo (R-CA) introduced their reform bill in September. Their bill sought to eliminate species recovery as the primary goal of the act, give more opportunities for states and landowners to be more involved in decisions related to endangered species, create biodiversity reserves, give more leeway to landowners, and reimburse private property owners for loss in land value resulting from endangered species regulation.[59] The House Resources Committee approved the bill in October. The House leadership refused to bring the bill to the floor for a vote in light of public perception that Republicans were attacking the environment. Representatives Jim Saxton (R-NJ) and Wayne Gilchrest (R-MD) worked to develop a more moderate bill in 1996, focusing on incremental changes dealing with the review of listing decisions and ways of encouraging private landowners to develop species conservation initiatives. Conservatives and property rights activists tried to pressure the leadership to schedule a vote on the bill, but there was little support for taking on the controversial measure during an election year.

Senator Slade Gorton introduced his ESA reform bill in May 1995.[60] It was discredited by revelations that it had been written by timber and other industry representatives and by the inability of Gorton's staff to explain the provisions of the bill. Senator Dirk Kempthorne's reform bill was used by Democrats and Republicans on the Environment and Public Works Committee as the beginning point for compromise legislation.[61] Negotiators had produced substantial agreement on three issues by July 1996. First, state and local governments and private landowners would develop multiple species conservation plans that would protect listed as well as other "rare or declining" species in an area. The plans would permit "low effect" conservation plans that allow for incidental takings of protected species as long as mitigation of the impact occurs, and the taking does not decrease the likelihood of survival of the species and does not result in the "destruction or adverse modification of designated critical habitat." The bill would also codify the Interior Department's "no surprises" policy, which ensures that parties to habitat conservation plans are not required to spend more money or have more restrictive land and water uses imposed than earlier provided for, and the "safe harbors" policy, which encourages private conservation efforts by protecting landowners who create or restore habitat from subsequent liability.

Second, Republicans want listing decisions to be based on the "best scientific and commercial data available," while Democrats would limit that requirement to decisions that expressly require that standard. The Interior Department would be given ninety days from the time a petition is filed to list, delist, or down-list species from endangered to threatened or from threatened to recovered. Agencies would be required to release all information used in making decisions unless there was a "good cause" to keep it confidential. Agencies would subject all listing decisions to peer review from a panel of three independent referees from a list compiled by the National Academy of Sciences; referees may not have any conflict of interest or be a party to a petition. Emergency listings would be redefined to be required when there is "an imminent threat to the continued existence" of a species; the current law requires only a showing of "significant risk to the well being" of a species.

Third, agencies would be required to publish draft recovery plans within eighteen months and final plans within thirty months of listing. For species listed before January 1, 1996, plans are to be developed within thirty-six months of enactment of the law. Recovery plans would be formulated by representatives from the state, federal agencies, tribal governments, local governments, academic institutions, private individuals, and commercial enterprises. Republicans favor specific recovery goals for species, while Democrats want goals that "achieve the timely recovery of the species." Republicans also want agencies to assess the economic effects of recovery plans and options for minimizing social and economic impacts; Democrats want such analyses only if the Interior

Department concludes that the plan will have a significant net economic impact on private interests. The bill would also permit states to develop their own recovery plans for threatened and endangered species on a showing of "adequate authority and capability" to meet federal standards.[62]

Congressional Republicans were temporarily successful in using the appropriations process to place a moratorium on listing threatened and endangered species and designating critical habitat,[63] but that moratorium was lifted in an April 1996 budget bill.[64] Republicans proposed a number of riders to Interior Department appropriations bills during the 104th Congress in response to their failure to reauthorize the ESA. These riders would have prohibited the Department of the Interior (DOI) from adding new species to the endangered list, transferred the National Biological Survey to the U.S. Geologic Survey and barred surveys without permission of landowners, reduced efforts to protect imperiled species in the Columbia River Basin, banned implementation of the Framework Convention on Biological Diversity, and provided for clear-cutting Apache sacred lands and home of the endangered red squirrel on Mt. Graham in Arizona in order to build a telescope. These riders were defeated when the president vetoed the appropriations bills (see Chapter 2). One rider was eventually enacted: in September 1996, Congress exempted construction of fences and roads along the U.S.–Mexican border from ESA requirements.

When the moratorium on new listings was lifted, there was a backlog of 242 proposed listings and 182 candidates for listing. The U.S. Fish and Wildlife Service announced in June 1996 a three-tier system for remedying the backlog. Highest priority is to be given species facing an imminent risk of extinction. The agency will then give priority to making final decisions on the 242 species proposed for listing. Lowest priority will be given reviews of listing petitions, proposals for new listings, delisting recovered species, down-listing species, and designating critical habitat for species that are already protected.[65]

Congress was successful in enacting one piece of legislation that might encourage protection of habitat by private landowners. In April 1996, it passed the Federal Agriculture Improvement and Reform Act, which made major changes in agricultural policy: it replaced the traditional price support subsidies to farmers with transitional payments. The act created the Farmland Protection, the Wildlife Habitat Incentives, and the Conservation Farm Option programs, but no funding was included in the House FY 1997 agriculture appropriations bill. It created the National Natural Resources Conservation Foundation as a nonprofit corporation to fund research and educational activities to promote conservation on private lands.[66]

The Importance of Biodiversity

Scientists debate the rate of species loss in the world. Part of the challenge is knowing how many species there are. Some estimates argue that we are losing in the world from 50 to 200 species a day and that if trends continue, and more habitats are destroyed, we may lose 1 million species in the next few decades, most of which are located in tropical areas. The speed and magnitude of this extinction dwarf extinctions in history. The decline of species represent threats to specific species but may also signal that entire ecoystems are at risk. Threatened species are a result of a loss and disruption of habitat, land degradation, and hunting and poaching.[67] A voluminous literature argues that the loss of biodiversity is one of the most serious problems we face and that we can no longer afford to look at the preservation of biodiversity narrowly. It is central to our survival.[68] Our genetic library is being depleted rapidly and irreversibly.[69] E. O. Wilson has warned that

the worst thing that can happen . . . is not energy depletion, economic collapse, limited nuclear war, or conquest by a totalitarian government. As terrible as these catastrophes would be for us, they can be repaired within a few generations. The one process ongoing in the 1980s that will take millions of years to correct is the loss of genetic and species diversity by the destruction of natural habitats. This is the folly that our descendants are least likely to forgive us.[70]

The debate over the Endangered Species Act has primarily focused on the impact of the law on human development and property use. But from a biological perspective, the agenda is much broader and much more important. Protecting biodiversity produces economic, medical, recreational, scientific, ecological, and aesthetic benefits. It reminds humans of their stewardship over the earth as its most powerful species and its opportunity to protect the place of each species as a unique part of the biosphere we inhabit. Each species can contribute to our understanding of how life evolves and is preserved and to the functioning of ecosystems. Wildlife is a source of beauty, joy, and wonder. There are opportunities for compromise, but the preservation of biodiversity is itself a tremendously important public policy goal. It is not simply one of several goals that should be balanced but is essential in ensuring our survival. The fate of the human species on earth is intricately intertwined with the fate of those who make up the biosphere.

There is some opportunity for common ground. Congressional reformers' interest in revising the ESA in order to permit priority setting focuses attention on the need for more research about the role of biodiversity in the ecosystem. Since we are not doing a very good job of protecting endangered species, there are opportunities to fashion agreements around more effective measures. But a conservative, cautious approach would be to err on the side of protection until these issues are better understood. Proposals to create incentives for private landowners to conserve species and their habitat can lead to more protection than is currently provided. Broadening the focus of our attention from individual species to broader habitats and ecosystems is essential. But reorienting the law in that direction will require a great deal of trust and good faith on the part of all parties and a strong commitment to the idea of preserving biodiversity. The political conflicts surrounding the Endangered Species Act reflect a recognition that the economic states involved in protecting species and their habitats are extremely high, but the ecological issues or stake are even more profound.

NOTES

1. For a history of biodiversity policy, see Jacqueline Switzer, with Gary Bryner, *Environmental Politics*, 2d ed. (New York: St. Martin's Press, 1998): Chapter 12.

2. Ibid.

3. For a history of these acts, see Elizabeth Foley, "The Tarnishing of an Environmental Jewel: The Endangered Species Act and the Northern Spotted Owl," *Journal of Land Use and Environmental Law* 8 (1993): 261–62.

4. U.S. General Accounting Office, "Endangered Species Act: Types and Number of Implementing Actions" (Washington, D.C.: U.S. General Accounting Office, 1992): 1.

5. David S. Wilcove, Margaret McMillan, and Keith C. Winston, "What Exactly Is an Endangered Species? An Analysis of the U.S. Endangered Species List: 1985–1991," *Conservation Biology* 7 (March 1993): 87–93, at 88.

6. 16 U.S.C. 1536(a)(2).

7. 437 U.S.C. 153 (1978).

8. 16 U.S.C. 1531(c).

9. 16 U.S.C. 1536(e).

10. George Cameron Coggins, Charles F. Wilkinson, and John D. Leshy, *Federal Public Land and Resource Law* (Westbury, NY: Foundation Press, 1993): 805–6.

11. 16 U.S.C. 1532(5)(B).

12. 16 U.S.C. 1533(f)(1).

13. Switzer and Bryner, *Environmental Politics*.

14. *Babbitt v. Sweet Home Chapter of Communities for a Greater Oregon*, 115 S. Ct. 2407 (1995).

15. Switzer and Bryner, *Environmental Politics*.

16. This discussion is based on Gary C. Bryner, *From Promise to Performance: Achieving Global Environmental Goals* (New York: W. W. Norton, 1997): Chapter 1.

17. Article 16.

18. These agreements are summarized in Fridtjof Nansen Institute, *Green Global Yearbook of International Co-Operation on Environment and Development* (New York: Oxford University Press, 1996).

19. United Nations Environment Programme, *Global Biodiversity Assessment* (Cambridge: Cambridge University Press, 1995).

20. Wilcove, McMillan, and Winston, "What Exactly Is an Endangered Species?

21. The Nature Conservancy, "Priorities for Conservation: 1996 Annual Report Card for U.S. Plant and Animal Species" (Arlington, VA: Nature Conservancy, 1996).

22. C. H. Flatner, L. A. Joyce, and C. A. Bloomgarden, "Species Endangerment Patterns in the United States," General Technical Report RM-241 (Fort Collins, CO: U.S. Department of Agriculture Forest Service, 1994).

23. Jonathan Adams, "Rescuing the Endangered Species Act," *WWF Conservation Issues* (August 1995):3.

24. U.S. General Accounting Office. "Endangered Species Act: Types and Number of Implementing Actions" (Washington, DC: U.S. General Accounting Office, 1992).

25. Ibid.

26. U.S. General Accounting Office, "Endangered Species Act: Information on Species Protection on Nonfederal Lands" (Washington, DC: U.S. General Accounting Office (1994): 2–3.

27. Ibid.

28. Ibid.: 11.

29. Ibid.: 12.

30. Thomas Lambert and Robert J. Smith, *The Endangered Species Act: Time for a Change*. (St Louis, MO: Center for the Study of American Business (1994): 19–20.

31. Ibid.: 12.

32. Ibid.: 44–53.

33. Wilcove, McMillan, and Winston, "What Exactly Is an Endangered Species?" : 92.

34. M. Lynn Corn, "The Listing of Species: Legal Definitions and Biological Realities," U.S. Congress, Congressional Research Service Report for Congress (December 1992):1.

35. Ibid.: 3.

36. Ibid.

37. Ibid.: 6.

38. Adams, "Rescuing the Endangered Species Act."

39. Foley, "The Tarnishing of an Environmental Jewel" : 253–55.

40. David Wilcove, "Toward a More Effective Endangered Species Act," *EDF Letter* (January 1997): 7.

41. Robert Reinhold, "U.S. Acts to Save Home of Rare Bird," *New York Times* (March 26, 1993): A11.

42. *Endangered Species Technical Bulletin* (1994): 3.

43. John Brinkley, " 'A Deal's a Deal' on Species Protection, Babbitt Says," *Washington Times* (August 12, 1994): A6.

44. William Claiborne, "In California Compromise, Developers and Environmentalists Benefit," *Washington Post* (August 18, 1996): A3; Switzer with Bryner, *Environmental Politics*: Chapter 12.

45. U.S. General Accounting Office, "Ecosystem Management: Additional Actions Needed to Adequately Test a Promising Approach" (Washington, DC: U.S. General Accounting Office, 1994): 6.

46. Ibid.: 3.

47. Ibid.

48. Ibid.: 6.

49. Ibid.: 6–7.

50. Ibid.: 7.

51. Reinhold, "U.S. Acts to Save Home of Rare Bird."

52. William K. Stevens, "Battle Looms on Plans for Endangered Species," *New York Times*, (November 11, 1993): B5, B8.

53. Allan K. Fitzsimmons, "Federal Ecosystem Management: A 'Train Wreck' in the Making," *Policy Analysis* No. 217 (1994): 1–2.

54. Ibid.: 5–6.

55. Ibid.: 9.

56. Ibid.: 10.

57. Ibid.: 13.

58. Ibid.: 16.

59. 104th Congress, H.R. 2275.

60. 104th Congress, S. 768.

61. 104th Congress, S. 1364.

62. Environmental and Energy Policy Institute, *Monthly PULSE* (July 1996): 12–13.

63. P.L. 104–6.

64. 104th Congress, H.R. 3019, P.L. 104–134, April 1996: omnibus FY 1996 spending bill for the Interior Department and other agencies.

65. Environmental and Energy Policy Institute: 12.

66. P.L. 104–127.

67. G. Tyler Miller Jr., *Living in the Environment* (Belmont, CA: Wadsworth, 1996): 635–64.

68. See Jonathan S. Adams and Thomas O. McShane, *The Myth of Wild Africa: Conservation without Illusion* (New York: W. W. Norton, 1992); David Attenborough, *Life on Earth* (Boston: Little, Brown, 1979); David Attenborough, *The Living Planet* (Boston: Little, Brown, 1984); James M. Broadus and Raphael V. Vartanov, *The Oceans and Environmental Security: Shared U.S. and Russian Perspectives* (Washington, DC: Island Press, 1994); Paul Erlich and Anne Erlich, *Extinction: The Causes and Consequences of the Disappearance of Species* (New York: Ballantine Books, 1981); Robert Goodland, ed., *Race to Save the Tropics: Ecology and Economics for a Sustainable Future* (Washington, DC: Island Press, 1990); Edward Goldsmith and Nicholas Hildyard, *The Earth Report: The Essential Guide to Global Ecological Issues* (Los Angeles: Price Stern Sloan, 1988); Suzanne Head and Robert Heinzman, eds., *Lessons of the Rainforest* (San Francisco: Sierra Club Books, 1990); Philip Hurst, *Rainforest Politics: Ecological Destruction in South-East Asia* (London: Zed Books, 1990); Jeffrey A. McNeely et al., *Conserving the World's Biological Diversity* (Gland, Switzerland: International Union for Conservation of Nature and Natural Resources, World Resources Institute, Conservation International, World Wildlife Fund–U.S. and the World Bank, 1990); Norman Myers, *The Primary Source: Tropical Forests and Our Future* (New York: W. W. Norton, 1990); Walter V. Reid and Kenton R. Miller, *Keeping Options Alive: The Scientific Basis for Conserving Biodiversity* (Washington, DC: World Resources Institute, 1989); Richard Tobin, *The Expendable Future: U.S. Politics and the Protection of Biological Diversity* (Durham, NC: Duke University Press, 1990); World Conservation Monitoring Centre, *Global Biodiversity: Status of the Earth's Living Resources* (London: Chapman and Hall, 1992); World Resources Institute, World Conservation Union, and United Nations Environment Programme, *Global Biodiversity Strategy: Guidelines for Action to Save, Study, and Use Earth's Biotic Wealth Sustainably and Equitably* (Washington, DC: World Resources Institute, 1992).

69. Sandra Postel, "Denial in the Decisive Decade," in Lester Brown et al., *State of the World 1992* (New York: Norton, 1992): 3.

70. E. O. Wilson, *The Diversity of Life* (Cambridge: Harvard University Press, 1992); see also E. O. Wilson, ed., *Biodiversity* (Washington, DC: National Academy Press, 1988).

5

National Forests and Timber Policy

THE POLICY FRAMEWORK

Like other natural resources, the United States seemed to enjoy a limitless supply of timber in the nineteenth century. The goal of forest policy on public lands has traditionally been to provide a continuous supply of lumber to meet the nation's needs. Criticism has generally focused on the failure of policies to ensure a sustainable yield. One of the first such calls was in 1873, when the American Association for the Advancement of Science asked Congress to enact legislation to protect the nation's forests. In 1876, the Agriculture Department established a forestry division to promote timber development. By the end of the nineteenth century, it became clear that forest resources were limited.

In response to destructive timber cuts in Michigan and other states, Congress passed the Creative Act of 1891, which authorized the president to withdraw lands open to preemption and homesteading rights as national forests. Democratic president Grover Cleveland, in an act of defiance as Republican William McKinley was elected in 1896, doubled the size of the forest reserves to 40 million acres in 1897 as he left office. Cleveland's action locked up forests in South Dakota and Montana that had been the source of timber for two mining companies. Congress repealed the act in 1897, because members had not been sufficiently consulted in the creation of these forests, and enacted the Organic Administration Act to provide objectives for the reserves and transfer them to the Department of Interior.[1] The act limited public lands designated by the president as forest reserves to the following condition: "No public forest reservation shall be established except to improve and protect the favorable conditions of water flows, and to furnish a continuous supply of timber for the use and necessities of the citizens of the United States."[2]

The Organic Act was written from the perspective of members of Congress worried about how the increase in the forest reserves would affect the mining industry. Congress declared its purpose in enacting the law to be that "no national forest shall be established, except to improve and protect the forest within the boundaries, or for the purpose of securing favorable conditions of water flows, and to furnish a continuous supply of timber for the use and necessities of the citizens of the United States."[3] But farmers and miners were authorized to harvest any size and species of trees, while commercial sales were limited to "dead, matured, or large growth of trees," which had to be marked before being sold.[4]

In 1905, Congress reversed itself again and transferred the reserves back to the U.S. Department of Agriculture (USDA) and created the U.S. Forest Service. President Theodore Roosevelt created twenty-one new national forests in 1907. Congress permitted the Forest Service a relatively free hand for more than a half century as its mission was primarily understood to be timber production. Gifford Pinchot, the first chief of the Forest Service, envisioned national forests as tree farms. His goal was to transform wild, natural lands into "cultivated" forests, managed for maximum sustainable yield. Subsequent Forest Service employees such as Aldo Leopold and Robert Marshall in the 1930s helped direct the agency toward preservation and administrative designation of 13 million acres as wilderness areas where logging was banned. But the demand for timber after World War 11 exploded, and timber sales from national forests increased by 800 percent from 1941 to 1966. Lumber companies and loggers in the West in particular became dependent on national forests, as did the counties that received 25 percent of the income from timber sales.

The Multiple Use-Sustained Yield Act of 1960 ordered the secretary of agriculture, in vague and imprecise terms, to administer the resources of the national forests for "multiple use and sustained yield of the several products and services obtained therefrom." Multiple use is defined as management that

will best meet the needs of the American people; making the most judicious use of the land for some or all of these resources or related services . . . and harmonious and coordinated management of the various resources, each with other, without impairment of the productivity of the land, with consideration being given to the relative values of the various resources, and not necessarily the combination of uses that will give the greatest dollar return or the greatest unit output.[5]

Sustained yield means "the achievement and maintenance in perpetuity of a high-level annual or regular periodic output of the various renewable resources of the national forests without impairment of the productivity of the land."[6] The act provided that national forests be created to foster recreation, timber, range, watershed, and wildlife but also reaffirmed the purposes of the 1897 Organic Act.[7] Subsequent legislation has never repealed the Organic Act.

The National Forest Management Act

By the 1970s, environmental damage in national forests prompted Congress to order the Forest Service, through the National Forest Management Act, to give more protection to nontimber resources. Senator Hubert H. Humphrey (D-MN), chief sponsor of the bill, argued that "the days have ended when the forest may be viewed only as trees and trees viewed only as timber. The soil and the water, the grasses and the shrubs, the fish and the wildlife, and the beauty of the forest must become integral parts of the resource managers' thinking and actions."[8] In 1974, Congress passed the Forest and Rangeland Renewable Resources Planning Act (RPA), which required the Forest Service to engage in long-term planning, assess its resources every ten years, and require management plans for each unit and update them every fifteen years. Two years later, Congress enacted the National Forest Management Act (NFMA) of 1976, which amended the planning process to restrict clear-cutting, limit logging on fragile lands, emphasize multiple use, and maintain a diversity of plants and animals. Congress provided three primary goals for the Forest Service when it enacted the NFMA. First, the law required the Forest Service to prepare forest plans for each national forest. Second, the law established standards for Forest Service timber sales. Third, it provided basic principles to guide Forest Service timber policy. While the 1897 Organic Act, the 1964 Multiple Use-Sustained Yield Act, and the 1974 Forest and Rangeland Renewable Resources Planning Act all govern the Forest Service, the National Forest Management Act is the primary law governing forest management practices. NFMA orders the Forest Service to conduct an assessment of public and private renewable resources in national forests every ten years, develop long-range plans for the Forest Service every five years, and create Land and Resource Management Plans for each forest.

NFMA outlines requirements for forest planning. Land and Resource Management Plans are required for individual forests, ten to fifteen-year plans that are to guide local management decisions and are to be consistent with NFMA and national timber sales targets. They are to be based on advice from a committee of scientists and subject to public review and participation. Forest plans must meet the requirements of the National Environmental Policy Act; the planning process is viewed as the equivalent of the environmental impact statement requirement. Wilderness preservation is to be given equal status with other uses of national forests in formulating plans.[9]

Timber sales must take place at no less than the appraised value and be publicly advertised, unless there are extraordinary circumstances, or the appraised value is less than $10,000. Bidding procedures must ensure open and fair competition and authorize the secretary of agriculture to prevent collusion in bidding. In western forests, bidding is primarily done orally; in eastern and southern forests, sealed bids are primarily used. Timber contracts must promote "orderly harvesting," usually completed within three to five years. Logging companies may construct access roads and be reimbursed by the Forest Service, or the service may construct the roads. Roads are to be built to standards that anticipate later uses such as recreation, wildlife management, and subsequent logging.[10]

NFMA places several constraints on Forest Service timber harvesting. The service is prohibited from logging lands that are "not suited for timber production, considering physical, economic, and other pertinent conditions."[11] NFMA was the first federal law to address biodiversity, as it required the Forest Service to promote biodiversity in forests when establishing plans, even if that limits timber sales. The agency, based on recommendations from independent scientists, was to maintain "viable populations" of existing vertebrate species and provide for "diversity of plant and animal communities . . . in order to meet over-all multiple use objectives . . . to the degree practicable."[12] Trees must not be cut until they reach the culmination of their mean annual increment of growth. The service must allow no more cuts than what is required to ensure a sustained yield. Clear-cuts can be approved only if the Forest Service finds that they are the optimal means of achieving the goals of the forest plan. Clear-cuts must ensure the protection of soils, watersheds, fish, wildlife, recreation, and forest aesthetics and ensure the regeneration of forests.[13]

The Forest Service issued regulations implementing NFMA in 1979, and the final planning regulations took effect in 1982. The agency conducted a major review of the planning process in 1989. That assessment, issued in 1990, recommended that the agency clarify what decisions are to be made in the forest plans, simplify and shorten the planning process, and provide for revisions of forest plans when needed. The agency proposed a new planning rule in 1995 and received more than 1,000 responses during the public comment period. The draft rule promised to streamline planning procedures, incorporate principles of ecosystem management into the forest-planning process, and clarify the nature of forest plan decisions and how they relate to other planning and decision-making processes.[14] Both "wise use" and environmental interests are demanding more opportunities for participation in Forest Service management decisions, and it will be increasingly difficult for the agency to satisfy these growing demands for access to decision makers and decision-making processes.

The goals of the NFMA were largely unrealized during the 1980s, as the Forest Service resisted making changes in timber policy. It increased timber sales, peaking at 12.7 billion board feet of timber in 1987, 40 percent of which came from the Pacific Northwest. Forest plans developed in the 1980s called for a doubling of timber production in Rocky Mountain and eastern national forests and the construction of more than 100,000 miles of new logging roads throughout the nation over the next half century. This would open to development millions of acres of forests that had been protected from cuts. Forest Service officials argued that this would actually increase biodiversity: new roads, for example, would create new habitat for edge-dwelling game species. The Forest Service's budget process encourages logging, as appropriations are tied to outputs such as board feet of timber cut or miles of roads constructed, rather than measures of biodiversity. Failure to meet timber targets is widely viewed in the agency as serious management failure.[15]

Proponents of continued emphasis on timber production argue that the 25 percent of revenues from timber sales that go to counties are a major source of funds for schools and roads in rural communities. These funds total more than $300 million a year. The plan to preserve northwest logging, discussed later, included an act passed by Congress in 1993 that guaranteed counties a minimum percentage of the funds they had traditionally received, despite a decline in actual revenues.

Clinton Administration Policy

The Clinton administration initiated a shift in Forest Service policy from giving priority to timber production to embracing a range of values, including protection of biodiversity. Until the Clinton administration, the Forest Service had largely been a timber management agency, with two-thirds of its budget and workforce dedicated to logging activities. The Northwest Forest Plan became the centerpiece of the Clinton approach.

The northern spotted owl lives in forests that stretch along the Pacific Coast from Canada to the San Francisco Bay Area. The owl's primary habitat is in the national forests and BLM lands in California, Oregon, and Washington that contain Douglas firs. Because of low reproductive rates and low survival rates of young owls, it was listed as a threatened species by the U.S. Fish and Wildlife Service in 1990 (see chapter 4). The owl may be an indicator species, since it feeds at the top level of the forest, and other species in these old-growth forests may also be threatened. The U.S. Fish and Wildlife Service developed a recovery plan for the owls that included the designation of critical habitat for its protection. In 1992, the Bureau of Land Management proposed that forty-four timber sales in western Oregon be exempted from the act, despite an opinion issued by the FWS that the proposal would threaten the owl's long-term survival. A federal court granted a motion by environmental groups to block the timber sales. The Endangered Species Committee was then convened to consider the BLM proposal. In order to exempt actions from provisions of the ESA, the committee must find that there is no reasonable or prudent alternative to the proposed action, that the benefits of the action "clearly outweigh" any other alternatives, and that the action is in the public interest. In 1992, the committee voted to deny thirty-one of the forty-four BLM timber sales. While the decision affected only 1,742 acres of timberland and a thousand jobs, it was the first exemption ever granted under the ESA and a major symbolic shift in policy.

The issue was further complicated by a May 1992 ruling by a federal judge that the Fish and Wildlife Service protection plan for the owl was inadequate because it did not address new information about the size of the owl's population.[16] The Forest Service's spotted owl management plan was rejected by a federal court because its EIS was incomplete and included outdated scientific evidence and false assumptions.[17] The Supreme Court prohibited the Forest Service from permitting timber cutting in areas that served as habitat for the spotted owl.[18] Logging of old-growth forests in the Northwest was described by Judge William Dwyer, a Reagan appointee, as "a remarkable series of violations of the environmental laws" and "a deliberate and systematic refusal to comply with the laws protecting wildlife."[19]

The Clinton administration held a summit meeting in Portland in April 1993 to try to come up with a compromise plan. The Clinton administration brought together biologists, hydrologists, economists, and other scientists in a Forest Ecosystem Management Assessment Team, which identified ten options for managing all or part of seventeen national forests that provide habitat for the spotted owl. The options ranged from preserving all remaining old-growth forests to reaffirming existing management plans and included alternative designations of reserve areas and levels of logging outside those protected enclaves. The team also assessed the impact of alternatives on biodiversity, finding that the viability of some 1,300 species was a direct function of the size of old-growth reserves. The option the Clinton administration ultimately selected was one of the least environmentally protective. It designated about half of the old-growth forest acreage outside wilderness areas as timber-producing lands. In exchange for opening lands to produce about 1.2 billion board feet of lumber a year, the plan increased the threat to some 400 species whose habitats became more isolated and fragmented.[20] The team also recommended the creation of a reserve system for many old-growth areas that would also protect watersheds and riparian areas, changes in tax policy to discourage the exporting of raw logs for processing in other countries, and financial assistance to logging communities. Neither the timber industry nor the conservation community was happy with the proposal: they did not agree on what level of timber cutting was sustainable; environmentalists pushed for a logging ban in old-growth forests, while timber companies were permitted to make thinning and salvaging cuts; and allowing cuts around salmon streams would favor logging at the expense of fishing jobs.[21]

Much of the debate among the Clinton administration, environmentalists, and timber stakeholders focused on the impact on timber jobs. The option selected was projected to result in a loss of 6,000 jobs. Preserving all old-growth forests was projected to cost 13,000 jobs. Industry representatives had projected a loss of 60,000 jobs. The plan also included federal assistance to help communities diversify their economies.[22] In October, the administration reached agreement with twelve different environmental groups. Logging would be permitted in some northwestern forests while the Clinton administration promised to work against any legislation in Congress that seeks exemption from environmental laws or promotes a long-term logging plan. In Clinton's proposed ten-year plan, logging would be reduced to 1.2 billion board feet per year. This is about a quarter of the timber that is usually extracted. (A board foot is one foot square by one inch thick.)[23]

The July 1993 Northwest Timber Plan included the following provisions:

• allows for logging of about 12 billion board feet of timber over ten years, or about 1.2 billion annually on federal lands in the Northwest that produced more than 5 billion a year in the 1980s

• establishes reserves for the threatened northern spotted owl in which logging would be limited to dead and dying trees and thinning of some live ones, but only where that poses no threat to the owl

• sets up ten special management areas where experimental harvesting techniques would be used

• establishes no-logging buffer zones around sensitive streams and protects entire watersheds to try to avoid endangered salmon and other wildlife

• asks Congress to spend $1.2 billion over five years, including $270 million in the fiscal year 1994, to assist the region's economy through economic development grants, small business zones, job training money, and funds to have loggers restore rivers damaged by excessive logging

• asks Congress to encourage more domestic milling by eliminating a tax subsidy for timber companies that export raw logs.[24]

The agreement has satisfied no one. Environmental groups continue to seek a ban on the logging of old-growth forests, and the timber industry has used a salvage logging provision passed by Congress in 1995 (see later) to expand logging in the area. Mark Rogers, a wood industry analyst, had argued in 1991 that "[n]o tonic could be better for the depressed wood-products industry than a decrease in capacity coinciding with an increase in demand. Thanks to the controversy over the spotted owl, industry capacity is almost certain to be cut just as the housing recovery begins to stimulate demand." This could certainly mean higher profits for the timber industry.[25] There have also been some challenges to the belief that the owls are endangered.[26] Some environmentalists admitted that the real agenda was the preservation of old-growth forests: "[T]he controversy surrounding the spotted owl involves more than the loss of one species of bird. It concerns the destruction of an entire ecosystem and the loss of many of the species that depend on it for survival." The owl serves as the "indicator species," a species whose own health reflects the health of all the species in the old-growth forest ecosystem.[27]

One of the most widely criticized environmental actions of the 104th Congress was the salvage logging rider attached to the 1995 Rescissions Act.[28] The act was an effort to cut spending that had already been appropriated by the 103d Congress. The salvage logging rider suspended the coverage of environmental laws in order to facilitate the logging of dead and dying trees. The actual language of the rider was quite expansive, allowing logging companies to remove healthy trees if they were associated with trees susceptible to fire or disease. As a result, the Forest Service expedited logging contracts and permitted some areas to be logged that likely would never have been approved if environmental reviews had been required. Industry groups defended the rider as an essential step to ensure supplies of timber and promote forest health by removing trees that were susceptible to fire and disease. However, there was little commercial interest in much of the salvage timber that was put on the market. By April 1996, there were more than one hundred sales announced that had not received any bids. The bids that were awarded included the price of some trees at less than a dollar each. Some areas that had been off-limits to loggers were suddenly made available. The rider seemed primarily aimed at opening old-growth forests to timber cuts. Logging occurred in areas that had previously been protected as habitat for grizzlies and other species. Environmentalists were unsuccessful in trying to get the Clinton administration to veto the Rescissions Act and just as fruitless in getting Congress to pass new legislation to curb the "logging without laws." The salvage timber rider expired on December 31, 1996, prompting a flurry of approvals for cuts before the end of the year.[29]

In October 1995, the Ninth Circuit Court of Appeals rejected a petition to stop the timber industry's logging of healthy, old-growth forests in the Pacific Northwest, under the salvage logging rider. The lower court's order required the Forest Service and the Bureau of Land Management to make available to the timber industry millions of board feet of timber, with no environmental protections. The federal government and environmental groups had requested the court to stop sales until all economic and environmental impacts could be determined. The lower court ruled that the 1995 law gave to timber companies broad logging rights.[30] Opponents argued that the ruling forced the Forest Service and the BLM to allow cuts at a fraction of their value and open to cuts forests that are home to the threatened marbled murrelet. In a 1995 Senate Energy and Natural Resources Oversight and Investigations Subcommittee hearing in October 1995, proponents of more logging criticized the administration's implementation of the rescission logging rider as delaying, rather than expediting, timber sales. In October, then forest chief Jack Ward Thomas confirmed the agency's commitment to produce 4.5 billion board feet (bbf) of timber under the logging rider and the targeted 1.1. bbf in the Northwest Plan by 1997 and noted that while the Forest Service had been opposed to the rescissions rider, it was subjected to intense pressure from both Congress and the White House to meet those targets.

Timber policy is occasionally the subject of broader political efforts. In Maine, for example, voters rejected in 1996 a referendum that proposed a ban on clear-cutting on 10 million acres of northern forests. Governor Angus King said the plan would have cost the state thousands of jobs. The paper industry spent more than $5 million in fighting the proposal, the most expensive referendum ever in Maine. Voters expressed strong support for a competing measure that would have reduced, but not eliminated, clear-cutting. This proposal will be put to the voters in a future election.[31]

Acid Rain and Global Forestry Agreements

The health of American forests is also affected by other public policies besides endangered species protection and timber harvesting. Low-level ozone pollution adversely affects trees and plants, for example, and air pollution programs have reduced emissions of ozone precursors. Much more attention has been given to the threat to many forests throughout the world from acid deposition, or, more commonly, acid rain.[32] Acid rain is a by-product of the burning of fossil fuels, which produces sulfur dioxide SO_2 and NO_x. These gases are transformed in the atmosphere into sulfuric acid and nitric acid. The acids usually remain in the atmosphere for weeks and may travel hundreds of miles before settling on or near the earth as dry particles or precipitation. Acidic particles and gases can also be formed at ground level and are absorbed directly by plants or oxidized into sulfates and nitrates and absorbed by the soil.

Most of the concern surrounding acid rain has focused on its danger to forests and aquatic resources. Studies conducted throughout the 1980s indicated that acid rain is a threat to watersheds, lakes, and streams in New England, forests and coastal plains in the mid-Atlantic region, and forests in northern Florida. Acid rain pollution is believed to harm red spruce and pine trees in the eastern and southeastern United States (low-level ozone pollution is also a threat to trees). The precipitation in many of the eastern states and Canadian provinces is thirty to forty times more acidic than it was in the 1980s.[33] Some areas are more susceptible to acid rain damage than others. The western and midwestern regions of the United States and Canada, for example, have a natural alkaline geological foundation, composed of limestone, that neutralizes acid rain. The granite foundation of eastern Canada and the northeastern states does not provide that natural buffer. According to some estimates, one-half of all the acid rain that falls on Canada comes from its southern neighbor; Canadian industries are responsible for 15 percent to 25 percent of the acid rain in the northeastern United States.[34] This dispersion of pollutants is largely a factor of prevailing wind patterns. Fossil fuel combustion not only contributes to acid rain but is also the major source of carbon dioxide, a greenhouse gas implicated as a primary cause in theories of global climatic change. Nitrogen oxide emissions from automobiles also contribute to the formation of urban ozone, which plagues most large cities in the United States.

The acid rain provisions of the 1990 Clean Air Act include an emissions trading program for sulfur dioxide (the major precursor of acid rain). The EPA is to allocate to each major coal-fired power plant an allowance for each ton of emission permitted; sources cannot release emissions beyond the number of allowances they are given. Allowances may be traded, bought, or sold among allowance holders. Additional allowances are to be given to certain midwestern utilities that they can sell to help finance their cleanup efforts. The EPA is required to create an additional pool of allowances to permit construction of new sources or expansion of existing ones. The sulfur dioxide emission allowances for each of the major power plants in twenty-one states are listed in the law. Emission allowances for other power plants are to be computed by means of detailed formulas that are provided. Sulfur dioxide emissions are to be cut in half by the imposition of these emission limitations. A reduction from 1980 levels of 10 million tons annually is to be achieved by the year 2000. Half of the reduction took place by January 1, 1995, when the 110 largest sulfur dioxide-emitting electric utility plants in twenty-one states were required to meet more stringent emission standards. Emissions of nitrogen oxides, the other major cause of acid rain, are to be reduced by 2 million tons a year from 1980 levels.

In the 1991 Canada–United States Air Quality Agreement, Canada promised to reduce SO_2 emissions by 1994 to 2.3 million tonnes from sources in the seven eastern provinces and agreed to a national cap of 3.2 million tonnes by the year 2000. The United States essentially agreed to make the reductions mandated in the 1990 Amendments to the Clean Air Act: a 10 million ton reduction in SO_2 emissions from 1980 levels by the year 2000 and a cap by 2010 of 8.95 million tons of SO_2 from electric utilities and 5.6 million tons from industrial sources. Several international agreements and national regulatory programs have been fashioned to reduce the risk of acid rain to human health and ecosystems. Thirty-five nations from Europe and North America signed the 1979 Convention on Long-Range Transboundary Air Pollution, which established a framework for subsequent negotiations.[35] In 1985 most of these nations, although not the United States, agreed to cut sulfur dioxide emissions, the primary precursor of acid rain, by 30 percent from 1980 levels by 1993. In 1988, a second agreement placed a cap on nitrogen oxide emissions, the other major contributor to acid deposition, at 1987 levels.[36] Sulfur dioxide emissions fell dramatically in Western Europe from 1980 to 1990 under a 1979 treaty on transboundary air pollution and subsequent tightening measures. However, these reductions have not been great enough to adequately protect some ecosystems: damage to plant and aquatic life continues.[37]

The International Tropical Timber Agreement (ITTA), adopted in 1983 in Geneva and entered into force in 1985, seeks to ensure cooperation and consultation between countries that produce and consume tropical timber; promote the expansion and diversification of international trade in tropical timber; promote and support research and development to improve sustainable forest management and wood utilization; encourage national policies aimed at sustainable utilization and conservation of tropical forests and their genetic resources; and ensure that all tropical timber entering international trade will be produced from forests under sustainable management by the year 2000.

International environmental agreements dealing with climate change and biodiversity have some impact on forests, as indicators of sustainable forests have become part of the implementation of these accords. Forests have become the subject of joint implementation projects under the climate change convention, such as tree planting or forest conversation, which are paid for by wealthy countries and benefit poorer nations. Both rich and poor countries can claim credit for actions that absorb CO_2. The International Tropical Timber Organization has developed criteria and indicators for sustainable forest management and has called on all nations to ensure that tropical forest products traded in international markets come from sustainably managed forests. The World Commission on Sustainable Development, established at the 1992 World Summit, created an International Panel on Forests to propose agreements for sustainable forest management and related issues of trade, scientific cooperation, and monitoring of forest conditions. Nongovernmental organizations are developing voluntary efforts to certify forest operations and use market incentives to promote sustainable forestry.[38]

THE DEBATE OVER U.S. FORESTRY POLICY

Those interested in forests usually take one of two positions. Preservationists believe that forests have intrinsic values as diverse ecosystems as well as instrumental environmental values such as stabilizing climates and serving as watersheds. Use of public forests should be limited to human activities that do not disrupt these critical ecological functions. But the predominant view has been that trees are crops, and public forests are to be harvested as a product. The Forest Service and other policy makers face a number of challenges in providing for each of these two values.

Forests as Crops

Logging dominates the use of forests. The Forest Service is the nation's largest road-building enterprise; the length of the roads it has built would circle the earth fourteen times. Roads provide access to timber cuts, but logging companies are not required to pay their cost. The roads disrupt ecosystems and promote erosion, stream pollution, and damage to fish and aquatic life. While its legal mandate is to promote multiple use of forests, the Forest Service, is largely in the logging business. Nearly three-quarters of its budget is directly or indirectly dedicated to timber sales. It is permitted by law to keep most of the proceeds from timber sales and to give counties in which the forests are located 25 percent of the gross proceeds, strong incentives to increase logging. Timber is sold at lower prices than that sold on private lands. Between 1978 and 1993, the Forest Service, according to varying estimates, lost from $4.5 to $7 billion. In recent years it has lost $200–350 million, according to one estimate, which found that fewer than 25 of the 120 forests open to logging typically make a profit on timber sales. A White House report found that the service spent $234 million more in services to logging companies in 1995 than it received from timber cuts.[39] Below-cost timber sales skew prices and resultant decisions about con-

Table 5.1
National Forest Recreation Use, 1980–1993

Year and Activity	Recreation visitor-days[1] 1,000	Percent
1980	233,549	100.0
1981	235,709	100.0
1982	233,438	100.0
1983	227,708	100.0
1984	227,554	100.0
1985	225,407	100.0
1986	226,533	100.0
1987	238,458	100.0
1988	242,316	100.0
1989	252,495	100.0
1990	263,051	100.0
1991	278,849	100.0
1992	287,691	100.0
1993 Total	295,473	100.0
Mechanized travel and viewing scenery	99,573	33.7
Camping, picnicking, and swimming	79,319	26.8
Hiking, horseback riding, and water travel	26,632	9.0
Winter sports	19,230	6.5
Hunting	17,279	5.8
Resorts, cabins, and organization camps	17,086	5.8
Fishing	16,299	5.5
Nature studies	2,711	0.9
Other[2]	17,343	6.0

[1]One recreation visitor-day is the recreation use of national forest land or water that aggregates twelve visitor-hours. This may entail one person for twelve hours, twelve persons for one hour, or any equivalent combination of individual or group use, either continuous or intermittent. [2]Includes team sports, gathering forest products, attending talks and programs, and other uses.
Source: U.S. Department of Commerce, *Statistical Abstract of the United States, 1996* (Washington, DC: U.S. Government Printing Office, 1996): 251.

sumption, recycling, and alternative uses of forests.[40] Tables 5.1 and 5.2 show the growing importance of recreation in national forests. Table 5.3 shows the distribution of funding for the National Forest System and compares the resources expended on major activities such as fire fighting, recreation, and administration of logging sales. Tables 5.4 and 5.5 provide recent figures on timber sales and timber management.

Several problems have emerged from the implementation of the National Forest Management Act.[41] Forest Service officials often lack complete information about forest resources, minerals, and wildlife in the forests, but forest plans require such information. It is difficult to quantify values such as preservation of wilderness and wildlife in forests. Decisions under the Endangered Species Act require information about species that is often lacking. There is little infor-

Table 5.2
National Forest Recreation Visitor Days, by Activity, Fiscal Year 1995

Dispersed recreation	55.3% of visits
Developed recreation	24.9%
Facilities operated by the private sector, such as ski areas and vacation cabins	11.6%
Other	8.2%

Source: U.S.D.A., *Report of the Forest Service, FY 1994* (June 1995): 7.

mation about the cumulative environmental effects of actions, making compliance with NEPA problematic. Federal forest resources interact with private forests, but there is no mechanism to integrate those two sets of resources. There is little agreement over what approach to forest policy best meets the needs of the nation.[42]

Planning has become an expensive process. Projected to cost $100 million and take five years, the development of forest plans became a ten-year, $2 billion enterprise. Some plans were obsolete before they were released and were not updated. Public participation opportunities were limited. The process did produce useful inventories of forestlands, but that information has not always been made available or communicated effectively. The laws and regulations are inconsistent, and the agency lacks the resources to comply with all of them. As a result, managers must choose which requirements to comply with and which ones to ignore.[43]

Forest Service management decisions have been challenged in court as inconsistent with forest plan provisions, but those challenges are usually rejected by federal judges who defer to Forest Service judgment and expertise.[44] Federal courts have generally given the Forest Service discretion to balance the relevant factors when signing timber contracts and have deferred to agency expertise in harvesting methods, protection of old-growth forests, and fostering biodiversity.[45] It can use cost-benefit analysis in determining which lands should be logged to achieve forest plan goals.[46] Below-cost timber sales are permissible, since the Forest Service can include nontimber benefits, such as access to recreation, that come from the construction of timber roads.[47] Timber harvesting can damage soil, for example, as long as it is not irreversible, but the Forest Service must show how irreversible damage is prevented.[48] It can pursue biodiversity goals by protecting many small areas of species habitat rather than fewer, larger habitat areas.[49] Occasionally, federal courts reject Forest Service decisions. However, some courts rejected Forest Service logging decisions as

Table 5.3
National Forest System Funding, Fiscal Years 1990–1994 ($ Thousands)

	1994	1993	1992	1991[a]	1990
Minerals area management	33,017	34,812	34,332	30,380	28,414
Real estate management	34,880	36,024	35,430	31,192	25,973
Landline location	28,783	30,873	32,251	29,844	30,710
Maintenance of facilities	26,476	26,495	26,283	24,866	21,142
Cooperative law enforcement	55,130	15,479	8,377	15,538	11,082
Forest road maintenance	79,180[b]	81,936	85,891	91,303	96,384
Forest trail maintenance	34,543	31,332	30,549	28,228	24,459
Sales administration and management	184,606	219,033	263,745	263,133	251,796
Reforestation and stand improvement[c]	62,339	92,306	96,521	101,960	99,995
Recreation use	224,522	229,742	216,396	198,817	153,613
Wildlife and fish habitat management	121,130	116,364	112,500	106,626	81,500
Range management	44,127	44,443	43,153	39,473	32,966
Soil, water, and air management	77,984	72,325	76,243	72,153	61,612
Subtotal	1,006,717	1,031,164	1,061,671	1,033,513	919,646
General Administration (subtotal)	298,174	305,941	303,786	292,333	272,154
Forest fire protection	190,108	189,163	187,411	179,899	177,792
Fighting forest fires	190,222	185,411	110,589	118,035	611,850
Subtotal	380,330	374,574	298,000	297,934	789,642
Youth Conservation Corps (subtotal)[d]	(1,000)	(1,000)	(1,000)	(1,000)	(1,000)
Construction					
Construction of facilities[e]	94,437	83,868	77,497	82,578	40,593
Forest road construction	97,345	140,586	168,989	173,072	164,356
Forest trail construction	32,310	27,233	21,667	21,479	18,611
Forest roads purchaser construction[f]	(60,000)	(110,669)	(113,000)	(118,690)	(120,310)
Transfer to salvage	0	-2,750	NA[g]	NA	NA
Watershed restoration	20,000	-	-	-	-
Subtotal	244,092	248,937	268,153	277,129	223,560
Land acquisition	64,250	62,412	83,306	88,695	63,433
Acquisition of lands for national forests, special acts	1,212	1,180	1,134	1,097	1,045
Early Winters land exchange	0	0	0	497	0
Gifts, donations and bequests	96	5	96	1	3

134

Range betterment	4,600	4,647	4,795	4,546	4,915
Permanent appropriations	542,774	539,240	550,562	569,144	638,040
Trust funds	298,404	310,191	303,379	281,974	260,137
Total	2,840,852	2,878,442	2,881,112	2,846,968	3,172,588

[a]Post sequestration with supplemental. [b]Does not include $1,171,590 of Washington Office and National Commitment funds.
[c]Includes reforestation trust fund dollars. [d]Appropriations Act required minimum level of funding from National Forest funds; amounts not included in totals.

    1990 - operated a $2.1 million program from available funds.
    1991 - operated a $1.8 million program from available funds.
    1992 - operated a $2.5 million program from available funds.
    1993 - operated a $2.1 million program from available funds.
    1994 - operated a $1.7 million program from available funds.

[e]Excludes construction of research facilities. [f]This account was taken off budget in 1982. For comparison, the amounts are shown as nonadd items.

[g]NA = not applicable; not available.
Source: U.S. Department of Agriculture, *Report of the Forest Service, Fiscal Year 1994* (June 1995): 74-75.

Table 5.4

U.S. Forest Service, Timber Offered, Sold, and Harvested, Fiscal Years 1990–1994

	1994	1993	1992	1991	1990
Offered					
Volume (billion board feet)	3.4	4.6	5.1	6.2	11.1
Volume (billion cubic feet)ª	(0.65)	(0.87)	(1.0)	(1.2)	-
Sold					
Number of salesᵇ	215,004	255,825	250,852	271,963	262,781
Volume (billion board feet)	3.1	4.5	4.4	6.4	9.3
Volume (billion cubic feet)	(0.57)	(0.85)	(0.86)	(1.2)	-
Value (million dollars)ᶜ	508.9	774.9	576.2	801.2	1,609.9
Harvested					
Volume (billion board feet)	4.8	5.9	7.3	8.5	10.5
Volume (billion cubic feet)	(0.94)	(1.2)	(1.4)	(1.6)	-
Value (million dollars)ᵈ	783.0	914.6	934.5	1,008.6	1,187.6

ªConversion from the 1990 RPA Program. ᵇThese figures do not include nonconvertible product sales.
ᶜThis is the high bid value from all sales and includes stumpage, cost of reforestation, stand improvement costs, and timber salvage. Does not include value of roads or brush disposal. ᵈThis is the current stumpage rate for the actual volume harvested and includes the reforestation and stand improvement costs and timber salvage. Does not include value of roads or brush disposal.
Source: U.S. Department of Agriculture, Report of the Forest Service, Fiscal Year 1994 (June 1995): 123.

inconsistent with federal law. Among the best-known cases are those dealing with endangered and threatened species. A federal judge in Texas ordered the Forest Service to stop clear-cutting near the habitat of red-cockaded woodpecker colonies since its numbers had significantly declined. Other logging practices threaten the grizzly bear and bull trout in Montana, black bear in the southern Appalachians, the northern goshawk in Arizona and New Mexico, the gray wolf in the upper Great Lakes, and other species.[50]

The NFMA has been flexible enough to accommodate the kind of planning, preservation of biodiversity, and balance of competing values that occurred in the formulation of the Northwest Forest Plan. Change in Forest Service policy away from logging to preservation of biodiversity would not require new legislation, since NFMA already provides that protecting biological diversity should be the primary objective of national forest management. Proponents argue that the best way to pursue that goal would be to abolish forest plans and replace them with ecosystem plans. Options include changing the appropriations for the Forest Service to reflect preservation of biodiversity and other values, rather than timber output, elimination of timber targets for each Forest Service region and national forests, replacing existing administrators with new staff members more oriented toward broader agency goals, hiring more ecologists and fewer foresters and civil engineers whose primary responsibility is to build roads, consolidating the national forest offices, formulating new management plans, putting a moratorium on the construction of new roads in roadless areas and timber sales in these areas, and removing some existing roads and restoring watershed areas.[51]

Table 5.5

U.S. Forest Service, Timber Sale Funding, Fiscal Years 1992–1994 ($ Thousands)

	1994	1993	1992
National Forest System			
Timber management	130,511	150,881	188,604
Harvest administration	54,095	68,152	75,141
Subtotal	184,606	219,033	263,745
Support to timber sales program			
Minerals	1,018	1,127	1,606
Forest fire protection	2,909	3,177	4,376
Recreation	6,567	12,179	15,827
Wildlife and fish	11,802	16,445	15,920
Range	166	862	1,243
Soil and water	4,371	7,929	9,804
Landline location	9,390	13,210	a
Subtotal	36,223	54,929	48,776
Road construction			
Forest Service construction	51,061	86,259	117,574
Purchaser construction	(60,000)	(110,669)	(113,000)
Purchaser construction by the Forest Service	8,457	8,546	5,806
Subtotal	59,518	94,805	123,380
Total, appropriated accounts	280,347	368,767	435,901
Special accounts[b]			
Timber salvage sales	186,737	193,747	120,358
Subtotal	186,737	193,747	120,358
Total	467,084	562,514	556,259

[a]All landline funds were spent in support of the stewardship program and resolving trespass cases.
[b]Includes General Administration expenses.
Source: U.S. Department of Agriculture, Report of the Forest Service, Fiscal Year 1994 (June 1995): 128.

Industry groups have been just as critical of Forest Service planning efforts as have been conservationists. The American Forest and Paper Association, for example, charged in a 1996 congressional hearing that the Forest Service had spent nineteen years and more than $250 million to prepare 123 resource management plans but failed to manage its forests consistent with the plans. Planning, the spokesperson for the association charged,

has become a never-ending desk-bound process that practically precludes on-the-ground management. . . . [B]ecause of its constantly changing, ephemeral condition, instead of providing secure, predictable guidance for management activities, planning heightens the insecurity of, and often paralyzes, managers attempting to make on-the-ground decisions.[52]

The real problem for the industry is that this "frenzy of additional planning" focuses on "watershed plans, landscape plans, [and] ecoregion-based ecological assessments" that focus on the protection of species rather than timber resources. The result is "management paralysis," inadequate provision for public participation, and a failure to carry out resource management plans. The agency

has failed to secure the allowable sales quantities of timber that had been promised in the plans: timber output has been authorized at 7.6 billion board feet a
year, but only about 4 billion board feet were made available in FY 1995, and
only 3.6 billion were requested by the Clinton administration in 1996. The Clinton administration's Pacific Northwest Forests Plan was singled out for criticism:
it projected yearly timber volume of only 20 percent of previous sale levels, but
during the first two years produced only 25 percent of the projected levels.[53]
The Forest Service's regulation implementing the statutory provision mandating
protection of the diversity of plant and animal communities, critics charge, permits injunctions that effectively shut down forests and provide for more protection of species than does the Endangered Species Act. The idea of ecosystem
management, they argue, is ill defined and gives managers the opportunity to
override long-standing statutory and administrative declarations aimed at promoting timber cuts. Administrative and judicial appeals of timber sales have
become almost automatic, further delaying cuts. Industry officials blame Congress for permitting attorneys bringing these challenges to be reimbursed under
the Equal Access to Justice Act, for failing to provide narrow standing requirements, and for not providing deadlines for bringing administrative or judicial
challenges.[54]

The timber industry has produced a long list of reforms, including requiring
the Forest Service to set time limits for preparing and amending resource management plans, reduce the levels at which planning occurs, require that policies
or guidances apply to forests only if the resource management plans are altered
accordingly, require resource management plans to discuss how they will be
implemented, define resource management plans as final agency decisions en-
forceable and subject to judicial review, permit the agency to waive guidances
if the waiver would not result in significant and permanent adverse environmental effects, require NEPA and other studies accompanying resource management plans to discuss the impact of planning alternatives on communities'
public service and employment and income prospects of its residents, amend
resource management plans where the agency is unlikely to meet timber targets
(allowable sales quantities), abolish the viability rule and not require every species within a unit to be viable within that unit, not adopt any policy or requirement inconsistent with NFMA and FLPMA, and refocus NEPA compliance so
that management activities are generally subject to environmental assessments
rather than full EISs. It also urged Congress to permit the land management
agency and not the FWS or other agency to prepare biological opinions required
by the ESA, provided that only the Forest Service and not other federal agencies
be empowered to make environment decisions concerning management activities
that are consistent with resource management plans, set minimum standing requirements for bringing an administrative or judicial challenge to a resource
management plan or revision, and set deadlines for challenging resource management plans and revisions.[55]

Other critics of the Forest Service also argue that the agency has ignored the purposes of the Organic Administration Act of 1897 to "furnish a continuous supply of timber for the use and necessities of the citizens of the United States."[56] They cite approvingly a 1978 Supreme Court case holding that Congress intended, under the Organic Act, that national forests be managed for watershed protection and timber supply.[57] They find in the legislative history of the act as well as in Forest Service regulations published in *The Use Book* a long-standing commitment to protect the economic stability of communities near national forests. That commitment to county welfare was reflected in the passage of the Twenty-Five Percent Fund Act, which ordered the Forest Service to distribute 25 percent of revenues from timber sales to surrounding counties. In 1913, Congress ordered an additional 10 percent of revenues from timber, mining, and livestock grazing on national forest lands be given to counties for schools and roads; in 1976, Congress ordered the 25 percent to be calculated from gross revenues rather than stumpage prices.[58] Nevertheless, critics charge that NFMA has been used to prevent multiple use of forests and has destroyed local communities.[59]

The Western Governors Association (WGA) has joined in the chorus of critics of the Forest Service. Activities on federal lands often require state permits, since states administer many federal environmental protection programs and are also responsible for public health and safety, water allocation, hunting and fishing, and fish and wildlife. State zoning decisions affect private lands adjacent to federal lands. States are dependent on trust lands for revenue as well as receive shares of federal leasing and sales programs. This results in inefficiency, frustration, uncertainty, delays and appeals, and perpetual planning that appears to avoid decision making. Lack of decisions about the use of public lands may place increased environmental pressure on private lands. NEPA analyses have become major burdens and stresses on government resources. The WGA has offered seven principles to guide public land management:

• Laws, policies, and management decisions must be based on sound resource stewardship that provides resource sustainability and protection to meet the diverse needs of present and future generations.

• Management of public lands should promote stability and predictability in the production of goods and services and sustainability of resources on the public lands. At the same time, management must be sufficiently flexible to adapt to changing social, economic, and ecological conditions.

• Federal administration of the public land laws should provide incentives for sustained management and encourage efficiency.

• The role of public involvement in the management of public lands should be meaningful, collaborative, and timely.

• The diversity and significance of natural resources must be acknowledged in land management decisions.

• When value is created by the use of the public lands and their resources, federal managers should be enabled to recover an appropriate amount of that value.

• Federal budgets, incentives for federal managers, and incentives for good stewardship to users of the federal lands should support these goals.[60]

Key changes include a planning process that is more timely and produces clear management directives, public participation that is more efficient and effective, meshing of public lands laws and policies, more incentives to encourage compliance with policies, streamlining of NEPA reviews, and the development of pilot projects and experiments to find more effective procedures and policies for balancing the competing purposes of public land management.

Critics argue that Forest Service timber policy has failed to adapt to changes in the lumber industry and in environmental conditions. Public lands provide only about 15 percent of the nation's timber supply. Many national forests are in mountain regions, where harsh climates and shorter growing seasons produce thin stands of small trees. Income from timber sales for low-value lumber fails to compensate for the increasing cost of access roads and reseeding in remote areas. Communities that have become dependent on federally subsidized timber cuts suffer from the boom and bust cycles that plague other extractive industries. Increasing timber cuts in economically depressed areas do not create more stable, economically healthy communities but simply delays the inevitable adjustment.[61]

There is no consensus over exactly how public forests can produce maximum yield. One approach seeks to manage trees of about the same age and size in a kind of industrial forestry approach where forests are tree farms. The biodiversity of old-growth forests is replaced with a monoculture of fast-growing trees that can be economically harvested. These forests are often logged through clearcutting, where all trees in an area are cut at the same time, and then the area is reseeded for the next generation of growth. Alternatively, forests could be harvested through the tree-seed approach, where some trees are left to provide seed for the next growth. Clear-cutting is a simple, easily managed, economically efficient logging approach that requires a minimum of management and planning. It facilitates the growth of desirable trees by ensuring they have access to sunlight. It also results in destroyed habitat and reduced biodiversity, soil erosion, water pollution, flooding, and reduced recreational uses of forests.

A second approach maintains trees at different ages and sizes. Selective timber cuts are aimed at mature trees with high economic value, but logging is carried out in a way that encourages the growth of smaller trees, promotes biological diversity, and accommodates multiple uses of forests. Vegetation is naturally regenerated, and less erosion and damage to watersheds occur than in clearcutting. Some foresters believe selective cuts are less profitable than clear-cuts. Strip cutting is a middle strategy, involving clear-cuts along sections of the forest but leaving surrounding areas intact; in this way, an entire forest could be eventually clear-cut, but over a long enough period of time that forest health is significantly preserved.[62]

It is difficult to estimate future demand for timber, a function of electronic communications and data storage, biotechnology, construction materials and demand, and other factors. But consumption has increased steadily for all major categories of wood products in the United States: per capita consumption of raw wood increased by 33 percent between 1970 and 1990; per capita consumption of paper and paperboard doubled between 1960 and 1995 and increased by 30 percent for lumber and by 163 percent for wood-based panels. It requires 1.8 acres of timberland to meet the annual timber needs of each American (one acre produces on average forty-four cubic feet of raw wood). There are 490 million acres of timberland that are productive enough for logging and not protected in wilderness areas or parks, just barely sufficient to meet the demand for wood products. The nation's overall forested areas have remained stable since 1920, at around 730–760 million acres. But it is not clear how future demand can be satisfied with current levels of productivity and land availability. The Forest Service projects demand for wood to increase by 26 percent between 1996 and 2020 and 40 percent by 2040 and a small decline (less than 5 percent) in forest area during the next thirty years. The volume of available timber doubled between 1952 and 1991, but a much slower net annual growth rate in timber is projected, as low as 0.3 percent, between now and 2040. Since 1986, net growth levels have declined by 2 percent. Timber growth rates exceeded harvest rates by 54 percent in 1976 but only by 30 percent in 1991. While there is an increase in growth over harvests in public lands because of the increasing protection of forests for nonconsumptive uses, harvests on private forestlands are expected to exceed growth soon after the year 2000. If these trends are realized, the United States will become a net importer of wood.[63] Timber, like other commodities, is subject to volatile price swings. Logging wages are higher than average, but changes in demand for wood throw thousands of workers out of jobs. During the 1980s, some 100,000 wood products jobs were lost.[64]

In October 1996, Forest Service chief Jack Ward Thomas resigned. His tenure was rocky as he clashed with the timber industry, environmentalists, western members of Congress, and other members of the Clinton administration. Forest Service output declined to one-fourth of the level in the 1980s as a result of court rulings that required more protection of wildlife. In announcing his resignation, Thomas stated that his agency was "somewhat confused," and he hoped that "after the election there will be time for everyone to sit down and talk about giving the Forest Service a clear mission."[65]

Forests as Ecosystems

Advocates of forest policy reform argue that timber harvests are not the greatest resources contained in national forests. They argue that forests are much more important as biodiversity preserves and watersheds. About 75 percent of the West's water supplies flow from national forests. These rivers are productive fisheries that are threatened by the runoff from clear-cuts and road building. Forests provide recreational opportunities. They help nourish the diversity of life on which all living things are dependent, help maintain soil fertility, recycle nutrients, produce oxygen and absorb carbon dioxide, filter water, and provide new products for medicine and agriculture. Old-growth forests are particularly important in promoting biodiversity, but most of the nation's old-growth forests have been cut down. Only small pockets remain, plus one large area in the Pacific Northwest and Alaska. Scientists working on the Clinton administration's forest plan for Oregon and Washington concluded that "old-growth forests in the Pacific Northwest may be unique ecosystems that developed under climatic and disturbance regimes that may never be duplicated." While some old-growth forests can regenerate over centuries, their loss will result in the extinction of some species.[66]

The Forest Service has undergone great changes. The traditional foresters came from similar backgrounds and training. Norms and values were reinforced as they rose through the ranks. The creation of the Association of Forest Service Employees for Environmental Ethics, Public Employees for Environmental Ethics, and Public Employees for Environmental Responsibility by Forest Service employees signaled a shift in organizational consciousness. The agency produced a new approach to forestry, ecosystem management, that focused on stewardship, conservation biology, ecological restoration, preservation of biodiversity, and the human dimensions of natural resources. Other federal agencies began to adopt the Forest Service approach. NFMA provides authorization for the agency to provide for plant and animal diversity. But critics argue that the Forest Service has failed to adequately protect viable populations. Planning efforts have failed to model the effects of habitat fragmentation, include insufficient data, and have not effectively integrated the efforts of different agencies. More successful planning efforts will likely require the agency to plan at the landscape level, rather than in response to ecologically artificial administrative boundaries, work more closely with other agencies, find ways to create incentives for private landowners to help achieve agency goals, and generate better information.[67]

Ecosystem management has become an important element in Forest Service policy. That clashes with earlier planning approaches that emphasized production of timber products. Traditional forest plans focus on a stable flow of timber and sustained yields to meet direct human needs. Forests are viewed much like other agricultural products. Production efficiency is limited by environmental constraints. These planning approaches are still in effect in many areas. But ecosystem management is a competing, alternative paradigm for agency management. It promises to help the agency deal with major disturbances such as floods and fires and manage forests more closely attuned to natural forces, integrate ecological and economic concerns, account for cumulative effects of timber harvesting and other activities, facilitate participation and collaborative learning, and still provide for the sustainable yield of forest products.[68]

The agenda of management has been greatly expanded from timber production to a much wider range of concerns and purposes. It challenges the presumption in the NFMA that planning achieve a ''non-declining yield'' of timber volume and requires the agency to justify departures. Since timber harvesting is only one of several goals, stable harvests cannot be assured. Ecosystem management also renders meaningless the division of forestlands into those suited for timber production and those that are not. Since no lands are primarily timber production lands, this distinction makes little sense. Much more needs to be learned about how to manage forest ecosystems. Tremendous challenges face the agency in learning how to develop the information necessary to achieve this goal and formulate specific management plans.

One important challenge is the importance of forests as recreational areas. Demand for recreational and other uses of national forests has increased dramatically; the number of recreational visitor days has increased tenfold since 1950. Increased demand for day hiking is expected to grow by 193 percent over the next fifty years, by 155 percent for backpacking, by 77 percent for developed campgrounds, and by 74 percent for wildlife observation and photography. The economic value of outdoor recreation was estimated in one study at more than $6.6 billion a year or about $20 a person for each visitor day. The value of nontimber forest products such as mushrooms, medicines, wild berries, and craft materials is difficult to estimate but appears to be growing dramatically.[69]

Fire is another primary determinant of forest well-being but also poses challenges for forest management. Surface fires burn the undergrowth and litter on the forest floor, release nutrients stored in the undergrowth, stimulate the release and germination of the seeds of some species such as the giant sequoia and lodgepole pine, check the growth of pathogens and insects, produce vegetation that some wildlife feeds on, and prevent more intense fires from occurring. If dead wood, leaves, and other material build up over many years, crown fires sometimes result, intense conflagrations that destroy trees, threaten wildlife, and contribute to erosion. Prevention of surface and other fires tends to make more serious and damaging fires more likely. The National Park Service policy is to allow lightning-initiated fires to burn themselves out unless they threaten humans, park facilities, or endangered species. The spectacular fire in Yellowstone National Park in 1988 triggered demands to change policy and stop fires from burning, but the size of that fire was a result of the buildup of material on the forest floor that would normally be cleared through occasional surface fires. Fire-prone forests can be thinned to help preserve forest health but can also be used as an excuse to log forests that otherwise are protected from timber cuts. Prescribed fires may also promote forest health and help prevent more damaging blazes.[70]

National forests are critical ecological resources. They provide habitats for more than 80 percent of the nation's wildlife. About 22 percent of the nation's commercially viable forests lie within the 156 national forests. They supply 13 percent of the nation's timber, as well as providing grazing lands for some 3 million cattle and mining operations. Logging in national forests raises profoundly difficult ecological and economic dilemmas. Forest in the Northwest play a key role in protecting the waters where salmon live and helping to maintain the $1.25 billion salmon sport and fishing industry, which employs about 60,000 people. The logging industry supplies jobs for some 100,000 workers. Logging of these forests releases sediment from erosion that disrupts spawning and feeding patterns of salmon. The logging/milling industry is in decline as supplies dwindle, logs are sent overseas for milling, timber is imported from Canada, and jobs are lost to automation. The U.S. Forest Service encourages timber sales because part of the revenue from the sales supplements its budget; local governments receive 25 percent of the gross proceeds from cutting, giving them a strong incentive to support heavy logging. Private landowners also face economic incentives to cut logs at unsustainable rates to generate cash quickly.[71] Species like the threatened northern spotted owl are also caught in the middle of the conflict over which jobs and industries will be advantaged as a result of public lands policy and the debate between loggers who want to clear-cut remaining forests in order to keep the timber industry healthy for several more years and environmentalists who want to preserve the forests. The Forest Service has shifted from traditional forest plans emphasizing consistent levels of timber harvest to ecosystem management. It has failed to meet these new ecological goals and satisfy demands of environmentalists, but it has shifted away from an emphasis on timber cuts sufficiently to raise the ire of the timber industry. No one is happy, but the direction the agency is moving is clear. The challenge will be to find ways of bringing the timber industry and community groups interested in maintaining their economic livelihood from forest products into planning and management efforts that are aimed at ecosystem restoration and preservation and a much broader vision of the economic and ecological value of national forests. Reforms have not reduced stakeholder dissatisfaction with the agency.

Legislation governing national forests has largely developed in response to domestic concerns, but forest policy is increasingly affected by global trends. The United States was self-sufficient in timber until 1940; since then, it has imported timber, primarily from Canada, to meet its needs. Demand for timber has increased as a result of population growth and deforestation and forest degradation in other lands, but primarily by growth in per capita income and consumption. Demand for wood and wood-based panels, the two fastest growing wood products, is expected to grow by 3 percent a year. Consumption in the more developed world drives demand: Americans consume 700 pounds of paper per person per year; Latin Americans consume 66 pounds. Forests throughout the world are increasingly threatened by air pollution, climate change, the spread of exotic species and diseases, diminished biodiversity, and decline in ecosystem processes such as fire suppression and flood control that contribute to forest health. Global climate change threatens the reproduction and growth of trees unable to adapt to rapid changes in climate. Environmental disruptions increase the threat of pests, microbial pathogens, fires, and flooding. Increased trade has introduced new insects and diseases to forests, threatening native forests that have not developed defenses. Intensive forest management efforts have changed the relationships between predators and their prey, and tree plantations have become more susceptible to pests and diseases.[72]

The global forests declined by 2 percent between 1980 and 1990 and tropical forests by 3.6 percent. Deforestation rates are higher in some areas than others— 11 percent in Asia, 8 percent in Latin America, and 7 percent in Africa. Many countries, such as the Philippines, Thailand, Nigeria, El Salvador, and Haiti, that were once timber exporters are now net importers. Some of this has been offset by an increase in tree plantations by 88 percent during the 1980s but still represent only about 20 percent of the forestlands lost to other uses. While plantations are less biologically diverse, they have the potential to meet demand for pulp and paper products. Nonwood sources of fiber are also being developed that may help meet growing demand.[73]

While much of the attention has been directed to deforestation of tropical rain forests, the reduction in the boreal forests of the far North that comprise nearly one-third of the world's forests is also a serious environmental threat. These forests are a major carbon sink as well as home to plants and animals and to a million indigenous people who have lived in the forests for centuries. Massive logging in Canada disrupts ecosystems, displaces native peoples, pollutes rivers with toxic chemicals used in the bleaching of pulp, and subsidizes the expenses of the large corporations, such as Mitsubishi and Daishowa, that have purchased leases. The subsidies are given to companies in exchange for jobs in logging and pulp mills, but the timber companies are reaping enormous profits at the expense of local residents. In Alberta, for example, the province collects $0.90 for sixteen aspen trees that are made into $590 worth of pulp; a foreign mill then transforms that into $1,250 worth of paper. Taxpayers end up paying some $176,500 in subsidies for each job created at Mitsubishi's Alberta-Pacific mill. About 90 percent of the logging is clear-cutting, and 25 percent of these areas do not regenerate, as topsoil erodes away during and after logging. Logging also destroys permafrost, the layer below the topsoil that acts as a heat reservoir in the winter, making it more difficult for vegetation to grow. As the permafrost retreats, risk to the forests from fires, pests, and species composition grows; the downward spiral contributes to the threat of global climate change as the carbon sink is lost, and carbon from dead trees is increasingly released into the atmosphere.[74] Throughout the world, below-cost timber subsidies that waste resources and enrich large corporations, little environmental review of proposed logging efforts, selling off forests that are home to indigenous peoples, large-scale clear-cutting that threatens the sustainability of forest production, and lack of recycling of paper and other products pose a major challenge to forests.[75]

Trees are a remarkably valuable economic resource. They produce nuts and fruits, chewing gum, ointments, perfumes, flavoring extracts, resins, adhesives, drugs, sugar and syrup, tannin, oils, dyes, veneer, turpentine, wood tar, pine oil, fuelwood, pulpwood, lumber, plywood, pressboard, poles, posts, and other products. A typical tree is worth about $590 if sold as timber. The value of trees increases dramatically when their ecological benefits are included: forests help produce oxygen, purify air, prevent soil erosion, recycle and purify water, help maintain humidity levels, and provide habitat for wildlife. Counting those benefits, one estimate of the value of a typical tree is $196,250.[76]

Most of the old-growth forests of the developed countries have been logged, and those that remain are always susceptible to new demands for scarce resources. Their value as sources of biodiversity is just beginning to be appreciated just as only a relatively few stands remain. Most forests in the United States are second-growth forests that have grown back after clear-cutting. Some second-growth forests were cut so long ago and have been protected from subsequent cuts that they have encouraged biodiversity as old-growth forests. Some forests are tree farms, where uniform trees are planted and harvested at the same time like any other agricultural crop. While the number of forested acres in the United States is actually greater today than in 1900, most of these forests are second- and third-growth forests. Only about 10 percent of the temperate-zone old-growth forests in the lower forty-eight states have been left unharvested. Old-growth forests—those that have been undisturbed for hundreds and even thousands of years—are particularly important because they are home to a great variety of wildlife species. They accumulate biomass more efficiently than any other ecosystem: decomposing trees recycle nutrients over hundreds of years, and old-growth forests act as sponges that trap water, protect against fires, and supply water to streams and aquifers. While there are more acres of forest today than before, forest biodiversity has been greatly diminished.[77]

The Debate in Congress

Republicans in the 104th Congress sought to reduce environmental restrictions on logging in order to increase timber output. In October 1995, the House Timber Salvage Task Force conducted an oversight hearing on the implementation of the logging rider. The Salvage Task Force, created by House Resources Committee chairman Don Young (R-AK), included no Democrats. Environmentalists boycotted the hearings after witnesses were insulted by task force members in a California field hearing. Republicans pushed for increased logging and argued that the Forest Service was not complying with the law.[78]

In June 1996, the Senate Energy and Natural Resources Committee marked up a forest policy bill sponsored by Senator Larry Craig (R-ID) that had been introduced in March.[79] The bill would require public lands agencies to catalog public forests according to their health: those where more than half the trees are damaged, diseased, or dead would be declared emergency areas, and actions taken in response would be exempt from environmental laws. Forest health management activities include thinning, salvage, timber stand improvement, reforestation, prescribed burning, insect or disease control, and riparian habitat improvement. The interior and agriculture secretaries would be required to report to Congress annually on the health of public forests. Both Democrats and Republicans worked on the bill but were divided by numerous issues, particularly how to deal with dozens of old-growth sales in Pacific Northwest forests.[80]

In 1996, several bills dealing with the Tongass National Forest were introduced. Ketchikan Pulp Company Contract Extension bill would have extended the company's fifty-year lease on federal lands by fifteen years and given additional benefits to the company. The Landless Natives Land Allocation Act would have given 500,000 acres of prime timberlands to five newly designated native communities. The Tongass Forest Plan appropriations rider would have delayed implementation of the new land management plan. The Tongass Transfer and Transition Act would have turned over the entire 17 million acres to the state of Alaska. The Tongass jobs bill would require the Forest Service to guarantee 2,400 new timber jobs. None of these bills passed, but Senator Frank Murkowski (R-AK) was able to negotiate a deal as part of the Omnibus Parks Bill enacted at the end of the 104th Congress to provide some transitional assistance to the Ketchikan Pulp Company, which operates in the Tongass.

Congress also considered the Northern Rockies Ecosystem Protection Act, which would prohibit development in virtually all Forest Service roadless areas in Montana, Idaho, Wyoming, and eastern Washington and Oregon, some 20 million acres in twenty-eight national forests. Proponents argue that many wildlife species such as grizzly bears, timber wolves, salmon, bull trout, and woodland caribou cannot be protected through piecemeal land designations but will survive only if large corridors are preserved. One study found that about 1,400 jobs would be lost in the timber industry, about one-tenth of 1 percent of jobs in the five-state region, and that would be balanced by at least as many jobs to protect the areas and offer new recreational opportunities. The timber industry is already in decline in this area, while recreation has become a much more important industry. The natural landscape is believed by many to be the key to the economic future of the regions. The Forest Service would be unable to meet the timber production goals it projected for the area because of water quality and fish habitat standards and protection of old-growth forests and threatened species. Logging has been in long-term decline and is an unstable source of income.[81]

Policy Options

Congress can make an important contribution to policy by clarifying the major expectations all parties ought to hold for forest policy. Congress ought to codify the ecosystem management policy, or provide its own set of expectations for national forests, and provide general principles and priorities for integrating the numerous goals of national forests. There is a great need to develop some agreement over a public lands ethic, and Congress, despite all its flaws, is inescapably the major institution for formulating such policies. Second, Congress should provide more guidance concerning the process by which the Forest Service is to conduct forest ecosystem management and can specify the mix of nationwide principles and tailoring of plans to local conditions. Congress can address the problem of competing laws and help the agency sort out the demands of NEPA, water and wetlands laws, and other agencies' policies, as well as state and local laws and planning processes. Congress can mandate that agreement-building processes are needed to help reduce the tension between agency officials and stakeholders.[82]

Truly sustainable forestry appears to require much more than current Forest Service policy. Additional steps would including growing more timber for longer periods of time before logging, selective cutting of individual or small groups of trees, strip cutting rather than clear-cutting, protecting large units of forests, minimizing soil erosion and damage from road building and logging methods, and allowing dead trees to remain in forests to promote biodiversity. One of the most important policy steps to take would be to ensure full-cost accounting, so prices reflect the ecological benefits of forests. Part of ensuring true cost pricing is to require companies to pay the full cost of production, including construction of roads, reforestation, and restoration of damaged areas. Policies can provide assistance to displaced workers and to sawmills to retool for smaller, second- and third-growth trees. Policies could allow parties to purchase protection right or easements in ecologically sensitive areas. Tax laws could tax exports of raw logs, but not finished products, to encourage value-added jobs and ban exports of raw logs.[83] But forestry policy is not enough to preserve forests. Other required actions include increased recycling of paper and other paper products and development of other sources of fiber for paper products; requiring the price of timber cut in national forests to include the true costs of forests, including the cost of road building, site preparation, and restoration; and ending the practice of keeping timber revenues in the Forest Service, because of the incentive it creates for overlogging. Ultimately, Congress can decide that the primary value and importance of national forests lie in their role as sustainers of biodiversity and environmental quality and place timber harvesting as a subordinate goal.[84]

NOTES

1. 16 U.S.C. 471.
2. 16 U.S.C. 475 (Organic Act of 1897).
3. Ibid.
4. 16 U.S.C. 473.
5. 16 U.S.C. 531(a).
6. 16 U.S.C. 531(b).
7. 16. U.S.C. 528.
8. Quoted in H. Michael Anderson, "Reforming National-Forest Policy," *Issues in Science and Technology* (Winter 1993–1994): 40–47, at 41.
9. 16 U.S.C. 1604.
10. 16 U.S.C. 472.

11. 16. U.S.C. 1604(k).

12. 16 U.S.C. 1604(g)(3)(B). The Forest Service regulation implementing this provision requires forest managers "to maintain viable populations of existing native and desired non-native vertebrate species in the planning area" (36 C.F.R. 219.19).

13. 16 U.S.C. 1604, 1611.

14. Jack Ward Thomas, "The Need for a New NFMA Planning Rule," The National Forest Management Act in a Changing Society 1976–1996: How Well Has It Worked in the Past 20 Years? Will It Work in the 21st Century? Natural Resources Law Center, University of Colorado School of Law (September 17, 1996).

15. Anderson, "Reforming National-Forest Policy," at 43–44, 46.

16. See Steven L. Yaffee, "The Northern Spotted Owl: An Indicator of the Importance of Sociopolitical Context," in Tim W. Clark, Richard P. Reading, and Alice L. Clarke, eds., *Endangered Species Recovery: Finding the Lessons, Improving the Process* (Washington, DC: Island Press, 1994): 47–71; Steven L. Yaffee, *The Wisdom of the Spotted Owl: Policy Lessons for a New Century* (Washington, DC: Island Press, 1994); Jacqueline Switzer with Gary Bryner, *Environmental Politics* (New York: St. Martin's Press, 1997): Chapter 11.

17. *Seattle Audobon Society v. Espy*, 998 F.2d 699 (9th Cir. 1993).

18. *Robertson v. Seattle Audobon Society*, 503 U.S. 429 (1992).

19. Quoted in Anderson, "Reforming National-Forest Policy," at 41–42.

20. Ibid., at 45–46.

21. G. Tyler Miller Jr., *Living in the Environment* (Belmont, CA: Wadsworth, 1996): 299.

22. Anderson, "Reforming National-Forest Policy," at 45.

23. Associated Press, "Environmental Groups Back Logging Accord," *New York Times* (October 8, 1993): A1.

24. "Upheaval in Forest from Compromise on Logging," *New York Times* (July 2, 1993):A1.

25. John M. Berry, "The Spotted Owl Lays a Golden Egg," *Washington Post National Weekly Edition* (August 12–18: 1991): 19–20.

26. Gregg Easterbrook, "The Birds," *The New Republic* (March 28, 1994): 22–29.

27. Elizabeth A. Foley, "The Tarnishing of an Environmental Jewel: The Endangered Species Act and the Northern Spotted Owl," *Journal of Land Use and Environmental Law* 8 (1992): 253–83, at 256–57.

28. H.R. 1944, P.L. 104–19.

29. Patti Goldman, "1995 Logging without Laws: Legislating by Budget Rider," *Environment* 38, no. 3 (April 1996): 41–43.

30. 1995 Rescissions Act, P.L. 104–19.

31. Robert Pear, "The 1996 Elections: The States—The Initiatives," *New York Times* (November 7, 1887): B7.

32. This section is based on Gary C. Bryner, *Blue Skies, Green Politics: The Clean Air Act of 1990 and Its Implementation*, 2d ed. (Washington, DC: Congressional Quarterly, 1995): 79–82

33. Cecie Starr and Ralph Taggart, *Biology*, 5th ed. (Belmont, CA: Wadsworth, 1989): 795.

34. John Carroll, *Acid Rain: An Issue in Canadian–American Relations* (Washington, DC.: National Planning Association, 1982).

35. Congressional Research Service, Library of Congress, "Environmental Protection

Laws and Treaties: Reference Guide'' (January 30, 1991): 33–35. See also U.S. Environmental Protection Agency, *U.S. Government Participation in International Treaties, Agreements, Organizations and Programs* (1984): A-2; U.S. Department of State, *Treaties in Force: A List of Treaties and Other International Agreements of the United States in Force on January 1, 1988* (Washington, DC: U.S. Government Printing Office 1988): 322–23.

36. For a review of these developments, see C. Ian Jackson, ''A Tenth Anniversary Review of the ECE Convention on Long-Range Transboundary Air Pollution,'' *International Environmental Affairs* 2, no. 3 (1990): 222–25.

37. Hilary French, *After the Earth Summit: The Future of Environmental Governance*, Worldwatch Paper 107 (Washington, DC: Worldwatch Institute, March 1992): 10–11.

38. Nels C. Johnson, ''Global Trends and the Future of National Forests,'' The National Forest Management Act in a Changing Society 1976–1996: How Well Has It Worked in the Past 20 Years? Will It Work in the 21st Century? Natural Resources Law Center, University of Colorado School of Law (September 17, 1996): 13–18.

39. The report is cited in ''What's News,'' *Wall Street Journal* (February 19, 1997): A1.

40. G. Tyler Miller Jr., *Living in the Environment* (Belmont, CA: Wadsworth, 1996): 620–21.

41. For a helpful review and critique of NFMA, see David H. Getches, ''Framework for Understanding NFMA in a Legal Context,'' presentation at National Forest Management Act in a Changing Society 1976–1996: How Well Has It Worked in the Past 20 Years? How Will It Work in the 21st Century?, Natural Resources Law Center, University of Colorado School of Law (September 16, 1996).

42. Perry R. Hagenstein, ''Understanding the Interplay among Many Laws: 1970 to 200,'' National Forest Management Act in a Changing Society 1976–1996: How Well Has It Worked in the Past 20 Years? How Will It Work in the 21st Century?, National Resources Law Center, University of Colorado School of Law (September 16, 1996).

43. Elizabeth Estill, ''Can Managers Adapt to New Relationships and Roles under NFMA? National Forest Management Act in a Changing Society 1976–1996: How Well Has It Worked in the Past 20 Years? How Will It Work in the 21st Century?, Natural Resources Law Center, University of Colorado School of Law (September 16, 1996).

44. See, for example, *Sierra Club v. Robertson*, 845 F.Supp. 485 (S.D. Ohio 1994) and *Sierra Club v. Marita (Chequamegon)*, 843 F.Supp 1526 (E.D. Wis. 1994), affirmed, 46 F.3d 606 (7th Cir. 1995).

45. See, for example, *Sierra Club v. Espy*, 38 F.3d 792 (5th Cir. 1994).

46. *Sierra Club v. Robertson*, 845 F.Supp. 485 (S.D. Ohio 1994).

47. *Thomas v. Peterson*, 753 F.2d 754 (9th Cir. 1985).

48. *Citizens for Environmental Quality v. United States*, 731 F.Supp. 970 (D. Colo. 1989).

49. *Sierra Club v. Marita (Chequamegon)*, 843 F.Supp. 1526 (E.D. Wis. 1994).

50. Anderson, ''Reforming National-Forest Policy,'' at 42.

51. Ibid., at 46–47.

52. Steven P. Quarles, ''The Failure of Federal Land Planning,'' testimony given at an oversight hearing of the Subcommittee on National Parks, Forests and Lands, Committee on Resources, U.S. House of Representatives (March 26, 1996): 4–5.

53. Ibid., at 6–7, 11–12.

54. Ibid., at 13–22. Congress did place some time limits on administrative appeals of Forest Service projects in a FY 1993 Interior Department appropriations bill.

55. Ibid., at 23–26.

56. 16 U.S.C. 475.

57. *United States v. New Mexico*, 438 U.S. 676, 1978.

58. 16 U.S.C. 500.

59. Dan S. Budd, "The National Forest Management Act: Managing the Use Out of Multiple Use Lands," National Forest Management Act in a Changing Society 1976–1996: How Well Has It Worked in the Past 20 Years? How Will It Work in the 21st Century?, Natural Resources Law Center, University of Colorado School of Law (September 16, 1996).

60. Western Governors Association, Resolution 96-011 (June 23, 1996).

61. Quoted in Anderson, "Reforming National-Forest Policy," at 41–42.

62. Miller, *Living in the Environment*: 614–16.

63. Nels C. Johnson, "Global Trends and the Future of National Forests," National Forest Management Act in a Changing Society 1976–1996: How Well Has It Worked in the Past 20 Years? Will It Work in the 21st Century? Natural Resources Law Center, University of Colorado School of Law (September 17, 1996): 5–6.

64. Thomas Michael Power, *Lost Landscapes and Failed Economies: The Search for a Value of Place* (Washington, DC: Island Press, 1996): 140–41.

65. Associated Press, "After a Rocky Tenure, Chief of Forest Service to Resign," *New York Times* (October 16, 1996): A16.

66. Anderson, "Reforming National-Forest Policy," at 42–43.

67. Richard L. Knight, "NFMA and Ecosystem Management," National Forest Management Act in a Changing Society 1976–1996: How Well Has It Worked in the Past 20 Years? How Will It Work in the 21st Century?, Natural Resources Law Center, University of Colorado School of Law (September 16, 1996).

68. John K. Sessions and K. Norman Johnson, "Forest Planning on the National Forests under Ecosystem Management," National Forest Management Act in a Changing Society 1976–1996: How Well Has It Worked in the Past 20 Years? How Will It Work in the 21st Century? Natural Resources Law Center, University of Colorado School of Law (September 16, 1996).

69. Johnson, "Global Trends and the Future of National Forests," at 7–8.

70. Miller, *Living in the Environment*: 617–18.

71. Ibid.: 296–97.

72. Johnson, "Global Trends and the Future of National Forests": 8–12.

73. Ibid.

74. Anjali Acharya, "Plundering the Boreal Forests," *World Watch* (May/June 1995): 21–29, at 21–26.

75. Ibid., at 27–29.

76. Miller, *Living in the Environment*: 278–79.

77. Ibid.: 278–79, 620.

78. Western Ancient Forest Campaign, Report from Washington, October 26, 1995, <mlist.wafcdc@conf.igc.apc.org>.

79. 104th Congress, S. 391.

80. Environmental and Energy Policy Institute, *Monthly PULSE* (July 1996): 15.

81. Power, *Lost Landscapes and Failed Economies*: 167–69.

82. R. Max Peterson, "What Can We Learn from Past Reform Efforts," National

Forest Management Act in a Changing Society 1976–1996: How Well Has It Worked in the Past 20 Years? How Will It Work in the 21st Century?, Natural Resources Law Center, University of Colorado School of Law (September 16, 1996).

83. Miller, *Living in the Environment*: 297–98.

84. Ibid.: 619, 621.

6

Grazing and Public Lands

THE POLICY FRAMEWORK

Throughout the nineteenth century, the federal government pursued a variety of means to encourage the settlement of the West. The push to develop resources, tame wilderness, and pursue wealth shaped these lands for more than a century. The Homestead Act authorized families to claim 160 acres of land to support themselves; some settlers received 320 or 640 acres. But ranching required thousands of acres in the dry West in order to be financially feasible, so many settlers selected lands near public lands and relied on the open range to graze their cattle. Competition over use of these lands became fierce, prompting range wars and conflict among ranchers seeking to expand their herds. Overgrazing occurred in many areas, damaging streams, destroying natural vegetation and encouraging mesquite and sagebrush to grow, producing near desert conditions, and threatening the viability of grazing on public lands.

In response, Congress enacted the Taylor Grazing Act of 1934 to govern the management and protection of "vacant" federal lands. It ended open grazing and created a system of grazing leases for public lands.[1] The act created a Division of Grazing to work with the General Land Office to establish grazing districts, fees, and a permit system. It provided that grazing fees be calculated on the basis of an animal unit month (AUM)—the amount of forage required to feed a cow and her calf and a horse or five goats or sheep for a month. In 1934, the fee was five cents per AUM.[2] The two agencies were eventually combined to form the Bureau of Land Management in the 1946 Anderson–

Mansfield Act, which created the BLM and authorized it to make improvements in public rangelands.

About one-third of the total land area of the United States is classified as rangeland, mostly located in the western states. More than half of these lands, 52 percent, are privately owned; 43 percent are federal lands, primarily managed by the Bureau of Land Management; the other 5 percent are owned by state and local governments. Some 120 million cattle graze on this land. Ownership of the land is about 55 percent private, 40 percent public. About 70 percent of the eleven western states are grazed by livestock. Most public rangeland is managed by the BLM. The Bureau of Land Management and the U.S. Forest Service manage some 260 million acres of public lands for grazing. About 27,000 ranchers, 2 percent of all ranchers in America, have grazing rights on public lands; some 19,000 ranchers hold 14 million AUMs on 159 million acres of BLM lands, and 12,000 ranchers hold about 4 million AUMs on Forest Service lands. Some 19,000 ranchers hold 14 million AUMs on 159 million acres of BLM lands; 12,000 ranchers hold about 4 million AUMs on Forest Service lands: 10 percent are held by small ranching families, and 90 percent are held by large corporations or "hobby" ranchers. Some 19,000 ranchers hold 14 million AUMs on 159 million acres of BLM lands; 12,000 ranchers hold about 4 million AUMs on Forest Service lands.

The grazing fee on public lands has been typically about $1.85 per animal unit month since 1981, although it fluctuates to a modest degree. Federal land forage makes up about 10 percent of all cattle forage in the West and 2 percent of the nation's total. Individual ranches may have permits to graze BLM, state, and national forest lands.[3] Grazing takes place on 89 percent of all BLM land and 69 percent of all Forest Service lands as well as many national wildlife refuges and national parks.[4]

Regulations by the Department of Interior have governed the issuance of grazing permits, which specify the kind and number of livestock allowed to graze, the times of the year grazing is permitted, and the determination of fees. Permit holders elect district Stockmen's Advisory Boards; these boards have largely controlled the management of federal grazing lands. The boards were authorized to draft a code of rules and regulations, supervised the expenditure of funds to improve rangelands, and played major roles in allocating permits, setting grazing fees, and selecting land managers. Agency officials who have opposed advisory boards have usually been unsuccessful; many officials have agreed with these groups and acted as their spokespersons and lobbyists.[5] Table 6.1 shows the distribution of BLM lands by state; as the table indicates, BLM lands exist throughout the nation but are concentrated in the West.

Ranchers soon came to believe that permits and leases granted them permanent property interests in public lands and that they were responsible for public land management, and consequently they oppose any regulation. Grazing permits have conferred different interests than have mining claims, oil and gas leases, and timber contracts. Federal courts have ruled that permits are not property interests protected against taking by the Fifth Amendment but are interests that some courts have ruled can be withdrawn without compensation.[6]

The passage of the National Environmental Policy Act in 1969 eventually led to the requirement that the BLM prepare environmental studies before issuing grazing permits.[7] In a 1974 case brought against the BLM by the Natural Resources Defense Council, the court ruled that the BLM must assess the specific environmental effects of the permits it issued, either by preparing a separate impact statement for each district or several statements for each district or by some other means.[8] Environmental impact studies have identified widespread land degradation that had occurred as a result of grazing. The Endangered Species Act, first enacted in 1973, also places limits on grazing in habitats that supported threatened or endangered species.

The Federal Land Policy Management Act of 1976 gave the BLM new powers to control grazing, improve rangeland health, and manage public lands for multiple uses, in response to congressional finding that federal rangelands were deteriorating.[9] FLPMA established ten years as the usual term for grazing permits or leases; a shorter term is permissible if the land may be disposed of or used for other purposes within ten years, or if it is "in the best interest of sound land management."[10] In issuing permits, the Interior Department either simply grants a permit, including prescriptions for appropriate livestock management, or issues a permit in conjunction with Allotment Management Plans that are land use plans tailored to individual permits. FLPMA required the United States to compensate permit holders whose lease is terminated with the fair market value of the terminated portion as well as the value of permanent improvements made.[11] It gives priority for the award of new permits and leases to holders of the expiring leases and permits as long as the rancher was in compliance with the relevant terms and conditions.[12] Permits can be canceled, suspended, or modified for violation of grazing regulations or terms in the lease or permit.[13] It orders the BLM to give "priority to areas of critical environmental concern" (ACECs) but gives little guidance about what management restrictions are appropriate for such designations.[14] FLPMA applies to grazing on BLM and Forest Service lands.

The 1978 Public Rangelands Improvement Act (PRIA) expressly reenacted the Taylor Grazing Act and FLPMA and also included a congressional finding that "vast segments of the public rangelands [were in] an unsatisfactory condition."[15] PRIA also revised the formula for calculating grazing fees that had been established in the 1934 law, tieing the fees to market conditions but maintaining an artificially low fee structure.[16] Until the act devised a uniform grazing fee, the Forest Service and BLM had at times charged different fees. Table 6.2 lists the number and size of grazing leases in force in the fourteen western states. Tables 6.3 and 6.4 outline trends in grazing on BLM and Forest Service lands.

Table 6.1
Public Lands under Exclusive Jurisdiction of the Bureau of Land Management, Fiscal Year 1996 (in Acres)

State	Vacant public lands[a] Outside grazing district	Within grazing district	Total	Reserved lands Lu[b]	Other	Grand total
Alabama	3,037	-	3,037	-	107,846	110,883
Alaska	87,261,605	-	87,261,605	-	-	87,261,605
Arizona	1,517,187	10,092,698	11,609,885	32,321	[c]2,610,458	14,252,644
Arkansas	1,865	-	1,865	-	289,107	290,972
California	7,379,753	1,725,343	9,105,096	-	5,404,986	14,510,082
Colorado	480,313	6,776,323	7,256,636	36,206	999,327	8,292,169
Florida	1,329	-	1,329	-	23,765	25,094
Idaho	423,361	10,737,038	11,160,399	72,276	619,679	11,852,354
Illinois	3	-	3	-	224	227
Iowa	-	-	-	-	378	378
Louisiana	4,351	-	4,351	-	305,260	309,611
Michigan	47	-	47	-	74,807	74,854
Minnesota	5,521	-	5,521	-	145,211	150,732
Mississippi	1,240	-	1,240	-	55,971	57,211
Missouri	107	-	107	-	2,174	2,281
Montana	1,151,333	4,940,103	6,091,436	1,807,278	170,288	8,069,002
Nebraska	6,780	-	6,780	-	-	6,780
Nevada	3,136,904	44,493,239	47,630,143	3,127	207,299	47,840,569

156

State	Vacant public lands[a]			Reserved lands		Grand total
	Outside grazing district	Within grazing district	Total	Lu[b]	Other	
New Mexico	1,355,504	11,112,990	12,468,494	229,500	135,884	12,833,838
North Dakota	59,371	-	59,371	-	181	59,552
Oklahoma	2,233	-	2,233	-	-	2,233
Oregon	578,315	12,458,443	13,036,758	78,124	3,104,594	16,219,476
South Dakota	272,078	-	272,078	-	7,592	279,670
Utah	-	21,159,385	21,159,385	45,033	1,677,604	22,882,022
Washington	361,427	-	361,427	-	3,189	364,616
Wisconsin	2,536	-	2,536	-	157,631	160,167
Wyoming	3,916,171	11,273,811	15,189,982	10,434	3,189,004	18,389,420
Total	107,922,371	134,769,373	242,691,744	2,314,299	19,292,419	264,298,462

[a]The following types of surveyed and unsurveyed public and ceded Indian lands are included: Areas withdrawn under the Executive Orders of November 26, 1934, and February 5, 1935 (43 CFR 2400.0-3 et seq.); areas embraced in mineral withdrawals and classifications; areas withdrawn for resurvey; and areas restored to entry within national forests (Act of June 11, 1906, 34 Stat. 233, 16 U.S.C. 506-509), within reclamation projects (Act of June 17, 1902, 32 Stat. 388), and within power site reserves (Act of June 10, 1920, 41·Stat. 1063; 16 U.S.C. 791). These lands are not covered by any non-Federal right or claim other than permits, leases, rights-of-way, and unreported mining claims. [b]"Land Utilization Project" lands, purchased by Federal government under Title III of the Bankhead-Jones Farm Tenant Act and subsequently transferred by various Executive Orders between 1941 and 1958 from jurisdiction of the U.S. Department of Agriculture to the U.S. Department of the Interior, now administered by the Bureau of Land Management. Acreages are within grazing districts unless otherwise noted. [c]Includes acreage on the Barry M. Goldwater Air Force Range.

Note: Lands under BLM's exclusive jurisdiction are those lands (and resources) managed solely by BLM. Table includes all unperfected entries except for those involving reclamation and forest homesteads. Differences in fiscal year 1996 acreage from the previous year is due to land acreage acquired by the BLM; exchange land acreage received by the BLM; exchange BLM acreage (surface estate only) patented out by the BLM; withdrawn land acreage restored to BLM's jurisdiction; withdrawals, rights-of-way and easements for which the BLM relinquishes exclusive jurisdiction; or land acreage disposed of by the BLM.

Source: U.S. Department of the Interior, Bureau of Land Management, *Public Lands Statistics 1996* (March 1997): 8-9.

Table 6.2
Summary of Authorized Use of Grazing Lease (Section 15) Lands, Fiscal Year 1993

State	Cattle and yearlings	Horses and burros	Sheep and goats	Total
Number of operators				
Arizona	313	72	0	-
California	183	1	17	-
Colorado	950	46	93	-
Idaho	1,326	95	109	-
Montana	2,511	129	134	-
Nevada	490	48	46	-
New Mexico	1,259	340	113	-
Oregon	676	32	8	-
Utah	1,265	69	212	-
Wyoming	872	142	120	-
Total number of operators[a]	9,845	974	852	[b]
Animal unit months (AUMs) authorized				
Arizona	361,557	4,553	0	336,110
California	168,575	7	19,673	188,255
Colorado	307,750	2,735	73,542	384,027
Idaho	1,013,277	5,215	115,284	1,133,776
Montana	1,082,166	4,051	40,324	1,126,541
Nevada	1,140,196	4,817	96,039	1,241,052
New Mexico	1,148,832	14,444	115,542	1,278,818
Oregon	783,589	2,195	4,075	789,859
Utah	663,487	3,068	201,608	868,163
Wyoming	860,540	8,296	177,907	1,046,743
Total AUMs authorized[a]	7,529,969	49,381	843,994	8,423,344

[a]Many operators own more than one kind of livestock. The operator is counted for each kind of livestock authorized for public lands. Because of these overlaps, a valid total cannot be obtained and is therefore not shown.
[b]Totals do not include authorized nonuse.
Source: U.S. Department of the Interior, Bureau of Land Management, *Public Lands Statistics 1996* (March 1997): 62.

Table 6.3
Grazing Permits in Force on Grazing Lease (Section 15) Lands as of September 30, 1993

Geographic State[a]	Number of Permits	AUMs of preference[b]
Arizona	422	518,703
California	235	215,044
Colorado	1,199	640,162
Idaho	1,592	1,323,055
Montana	2,713	1,152,200
Nevada	732	2,297,143
New Mexico	1,543	1,656,658
Oregon	749	980,453
Utah	1,642	1,285,528
Wyoming	1,073	1,539,420
Total	11,900	11,608,366

[a]Administrative state boundaries differ slightly from geographic state boundaries: for example, California BLM administers some of the public lands within the state of Nevada; these figures show the number of permits within actual state geographic boundaries. Animal Unit Months (AUMs) of preference held by lessees on public lands. [b]AUMs (animal unit months) of preference held by permittes on public lands.

Source: U.S. Department of the Interior, Bureau of Land Management, Public Lands Statistics 1996 (March 1997): 64.

The Clinton Administration's Rangeland Reforms

Critics of grazing policy in Congress began proposing reform legislation in 1990. Then Representative Mike Synar (D-OK), a leader in the reform movement, argued that the grazing fee formula was "an experiment that failed." It had been adopted "to protect western livestock grazing operators from the rigors of the market place" and was based on the belief that "the economic stability of the industry could only be protected through low grazing fees." But it has been an inherently unfair system, causing the taxpayers millions of dollars to subsidize the 2 percent of the nation's livestock producers who use public lands. The federal subsidy has risen to $50 million a year, argued Synar, since the federal government receives only twenty cents in grazing fees for every dollar it spends managing the public range. Grazing fees were about one-fifth the price of fees charged by private land owners, but public lands' ranchers were responsible for providing wells, fences, and other structures necessary for grazing. As a result, "much of the public rangeland is still in poor or unsatisfactory condition."[17] In 1990, 1991, and 1992, the House passed grazing fee increases (as high as $8.70/AUM), but the bills died in the Senate or were stripped from the bills in the conference committees. In January 1993, Representatives Synar and Ralph Regula (R-OH) proposed to increase fees 33 percent a year for several years, to $5.83 by 1997, based on a "modified market value" formula that would take into account the condition of the land.[18]

The Clinton administration then entered the grazing lands reform debate through the budget process, proposing to raise the grazing fee from $1.92 to $5.00/AUM as part of its fiscal stimulation package (grazing fees are calculated in animal unit months, or AUMs, the amount charged for each cow and calf grazed on public lands). Western senators quickly opposed the administration's initiative, and the president just as quickly retreated, dropping his demands for public land reform and reduction of subsidies. Reform efforts shifted from the budget process to proposals made by the Secretaries of the Interior and Agriculture Departments. In August 1993, the administration proposed raising the grazing fee to $4.28 over three years and making other changes such as expanding membership in the advisory boards, compensating ranchers for improvements made on public lands, giving increased protection to riparian areas, shortening the grazing season, reducing the use of pesticides, and empowering federal land managers to revoke leases for mismanagement. By October, a compromise package had been crafted that would have raised fees to $3.45 over three years, but the effort was killed by a Senate filibuster led by Pete Domenici (R-NM), the leading proponent of grazing interests in Congress.

The authorization for the BLM expired in 1981, and Congress has not been able to agree since then on what new instructions to give the agency. Representative Jim Hansen (R-UT) proposed a six-year reauthorization but was blocked by other Republicans who believed a permanent reauthorization was not in the best interests of the people of the West. The House failed to pass the

Table 6.4
Annual Grazing Statistics, National Forests, Fiscal Year 1994

	Permittees	Cattle Number	Cattle HM's[a] / AUM's[b]	Horses and burros Number	Horses and burros HM's / AUM's	Sheep and goats Number	Sheep and goats HM's / AUM's	Total Number	Total HM'S / AUM's
Permitted to graze		1,301,922	6,573,952 / 8,261,577	10,858	50,590 / 59,953	1,069,129	3,319,676 / 968,340	2,381,909	9,944,218 / 9,289,870
Authorized to graze: Paid permits[c]	8,970	1,213,689	5,790,986 / 7,234,697	10,502	49,402 / 58,541	924,959	2,693,255 / 782,125	2,149,150	8,533,643 / 8,075,363
Free use	46	1,838	3,596 / 4,666	626	6,604 / 7,919	2,110	18,611 / 5,198	4,574	28,811 / 17,783
Private land permits	123	47,904	252,518 / 316,812	528	4,973 / 5,944	11,197	45,597 / 13,042	59,629	303,088 / 335,798
Crossing	3	1,736	234 / 281	204	10 / 13	14,189	6,101 / 1,669	16,129	6,345 / 1,963
Total authorized[d]	9,019	1,217,263	5,794,816 / 7,239,644	11,332	56,016 / 66,473	941,258	2,717,967 / 788,992	2,169,853	8,568,799 / 8,095,109
Wild horses				2,080	23,930 / 23,930			2,080	23,930 / 23,930
Wild burros				142	1,704 / 1,704			142	1,704 / 1,704

[a] A head month (HM) is the billing unit for permitted grazing and is equal to one month's occupancy. [b] An animal unit month (AUM) is the amount of forage required by a 1,000-pound cow, or the equivalent for one month. [c] Includes term and temporary grazing permits and all other paid permits (e.g., transportation, research, working animals, special uses, etc.). [d] Private land permit data not included in totals.

Source: U.S. Department of Agriculture, *Report of the Forest Service, Fiscal Year 1994* (June 1995): 130.

FY 1996 appropriations bills for the Interior Department two times because conferees had deleted the moratorium on issuing new mining patents and had agreed to increase logging in the Tongass National Forest. Once those provisions were changed, the bill was passed, but then it was vetoed by the president.[19] The failure of congressional reform prompted a series of twenty meetings throughout the West between November 1993 and January 1994 by Interior Department officials. The meetings produced recommendations for a proposed Interior Department regulation in March 1994 that would raise the grazing fee, broaden public participation in rangeland management, and require environmental improvements on rangelands. Secretary Babbitt's call for raising the grazing fee was popular throughout the country, except among ranchers, as an example of undeserved subsidies that contributed to the budget deficit. Babbitt's proposal, called Rangeland Reform '94, had a much broader agenda than grazing fees. Rangeland Reform '94 included the following policy changes:

- Creates Resource Advisory Councils (RACs), made up of ranchers, conservationists, and other stakeholders to help make grazing policy, and eliminated Grazing Advisory Boards,
- Authorizes permit holders to not use land for up to ten years for conservation purposes and to graze fewer animals than permitted without losing leases,
- Allows federal officials to consider a permittee's past performance when determining future permits,
- Requires grazing land improvements to be owned by the federal government,
- Orders the Interior Department to issue range health guidelines,
- Raises fees to about $3.68/AUM and subsequent fees to be negotiated, and
- Requires changes in grazing practices to ensure recovery and protection of endangered species, restore and/or maintain water quality, encourage grazing during times of low impact on vegetation, limit use of pesticides, protect riparian zones by placing salt licks and water troughs at least one-fourth mile from riparian areas and prohibiting all structures but fences in these areas.

As Rangeland Reform '94 was evolving through the administrative process, finally gaining approval in 1994, opponents in Congress tried to enact legislation to overturn it. In May 1995, Senator Domenici and Representative Wes Cooley (R-OR) introduced their Public Grazing Act of 1995.[20] The Senate version was reported out of the Energy and Natural Resources Committee in June. Negotiations continued, and a substitute bill, the Public Rangelands Management Act, was reported by the committee in November and passed by the Senate in March 1996.[21] The Senate bill would have placed BLM and Forest Service grazing lands under one law, removed the national grasslands from the National Forest System, lengthened grazing permits from ten to twelve years, limited the application of NEPA reviews to land use plans and not grazing permits, given ranchers more control over management of the lands they use and more influence in agency decision making, created local advisory councils of ranchers and other interests (but not the "interested public"), and increased fees by 30 percent. The House Resources Committee approved a similar bill in April 1996, but opposition from Democrats and moderate Republicans kept it from coming to the House floor. In June 1996, House Parks Subcommittee chair Jim Hansen attached the grazing bill to the omnibus parks bill that had been passed by the Senate in May. Interior Secretary Babbitt threatened that the president would veto the entire parks bill if the grazing provisions were attached, and House leaders stripped them before the parks bill was brought for a final, successful vote.

THE POLICY DEBATE

Conservatives and ranchers have long been dissatisfied with the policies of the Bureau of Land Management. The Sagebrush Rebellion of the 1970s and 1980s demanded that Bureau of Management and Forest Service lands be transferred from the federal government to states as a way to increase ranchers' control over their lands.[22] The Wise Use movement has offered similar criticisms of public lands agencies, as discussed in Chapter 1. Until the 1960s, grazing interests were so closely in harmony with public lands policies that conflict was uncommon. A 1988 General Accounting Office report found that "the BLM is not managing the permittees, rather, permittees are managing the BLM."[23] As the health of public lands deteriorated, and environmental values became more politically powerful, grazing policy began to shift toward giving more protection to environmental values.[24]

Some advocates of grazing argue that it can enhance public lands: grazed plants may be more productive than ungrazed plants, grazed areas accumulate less dead vegetation and mulch, which inhibits plant growth, and grazing tramples seeds into the ground. Nonuse of grazing lands can lead to their deterioration just as overgrazing can, according to these advocates. They argue that BLM lands are marginal and can produce beef where nothing else of value could be produced. Ranchers rely on the subsidies as a way of providing their industry with a stable source of forage for their livestock. They also believe that public subsidies keep the cost of meat at a reasonable level for consumers and help to sustain the economic base for the rural West. Perhaps just as important, grazing on public lands preserves part of America's cultural past.

Most evidence, however, points to the adverse impact grazing has had on the native ecosystems of western North America.[25] More than one-half of private cropland is planted in livestock feed, and livestock production uses one-half of all the water consumed in the United States, mainly through growing hay and other feed. Natural grasslands have evolved as grazing systems, and many require some level of grazing to maintain their vigor. But ecosystems have a carrying capacity, which is the number of animals an ecosystem can tolerate without long-term damage. Damage to rangeland systems may originate from overgrazing (primarily), off-road vehicle use, human foot traffic, and other causes. When carrying capacity of grazing lands is exceeded, desertification often ensues. Damage to rangelands results in soil erosion and compaction, loss of species, encroachment of shrubs, loss of riparian vegetation, invasion of exotic (weed) species, and other problems. Damage often causes loss of cryptobiotic crusts (and therefore lowered nitrogen fixation, decreased soil organic matter, and diminished water infiltration).

Rangeland grasses can be a renewable resource, since their roots are generally deep, and blades of grass grow from the base, not the tip: if grazing animals eat only the top of the grass, it can be grazed over and over. Overgrazing results when too many animals graze for too long, exceeding the carrying capacity of the land, compacting the soil and reducing its capacity to hold water, reducing grass cover, and increasing soil erosion. Overgrazing leads to the invasion of woody shrubs, like mesquite, that take over the lands and to desertification in arid and semiarid lands. Once initiated, the cycle requires careful management to break it and to restore lands. The quality of rangelands in the United States has been improving. Excluding arctic lands, in 1936, 84 percent of public grazing lands were classified as unsatisfactory; in 1990, that percentage had fallen to 50 percent. Only 4 percent are classified as excellent, and 15 percent are considered poor. Much of the environmental damage from grazing occurs in riparian zones. Cattle congregate to drink water, trample and overgraze the vegetation near streams, and cause erosion. Streams widen, become more sediment-laden, and are less hospitable for fish. Streambeds become more susceptible to flooding and drying out. Riparian areas represent 1 percent of the land but are critical for plants and animals. As much as three-fourths of the wildlife in western range areas is completely dependent on riparian areas.[26] No one has described the damage from grazing more effectively than Edward Abbey:

[M]ost of the public lands in the West, and especially in the Southwest, are what might be called "cowburnt." . . . [Cattle] are a pest and a plague. They pollute our springs and streams and rivers. They infest our canyons, valleys, meadows, and forests. . . . They trample down the native forbs and shrubs and cactus. They spread the exotic cheat grass, the Russian thistle, and the crested wheat grass. *Weeds*.[27]

There have been other problems with grazing policy. Ranchers have regularly allowed more cattle to graze than the permits they hold provide and have permitted them to graze beyond the borders of the lands for which they hold permits. Enforcement has been inconsistent. The BLM has never developed a systematic, comprehensive inventory of the resources under its jurisdiction. Policies have been inconsistently applied across BLM districts because of its decentralized management structure. The BLM's lack of planning was in part due to inadequate resources from Congress and no congressional mandate for overall planning until FLPMA was passed in 1976. The BLM still lacks a coordinated, consistent, rational planning and management effort, critics charge. When it has engaged in long-range planning for specific areas, it usually ends in litigation. It has been inconsistent in its creation and management of areas of critical environmental concern or ACECs.[28] A number of U.S. General Accounting Office reports have been critical of federal grazing programs; grazing in the Southwest, for example, was characterized as leading to ''long-term environmental damage,'' failing to ''generat[e] revenues sufficient to provide for adequate management,'' and yielding ''minimal'' economic benefits.[29] A General Accounting Office study, for example, found that more U.S. plant species are destroyed or threatened by grazing than by any other cause. Grazing also displaces wildlife populations.[30]

In the past, range management emphasis has focused mostly on increasing livestock production, manipulating the successional stage of grassland communities to increase production of livestock. Methods have included adjusting stocking rates, rotating pastures or ranges, applying fertilizers and herbicides, removing predators, manipulating livestock species, and protecting riparian areas. Most methods require large energy inputs. Some improvements have been made to prevent soil and ecosystem degradation, enhance wildlife habitat, and improve recreational opportunities.

Studies have estimated that the average market value of a grazing permit is from $6 to $9 per AUM. Private grazing land is leased in the West for between $4 and $14 per AUM. Some studies have indicated that the difference between what permit holders pay and the actual value of grazing permits amounts to around $150 million per year or about $5,000 per permittee, meaning that the value of grazing on public lands may be about $1,000–$1,500 per animal. The federal government spends hundreds of millions of dollars a year on rangeland improvement, predator control, and other management techniques that are all part of the real cost of grazing on public lands. Federal agencies collect about $1 for every $3 they spend on direct range improvement; when indirect costs are included, some studies have indicated that $1 in $10 may be collected by the federal government to lease federal lands to ranchers. When all costs are factored in, some argue that taxpayers provide a $2 billion subsidy for 30,000 ranchers—mostly wealthy corporations or ranchers—to promote the production of 3 percent of the country's beef. Low fees encourage overgrazing, discourage wildlife management, curtail habitat improvement, and de-emphasize conservation issues.

The federal government has issued 29,000 grazing permits, affecting about 3 million cattle and 1 million other livestock on BLM and Forest Service land in western states. Only 10 percent of the ranchers holding permits are small operations; 90 percent are held by large livestock operations, including oil and insurance companies. These ranchers represent only about 1 percent of all ranchers in the nation; they raise about 2 percent of the beef produced each year. The grazing fees charged to public land users represent a subsidy of about $150 million a year, since fees are only about 15 to 25 percent of what ranchers pay on private lands. When additional benefits are added, such as predator control, fences, water supply, weed control, planting grass, and reduced biodiversity, the subsidy grows to $2 billion or $69,000 per rancher.[31]

Thomas Michael Power's study of the economics of federal grazing policy demonstrates the very small impact of this sector on the economies of the West. Studies done for the ranching industry usually define ranches that make any use of public land for grazing, or get as little as 5 percent of their forage from public lands, as "dependent" on federal land. This tremendously exaggerates the role of federal grazing in western state economies. In Nevada, for example, 100 percent of ranches are defined as dependent on federal grazing, but only 43 percent of feed comes from public lands, exaggerating dependency by more than 200 percent. In California, 94 percent of the ranches claim dependence on federal grazing, but these lands provide only 4 percent of feed, overstating dependency by more than 2,000 percent. The experiences of other states in the West fall between these two figures, reflecting very misleading data concerning the economic importance of grazing. In Montana, for example, Power found that forage on federal lands provided 7 percent of total livestock feed; cattle and sheep operations generate about 50 percent of agricultural sales; and agriculture provides about 7 percent of total personal income in the state. Grazing on federal lands thus accounts for about one-fourth of 1 percent of all income in the state. In the western states as whole, federal land grazing produces about $1 of every $2,500 in personal income and about one of every 2,000 jobs. If federal grazing fees were raised, grazing on federal lands would continue but would simply be less attractive. There would be little impact on state economies: it would take western states only about six days of normal economic growth to replace the total value of grazing on federal lands if it was completely eliminated.[32]

The federal land agencies are caught in the middle of the debate. For decades, environmentalists have criticized them for being too accommodating toward the extractive industries. Environmentalists have derided the BLM by referring to it as the Bureau of Lumber and Mining and have sought changes in Congress, the executive branch, and the federal courts. While preservationists are far from having achieved their goals, they have had a significant impact on policy and have reshaped it in some important ways, particularly through NEPA's environmental assessment and public participation requirements and the Endangered Species Act's protection of habitat. Agencies must balance recreation, preservation, hunting, grazing, mining, and other values in pursuing their multiple use mandate, and it is virtually impossible to make everyone happy.

Grazing policy raises the same set of questions arising on other public lands. Should grazing lands be primarily managed for cattle production, or should wildlife habitat and other purposes be pursued? Even if grazing continues to be given priority, is it being managed sustainably, or are short-term economic profits dominating management decisions? There are several management options for protecting grazing lands. Reducing the stocking rate, or the number of animals permitted to graze in a particular area, is one obvious option, but determining the carrying capacity of grazing areas is difficult, since it is a function of changing conditions such as rainfall, soil moisture, kinds of animals, soil type, and type of vegetation. Fences can be built to protect riparian areas. Livestock can be rotated through different lands to allow grasses to recover. Unwanted plants can be suppressed through the use of herbicides.[33]

Predators raise another difficult issue. The federal Animal Damage Control Agency, along with state predator control officials, kills some 2 million birds that threaten crops or are otherwise considered pests and 250,000 wild animals. Predator control programs led to the near extinction of the gray wolf and grizzly bear. Predator control focuses on coyotes, but there is little agreement over how much of a threat they pose. While they are responsible for killing some sheep, they also kill small animals and thereby reduce pressure on rangeland vegetation. Environmentalists have suggested ways ranchers can protect their cattle without widespread killing of coyotes, while ranchers favor the federal predator program since it costs them little or nothing. The other issues central to grazing reform include limiting grazing in riparian areas, limiting grazing on damaged lands, opening permits to competitive bidding or at least raising fees to market rates, and broadening representation on grazing boards to others besides ranchers. Ranching has been sustainable in some areas. Sustainable ranching may help preserve open lands and resist commercial and residential development.[34]

Rangelands are important ecological resources. They provide habitat for 84 percent of wild mammal species and 74 percent of wild bird species in the United States. They serve as watersheds for surface and groundwater.[35] Protection of soils is a fundamentally important environmental value. Soil and water are the two resources on which we are most dependent. Fertile soil is a rich, living system, comprising millions of bacteria, yeast cells, invertebrates, and fungi, the product of an ecological process: rocks are weathered into tiny fragments, mixed with decaying plants and animals, and moistened by rainfall and runoff. Topsoil takes from 200 to 1,000 years to create in temperate and tropical areas, depending on the type of soil and climate. Soils are fragile, highly dependent on their surrounding ecosystems for their survival—roots of grass protect soils in grassland, and leaf drops protect the soils of temperate forests, for example. Like everything else in nature, soil is part of an interconnected, interdependent relationship, connected with other environments through feedback loops and linkages. If one element is altered, the entire system may be disrupted.[36] Fertile soil requires nitrogen, organic matter, and moisture; the best soil is porous (can hold more water and air); permeable (water and air move slowly through it); permeated by water and air; a mixture of clay, sand, silt, and humus; and neither too acidic nor too alkaline. Acid deposition depletes some of the minerals in soils, making them less fertile and making plants and trees grow more slowly and become more susceptible to drought, disease, and pests. Topsoil is constantly eroding and moving from one location to another by wind and flowing water. It is a potentially renewable resource, but topsoil erosion occurs at many times the renewal rate. Erosion is caused by construction, deforestation and loss of vegetation that stabilizes the soil, overgrazing, and unsustainable farming—poor irrigation practices that lead to waterlogged soil and concentration of salts, soil compaction by farming machinery and cattle hoofs, and farming on poor soil and terrain. The world is losing about 7 percent of its topsoil every decade, and in some areas the rates are much faster. Extreme soil erosion results in desertification.[37]

In the United States, about one-third of the nation's original topsoil has been lost. Overgrazing, unsustainable agricultural practices, and a severe drought combined in the 1930s to create a dust bowl that displaced thousands of families and inundated the eastern United States in a blanket of dust. The Soil and Conservation Service was created in 1935 to help prevent further erosion and promote conservation. But some areas are not well suited to farming, and if global climate change results in warmer, drier weather, farming in the Great Plains may not be feasible. Agricultural topsoil is eroding in the United States at a rate sixteen times greater than it is being created. In some areas, like California, the depletion rate is eighty times the formation of new topsoil. Optimists believe that current conservation measures are sufficient and, along with fertilizer use, will ensure that we continue to produce enough food. Others argue that the risks are too high, and major conservation efforts should be undertaken, such as minimum or no-tilling farming that does not disturb cover vegetation, terracing, contour farming, planting different crops in the same field, restoring gullies where runoff occurs, building windbreaks, and planting trees and vegetation to stabilize soils. Federal farm policies encourage farmers to take out of production lands highly susceptible to erosion, require they develop conservation plans, and forgive debt for farmers who agree not to farm highly erodible croplands or wetlands for fifty years.[38]

Policy Options

Environmental organizations have urged federal agencies to take an ecosystem management approach to grazing on public lands. They favor agencies' raising fees to bring the charges more in line with what it costs to graze animals on the private market, rather than subsidizing ranchers.[39] Some groups call for a complete ban on grazing federal lands, while others call for increased spending to repair damage from overgrazing. One option is to allow grazing on healthy lands but prohibit it on marginal and fragile lands. Options for reform include prohibiting grazing in damaged, ecologically sensitive, or riparian zones; reducing the number of animals grazed; reducing or eliminating predator control; and increasing funding to restore areas damaged by grazing. One market option proposed would replace grazing permits with forage rights.[40] A market in forage rights would be established, permitting ranchers, conservationists, recreation interests, or any interested party to buy or sell rights. The rights would initially be sold by federal agencies to reflect future rents, much as apartments are converted to condominiums, and the future rents are capitalized into the sale price. Monthly fees would cover associated management expenses of public lands agencies. Users would be required to comply with environmental and other rules established by the agency and Resource Advisory Councils. Forage rights would raise the cost of grazing on public lands and eliminate the need for a public subsidy. Forage rights are attractive because they protect the interests of ranchers who bought ranches at high prices because they included federal grazing rights.

Other proposals have called for a reduction in total number of grazing animals; no grazing in damaged, sensitive, or riparian zones; no predator control; funding for restoration of areas damaged by grazing; stronger regulation and enforcement of responsible grazing management; control of ORVs on public lands; changes in grazing practices to ensure recovery and protection of endangered species; maintaining and restoring water quality; allowing grazing during times of low impact on vegetation; and allowing for more discretion to land managers when problems arise. As politically potent as grazing fees are, more important than changes in the grazing fees will be reforms that give increased protection to the soils, riparian areas, and ecosystems that are part of public lands subject to grazing.

The power of public lands grazing interests to preserve their subsidies is remarkable, given their small numbers. But it is also a clear example of what James Q. Wilson describes as the politics of regulation: subsidies that accrue to a small group of beneficiaries and whose costs are widely distributed are usually quite secure, since there is great incentive by the beneficiaries to protect the subsidies, with little incentive for those who pay the costs to try to end them.[41] Policy entrepreneurs who call for an end to subsidies as a way to pursue good government, reinvent government, or even end corporate welfare have to overcome significant political barriers. That they sometimes succeed is evidence that an interest group approach to understanding public policies is useful but limited in explaining policy outcomes. Public opinion polls show that "corporate welfare" is one of the top three things that the public "flips out on," right after "foreign aid" and "waste, fraud, and abuse." But there is little agreement on what exactly constitutes corporate welfare. Studies have proposed as candidates some sixty major tax breaks, including fourteen that each cost the U.S. Treasury at least $1 billion annually and spending programs ranging from $87 to $150 billion a year. Advocates range from the libertarian Cato Institute, to the corporate critic Ralph Nader, to John Kasich (R-OH), chair of the House Budget Committee. Defenders argue that corporate welfare is really "competitive equity," or that "one man's corporate welfare is another man's paycheck."[42]

Some studies have argued that from $500 billion to $1 trillion in resources could be made available worldwide for environmentally sustainable economic activity by ending subsidies on fossil fuels, pesticides and fertilizers, agriculture, irrigation, logging, resource development, and other actions that contribute to environmental harm.[43] Many such subsidies seek to protect jobs and profits that will inevitably decline as natural resources are exhausted. Price controls and other subsidies that seek to keep prices of food, energy, water, and other products artificially low also encourage excess use and fail to encourage more environmentally safe alternatives, and also represent significant opportunity costs. Ending subsidies is a tremendously powerful way to protect resources and generate funds for environmentally sustainable growth.[44]

However, there are tremendous challenges in ending subsidies. It is difficult to ensure that such changes achieve their goals: ending subsidies for resource development would cause some job loss. Some subsidies encourage energy conservation and the development of renewable energy sources, but distinguishing between good and bad subsidies, and anticipating the consequences of ending them, is an extremely difficult policy task. One approach is simply to try and eliminate subsidies: even though environmentally beneficial subsidies might be lost, they will be overwhelmed by damaging ones, and efforts to distinguish the two will be so difficult that a straightforward opposition to all subsidies is more feasible. But it is clear that some subsidies are environmentally valuable, such as those that help overcome the barriers facing new technologies. Subsidies should be narrowly tailored and applied and involve the least cost possible. All the costs, particularly the environmental ones, of giving subsidies should be included in the assessments of costs and benefits. Much work needs to be done in developing complete cost-benefit analysis of existing and proposed subsidies in order to be able to determine which subsidies should be provided and which should be dropped.[45] Can we disentangle the effects of subsidies and make good decisions about what subsidies to continue and what to eliminate?

More daunting is the political challenge. Beneficiaries of subsidies are concentrated and have great incentives to ensure their perpetuation, while those who pay the higher prices and are concerned by the environmental damage are widely dispersed and have only weak incentives to act. Those subsidies are politically quite entrenched and take enormous political entrepreneurship to end them. In the United States, subsidies are not likely to be reversed until the campaign financing system is overhauled to reduce the ability of economic interests to buy access and influence and shape policies to their benefit. But there are some promising alliances between environmentalists and fiscal conservatives, for example, that can identify wasteful and harmful subsidies and generate support for their elimination. How can the political support for reducing subsidies be generated?

Second, as difficult as subsidies are to eliminate, even more difficult are tax-based policies that represent powerful tools in reducing environmental problems and generating resources for investments in environmentally sustainable economic activity. Tax policy is a critical area of public policy: it creates incentives and disincentives for a host of activities that have environmental and economic impacts. Taxes on sales, income, payrolls, and profits create a disincentive for these activities; it makes little economic sense to tax activities that are socially beneficial. The environmental consequences of tax policy are equally unfortunate. Governments "tend to undertax destructive activities, such as pollution and resource depletions and environmental quality."[46] Policies that permit industries to dump their waste on other people encourage pollution production, which also results in economic costs being imposed on others, such as reduced property values, clean up costs, and medical expenses, not to mention the adverse impact on health itself. The failure to tax air and water pollution ensures that polluters will avoid the full costs of production.

Tax policy provides a clear means of integrating and improving economic and environmental policy. Shifting taxes away from desirable actions such as earning profits and paying salaries and directing them toward undesirable actions of producing pollution and harvesting scarce resources can strengthen economies and make them more ecologically sustainable at the same time. Several kinds of policies are critical. Exploitation of resources that generate windfall profits should be taxed, instead of income and sales. Wood from virgin forests, ocean fish, and other resources are become increasingly scarce, while harvesting costs have often fallen due to economies of scale and new technologies. Profits often exceed fair rates of return, and those excess profits should be taxed and shared with the entire society. Political leaders of many countries use access to public resources as political payoffs, through leases to mining and timber companies, for example, rather than as a way to raise needed revenue.

Pollution and depletion of scarce resources clearly should be taxed. It ensures that producers of pollution take some responsibility for the harms they create, it guarantees that those who benefit economically from industrial production also pay the costs and do not impose them on others who do not enjoy the benefits, it creates clear incentives for people to reduce harmful activities without the heavy hand of government regulators and the inherent loss of flexibility and freedom that comes from command and control regulation, and it encourages pollution reduction to be efficient. Examples of these include taxes on fish catches, building homes on habitats of endangered species or other actions that harm ecosystems and threaten biological diversity and stability, and timber sales in virgin forests. Taxes can permit us to include in current price calculations the interests of future generations who, if present, would also demand clean air and water and old growth forests and force up the prices for them. It is difficult to calculate the appropriate level of these taxes, since pollution levels differ significantly across similar sources (motor vehicles vary tremendously in their emissions, for instance, as a result of kinds of fuel, meteorological conditions, driving patterns, and other factors). Placing economic values on environmental quality or scarce resources is similarly difficult. Taxes must be integrated with other laws and policies. The benefits of increased gasoline taxes, for example, are countered by land use decisions that encourage urban sprawl and more driving. Increasing taxes may not solve problems of how pollution sources are distributed and their tendency to be concentrated in low-income communities. Some species will require absolute protection and a ban on their killing.[47]

Making markets work through true cost pricing is critical, but may not be enough. Markets have several important flaws. One is that they understate or discount the value of things in the future. Costs and benefits that extend very far into the future are discounted and devalued. As a result, "critical ecological resources that will be essential for our well-being even 30 years from now not only have no value to rational economic decision makers, but scarcely enter their calculations at all."[48] Markets don't account for real scarcity: "Although the market price mechanism handles incremental change with relative ease," some economists argue, "it tends to break down when confronted with absolute scarcity or even marked discrepancies between supply and demand." In cases such as famines, markets may simply collapse or "degenerates into uncontrolled inflation, because the increased price is incapable of calling forth an equivalent increase in supply."[49] Markets also fail to respond to the problems of ecological scarcity because scarcity "tends to induce competitive bidding and preemptive buying, which lead to price fluctuations, market disruption, and the inequitable or inappropriate distribution of resources." Consumers may not respond to rising prices in ways predicted by economic theory. Some consumer decisions are rather independent of price increases; increasing the price of gasoline is likely to have little impact, in the long run, on driving, unless the price increases are so dramatic that they discourage people from driving their own vehicles. If such price increases occurred, the resultant concerns about social equity and resource allocation would be daunting. Other consumer decisions, such as the kind of energy used to heat a home, are essentially locked in because of the high capital costs involved in converting to another energy system. High prices may not be enough to deter ecologically unsustainable activities.[50]

This agenda, of course, goes well beyond grazing reform. But the history of grazing policy in the United States provides a clear example of the ecological and political problems of subsidies. From an ecological perspective, it is surprising that grazing and other public lands and natural resource subsidies have lasted as long as they have. Their durability is evidence of a flawed policy making process. These subsidies are increasingly vulnerable, but the experience of the past few years demonstrates that the political relationships that form around subsidies are quite durable and require a sustained effort to demonstrate their ecological and economic costs.

NOTES

1. 43 U.S.C. 315.

2. Jacqueline Switzer, with Gary Bryner *Environmental Politics* (New York: St. Martin's Press, 1998): Chapter 4.

3. George Cameron Coggins, Charles F. Wilkinson, and John D. Leshy, *Federal Public Land and Resources Law* (Westbury, NY: Foundation Press, 1993): 688, 691.

4. George Wuerthner, "How the West Was Eaten," *Wilderness* 54, no. 192 (Spring 1991): 28–37.

5. Coggins, Wilkinson, and Leshy, *Federal Public Land and Resources Law*: 694, 705.

6. See *Red Canyon Sheep Company v. Ickes*, 98 F.2d 308 (D.C.Cir. 1938); *United States v. Cox*, 190 F.2d 293, 296 (10th Cir. 1951), cert. denied, 342 U.S. 867 (1951).

7. 42 U.S.C. 4321–4347.

8. *Natural Resources Defense Council, Inc., v. Morton*, 388 F.Supp. 829, affirmed, 527 F.2d j1386 (D.C. Cir. 1976), cert. denied, 427 U.S. 913 (1976).

9. 43 U.S.C. 1701–1784.

10. 43 U.S.C. 1752.

11. 43 U.S.C. 1752(g).

12. 43 U.S.C. 1752(c).

13. 43 U.S.C. 1752(a).

14. 43 U.S.C. 1712(c)(3).

15. 43 U.S.C. 1901(a)(4).

16. 43. U.S.C. 1901 et seq.

17. Testimony of Representative Mike Synar, *H.R. 643, Fair Market Grazing for Public Rangelands Act of 1993*, Committee on Natural Resources, U.S. House of Representatives (Washington, DC: U.S. Government Printing Office, 1993): 28–29, 31.

18. 104th Congress, H.R. 643.

19. 104th Congress, H.R. 1977.

20. 104th Congress, S. 852, H.R. 1713.

21. 104th Congress, S. 1459.

22. William L. Graf, *Wilderness Preservation and the Sagebrush Rebellions* (Savage, MD: Rowman and Littlefield, 1990): 229.

23. This report is discussed in Switzer, and Bryner *Environmental Politics*: Chapter 4.

24. I am greatly indebted to my colleague Samuel Rushforth for the information on the environmental consequences of grazing I use here.

25. Thomas L. Fleischner, "Ecological Costs of Livestock Grazing in Western North America," *Conservation Biology* 8, no. 3 (September 1994): 629–38.

26. G. Tyler Miller, Jr., *Living in the Environment* (Belmont, CA: Wadsworth, 1996): 623–24.

27. Quoted in Coggins, Wilkinson, and Leshy, *Federal Public Land and Resources Law*: 689–90.

28. Ibid.: 708, 742–44, 752.

29. U.S. General Accounting Office, *BLM's Hot Desert Grazing Program Merits Reconsideration* (1991); quoted in Coggins, Wilkinson, and Leshy, *Federal Public Land and Resources Law*: 769.

30. George Wuerthner, "The Price Is Wrong," *Sierra* 75, no. 5 (September–October 1990): 38–43.

31. Ibid.: 625–26.

32. Thomas Michael Power, *Lost Landscapes and Failed Economies: The Search for a Value of Place* (Washington, DC: Earth Island Press, 1996): 181–86.

33. Miller, *Living in the Environment*: 623–24.

34. Ibid.: 626–27.

35. Miller, Living in the Environment: 622–26.

36. Clive Ponting, *A Green History of the World: The Environment and the Collapse of Great Civilizations* (New York: Penguin, 1991): 15–16.

37. Miller, *Living in the Environment*: 511–19.

38. Ibid.: 519–24.

39. Phillip A. Davis, "Grazing Fee Increase OK'd by Interior Subcommittee," *Congressional Quarterly Weekly Report*, June 8, 1991: 1497.

40. I appreciate research done by a student of mine, David Curtis, whose work I have relied on in this section on policy options.

41. James Q. Wilson, *The Politics of Regulation* (New York: Basic Books, 1980).

42. David E. Rosenbaum, "Corporate Welfare's New Enemies," *New York Times* (February 2, 1997): E1.

43. Paula DiPerna, "Five Years After the Rio Talkfest: Where is the Money?" *Earthtimes* (25 January 1997), http://earthtimes.org

44. David Malin Roodman, "Paying the Piper: Subsidies, Politics, and the Environment," WorldWatch paper #133 (Washington, DC: WorldWatch Institute, December 1996).

45. DiPerna, "Five Years After the Rio Talkfest."

46. David Malin Roodman, "Public Money and Human Purpose: The Future of Taxes," *World Watch* 8 (September–October 1995): 10–19, at 13.

47. Taxes can be used to help workers. Pollution taxes are often regressive since they raise the price of energy, transportation, manufactured goods, and other essentials, and take a larger bite out of the total income of poor households than of more wealthy ones. They must be combined with wage and income tax cuts aimed at low income families, rebates for energy taxes, and other adjustments. See Roodman, "Public Money and Human Purpose."

48. William Ophuls and A. Stephen Boyan, Jr., *Equality and the Politics of Scarcity Revised* (New York: W. H. Freeman, 1992): 219.

49. Ophuls and Boyan, *Equality and the Politics of Scarcity Revised*, 219.

50. Ophuls and Boyan, *Equality and the Politics of Scarcity Revised*, 220.

7

Mining and Energy

THE POLICY FRAMEWORK

The federal government owns nearly 600 million acres of land that are subject to mineral and energy development. These lands hold a large part of the nation's natural resources: 21–80 percent of its recoverable petroleum, 16–40 percent of its natural gas, and 33 percent of its coal, according to different estimates. These lands were heavily mined through the 1960s. By the 1970s, environmental and financial concerns combined to slow development of these resources. Mining has traditionally been seen in the West as the ultimate value, the most desirable use of public lands. Gold, silver, and copper mining has created many of the expectations that have made the West so attractive to wealth seekers and underlie many of its myths and stories.

Coal was the first mineral resource to be regulated by the federal government, when Congress passed the Coal Act of 1864. Mining was regulated by states until 1872, when Congress enacted a broad law aimed at encouraging mining in nearly all of the public lands. The General Mining Law of 1872 was enacted in the Ulysses S. Grant administration to encourage western settlement and spur development of the nation's mineral wealth. It permitted prospectors to make claims on practically any parcel of federal land and to obtain title to the land for a nominal fee. The law worked exactly the way proponents had hoped and encouraged the settlement of the West and development of energy and mineral resources.

The mining law was also the last of the homesteading acts. It applies to BLM and USFS lands: national parks, wilderness, and wildlife refuge lands contain mining claims, and, under the law, mining is considered highest use of the lands. The 1872 mining act permits any person or corporation to file a claim on any federal land not within a protected area such as a wilderness or park if they declare they believe the land contains valuable hard-rock minerals. Miners may patent or buy land if they demonstrate a legitimate mineral discovery; spend $500.00 on "assessments" that prepare the land for mining; spend at least $100.00 a year on developing the claim, and pay $2.50/acre for placer deposits and $5.00/acre for lodes. Once those steps are taken, the land is theirs—they receive a patent or title to the land and are not required to pay any royalties on proceeds from the mining and can sell or lease land and charge royalties. As discussed later, royalties are required of other developers of mineral resources on federal lands; mining royalties on private lands are as high as 18% of gross proceeds.

The mining law provides that

all valuable mineral deposits in lands belonging to the United States, both surveyed and unsurveyed, shall be free and open to exploration and purchase, and the lands in which they are found to occupation and purchase, by citizens of the United States and those who have declared their intention to become such.[1]

The law requires miners to forfeit unpatented claims unless "not less than $100 worth of labor shall be performed or improvements made during each year."[2] The Interior Department has the authority to raise this $100 threshold but has never done so. Miners who fail to continue with assessment efforts do not automatically lose their claims; they usually lie dormant until miners recommence their work or until other miners begin. The federal government has occasionally challenged mining claims for failure to conduct assessment work when it proposes to withdraw the land from the Mining Law's jurisdiction.[3]

Patents usually grant a fee simple in the land, and they can be sold, transferred, and inherited. When granted in wilderness and other protected areas, Congress has sometimes provided that the patents extend only to the minerals and not the surface lands. Claims are believed by some to grant absolute rights in holders to do whatever they wished with their lands, but courts have generally held that federal land management agencies have some authority to regulate the use of these lands and require that they be used only for mining purposes. Unpatented lands can be open to the public for recreation uses as long as that does not materially interfere with mining activity. Since claims can be so easily filed, they can pose challenges to the management of public lands.[4] Federal agencies can use administrative or judicial proceedings to challenge the validity of unpatented claims and clear the titles.

The Forest Service has issued regulations aimed at minimizing the environmental impact of mining on national forestlands. While the Organic Act provides that mining can occur in national lands, miners "must comply with the rules and regulations covering such national forests." The Forest Service is to issue regulations to "preserve the forests . . . from destruction." Miners must file an operating plan with the Forest Service that specifies environmental protection and reclamation efforts, such as the location and number of trees that can be cut down, and must post a bond to cover the costs of damage or reclamation that is not completed.[5]

The BLM also regulates mining on lands under its jurisdiction in order to "prevent unnecessary or undue degradation of the lands." Mines that disturb more than five acres in any calendar year must be approved by the BLM, including an environmental assessment. Mines disturbing less than five acres require only notice to the BLM of the location and extent of the mining activity and a statement promising to complete reclamation of disturbed areas.[6] Finally, mining claims are defined by courts as real property; even though the United States retains title, claimants have possessory title. But claim holders do not have a vested right to patents issued for those claims. Lands on which claims lie may be withdrawn from patent without triggering a taking of private property requiring compensation.[7]

Determining what materials are defined as a mineral has been an important part of mining law development and implementation: if materials on public lands are defined as minerals, then private interests can mine them, patent or buy the land, and pay no royalties. Courts have ruled that water drilled on federal lands, peat and organic soil, fossils of prehistoric animals, radon gas, silt or drilling mud, quartzite, and stalactites, stalagmites, and other natural "curiosities" are not defined as minerals.[8] Legal and policy questions have also arisen over when the provisions of the law apply and when miners can claim legal protection. The Mining Law has been interpreted to give some protection to prospectors before mines are actually discovered, and the lands are patented. Miners prospecting in good faith are protected from claim jumpers. But no claim can actually be made until the discovery of the vein or load.[9] Claims can also extend beyond the sidelines of a claim in order to follow a vein or lode. But since veins often intersect and rarely match the irregular claims indicated on the surface of the land, conflicts among claim holders concerning the extension of their claims underground have spawned thousands of court decisions.[10]

USDA and DOI reclamation regulations put in place in 1974 and 1981 require a plan of operations for mining that disturbs more than five acres. Some state reclamation laws require plans, bonds, and permits to protect air, water, and cultural resources. Some regulation of mining also occurs through surface water and groundwater quality protection permits required by the Clean Water and Safe Drinking Water Acts. The National Environmental Policy Act applies to mining, but few environmental impact statements (EISs) and environmental assessments (EAs) are done.

By 1920 the mining law had become so successful in encouraging resource development that critics feared the United States was selling off its critical natural resources, and Congress passed the Mineral Lands Leasing Act of 1920 (see later). That act ordered federal agencies to maintain title to lands with energy resources and lease them to developers, who would pay a royalty on coal, oil, and gas, to be equally shared by the federal and affected state governments. Hard-rock mining for gold, silver, copper, lead, iron ore, zinc, and other minerals remained under the old patenting system.[11] The 1947 Materials Disposal Act ended the patenting of mining claims for sand, gravel, and other materials. Developers must pay a royalty on energy development to be shared by the federal governments and the states in which the lands are located. The 1947 act and the Common Varieties Act of 1955 provide for the mining and sale of sand, stone, gravel, pumice, cinders, and other minerals on federal lands.[12] Mining is limited in federal lands withdrawn by executive or legislative action, such as national parks and wilderness areas, although mining claims in effect when protected areas are designated are valid and can continue to be developed.

Fossil Fuels

A thorough discussion of energy policy is well beyond the scope of this book. But development of energy resources on public lands is an important element of public lands policy, and deserves a brief discussion. The 1920 Mineral Leasing Act applies to fossil fuel minerals such as oil, gas, oil shale, coal, native asphalt, bituminous rock, and solid and semisolid bitumen; the fertilizer and chemical minerals such as phosphate, potash, sodium, and sulfur; all minerals on the Outer Continental Shelf (in practice, oil and gas); and geothermal resources. Unlike hard-rock mining, parties must obtain permission from federal agencies before beginning exploration. Agencies usually have discretion to approve or reject applications and are empowered to regulate exploration and development efforts. Royalties are charged on all resources developed from federal lands. All offshore oil and gas leasing is done through competitive bidding; onshore leasing must also begin competitively, but if no bids are received, noncompetitive bids are permitted. Royalties for oil and gas range from 12.5 to 25 percent, depending on levels of production; 12.5 percent for surface-mined coal; and 10–15 percent for geothermal steam.[13] Federal lands have become increasingly important sources of fossil fuels. Table 7.1 provides data on the history of fossil fuel production on federally administered lands. In 1949, crude oil from federal lands provided 5.2 percent of the nation's total; in 1994, 18.1 percent. The share of natural gas supplies (liquid and gas) from federal lands grew during the same forty-five year period from 5.6 percent to 45.7 percent; the amount of coal from federal lands grew from 2.0 percent to 31.1 percent. Total fossil fuel production from federal lands grew from 3.2 percent of total production in 1949 to 29.4 percent in 1994.

Coal. Coal from federal lands provided only a small amount of the total annual production in the United States until the late 1970s, when it increased from about 7 percent of all coal produced in the nation in 1976 to nearly one-third in 1994. The Surface Mining Control and Reclamation Act regulates all

Table 7.1

Fossil Fuel Production on Federally Administered Lands, 1949–1994

Year	Crude Oil and Lease[1] Condensate Million Barrels	Percent U.S. Total[5]	Natural Gas Plant Liquids[2] Million Barrels	Percent U.S. Total[5]	Natural Gas[3] Trillion Cubic Feet	Percent U.S. Total[5]	Coal[4] Million Short Tons	Percent U.S. Total[5]
1950	105.9	5.4	4.4	2.4	0.14	2.4	7.7	1.4
1955	159.5	6.4	6.0	2.1	0.43	4.8	5.9	1.2
1960	277.3	10.8	11.6	3.4	0.95	7.8	5.2	1.2
1965	378.6	13.3	14.3	3.2	1.56	10.2	8.2	1.6
1970	605.6	17.2	40.6	6.7	3.56	16.9	12.0	2.0
1975	531.5	17.4	59.7	10.0	4.57	23.8	43.6	6.7
1980	510.4	16.2	10.5	1.8	5.85	30.2	92.9	11.2
1981	529.3	16.9	12.3	2.1	6.15	32.1	138.8	16.8
1982	552.3	17.5	15.0	2.7	5.97	33.5	130.0	15.5
1983	568.8	17.9	14.0	2.5	5.17	32.1	124.3	15.9
1984	595.8	18.3	25.4	4.3	5.88	33.7	136.3	15.2
1985	628.3	19.2	26.6	4.5	5.24	31.8	184.6	20.9
1986	608.4	19.2	23.3	4.1	4.87	30.3	189.7	21.3
1987	577.3	18.9	23.7	4.1	5.56	33.4	195.2	21.2
1988	516.3	17.3	37.0	6.2	5.45	31.9	225.4	23.7
1989	488.9	17.6	45.1	8.0	5.32	30.7	236.3	24.1
1990	515.9	19.2	50.9	8.9	6.55	36.8	280.6	27.3
1991	491.0	18.1	72.7	12.0	5.99	33.8	285.1	28.6
1992	529.1	20.2	70.7	11.4	6.25	35.0	266.7	26.7
1993	529.3	21.2	64.4	10.2	6.56	R36.3	285.7	30.2
1994	527.7	21.7	60.0	9.5	6.78	36.2	321.4	31.1

[1] Production from Naval Petroleum Reserve No. 1 (NPR#1) for 1974 and earlier years is for fiscal years (July through June). [2] Includes only those quantities for which the royalties were paid on the basis of the value of the natural gas plant liquids produced. Additional quantities of natural gas plant liquids were produced; however, the royalties paid were based on the value of natural gas processed. These latter quantities are included with natural gas. [3] Includes some quantities of natural gas processed into liquids at natural gas-processing plants and fractionators. [4] Converted to British thermal units (Btu) on the basis of an estimated heat content of coal produced on federally administered lands of 21.0 million Btu's per short ton. [5] Based on physical units. Note: Federally administered lands include all classes of land owned by the federal government, including acquired military, Outer Continental Shelf, and public lands. R=Revised data.
Source: U.S. Department of Energy, Energy Information Administration, *Annual Energy Review 1995* (Washington, DC: U.S. DOE, 1996): 31.

coal-mining operations producing more than 250 tons a year.[14] It is a complex, comprehensive law, imposing specific requirements for environmental protection and reclamation. The Reagan administration fought to reduce the requirements imposed on coal companies in order to increase coal production. Litigation blocked some administrative efforts, but budget cuts and personnel decisions weakened the law.

In the early 1970s, the federal government suspended its coal and simultaneous onshore oil-and gas-leasing programs in response to criticism that the leases were underpriced and failed to protect environmental conditions. Congress passed two acts in 1976 in order to resurrect the leasing program and to provide for environmental protection for federal lands affected by mining. Congress subsequently passed two laws in 1976, the Federal Coal Leasing Amendments

Act[15] and the Federal Lands Policy and Management Act[16]; the first act required coal lease bids to be based on fair-market values and leaseholders to develop their leases and not simply hold them for speculative purposes; FLPMA ordered the Interior Department to examine the environmental impact of leasing. As a result, leasing activity declined on federal lands.

The Surface Mining Control and Reclamation Act of 1977 established environmental standards for surface mining of coal and a fund to help finance reclamation of abandoned mines and to protect other lands. The levy on coal mining for the reclamation fund was reauthorized in 1992 through the year 2004; part of the interest from the fund goes to provide health benefits to retired miners; funds also go to compensate landowners whose drinking water is contaminated by mining wastes.

Oil and Gas. In 1981, the Reagan administration, led by Interior Secretary James Watt, proposed to double the rate of leasing of oil, gas, and mineral resources and open some wilderness areas to exploration. Congress blocked the administration from pursuing most of those changes. In 1987, Congress revised the oil-and gas-leasing system in the Interior Department in the Federal Onshore Oil and Gas Leasing Reform Act. Passed as part of the Omnibus Budget Reconciliation Act,[17] the new law required all lands to be subject to competitive bidding; lands that fail to attract a bid of at least $2.00/acre go to the first bidder in a second, noncompetitive round. If there is no bidder after two years, the land returns to the competitive bidding process. The percentage of land subject to competitive bids increased from 9 percent to 65 percent by FY 1993. The new law also prohibits the federal government from issuing drilling permits unless the company has prepared a plan of operations that describes all activities that will disturb the surface lands and posts a bond to ensure restoration of disturbed lands. It also established an annual rent of $1.50 an acre and a royalty of 12.5 percent. The 1992 Energy Policy Act[18] amended the 1987 law to require ten-year leases for energy development on federal lands, in response to criticism that the five-year leases mandated by the 1987 law had discouraged drilling activity. The 1992 act also provided that holders of pre-1920 oil shale claims be permitted to receive patents only for the oil shale itself and not for the surface lands or other minerals. That action had been prompted by the sale of oil shale lands in Colorado that had been patented for $2.50 an acre, then sold for $2,000.00 an acre.[19]

After nearly a decade of trying to overhaul the leasing program, Congress passed in 1987 the Federal Onshore Oil and Gas Leasing Reform Act (the act was passed as part of that year's Omnibus Budget Reconciliation Act).[20] Under the old law, only lands with proven resources were subject to competitive bids; other lands were leased to the first bidder. The new law required all lands to be offered for competitive bids. Lands that fail to attract a bid of at least $2.00 an acre go to the first bidder in a second round of noncompetitive bidding. After two years, lands that are not leased are returned to competitive bidding. Under the old law, only 9 percent of available lands were leased competitively; under the new law, that percentage rose to 65 percent in 1993. The 1987 act also included several other important provisions: it required federal agencies to make greater efforts to comply with the land use planning provisions of existing law, prohibited agencies from issuing permits to drill for oil and gas unless the company submits a document identifying the disturbance the drilling will create and posts a bond to ensure reclamation occurs, and established a uniform annual rent of $1.50/acre and a 12.5 percent royalty on oil and gas leases.[21] The 1992 Energy Policy Act authorized federal agencies to grant ten-year development terms for all competitive and noncompetitive leases. The act also resolved years of conflict over the leasing of oil shale lands by placing limits on patenting pre-1920 oil shale claims and allowing claimants to obtain rights to the oil shale itself and not to other minerals or other surface lands.

Natural Gas. The federal government first began regulating natural gas prices as a way to stabilize prices and supply in the face of an unstable global market. In 1938, the Natural Gas Act authorized the Federal Power Commission to regulate interstate transportation of natural gas and eventually led to the regulation of wellhead prices as well. Shortages of natural gas occurred in the 1970s, and international supplies were disrupted, and prices soared, while domestic production was artificially held low. In response, Congress provided for higher prices for new gas produced in the Natural Gas Policy Act of 1978.[22] Gas produced after enactment was fully decontrolled in 1985; gas produced before 1978 was still subject to price controls. Gas production increased as a result of the 1978 act. Marketing agreements between producers and users resulted in higher gas prices as the 1980 recession resulted in reduced consumption, leading eventually to the decision in Congress in 1989 to end controls on wellhead prices.[23] By 1993, all wellhead prices controls were lifted, and prices declined as new contracts were signed amid an oversupply of gas.

Other issues have arisen concerning natural gas, and some were not resolved as of 1997. The Federal Energy Regulatory Commission (FERC) has explored ways of streamlining the process for gaining approval to construct new pipelines and requiring energy companies to assume more of the cost of construction of new pipelines. The 1992 Energy Policy Act, in response to northeast residents who import much of their natural gas from Canada, prohibited FERC from discriminating against imported oil in setting interstate pipeline rates or in regulating other activities. The act also indirectly encouraged natural gas production by encouraging the use of alternative motor vehicle fuels and increasing competition in the electric power industry.[24]

The 104th Congress cut research and development spending for natural gas in FY 1996 to 75 percent of what it was in 1975. It also considered a new pipeline safety act that would reauthorize the 1968 Natural Gas Pipeline Safety[25] and the 1979 Hazardous Liquid Pipeline Safety[26] Acts. The bill proposed would require federal agencies to conduct cost-benefit analyses of proposed regulations with compliance costs of at least $25 million a year and to submit risk and cost-benefit assessments to peer review committees; require new pipelines to accom-

Table 7.2
Producing Federal and Indian Onshore Coal Leases, December 31, 1993

	Indian		Federal		Total Onshore	
	No.	Acres	No.	Acres	No.	Acres
Alabama	2	3,456	—	—	2	3,456
Arizona	—	—	3	64,858	3	64,858
Colorado	27	38,399	—	—	27	38,399
Kentucky	1	818	—	—	1	818
Montana	13	36,728	1	14,746	14	51,474
New Mexico	7	14,142	2	44,394	9	58,536
North Dakota	5	5,714	—	—	5	5,714
Oklahoma	3	2,760	—	—	3	2,760
Utah	38	51,243	—	—	38	51,243
Washington	1	241	—	—	1	241
Wyoming	36	114,529	—	—	36	114,529
Total	**133**	**268,030**	**6**	**123,998**	**139**	**392,028**

Source: U.S. Department of the Interior, Mineral Revenues 1993 (Washington, DC: U.S. DOI, n.d.): 98.

modate "smart pigs," devices that travel through pipelines and locate pipeline sections and joints that are weakened; and no longer require that pipelines be inspected by owners every two years.[27] Tables 7.2, 7.3 and 7.4 describe the extent of leases on federal and Native American lands, by state, for coal, oil and gas, and other minerals.

Nuclear Policy and Energy Production

Coal is the largest single source of energy produced in the United States. In 1994, 22.0 percent of total energy production was based on coal; dry natural gas provided 19.4 percent; crude oil, 14.0 percent; nuclear power, 6.8 percent; hydroelectric, 2.7 percent; natural gas liquids, 2.4 percent; and other sources, 3.1 percent.[28] In 1970, nuclear power plants generated about 1 percent of the electricity produced in the United States. By 1996, that figure grew to nearly 22 percent of total electrical generation. The role of nuclear power is expected to fall after the year 2010, when plants built in the 1970s come to the end of their expected forty-year lifetimes. The number of plants increased from 70 in 1980 to 109 in 1994. Eight plants have been given construction permits, but no new plants have been ordered since 1978, and all plants ordered since 1973— more than 100 were planned—have been canceled. Construction cost overruns, reduced demand for electricity, and concerns about plant and waste safety have all combined to reduce interest in nuclear power. The problems facing nuclear power are closely linked to widespread public fears about nuclear plant safety that were intensified by the 1978 Three Mile Island nuclear plant accident, which released radioactive material into the atmosphere from a coolant system break- down, and the 1986 accident at the Chernobyl plant in the Ukraine, which

Table 7.3
Producing and Producible Federal and Indian Onshore, and Federal Offshore, Oil and Gas Leases, December 31, 1993

| | Indian | | Federal | | Total Onshore | |
	No.	Acres	No.	Acres	No.	Acres
Alabama	—	—	29	14,608	29	14,608
Alaska	—	—	35	61,326	35	61,326
Arizona	15	69,096	—	—	15	69,096
Arkansas	—	—	184	90,404	184	90,404
California	—	—	353	82,368	353	82,368
Colorado	170	457,362	1,980	1,390,421	2,150	1,847,783
Florida	—	—	3	5,778	3	5,778
Illinois	—	—	4	1,143	4	1,143
Kansas	—	—	459	127,375	459	127,375
Kentucky	—	—	55	30,352	55	30,352
Louisiana	—	—	180	51,539	180	51,539
Maryland	—	—	3	35,135	3	35,135
Michigan	3	60	47	74,132	50	74,192
Mississippi	—	—	118	56,818	118	56,818
Missouri	—	—	1	200	1	200
Montana	444	106,743	1,310	783,552	1,754	890,295
Nebraska	—	—	24	36,959	24	36,959
Nevada	—	—	42	23,493	42	23,493
New Mexico	465	555,296	5,903	3,406,874	6,368	3,962,170
New York	—	—	4	1,009	4	1,009
North Dakota	36	7,511	501	339,349	537	346,860
Ohio	—	—	108	12,775	108	12,775
Oklahoma	2,087	201,649	815	128,446	2,092	330,095
Pennsylvania	—	—	61	26,768	61	26,768
South Dakota	1	160	70	37,288	71	37,448
Tennessee	—	—	7	2,446	7	2,446
Texas	8	3,267	173	63,516	181	66,783
Utah	789	255,437	1,098	825,662	1,887	1,081,099
Virginia	—	—	11	5,717	11	5,717
West Virginia	—	—	160	152,445	160	152,445
Wyoming	91	51,447	5,805	2,809,578	5,896	2,861,025
Subtotal			19,543	10,67,476	23,652	12,385,504
Total	**4,109**	**1,708,028**				
California OCS Area			43	217,668	43	217,668
Gulf of Mexico OCS Area						
Central OCS Planning Area			1,810	5,867,853	1,310	5,867,853
Eastern OCS Planning Area			—	—	—	—
Western OCS Planning Area			378	2,013,459	378	2,013,459
Subtotal			1,731	8,098,980	1,731	8,098,980
Total			**21,274**	**18,776,456**	**25,383**	**20,484,484**

Source: U.S. Department of the Interior, *Mineral Revenues 1993* (Washington, DC: U.S. DOI, n.d.): 96.

included an explosion and fire, and heightened fears of nuclear power.[29] Industry officials, however, place the blame on burdensome licensing procedures that require decades, delay construction, and increase costs.

Congress passed the 1957 Price–Anderson Act to limit the liability of nuclear power companies for off-site damage that might occur as a result of a power plant accident. The limitation on liability was a major inducement required to

Table 7.4
Producing Federal and Indian Onshore Leases of Other Minerals, December 31, 1993

	Federal		Indian		Total	
	No.	Acres	No.	Acres	No.	Acres
Alabama						
Clay	1	40	---	---	1	40
Arizona						
Copper	---	---	3	6,734	3	6,734
Sand-Gravel	---	---	4	796	4	796
Silica Sand	---	---	1	640	1	640
Arkansas						
Quartz Crystals	2	162	---	---	2	162
California						
Geothermal	21	23,320	---	---	21	23,320
Sand-Gravel	---	---	4	1,545	4	1,545
Sodium	1	15,109	---	---	1	15,109
Colorado						
Sodium	1	2,483	---	---	1	2,483
Florida						
Phosphate	1	40	---	---	1	40
Idaho						
Garnet Sands	1	75	---	---	1	75
Phosphate	7	6,842	20	4,022	27	10,864
Illinois						
Fluorspar/Zinc	1	45	---	---	1	45
Minnesota						
Iron Ore	1	160	---	---	1	160
Missouri						
Copper	1	120	---	---	1	120
Lead/Zinc	9	24,809	---	---	9	24,809
Montana						
Phosphate	6	2,815	---	---	6	2,815
Nevada						
Geothermal	20	29,149	---	---	20	29,149
Sand-Gravel	2	1,100	1	100	3	1,200
New Mexico						
Gypsum	---	---	1	800	1	800
Hot Water	4	4,221	---	---	4	4,221
Langbeinite	2	5,116	---	---	2	5,116
Potash	34	55,067	---	---	34	55,067
Sand-Gravel	---	---	9	1,870	9	1,870
Sodium	4	4,072	---	---	4	4,072
Oklahoma						
Chat	---	---	3	265	3	265
Limestone	---	---	1	18	1	18
Sand-Gravel	---	---	5	4,556	5	4,556

Table 7.4 continued

Utah						
Geothermal	6	11,559	---	---	6	11,559
Gilsonite	1	197	---	---	1	197
Potash	10	24,700	---	---	10	24,700
Sodium	50	126,191	---	---	50	126,191
Virginia						
Limestone	1	355	---	---	1	355
Washington						
Sand-Gravel	---	---	7	224	7	224
Wyoming						
Sodium	14	23,611	---	---	14	23,611
Trona	1	1,933	---	---	1	1,933
Total	202	363,291	59	21,570	261	384,861

Source: U.S. Department of the Interior, *Mineral Revenues 1993* (Washington, DC: U.S. DOI, n.d.): 100-101.

encourage electric power companies to build nuclear plants, since insurance companies would not insure them because of the inability to predict the likelihood of accidents and the resultant costs. Companies feared to take on the risk of building a plant since any accident could result in financial ruin. Congress reauthorized the act in 1965, 1975, and 1988. The 1988 reauthorization[30] required each of the 110 commercial nuclear power plants to carry $200 million in private liability insurance and to contribute up to $75 million in retrospective premiums (with annual premiums not to exceed $10 million). The $200 million private policy and the additional premiums paid will result in $8.45 billion to be available in the case of an accident. Under a Nuclear Regulatory Commission regulation issued in 1993, plants that have been decommissioned or are shutting down must maintain $100 million in insurance but no longer make contributions to the fund. The 1988 law provides that if a court finds the liability resulting from an accident to exceed $7 billion, the president is to propose, and Congress would give, expedited attention to a plan for additional compensation. The same liability applies to companies, universities, and other organizations that operate nuclear facilities under Department of Energy (DOE) contracts; the DOE must indemnify these organizations up to the $7 billion cap. The liability for accidents involving nuclear wastes is also capped at $7 billion; compensation would be paid out of the Nuclear Waste Fund, which collects fees from a tax on nuclear power and finances DOE's nuclear waste disposal program. The law also authorizes civil penalties of up to $100,000 a day for violations of nuclear safety rules (but exempts some university and nonprofit contractors) and criminal penalties for knowing violations of safety laws and regulations.[31]

The 1992 Energy Policy Act also codified a Nuclear Regulatory Commission (NRC) rule that combined the process for obtaining construction and operating permits for commercial nuclear reactors and provided for preapproved, standardized design for reactors. Until 1989, the NRC required nuclear power plants to obtain separate permits for construction and operation. In 1989 the agency issued a rule that combined the two processes. The rule was unsuccessfully challenged in federal court, and Congress included the rule in the 1992 law. Utilities can now obtain a single license for both construction and operation. This streamlined the approval process for new power plants, requiring utilities to hold a public hearing before applying for the combined license. Opponents may petition for a second hearing if they can provide convincing evidence that the plant has not satisfied, or will fail to satisfy, at least one of the conditions specified in its license. Evidence must include specific operational consequences that would threaten public safety. The NRC can determine whether the hearing is informal or is bound by more formal, trial-type hearings. It can also allow interim operation of plants while the hearing takes place if it determines public safety will be protected. The law gives NRC the option to hold an informal or a more formal, trial-type hearing and whether to permit the utility to begin operating on a temporary basis during the hearing period.[32]

The 1992 Energy Policy Act also restructured the production of uranium enrichment, the process by which raw uranium is converted into fuel for nuclear reactors. It created the U.S. Enrichment Corporation, a federally owned corporation that was to eventually be privatized, to manage uranium enrichment efforts. The corporation was given exclusive rights to commercialize a new uranium enrichment technology called atomic vapor laser isotope separation in exchange for making royalty payments to the federal government. The Department of Energy will maintain control over the existing enrichment facilities: the federal government will finance 70 percent of the cleanup costs, and the nuclear power companies will finance the balance up to $2.25 billion over fifteen years, adjusted for inflation. The federal government is also funding research into the development of alternatives to the light-water nuclear reactors currently being used.[33] National energy laboratories have experimented with breeder reactors, which convert or breed uranium into plutonium, but funding for the research and development was cut in 1993.[34]

Finally, the 1992 energy law transferred the Department of Energy's uranium enrichment facilities to the U.S. Enrichment Corporation, a federally owned corporation that was given exclusive rights to commercialize a new uranium enrichment technology; in return, the corporation pays royalties to the federal government. The DOE retained ownership of existing enrichment facilities and leased them to the corporation. Seventy percent of the cost of cleanup of those facilities will be borne by the federal government, with nuclear power utilities providing the balance (their share is capped at $2.25 billion, indexed for inflation, over fifteen years). The 1992 act also directed DOE to develop two advanced-reactor prototypes by 1998. The department and other researchers have been working for years to develop a breeder reactor that produces or breeds plutonium from uranium that can be used in nuclear weapons or power plants. A liquid-metal breeder reactor demonstration project was canceled in 1983 because of concerns over cost and nuclear proliferation. Attention shifted to the development of the Integral Fast Reactor in federal labs. However, by 1993, advanced reactors fell victim to federal budget constraints, and funding was given low priority. The Clinton administration proposed eliminating this research effort in its 1993 economic plan, and DOE proposed ending funding for the latest reactor by 1998. Congress obliged in FY 1996, cutting spending for light breeder reactors to $40 million from FY 1995 spending of $49 million.[35]

High-Level Nuclear Waste. The storage of nuclear waste has become a major public policy challenge, and many proposals focus on the use of public lands as waste repositories. Three kinds of radioactive waste result from nuclear power: (1) high-level waste, such as spent reactor fuel rods; (2) transuranic (TRU) waste, made up of radioactive heavy elements, but less dangerous than high-level waste, and (3) low-level waste, including materials like clothing that have been exposed to radiation. High-level wastes remain radioactive for at least 10,000 years. The average reactor produces about 30 tons a year of high-level waste; more than 20,000 metric tons of waste have been generated since nukes began operating in the 1950s. By the year 2000, 40,000 metric tons are expected to have accumulated, and between 75,000 and 125,000 metric tons by the year 2020. These figures do not include the high-level waste produced in the manufacturing of nuclear weapons. Transuranic wastes contain radioactive elements that are heavier than uranium and are more dangerous than low-level wastes but less dangerous than spent nuclear fuel and other high-level wastes. TRU wastes are generated by the government's nuclear defense program.

The 1982 Nuclear Waste Policy Act ordered DOE to open a permanent, underground repository for high-level waste by 1998.[36] The act imposed a fee on electrical production by nukes; the fees accumulate in the Nuclear Waste Fund. The 1993 energy and water appropriations act[37] established the Defense Nuclear Waste Fund to fund development of a storage facility for nuclear weapons waste. The Department of Energy has constructed a disposal area near Carlsbad, New Mexico, that is designed to store about 850,000 fifty-five-gallon drums of TRU wastes in shafts and caverns in salt beds 2,200 feet underground.

The 1987 reconciliation act ordered the department to begin assessing the suitability of Nevada's Yucca Mountain, located one-hundred miles northwest of Las Vegas, serving as a permanent repository for the wastes and established the office of nuclear waste negotiator, who is responsible to find either a permanent repository for the waste or a temporary repository until a permanent site is established.[38] The site characterization studies of the suitability of the geological and hydrological features of Yucca Mountain for long-term storage were expected to take a decade. The DOE fell behind in its assessment schedule and postponed the date for opening the repository to 2010. The 1987 act also provides that if the study determines that Yucca Mountain is suitable, the DOE must then decide whether to select the site. The state can veto the decision, but Congress can override the veto. The site would also be subject to NRC and EPA regulations. If the site is found to be unsuitable, Congress must select another site. The 1992 Energy Policy Act ordered the DOE to promulgate nuclear waste disposal standards that would protect the public from any wastes stored at Yucca Mountain.

The future of Yucca Mountain is uncertain. The state of Nevada is actively opposing the site. Some nuclear power plants are running out of storage space for spent fuel rods and are demanding that the DOE accept the waste. One possible solution is to ship these wastes to federal nuclear weapons production facilities for temporary storage, but some residents of the affected states are opposed because they fear the storage could become permanent. The 1987 law authorized the creation of a monitored retrievable storage facility, but no suitable site has been found. The DOE recommended the development of interim storage of high-level waste along the Yucca Mountain site, but the 1982 law prohibits the siting of a temporary site in the same state as the long-term facility. Another option proposed during the 104th Congress is to build an interim storage facility before a permanent site is developed.[39]

The FY 1997 defense authorization bill included an amendment by Senators Craig and Kempthorne to exempt transuranic (TRU) wastes from some land disposal regulations and open the Waste Isolation Pilot Project (WIPP) facility in 1997.[40] Congress also considered legislation to create an interim high-level nuclear waste facility next to Yucca Mountain, Nevada. In March 1996, the Senate Energy and Natural Resources Committee passed such a bill.[41] The Clinton administration and Nevada senators opposed the legislation. The Clinton administration preferred instead the selection of a permanent site in Yucca Mountain but believes that site requires additional testing that will not be completed until 1998 or 1999. Despite decades of debate, there are no permanent storage facilities except for low-level wastes.[42]

Low-level Radioactive Waste. During the 1970s, low-level radioactive wastes were sent to one of six sites across the country. Environmental problems caused three of the sites to be closed down by the end of the decade. The three sites that remained—Hanford, Washington; Barnwell, South Carolina; and Beatty, Nevada—threatened to refuse shipments from other states and even close down their facilities. The Low-Level Radioactive Waste Policy Act of 1980 affirmed the responsibility that states had to develop solutions to the problems of low-level radioactive waste and gave states six years to establish regional sites for their disposal. Once approved by Congress, these regional compacts could reject wastes from outside the region. By that date, states would no longer be permitted to send waste to the three existing waste sites in Washington, Nevada, and South Carolina, and states would be required to either join a regional disposal system or dispose of their own waste. North Carolina, Nevada, and Washington established regional compacts with neighboring states, but other states failed to act.

Congress refused to ratify the three compacts so that the three states could not reject waste shipped from other areas. The three sites again threatened to shut down, prompting Congress in the Low-level Radioactive Waste Policy Amendments Act of 1985 to extend the deadline for the creation of other regional compacts to the end of 1992, and it approved seven regional compacts for the Northeast, Southeast, central states, Midwest, central Midwest, Northwest, and the Rocky Mountains.[43] The three compacts that include the existing waste sites (Southeast, Rocky Mountains, and Northwest) cannot refuse shipments from other areas. The existing sites can, however, charge higher fees for disposal of wastes from states outside their compact. The 1985 law required that by the beginning of 1993, the existing disposal sites were to accept shipments only from member states. If a region does not open disposal facilities by 1993, its member states were to take title to, and possession of, the waste (however, in 1992, the Supreme Court struck down this provision). The NRC could grant access to the existing sites if undisposed wastes posed a threat to public safety. Finally, the 1985 act required power plants to reduce their shipments to the three existing disposal sites by one-third between 1985 and 1992. Plants within the compact states were required to meet less stringent reductions. Plants could buy or sell unused waste disposal capacity. Nine groups of states have formed waste disposal compacts, and eight states are developing their own facilities, but no facilities were opened by the 1992 deadline. South Carolina agreed to continue to accept wastes but increased the disposal fees for sources outside the southeast compact region. The Hanford site accepted waste only from states in the Rocky Mountain and northwest compacts. Nevada closed its site in 1992 to further shipping.

The volume of low-level waste fell from 3.4 million cubic feet in 1980 to 1.1 million cubic feet in 1990 and is expected to continue to decline into the next century. The 1985 law also ordered the NRC to develop a policy that would deregulate the storage of some low-level radioactive waste and permit it to be incinerated or deposited in ordinary landfills. A regulation was proposed in 1990, but it met with strong criticism and was not implemented.[44]

Transuranic Wastes. Transuranic wastes are by-products of the production of nuclear weapons and are stored at nuclear weapons plants and laboratories. More than 6 million cubic feet of TRU waste is stored in nineteen nuclear weapons plants and laboratories. The Department of Energy constructed a Waste Isolation Pilot Plant near Carlsbad, New Mexico, underground shafts and caverns carved out of thick salt beds 2,200 feet beneath the earth's surface. The Waste Isolation Pilot Plant Land Withdrawal Act of 1992 transferred ownership of the land from the Interior Department to DOE and withdrew it from public use after a federal court had ordered the DOE to seek congressional approval before it could begin to bury waste on the site.[45] The 1992 act also prohibited the department from burying waste at the site until the EPA had issued new waste disposal regulations; the regulations had been invalidated by a federal court in 1987 for failing to protect groundwater from radioactive contamination. The EPA must also approve DOE's testing program and its plan to retrieve waste if the site proves to be inappropriate. The EPA rejected DOE's proposal to conduct a test burial of wastes in 1993 because the plans were incomplete and failed to demonstrate compliance with waste disposal standards. In 1994

DOE announced that it would stop tests and rely on laboratory experiments to determine compliance with EPA standards. In 1995, Representative Joe Skeen (R-NM) introduced a bill that would transfer responsibility from the EPA to the DOE for determining compliance with disposal standards.[46]

THE DEBATE OVER ENERGY AND MINERAL POLICY

Mining Reform

Reforming energy and minerals policy has been extremely difficult. Industries have had strong allies in Congress. Efforts to reform mining law have occurred for a century, but they were traditionally the domain of competing mining interests that wanted more protection of claims during exploration and statutory language to reduce litigation surrounding lodes that extended beyond the lateral boundaries of claims. Conservationists began demanding royalties, more guarantees of reclamation, and leasing of minerals rather than patenting of lands, but the mining industry has always strongly resisted such changes as inconsistent with the incentives required to encourage mining. Congressional reforms proposed during the last decade have been regularly stymied by Democratic and Republican senators from the West. In 1991, Senator Dale Bumpers (D-AR) began introducing bills to update the mining law, as he and others had done for oil and gas drilling on federal lands. The Senate Energy and Natural Resources Committee placed a one-year moratorium on mining patents in an interior appropriations bill but removed it on the floor under the threat of a filibuster. In the House, amendments to the Interior Department appropriations bill prohibited spending money to process patent applications. Representative Nick Joe Rahall (D-WV) introduced reform legislation as chair of Interior Committee's Mining Subcommittee that was debated on the floor but died at adjournment.

In January 1993, Rahall reintroduced legislation that would eliminate patenting, impose an 8 percent royalty on gross proceeds, mandate federal environmental standards for restoring mine sites, and authorize DOI and USDA officials to withdraw lands from exploration that were environmentally unsuitable for mining. Senator Bumpers proposed similar legislation in the Senate.[47] In February, the Clinton administration announced plans to use the budget process to reform public lands policy and, in particular, to impose a 12.5 percent royalty on hard-rock mining, which would raise $500 million over four years. Western senators, led by Max Baucus (D-MT), revolted against the budget proposal, and the Clinton administration beat a hasty retreat. That opened the door to mining legislation proposed by members of Congress sympathetic to industry concerns as a way to deflect more ambitious reform. Senators Larry Craig (R-ID), Harry Reid (D-NV), and other Western senators cosponsored legislation that would impose a 2 percent royalty on net proceeds from hard-rock mining, require miners to pay the fair market value of surface lands (not including value of minerals) in order to patent lands, pay a $25 fee for each claim and $100/claim/year to maintain the claim; and exempt from paying fees miners who filed fewer than ten claims. Two-thirds of the resulting revenue would go to the federal government, and one-third to the state in which the mines were located. Mines would be required to adhere to state reclamation standards (no effort was made to reconcile these widely divergent laws). The Senate passed the Craig bill in May 1993.[48]

In October 1993, the conference committee formed to complete work on the Interior Department's appropriations bill and considered, but failed to pass, a proposal to ban the processing of new patents. Legislation promoted by environmentalists was introduced in the House and passed by an overwhelming margin, 316 to 108, in November. The House bill would impose an 8 percent royalty (after shipping and smelting costs), dedicate the revenues to cleaning up abandoned mines, end patenting and keep ownership of mines in the hands of federal agencies, impose more stringent federal environmental standards, and allow DOI to protect some areas as unsuitable for mining.[49] House–Senate conferees met throughout the summer of 1994, but the threat of a filibuster by western senators caused them to abandon their efforts in October as the session drew to a close. However, in the Department of Interior appropriations bill passed in September, a provision imposed a one-year moratorium on new mining patent applications but permitted 420 of the existing 625 patent applications to be processed.

The Republican takeover of Congress in November 1994 blocked any chance of passage of an ambitious mining reform bill. Representatives Ken Calvert (R-CA), Barbara Vucanovich (R-NV), and Bill Orton (D-UT) introduced an industry-backed bill, but no action was taken.[50] Senator Craig reintroduced his bill in March 1995: it would require payment of "fair market value" rather than the fixed patenting fee and would set a 3 percent net royalty.[51] Mining reform engendered some political tension. House Resources Committee chair Don Young argued that the current law was satisfactory and should not be changed. Conflict between Senator Craig and Secretary Babbitt made it more difficult to build bipartisan bridges. A mining reform bill acceptable to industry interests was fashioned in the fall of 1995. It would have imposed a 5 percent net proceeds royalty; companies could deduct the cost of mining, transportation, processing, maintaining equipment, compliance with environmental regulations, and personnel and office expenses before calculating the royalties, and royalties would have been waived for net earnings less than $50,000. Patenting would be permitted at fair market value minus the value of the underground minerals. The mining reform bill was added to the Balanced Budget Act of 1995, a reconciliation bill that was vetoed by President Clinton in December 1995.[52] The Interior Department's appropriations bill was voted down by the House twice because it did not continue the moratorium on patents, and the provision was eventually included in the bill.[53]

The 1872 Mining Law has resulted in transferring more than $270 billion in mineral resources on federal lands to private interests. About $3.6 billion worth of minerals are removed each year from these lands. Almost half of the owners of these patents are companies controlled by foreign corporations. The examples provide tremendous targets for would-be reformers, but the mining industry has been remarkably adept at countering the attacks. The Interior Department took some initiative to reform mining policy by slowing down the process of reviewing patent claims. It negotiated with Kennecott Copper Corporation an agreement to pay a 3 percent royalty on mining profits in exchange for permission to expand its gold and silver mine into the Tongass National Forest in Alaska, the first hard-rock royalty ever paid to the federal government. The DOI negotiated with Noranda Incorporated, a Canadian company, to not dig a gold mine within three miles of Yellowstone Park. However, a federal judge ordered DOI to issue patents to the American Barrick Resources Corporation for 1,950 Nevada acres, containing an estimated $10 billion in minable gold, for $9,765—$5 an acre. The department also sold 110 acres of land in Idaho to an American subsidiary of Faxe Kalk Incorporated, a Danish company, for $275; the minerals were worth an estimated $1 billion. In 1993, the Manville Corporation purchased for $10,000, 2,000 acres of federal land in Montana that contained an estimated $32 billion of platinum and palladium. Companies need not mine the land themselves but can sell the land to others: in 1986, a mining company patented 17,000 acres in Colorado for $42,500 and immediately resold it for $37 million. Patented lands have been used for ski resorts, casinos, vacation homes, and golf courses.[54]

The 1872 law does not impose any reclamation requirements on miners. There are more than 550,000 abandoned hard-rock mines in the United States, primarily in the western states. More than 12,000 miles of streams have been contaminated by mining waste. The largest Superfund site—hazardous waste sites that are given priority for cleanup—is an abandoned mine in Montana; 55 other mines are on the Superfund list. Many of these sites are the result of a mining company mining a site, then abandoning it, declaring bankruptcy, and leaving the cleanup to others. One estimate of the cost of cleaning up mining wastes on public lands is $33 billion to $72 billion, depending on whether cleanup efforts include groundwater and toxic wastes.[55]

Environmentalists argue that current mining regulation has failed to protect against environmental damage to land and water. Other critics charge that the government is forced to virtually give land away and receives no royalties. Mining companies respond that the enormous costs of mining and the risks of finding profitable strikes preclude them from being able to afford royalties. Having to pay royalties, they warn, would result in loss of jobs and economic activity in the West, because production costs are so high. They also argue that they are already subject to numerous state and federal environmental laws. But 70 abandoned hard-rock mines are on the Superfund priority list; more than 130,000 mines pose safety and health hazards; and more than 10,000 miles of rivers have been damaged by mine wastes. A Congressional Budget Office study concluded that increased regulation would produce a net job gain because of work in land reclamation.[56]

Mining was at one time a major component of the economies of western states. But no longer. Mining of metals provides only about one-tenth of 1 percent of the jobs in the twelve western states. Mining jobs in the West have declined by 50 percent between 1980 and 1990. Only in Alaska, Montana, and Nevada has mining employment remained relatively constant. As mining jobs have been lost, the overall economies of these areas have boomed, clear evidence that mining has little impact on the economy of western states. While it is true that mining jobs pay relatively high wages, income from mining of metals still accounts for only less than 0.2 percent of total income in the western mining states. More significantly here, hard-rock mining on federal lands is only a fraction of the total mining activity in the West. Since the 1872 Mining Law permits miners to gain private ownership of the land, much of the mining occurs on private lands. A 1992 U.S. General Accounting Office study estimated that only about 15 percent of mining production took place on federal lands. Mining on public lands may represent no more than only four-hundredths of 1 percent of total employment, one of every 2,500 jobs.[57]

Mining is not likely to be a stable source of jobs and incomes for communities in the future. Mining has been a traditionally unstable industry, plagued by roller-coaster prices. The fall of real copper prices by 50 percent in the first half of the 1980s caused tens of thousands of miners to lose their jobs. Prices then increased by 70 percent between 1987 and 1989, fell by 40 percent in 1989, and then doubled by 1995. Gold prices peaked at more than $1,000 an ounce in 1981, then fell to one-half that price within a few years and in the mid-1990s was about one-third the peak price. Modest changes in prices that would result from imposing royalty fees on hard-rock mining would have a much smaller impact than these market-driven price changes. Mining jobs are also lost to automation and new extraction technologies as well as to falls in demand. When mining jobs are found, they often go to nonresident immigrants rather than locals. Exploration may result in a temporary increase in employment but end up disrupting the economy. There is no question that the transition to more sustainable, diverse economies is difficult. Mining jobs are often located in areas where few alternatives exist, and new jobs require relocation. Mining job loss can be devastating to workers and families, but these job losses have little impact on states' economies. When the Anaconda Copper Mine closed in Montana, employment fell by 20 percent, and real income by 15 percent. But five years later and after a much more diverse economy developed, one local government official observed, ''Now that I look back at it, one of the best things that ever happened to this community was Anaconda's leaving.''[58]

Mining is not only a minor element of western economies; the environmental damage that mining produces poses a major threat to their long-term economic viability. Mining often causes communities to sacrifice clean air, clean water, wildlife and recreation areas, and beautiful landscapes. As the supply of undisturbed landscapes decreases, the cost of environmental damage from mining and other extractive industries increases over time. The value of protected lands will increase as fewer such lands are found. The supply of wildlands cannot increase over time but will certainly decline, and their value will just as certainly increase over time. Communities that invest in mining sacrifice future opportunities that come from healthy landscapes.[59]

Opponents of reform argue that mining reforms such as charging royalties would devastate the western mining industry. But history shows such an outcome to be unlikely. The mining industry has always had to adjust to wide swings in commodity prices. Gold prices rose from $330 to $405 during the first six months of 1993, for example, six times the increase that would result from the imposition of an 8 percent royalty. An estimate of the impact of an 8 percent royalty increase on gold mining concluded that, at current prices, gold production would fall by only a slight amount, perhaps 1 percent, over the next decade. Other users of federal lands, such as energy developers, pay royalties. Only a small part of mining takes place on public lands, and federal land mining is such a small part of western states' economies that a decline in employment would be unnoticeable. An imposition of a royalty on gross proceeds would not raise prices by the amount of the royalty, since royalties can be deducted from state and federal taxes and are paid on the value of mined, not smelted and refined, minerals. Mine reclamation efforts will contribute to local economies and provide jobs and income.[60]

Future shortages of essential minerals are a major national concern. Estimates of mineral reserves are a function of several factors, including the rate of resource use, the amount of resources that can be economically mined (usually about 80 percent), the price, and the availability of substitutes. New reserves may be discovered that increase the available supply. Optimists believe that as resources become more scarce, prices will increase, fostering conservation, recycling, and the development of alternatives. Mining is also a risky enterprise. According to one formulation, for every 10,000 possible mining sites, only 1,000 are worth exploring, drilling or tunneling is worthwhile at only 100 sites, and only 1 site will be productive. Some increase in supply will likely come from more efficient extraction technologies that will permit us to use lower grades of ores, but extraction may still be limited by the availability of sufficient quantity of water, particularly in the Colorado Plateau, and the environmental consequences of waste may increase. Development of ocean floor resources and new materials to replace scarce minerals may also help meet demand, but perhaps at higher costs and inferior performance.[61]

But the costs of resource extraction must include environmental consequences. Mining consumes massive amounts of energy and water and produces massive amounts of waste. The development of new technologies in the 1980s, along with opening new areas to development, helped contribute to a decline in the price of many minerals (also a function of the global economic downturn in the early part of the decade). But these trends of lower prices are not likely to continue. As resources become less accessible, the energy and environmental costs of extraction increase. Cyanide heap leaching, for example, a new technology to retrieve gold from low-grade ore, involves spraying cyanide on massive piles of crushed rock, collecting the gold that is separated during the process, and storing the cyanide in collecting ponds that then contaminate wildlife and surface and subsurface water sources.[62]

Costs of products produced from mineral resources should also include the subsidies offered by governments to extractive industries. Supply and demand are so affected by subsidies that prices do not send accurate signals that permit rational, economically efficient choices about resource use. The federal government permits companies to deduct from their tax liability from 5 to 22 percent of their gross income, depending on the type of mineral, as a depletion allowance. Companies can deduct most of the expenses involved in exploration and development. Those costs are part of the true costs of having the minerals we use and should be accurately reflected in prices. Low prices for mineral extraction are also a problem since most of the costs of products come from manufacturing and distribution, and prices may not increase significantly as supplies dwindle until shortages occur. Much more beneficial to society would be to tax extraction of resources in order to send stronger market signals to conserve, recycle, and produce less pollution and waste.[63]

The agenda for federal mining law is straightforward: giving land managers discretion to prohibit mining that would result in serious adverse environmental consequences, requiring realistic reclamation bonds to ensure reclamation, and charging royalties to those who mine on public lands, and replacing the patenting of claims with leases.[64] Industry lobbyists are not likely to be able to block reform much longer. Indeed, some of them have acknowledged that the law needs to be changed. But fierce battles are likely when Congress eventually decides to pass a new mining law, and the negotiations focus on the details of legislation.

Energy Policy

Early in his presidency, Bill Clinton proposed a broad tax on all forms of energy in order to raise federal revenue to reduce the budget deficit. The proposed tax, called a Btu tax because it was based on the heating ability of different fuels, as measured by British thermal units, would have raised the prices of gasoline, electricity, and other energy sources. Environmentalists supported the measure as a way to promote conservation and to begin to move away from fossil fuel consumption. The tax would have raised only about $22 billion a year, only a tiny fraction of the $6 trillion U.S. economy, but opposition from Democratic and Republican senators representing energy-producing states killed the idea.[65] The administration was successful in raising gasoline taxes by 4.3 cents a gallon in 1993 as part of its deficit reduction plan. During the 1996 campaign, when gas prices jumped 17 percent during the summer, Republican candidate Bob Dole called for a repeal of the gas tax, and President Clinton called for an investigation of the oil companies and ordered the release of 12 million barrels of oil from the nation's Strategic Oil Reserve in order to soften the price increase.[66]

Increasing energy taxes sufficiently for significant conservation or revenue purposes requires more political skill than recent presidents and their congressional allies have been able to muster. The failure of policy debate here has been particularly remarkable. After adjusting for inflation, the price of crude oil in 1996, not including taxes, is less than one-half what it was in 1981. The average fuel efficiency of passenger vehicles climbed from 5.9 miles per gallon (mpg) in 1981 to 21.4 mpg in 1994; as a result, the average fuel cost per mile driven dropped during those years from 12.11 cents per mile to 3.38 cents per mile.[67]

Politically more popular have been proposals to deregulate the electric power industry, the last government-sanctioned monopoly. Deregulatory proposals have been made since the 1970s, as economists and power producers argued that increased competition would result in lower prices and improved efficiency. Large consumers such as industries are also active proponents of electricity deregulation. The agency responsible for regulating electricity production, the Federal Energy Regulatory Commission, issued in 1996 an order to utilities to open their transmission lines to any competing electric generator willing to pay fair transmission costs, paving the way for real competition in the industry. In 1996, two states, California and Rhode Island, enacted laws that brought competition into the industry, and almost every state was at least studying the idea. A number of deregulation bills was introduced in the 104th Congress and was a high priority of the Republican leadership's plan for the 105th Congress. The Clinton administration has promised its own plan. But the politics of energy policy is complicated: utilities want compensation for old investments such as nuclear power plants that will likely be unprofitable, the natural gas industry warns of increased profits to the electric companies and no benefits to consumers, westerners who enjoy cheap hydroelectric power fear national plans proposed by states whose residents have high electricity bills, and midwesterners want to burn more of their coal to produce power while northeasterners fear increased air pollution if they do. Environmentalists fear that deregulation will increase consumption and thereby increase fossil fuel emissions since coal-fired power plants are among the cheapest energy sources. As companies focus on the bottom line, they will be less willing to invest in research and production of more expensive renewable energy sources. Others argue that it is a mistake to tamper with the nation's electric power system when there is no pressing need to do so, and the system is arguably the best in the world.[68]

The recent debate over energy policy misses the evidence of a much broader policy failure. The mineral and energy resources of the United States played a key role in its emergence as a world power. However, the rise in the country's wealth has been built on an unsustainable rate of consumption of key resources. Each year, the nation imports more than 5 billion tons of fuel and nonfuel minerals to sustain its standard of living, about 21 tons for each person. The United States is the largest producer of nonfuel minerals but still must import half or more of twenty-four of forty-two key nonfuel minerals. Domestic reserves of many nonfuel minerals, such as manganese, cobalt, tantalum, niobium, platinum, chromium, nickel, aluminum, tin, antimony, and fluorine, will meet only about 10 percent or less of demand through the year 2000. Manganese, cobalt, platinum, and chromium are critical components of products such as home appliances, motor vehicles, and airplanes, and the United States is greatly dependent on imports from politically uncertain sources, primarily the former Soviet Union, South Africa, Zambia, and Zaire. About 62 percent of imports come from the more developed nations; 38 percent are imported from the less-developed nations.[69] The tremendous use of mineral and other resources by Americans raises profound issues of equity and fairness: less-developed countries provide the resources, usually at low prices forced on them by the economic clout of transnational corporations and the industrialized nations, and suffer the resulting environmental degradation, while the residents of the wealthy world continue to enjoy a high standard of living and consume many, many times the share of scarce resources used by those in the poorer nations.

Estimating the reserves of oil available for pumping and refining is difficult. The thirteen countries that form the Organization of Petroleum Exporting Countries (OPEC) control about two-thirds of all known reserves and each year supply 41 percent of total global production. That share continues to grow as more oil is discovered in the Middle East, and production declines from other fields in Alaska, Russia, and Mexico. The United States has about 4 percent of the known reserves, supplies about 13 percent of the total oil produced each year, and consumes about 30 percent of total world production. Petroleum production in the United States is declining: U.S. production has declined since 1985 and in 1993 fell to the lowest level since 1955. The United States imported 54 percent of the oil it used in 1994, and that figure is projected by some to rise to 70 percent by the year 2010.[70]

Crude oil or petroleum is dispersed in pores and cracks in rock formations throughout the earth's crust. Recovery of oil typically includes drilling a well and pumping out oil, then flooding the well with water to force out some of the remaining heavy oil. For each barrel of crude oil extracted, two additional barrels of heavy crude usually remain in the well. Extracting the remaining heavy crude is difficult and expensive: steam or carbon dioxide is pumped into the well to force the heavy oil into the well cavity where it can then be pumped out. The energy equivalent of one-third barrel of oil is needed to recover each barrel of additional heavy oil, and it may be economically feasible to recover only about 10 percent of the remaining heavy crude. More than half of American oil fields are at least 80 percent depleted and considered completely economically depleted. At current rates of consumption, current U.S. reserves will be depleted by the year 2018, and known global reserves will be exhausted by about 2040. One estimate is that even with the development of new oil fields and enhanced recovery processes, we may see depleted global oil resources within thirty-five to eighty years. These projections are quite uncertain. If consumption rates increase, reserves will be exhausted sooner. Rising prices may make more expensive extraction economically feasible, such as digging wells twice as deep as current ones.[71]

Oil continues to be a cheap source of energy. Average crude oil prices have not increased appreciably, in real terms, during the past twenty-five years. Its low price has encouraged waste and discouraged conservation. Its environmental costs are growing. They include the release of carbon dioxide, a greenhouse gas that is produced when oil is burned; localized air pollution that threatens human health, animals, and plants; oil spills; and contamination of groundwater by toxic wastes from drilling and exploration. Oil and gas leasing on federal lands is regulated through land use planning, leasing, exploration permits, and development permits. Much disagreement has arisen over how to integrate these reviews with environmental assessments required under the National Environmental Policy Act and federal agency planning statutes. Since the exact location of underground resources is often unknown initially, it is difficult to assess the environmental impacts of exploration and development. The effects of oil and gas exploration may occur after planning has been completed.[72] If the price charged for oil included all the costs of production and transportation, the cost of securing foreign supplies through military activity, and the environmental impacts, these true costs would likely encourage conservation and the development of alternative sources.[73]

One important alternative to petroleum, oil shale, is largely located on federal lands in the West, primarily in Colorado, Utah, and Wyoming. These reserves, some believe, could supply national demand for crude oil for forty years at current consumption rates. Canada, China, and areas in the former Soviet Union also contain large amounts of oil shale, and production from them might dwarf conventional petroleum supplies. Oil shale is rock that contains kerogen, a solid mixture of hydrocarbon compounds. The process of producing oil from shale is energy-intensive: the rock must be pulverized and heated underground to vaporize the kerogen; the vapor is condensed to produce thick shale oil and is then heated to remove impurities and make it flow in pipelines to refineries. The process of mining and preparing shale oil requires the equivalent of about one-half barrel of energy for every barrel produced, as well as large quantities of water, a formidable challenge in the western states. The process produces heaps of oil shale as well as salts and toxic chemicals that pollute groundwater.[74]

Tar sands, made up of clay, sand, water, and a heavy oil called bitumen, are another potential source of energy. Most reserves are located in Canada, Venezuela, Columbia, and the former Soviet Union; small reserves lie in the United States, primarily in Utah. The known reserves in the United States could supply total oil needs of the United States for about three months. Tar sands are removed by surface mining and heated with pressurized steam to soften the bitumen; the bitumen is then made into a synthetic crude oil that can be refined. As for oil shale, tar sands require the equivalent of one-half barrel of oil for each barrel produced and large quantities of water. The process also produces air pollution and waste disposal ponds.[75]

Crude oil and natural gas are often found together in the earth's crust. Conventional natural gas is found above crude oil reservoirs and is the source of the gas that is recovered. Unconventional natural gas is found by itself in coal seams, shale rock, deep underground deposits of tight sand, and deep zones where it is dissolved in hot water and is currently not extracted at economically feasible prices. About 40 percent of the world's natural gas reserves are in the former Soviet Union; the United States has about 5 percent of global reserves. Conventional deposits in the United States, if use continues at current levels, are expected to last for about 60 years. World conventional supplies are expected to last 80 years. If unconventional supplies are developed, and consumption rates remain unchanged, natural gas supplies might last for 200 years. Most natural gas reserves are located near crude oil, and many reserves in less-developed regions may be undiscovered. Natural gas fields include propane and butane gases that are liquefied, producing liquefied petroleum gas or LPG, typically used in rural areas that do not have access to natural gas pipelines. The remaining gas, primarily methane, is treated to remove water vapor and impurities and pumped into pipelines. Natural gas can be converted at low temperatures to liquefied natural gas (LNG) that can be shipped in refrigerated tanker ships. Natural gas is less expensive to produce than is petroleum, is easily transported via pipeline, and produces less air pollution when burned than does oil. Natural gas has promising uses in combined-cycle natural gas systems that produce electricity more efficiently and at lower cost than other sources (natural gas is burned in a gas turbine to produce electricity; then the excess heat in the turbine powers a second, steam turbine that produces more electricity), in co-generation facilities that produce heat and electricity, and in fuel cells. It poses risks when it is converted to LNG and is highly flammable, but the conversion is required in order to ship the gas by tanker. Leaks in pipelines and storage tanks release methane, a greenhouse gas. But natural gas is widely viewed as an important element in the transition from fossil to renewable energy sources.[76]

Coal is used to produce about one-fourth of the world's energy. China, the United States, and the former Soviet Union countries contain nearly 70 percent of the world's known coal reserves and some 85 percent of the estimated undiscovered reserves. At current rates of mining, existing world coal reserves will last for some 200 years, and unidentified reserves might last another 900 years. U.S. reserves are projected to last 300 years, at current rates of use, and may be augmented by another 100 years' worth of undiscovered reserves. In the United States, coal is the major fuel used to produce electricity (57 percent of the total produced); nuclear power plants provide 20 percent; natural gas provides 11 percent; hydropower, 9 percent; oil, 3 percent, and geothermal and renewal sources such as solar and wind energy, about 1 percent. Coal is roughly evenly divided between the eastern and western states: 45 percent of the nation's reserves are high-sulfur bituminous coal, found primarily in Illinois, Kentucky, Ohio, Pennsylvania, and West Virginia; the balance is located in Utah, Colorado,

Montana, and other intermountain states and Texas, primarily low-sulfur bituminous coal (low-sulfur coal produces less sulfur dioxide when burned).[77]

Coal is the most plentiful and least environmentally friendly fossil fuel. It produces particulate air pollution, which has been blamed for thousands of deaths each year and many times that number of cases of respiratory disease and distress. Coal-burning emissions also include radioactive matter that falls to the earth and is thousands of times more radioactive than the typical radioactive releases from nuclear power plants. It produces more carbon dioxide emissions per unit of energy produced than any other fossil fuel and is thus a major source of greenhouse gases. Coal mining disturbs land, contaminates streams and groundwater, causes land to sink from underground mining, and causes soil erosion. Coal emissions can be significantly reduced by installing sulfur dioxide scrubbers, fluidized-bed combustion systems, and other devices to remove sulfur dioxide and cause the coal to be burned more cleanly and completely. One study compared the *environmental* costs of producing electricity from different sources:

Source of energy	Cost in cents per kilowatt-hour[78]
coal	5.7
nuclear	5.0
oil	2.7
natural gas	1.0
biomass	0.7
solar cells	0.4
wind, geothermal	0.1

There are tremendous opportunities for increasing energy conservation and efficiency. Americans use only a small fraction of the energy they produce. According to one estimate, only 16 percent of commercial energy produced is actually used to perform tasks or produce petrochemicals; about half of the remaining 84 percent is unavoidably wasted (degraded as a result of the second law of energy), and the other half (43 percent of total production) is avoidably wasted through poorly insulated buildings, inefficient equipment, transmission, and other problems. A number of appliances and devices wastes much of the energy they receive: incandescent light bulbs (95 percent of energy is wasted), internal combustion vehicle engines (86–90 percent is wasted), and electricity-producing nuclear power plants (86 percent). Improving energy efficiency is one of the win-win-win natural resource options: investing in conservation can save money, improve environmental quality, and preserve nonrenewable fossil fuels longer and provide more time to move to renewable energy sources. The candidates for energy conservation have been clearly identified: cogeneration or production of two forms of energy such as steam and electricity in industry, switching to high-efficiency lighting, using more efficient motors and appliances, reducing air leaks in homes, increasing fuel efficiency of vehicles, shifting to mass transit, redesigning buildings to capture more solar energy, and increased use of insulation, among other efforts. Shifting from wasteful energy uses such as electricity for water and space heating would also reduce the demand for fossil fuels.[79]

Amory Lovins argues that cars waste 99 percent of the gasoline that they consume, that only 3 percent of the fuel burned in a power plant actually produces light in an incandescent bulb, and that the total waste of water, energy, mobility, and materials in the world may cost as much as $10 trillion a year. He argues that some 94 percent of the mass flow of materials used to produce American goods is jettisoned before manufacturing is completed, and about 80 percent of finished products are scrapped after just one use: "Somewhere near 99% of all the original materials used to manufacture goods in the United States ends up as waste within six weeks of sale."[80] One of Lovins' projects is the design of hypercars: "vehicles that are fully recyclable, 20 times more energy efficient, 100 times cleaner, and cheaper than existing cars. These vehicles retain the safety and performance of conventional cars but achieve radical simplification through the use of lightweight, composite materials, fewer parts, virtual prototyping, regenerative braking, and very small, hybrid engines."[81]

Nuclear Wastes. The production of electricity through nuclear power has failed to include the true cost of production, including the permanent, safe storage of waste. Light water reactors are made up of from 35,000 to 40,000 fuel rods that absorb neutrons as they are moved in and out of the core of the reactor. The fissionable uranium in fuel rods usually dissipates after three or four years, and spent fuel rods, as well as those damaged by ionizing radiation, must be removed and stored for at least 240,000 years. The waste resulting from the production of uranium fuel is radioactive for at least 10,000 years. Some plants to reprocess fuel rods have been built, but they have been plagued by problems, including the fear that materials could be diverted for the construction of bombs by terrorists and high construction and operating costs. The storage of radioactive waste has been similarly difficult.[82]

Low-level waste emits low levels of ionizing radiation and poses a threat for decades. Much of this waste has been encapsulated in steel drums and dumped in the ocean. Wastes from military weapons production are buried in government landfills. Commercial low-level wastes are increasingly shipped to regional dumps for storage, but these landfills eventually leak. One option for storing these wastes is to keep them on-site, where tests have already been conducted for construction of the plant on seismic stability, security, and trained personnel, and so avoid the need to transport them. But power companies have resisted being responsible for managing the wastes they produce. The NRC simply proposed that low-level waste be redefined as solid waste and disposed of like other household and industrial wastes. High-level wastes pose more daunting problems, and solutions range from burial deep underground in salt, granite, or other stable areas, to blasting the waste into space, to burying it deep in the ocean floor. A 1992 estimate found that some 45,000 sites in the United States contain contaminated material, nearly half of which are owned by the Energy and Defense Departments. The cost of cleanup may be from $400 to $900 billion over the next thirty years. The United States must also decommission and protect for thousands of years commercial reactors: as of 1994, twelve reactors in the United States were awaiting cleanup, and another twenty are expected to be decommissioned by 2012. Shutdown may cost a half a billion dollars per plant. As high as these costs are, they are dwarfed by the cost of cleaning up nuclear waste in the former Soviet Union.[83]

The first commercial nuclear power plants were built in the 1950s, encouraged by the federal government, which paid one-fourth of the construction costs of the first reactors and limited their liability in the case of accidents. One estimate found that the U.S. government has contributed about 20 percent or $100 billion to the $500 billion spent between 1950 and 1994 to develop commercial nuclear power. One reason there was so much investment in nuclear power was the belief that it would become the least expensive way to produce electricity and, except for the threat of accidents and the disposal of waste, is less environmentally threatening than the use of fossil fuels (the nuclear fuel cycle produces only one-sixth the level of greenhouse gases produced by burning fossil fuels to produce the equivalent of electricity). The most serious nuclear accident, at Three Mile Island (TMI) in Pennsylvania, in March 1979, occurred when, as a result of mechanical and human failures, the reactor's core became partially uncovered, about half of it melted and fell to the bottom of the reactor, and radioactive materials were released into the atmosphere. There is little agreement over the health effects of TMI, but the partial cleanup that has occurred has cost $1.2 billion. Critics of nuclear power point to the cost of this accident, studies that conclude there is a 15 to 45 percent chance of a complete core meltdown in a U.S. plant during the next twenty years, and obstruction of investigations by the body that regulates plant safety and waste disposal, the Nuclear Regulatory Commission.[84]

Policy Futures

The United States has no comprehensive strategy for dealing with the dwindling supply of fossil fuels, the problems with nuclear power and waste, and the shift toward renewable energy. But the prospects for such an expansive policy effort are not promising, given the failure of mining reform. Western senators' opposition to a compromise bill was deadly, even though the issues seemed manageable, at least in comparison with energy policy: federal, uniform cleanup standards versus state regulation; federal standards for protection of surface and groundwater from contamination by mining activities versus state regulation; administrative discretion and the power of federal land managers to deny permit applications for mines that would threaten sensitive lands and to create buffer zones; royalties; help for marginal operations; and patenting. Two members of Congress summarized the debate: "The time has come to end the policy of privatizing all the profits but socializing all the costs," said Representative George Miller (D-CA). "There is a point where [we] can't go farther, and that is when a bill is created that would cause a loss of more jobs. That is the point where we are going [to] stop," countered Senator Larry Craig.[85] That debate will continue. But there is some hope that it will shift to a debate between short-term, narrow perspectives and long-term, sustainability concerns. As soon as policymakers can be encouraged to take a longer view, the short-term disruptions involved in the move to long-term energy and environmental sustainability will become more manageable.

NOTES

1. 30 U.S.C. 22.
2. 30 U.S.C. 28.
3. George Cameron Coggins, Charles F. Wilkinson, and John D. Leshy, *Federal Public Land and Resource Law* (Westbury, NY: Foundation Press, 1993): 462.
4. Ibid.: 467–81.
5. 16 U.S.C. 478, 551. These regulations were promulgated under the 1897 Organic Act and are published at 36 C.F.R. 228.
6. FLPMA, 43 U.S.C. 1732(b); 43 C.F.R. 3809.
7. Coggins, Wilkinson, and Leshy, *Federal Public Land and Resource Law*: 506–8.
8. These cases are briefly reviewed in ibid.: 426–30, 445–47.
9. For a discussion of the cases specifying these exploration rights, see ibid.: 430–36.
10. Ibid.: 452–53.
11. 30 U.S.C. 181 et seq.
12. 30 U.S.C. 601–02, 611.
13. Coggins, Wilkinson, and Leshy, *Federal Public Land and Resource Law*; 512.
14. 30 U.S.C. 1201–1328.
15. P.L. 94–377.
16. P.L. 94–579.
17. P.L. 100–203.
18. P.L. 102–486.
19. Energy and Environment Study Institute (EESI), "Mining and Minerals," *1996 Briefing Book on Environmental and Energy Legislation* (Washington, DC: EESI, 1996): 44–45.
20. P.L. 100–203.
21. P.L. 102–486.
22. P.L. 95–621.
23. P.L. 101–60.
24. EESI, "Natural Gas," *1996 Briefing Book on Environmental and Energy Legislation* (Washington, DC: EESI, 1996): 46–48, at 46–47.
25. P.L. 90–481.
26. P.L. 96–129.
27. EESI, "Natural Gas": 47–48.

28. U.S. Bureau of the Census, *Statistical Abstract of the United States, 1996* (Washington, DC: U.S. Government Printing Office, 119): 578.

29. EESI, "Nuclear Policy," *1996 Briefing Book on Environmental and Energy Legislation* (Washington, DC: EESI, 1996): 51–52.

30. P.L. 100–408.

31. EESI, "Nuclear Liability," *1996 Briefing Book on Environmental and Energy Legislation* (Washington, DC: EESI, 1996): 49–50.

32. P.L. 102–486; EESI, "Nuclear Policy": 52.

33. The core of a typical light-water reactor is made up of from 35,000 to 40,000 fuel rods that are packed with uranium oxide pellets. The pellets are produced by combining nonfissionable and fissionable uranium and increasing the concentration of, or enriching, the fissionable uranium. Control rods that absorb neutrons are moved in and out of the core to absorb neutrons and control the fission and the amount of heat produced. Water, graphite, or some other material is used as a moderator to slow down the neutrons emitted and maintain the chain reaction. Water is typically used as a coolant to keep the fuel rods and other materials from melting and is also converted into steam.

34. EESI, "Nuclear Policy": 51–52.

35. Ibid.: 52.

36. P.L. 97–425

37. P.L. 102–337.

38. P.L. 100–203.

39. See 104th Congress, H.R. 1020, the Integrated Spent Nuclear Fuel Management Act.

40. Ibid.

41. 104th Congress, S. 1271.

42. P.L. 102–377.

43. P.L. 99–240.

44. EESI, "Nuclear Waste": 54, 105–6.

45. P.L. 102–579.

46. 104th Congress, H.R. 1663. See EESI, "Nuclear Waste": 54–55.

47. 103d Congress, H.R. 322, S. 257.

48. 103d Congress, S. 775.

49. 103d Congress, H.R. 1708.

50. 104th Congress, H.R. 1580.

51. 104th Congress, S. 506.

52. 104th Congress, H.R. 2491.

53. 104th Congress, H.R. 1977.

54. G. Tyler Miller Jr., *Living in the Environment* (Belmont, CA: Wadsworth, 1996): 502.

55. Ibid.: 502–3.

56. Catalina Camia, "Study of Abandoned Mines Stirs an Already 'Spirited Debate,' " *Congressional Quarterly Weekly Report* (July 24, 1993): 1951–52.

57. Thomas Michael Power, *Lost Landscapes and Failed Economies: The Search for a Value of Place* (Washington, DC: Island Press, 1996): 92–102.

58. Ibid.: 91.

59. Ibid.: 117–18.

60. Ibid.: 122–26.

61. Miller, *Living in the Environment*, 509–10.

62. Ibid.: 505–6.

63. Ibid.: 507–8.

64. Power, *Lost Landscapes and Failed Economies*: 120.

65. Susan Dentzer, "R.I.P. for the Btu tax," *U.S. News and World Report* (June 21, 1993): 95.

66. Howard Gleckman, "Gas Pump Politics," *Business Week* (May 13, 1996): 40–41.

67. "Resource Facts," *Resources*, no. 124 (Summer 1996): 4.

68. Jonathan Weisman, "Drive to Open Power Industry to Competition Gains Steam," *Congressional Quarterly Weekly Report* (October 12, 1996): 2911–17.

69. Miller, *Living in the Environment*: 504–5.

70. Ibid.: 374.

71. Ibid.: 374–76.

72. Coggins, Wilkinson, and Leshy, *Federal Public Land and Resource Law*: 556–58.

73. Miller, *Living in the Environment*: 376–77.

74. Ibid.: 377–78.

75. Ibid.: 378.

76. Ibid.: 378–82.

77. Ibid.: 381–84.

78. Ibid.: 383.

79. Ibid.: 332–43.

80. Lee Goldberg, "Green Engineering: Designing for a Brighter Future, Part 1," *Electronic Design* 45, no. 1 (January 6, 1997): 108.

81. Stuart L. Hart, "Beyond Greening; Strategies for a Sustainable World," *Harvard Business Review* (January 1997): 66.

82. Miller, *Living in the Environment*: 384–86.

83. Ibid.: 390.

84. Ibid.: 387–88.

85. Source of quotes: Camia, "Study of Abandoned Mines," at 1951.

8

Water Resources

THE POLICY FRAMEWORK

Water covers 71 percent of the earth's surface. Almost all of that water—97 percent—is located in the oceans; only 3 percent of the planet's water is freshwater, and 2.997 percent of that is located in ice caps or glaciers or otherwise inaccessible. The amount available for our use is only 0.003 percent of the earth's water supply, located in streams and lakes, water vapor, accessible groundwater, and soil moisture. Each day, 40 trillion gallons of water vapor pass over the United States. More than 4 trillion gallons fall as precipitation; two-thirds return to the atmosphere through evaporation and transpiration from bodies of water, vegetation, and the land. The balance passes into streams, lakes, underground water bodies, and the oceans. Precipitation is the source of nearly all freshwater and is the primary determinant of its availability.[1] Water constantly circulates among the land, the oceans, and the air through the hydrologic cycle, a continuous process of collecting, purifying, and distributing water that is sustainable as long as it is not interrupted by excessive pollution or withdrawn from underground sources at rates faster than they are recharged. Some 1,500 gallons for each American are withdrawn, used, and returned to the cycle each day. Each American uses about 90 gallons of water each day; another 600 gallons per person per day are used in manufacturing, and 800 gallons are used in agriculture.[2] In general, Americans use 41 percent of their water for irrigation, 38 percent for power plant cooling, 11 percent for other industrial uses, and 10 percent for municipal and household use. In the western United States, 85 percent of the water used goes for irrigation.

Water in the United States is provided either as surface water (streams, lakes, and wetlands formed by precipitation that is not absorbed by the ground or evaporated into the atmosphere) or groundwater (precipitation that is trapped in spaces between rocks and soil or water-saturated layers called aquifers). Aquifers are continually recharged by precipitation. Groundwater sources contain forty times the amount of water available from surface waters, but much of the groundwater that has been identified is not economically recoverable. Some aquifers are called fossil aquifers because they trap water in deep spaces that are recharged only after long periods of time and are essentially, for human purposes, nonrenewable resources.[3] Tables 8.1 and 8.2. provide an overview of the withdrawal of water in the United States.

Two major water policy questions are part of the overall agenda of public lands and natural resources policy. First, state (and federal) water laws, regulations, and programs are criticized for being inefficient, for failing to ensure that water is allocated in ways that maximize its value to society. Critics argue that water is wasted and that aggressive conservation efforts are required to prevent major shortages of water from occurring in areas of population growth.[4] In the West, these problems are aggravated by years of severe droughts. Second, efforts to ensure an adequate supply of water are often insufficiently coordinated with actions to protect water quality and water ecosystems.[5]

Water Supply

Ensuring an adequate supply of water, particularly in the arid West, has been the responsibility of two federal agencies, the Army Corps of Engineers and the Bureau of Reclamation, as well as state water boards, local irrigation companies, and a wide range of other institutions. The Corps of Engineers was established in 1802 as a branch of the Department of the Army. Its original jurisdiction over general construction for the military expanded over time. It was given responsibility for naval facilities in 1824 and for flood control and dam building in 1936. From the 1930s to the 1980s, it averaged construction of about ten large dams a year. In 1972, the corps was given responsibility for managing the nation's wastelands under the Clean Water Act. The Reclamation Service (later renamed the Bureau of Reclamation) was established by Congress in 1902 to assist settlers in the seventeen western states.[6] The bureau constructed massive water development projects in the West, including dams and canals such as Washington's Grand Coulee Dam and California's Central Valley Project. One other agency, the Federal Power Commission, created in 1920 and renamed the Federal Energy Regulatory Commission in 1977, is involved in water projects through its regulation of the hydroelectric and other electric power-producing industries. The two construction agencies became targets of congressional pork barrel projects, water developments in the districts of influential members of Congress. As a result, there have been close ties between congressional committees, water users, and the agencies. Appropriations bills have traditionally been filled with such projects. Projects have been built in most congressional districts, and funding often continued for projects even after they were completed, as members of Congress and lobbyists have ensured that benefits continue to flow to districts. The commission initially was responsible for regulating the nation's water resources, but its charter was eventually redirected to oversight of the electric power and natural gas industries.[7]

Agriculture in the West boomed after World War II, a result of new farming techniques, growth in the use of pesticides and fertilizers, and cheap, plentiful water from reclamation projects. The constituency for federally subsidized water projects expanded to serve municipalities, industries, and recreationists. Projects began to raise environmental concerns in the 1960s and 1970s as they infringed on areas preservationists sought to protect, such as a proposal to build Echo Park Dam in Dinosaur National Monument. The National Environmental Policy Act's requirements for environmental assessments gave environmentalists the opportunity to challenge proposed projects through litigation. Sometimes efforts backfired. Environmentalists successfully blocked plans to build a hydroelectric plant in the Grand Canyon; to offset the lost energy, the Mojave coal-fired power plant, located northeast of the canyon, increased its output. However, the Mojave eventually came to be blamed for producing emissions that harmed the visibility over the Grand Canyon.[8]

Support in Washington, D.C., for big western water projects began to falter in 1977, when the Carter administration created a ''hit list'' of nineteen water projects to be defunded, including the Central Arizona Project. But Congress refused to cut spending on any of the projects, although it did accept the administration's proposal for requiring states to share project costs. The Reagan administration continued the cost-sharing requirements on water projects, and some projects became less attractive to state and local governments as urban officials began to resist payments for projects that produced cheap water for farmers.[9] Bureau of Reclamation projects also became increasingly controversial as they were tied to environmental disasters such as dead waterfowl. In 1987, the bureau announced a formal shift in policy from construction to resource management and gave priority to ensuring continued production of water for urban areas. Even though the era of massive construction projects was over, there were still questions raised about how to fund water produced by these federal facilities. Years of subsidies have masked the true cost of producing water, and policymakers have been willing to use general tax revenues to meet the special water needs of westerners. Rate policies often encouraged development by giving high-quantity users discounted rates. Residential users often end up subsidizing industrial and agricultural water users by paying more for water than production costs would require.[10]

Despite the decline in big water projects, Congress continues to favor water projects. The Water Resources Development Act of 1986 authorized 262 new corps projects costing $16.3 billion. The federal government's share was $12 billion; nonfederal parties were to pay from 20 to 60 percent of the costs for

Table 8.1
Water Withdrawals and Consumptive Use—States and Other Areas, 1990 (in Millions of Gallons per Day, except as Noted)

State or other Area	Water Withdrawn		Source		Consumptive use freshwater[1]
	Total	Per capita	Groundwater	Surface water	
U.S.[2]	407,900	1,340	80,640	327,260	93,980
Alabama	8,090	2,000	403	7,680	454
Alaska	641	517	112	529	26
Arizona	6,570	1,790	2,740	3,830	4,350
Arkansas	7,840	3,330	4,710	3,130	4,140
California	46,800	1,180	14,900	31,900	20,900
Colorado	12,700	3,850	2,800	9,910	5,250
Connecticut	4,840	325	165	4,680	103
Delaware	1,370	1,540	89	1,280	59
District of Columbia	9	15	1	8	16
Florida	17,900	582	4,660	13,200	3,130
Georgia	5,350	816	996	4,360	822
Hawaii	2,740	1,070	590	2,150	627
Idaho	19,700	19,600	7,590	12,100	6,090
Illinois	18,000	1,570	945	17,100	750
Indiana	9,430	1,700	621	8,810	451
Iowa	2,860	1,030	495	2,370	271
Kansas	6,080	2,460	4,360	1,720	4,410
Kentucky	4,320	1,170	247	4,070	309
Louisiana	9,350	2,200	1,340	8,010	1,590
Maine	1,140	433	85	1,060	51
Maryland	6,420	307	239	6,180	126
Massachusetts	5,520	338	338	5,180	195
Michigan	11,600	1,250	707	10,900	738
Minnesota	3,270	748	797	2,480	872
Mississippi	3,640	1,290	2,670	963	1,800
Missouri	6,930	1,150	728	6,200	529
Montana	9,320	11,600	218	9,100	2,090

210

Water Withdrawn

State or other Area	Total	Per capita	Source Groundwater	Source Surface water	Consumptive use freshwater[1]
Nebraska	8,940	5,660	4,800	4,150	4,230
Nevada	3,350	2,780	1,070	2,280	1,690
New Hampshire	1,310	378	64	1,250	26
New Jersey	12,800	287	566	12,200	211
New Mexico	3,480	2,300	1,760	1,720	2,060
New York	19,000	583	840	18,100	562
North Carolina	8,940	1,350	435	8,510	390
North Dakota	2,680	4,190	141	2,540	228
Ohio	11,700	1,080	904	10,800	901
Oklahoma	1,670	452	905	760	659
Oregon	8,430	2,970	767	7,660	3,160
Pennsylvania	9,830	827	1,020	8,810	581
Rhode Island	526	132	25	501	18
South Carolina	6,000	1,720	282	5,720	293
South Dakota	592	851	251	341	345
Tennessee	9,190	1,880	503	8,690	252
Texas	25,200	1,180	7,880	17,300	9,020
Utah	4,480	2,540	971	3,510	2,230
Vermont	632	1,120	45	587	29
Virginia	6,860	762	443	6,420	224
Washington	7,940	1,630	1,450	6,490	2,830
West Virginia	4,580	2,560	728	3,860	509
Wisconsin	6,510	1,330	681	5,830	461
Wyoming	7,600	16,700	403	7,200	2,730
Puerto Rico	3,040	163	157	2,880	199
Virgin Islands	164	91	3	160	2

[1]Water that has been evaporated, transpired, or incorporated into products, plant, or animal tissue and therefore is not available for immediate reuse.

[2]Includes Puerto Rico and Virgin Islands.

Note: Figures may not add due to rounding. Withdrawal signifies water physically withdrawn from a source. Includes fresh and saline water. *Source:* U.S. Department of Commerce, *Statistical Abstract of the United States, 1996* (Washington, DC: U.S. Government Printing Office, 1996): 232.

Table 8.2
U.S. Water Withdrawals and Consumptive Use per Day, by End Use, 1940–1990

Year	Total bil. gal.	Per capita[1] gal.	Irrigation bil. gal.	Public Supply[2]		Rural[4] bil. gal.	Industrial and misc.[5] bil. gal.	Steam electric utilities bil. gal.
				Total bil.gal.	Per Capita[3] gal.			
Withdrawals								
1940	140	1,027	71	10	75	3.1	29	23
1950	180	1,185	89	14	145	3.6	37	40
1955	240	1,454	110	17	148	3.6	39	72
1960	270	1,500	110	21	151	3.6	38	100
1965	310	1,602	120	24	155	4.0	46	130
1970	370	1,815	130	27	166	4.5	47	170
1975	420	1,972	140	29	168	4.9	45	200
1980	440	1,953	150	34	183	5.6	45	210
1985	399	1,650	137	38	189	7.8	31	187
1990	408	1,620	137	41	195	7.9	30	195
Consumptive Use								
1960	61	339	52	3.5	25	2.8	3.0	0.2
1965	77	403	66	5.2	34	3.2	3.4	0.4
1970	87	427	73	5.9	36	3.4	4.1	0.8
1975	96	451	80	6.7	38	3.4	4.2	1.9
1980	100	440	83	7.1	38	3.9	5.0	3.2
1985	92	380	74	(6)	(6)	9.2	6.1	6.2
1990	94	370	76	(6)	(6)	8.9	6.7	4.0

[1]Based on Bureau of the Census resident population as of July 1. [2]Includes commercial water withdrawals. [3]Based on population served. [4]Rural farm and nonfarm household and garden use, and water for farm stock and dairies. [5]For 1940 to 1960, includes manufacturing and mineral industries, rural commercial industries, air-conditioning, resorts, hotels, motels, military and other state and federal agencies, and miscellaneous; thereafter, includes manufacturing, mining and mineral processing, ordinance, construction, and miscellaneous. [6]Public supply consumptive use included in end-use categories. Note: Includes Puerto Rico. Withdrawal signifies water physically withdrawn from a source. Includes fresh and saline water; excludes water used for hydroelectric power.
Source: U.S. Department of Commerce, *Statistical Abstract of the United States, 1996* (Washington, DC: U.S. Government Printing Office, 1996): 233.

deepening harbors and 25 to 50 percent of flood-control costs. The act also imposed a tax of 0.04 percent on the value of cargo passing through U.S. ports; that was raised in 1990 to 0.125 percent. Funds go to a harbor maintenance trust fund to pay for harbor operations and maintenance expenses. The 1988 Water Resources Development Act (WRDA) authorized sixteen new projects; the 1990 WRDA, twenty-six new projects; and the 1992 WRDA, twenty-three new projects. Each legislation raised questions about cost sharing, user fees, and how to pay for projects; the appropriateness of subsidized water for farmers to grow certain crops that are highly dependent on federal subsidies; the failure to promote conservation; and pollution and water quality resulting from the projects. Table 8.3 provides illustrations of how Congress has allocated costs to water users in different statutes.

Regulating Water Use

The scarcity of water in the West is one of its most critical characteristics. Subsidizing the production of water is one response. A second policy that deserves brief mention here is the way in which water is allocated among users on public as well as private lands. A system of riparian rights is built on the assumption that there is sufficient water to meet the needs of all those who have rights to it if they will limit their demands to reasonable uses. In contrast, appropriation law was developed to manage the distribution of water in arid areas, primarily in the western states.[11] Nine states rely on appropriation law,[12] and ten recognize both riparian rights and appropriation (often referred to as the "California Doctrine")[13]; the balance of the states are considered riparian states.

Riparianism is ultimately grounded in the idea of utilitarianism: each riparian rights holder is to make a reasonable use of his or her water and, in so doing, contributes to the most beneficial use of the resource as a whole.[14] What constitutes reasonable use has been widely discussed in court decisions and in legal commentary. One summary of the law on the reasonable use of water argued for a consideration of:

(a) The purpose of the use, (b) the sustainability of the use to the watercourse or lake, (c) the economic value of the use, (d) the social value of the use, (e) the extent and amount of the harm it causes, (f) the practicality of avoiding the harm by adjusting the use or method of use of one proprietor or the other, (g) the practicality of adjusting the quantity of water used by each proprietor, (h) the protection of existing values of water uses, land, investments and enterprises, and (i) the justice of requiring the user causing harm to bear the loss.[15]

Among riparian users, priority is given to the use of water for domestic purposes; after that, all other uses are to be recognized as equally valid.[16]

A number of challenges confront states that recognize and rely on riparian rights in allocating water.[17] One concern is how to provide water to nonriparian

Table 8.3
Some Significant Changes in Reclamation Law regarding Allocation of Project Costs to Irrigators and Their Repayment of These Costs

Statute	Change
Reclamation Act of 1902 (32 Stat. 388)	• Irrigation projects are authorized. • Construction is funded via a revolving fund. • Repayment of costs takes place over 10 years. • Repayment is interest-free.
Town Sites and Power Development Act of 1906 (34 Stat. 116)	• Establishment of towns and provision of water are authorized. • Projects' surplus power can be sold to towns and the revenues credited to repayment of irrigation costs.
Advances to the Reclamation Fund Act of 1910 (36 Stat. 835)	• U.S. Treasury is directed to loan up to $20 million to the fund to finance completion of the construction of water projects.
Reclamation Extension Act of 1914 (38 Stat. 686)	• Repayment period is extended from 10 to 20 years
Fact Finders' Act of 1924 (43 Stat. 672)	• Irrigators' repayments are amended to 5 percent per year of their average crop value based on the preceding 10 years. • Use of project revenues from nonirrigation activities, such as power sales and surplus water sales, is authorized for repayment of irrigators' construction costs and payment of operation and maintenance costs.
Omnibus Adjustment Act of 1926 (44 Stat. 636)	• Repayment period is extended from 20 to 40 years. • Irrigators are relieved of parts of their repayment obligations because of nonproductive land at specified projects.

Five Million Dollar Advance to the Reclamation Fund Act of 1931 (46 Stat. 1507)	• U.S. Treasury is directed to loan up to $5 million to the fund to finance completion of the construction of water projects.
Reclamation Project Act of 1939 (53 Stat. 1187)	• Multipurpose water projects are authorized, allowing for power, municipal and industrial water supply, navigation, and flood control as project purposes. • Construction of projects is financed by appropriated funds. • Development period of up to 10 years is added to the irrigators' repayment schedule. • Some construction costs are designated as nonreimbursable. • Power costs are to be repaid with interest. • Municipal and industrial water supply costs can be repaid with interest. • Repayment of irrigation costs remains interest-free.
Rehabilitation and Betterment Act of 1949 (63 Stat. 724)	• Repayment of expenditures is authorized for the rehabilitation and betterment of the irrigation systems of existing Bureau projects in installments fixed according to the water user's ability to pay.
Federal Water Project Recreation Act of 1965 (P.L. 89-72, 79 Stat. 213)	• Up to 50 percent of the separable construction costs for recreation and fish and wildlife enhancement are deemed nonreimbursable. • Reimbursable costs for these purposes are to be repaid with interest over 50 years.

Source: U.S. General Accounting Office, "Bureau of Reclamation: Information on Allocation and Repayment of Costs of Constructing Water Projects" (Washington, DC: U.S. GAO, July 1996): 34.

lands; water may be wasted in some areas, while in other areas land may be unusable without water. That concern raises a broader one: what if the community or society as a whole that extends beyond riverbanks and lakeshores may benefit from a wider distribution of water? The wider the basis for calculating social benefit, the less compelling is the argument that the most beneficial use of water is to limit its use to riparian rights holders. Once riparian rights holders are satisfied, water rights may then be allocated to nonriparians. But some protection is afforded nonriparians: they can make a beneficial use of water as long as they do not adversely affect riparian proprietors, and nonriparians who are reasonably using water in ways that do not adversely affect riparians are entitled to protection from wasteful use of water. But riparian rights systems apparently do not provide for a resolution of conflicts between nonriparians.[18]

In response to these and related problems, some states have superimposed administrative mechanisms on the common law structure. Eleven states, for example, require administrative permits for new uses.[19] The other riparian states (except Louisiana and Hawaii, which have unique systems) have enacted statutes to balance riparian rights with other public concerns, such as the building of dams and storage of water, the use of water by municipalities and states, and the maintenance of minimum instream flows. According to Trelease and Gould, "These statutes, rather than the common law, have become the important features of modern water law" in these states.[20]

Another set of challenges in regulating water use in riparian states is the interaction of riparian and underground water sources. Regulating the use of groundwater poses a number of difficulties. Since it is not visible, there is usually great uncertainty in estimating the volume of available water. The amount of water is a function of the size of the underground stock as well as the rates by which it is recharged and the withdrawals of surface water that would otherwise recharge the underground stock.[21] The law must achieve some balance between withdrawals and the maintenance of an adequate stock for future use. The cost of extracting water varies according to a number of factors, such as the depth of the groundwater; the feasibility of pumping water for one owner might differ significantly from that of another.[22] Water withdrawals could be regulated according to a number of different criteria; ranging from withdrawing as much as can be withdrawn each year ("maximum sustained yield"), to withdrawing the "maximum volume of water in storage in a particular source that can economically and legally be extracted and utilized for beneficial purposes, without bringing about some undesired result" ("permissive mining yield"), to withdrawing until it is "harmful to the aquifer itself, or to the quality of the water, or is no longer economically feasible."[23]

There is great variety in the approaches taken by the fifty states. Seven states rely on the ownership rule, where the underground water is owned by the landowner, who can withdraw as much water as he or she wishes.[24] Eighteen states have accepted the reasonable use rule, where the withdrawal of groundwater must be for reasonable uses that are connected to the land itself (Louisiana's civil code has a similar provision).[25] Four states have correlative rights for underground water that are similar to riparian requirements of reasonable sharing.[26] Permits are used to regulate water withdrawal in all or part of fourteen states.[27] In five states, the same law applies to surface and subsurface water[28]; nine states have a separate code for underground water.[29] Many states do not regulate surface and underground water together, despite their interrelationship. Most require that a landowner's withdrawal of underground water be "reasonable," but withdrawals from surface water may affect recharging of underground aquifers.[30]

Water Quality

The Clean Water Act (CWA) of 1948, amended in 1956, 1961, 1965, 1966, 1970, 1972, 1977, 1980, 1981, 1983, and 1987,[31] seeks to "maintain . . . the integrity of the Nation's waters" and to eliminate discharge of pollutants into navigable waters . . . , including the discharge of toxic chemicals."[32] The law instructs the EPA to regulate industrial and municipal discharges into surface waters of conventional, toxic, and certain nonconventional pollutants. Conventional pollutants deplete oxygen in the receiving waters, alter the pH level, contribute suspended solids, or are fecal matter or oil and grease. Toxic pollutants comprise sixty-five chemicals and classes of chemicals, which form about 130 priority pollutants; the EPA has established ambient water quality criteria for these chemicals and chemical classes and has issued industrial and municipal effluent guidelines and pretreatment standards to ensure these criteria are met. Nonconventional pollutants include ammonia, phosphorus, and other chemicals that do not fit into either of the previous categories.[33] All industries and governments that discharge effluent and storm water directly into surface waters must have a permit issued as part of the National Pollution Discharge Elimination System. Permits are written specifically for each source and are based on the effluent guidelines the EPA has established for each industry as well as on the quality of the water in which the discharge occurs. The CWA requires the EPA to establish limits on discharges of pollutants from specific industrial sources; different sources must meet different levels of best or available technology. Existing facilities that discharge directly into surface waters must treat effluents using the best practicable technology. Sources of conventional pollutants must employ best conventional technology. Sources of toxic and nonconventional pollutants must meet the more stringent best available technology standard. Because state-of-the-art control technologies are believed to be easier and cheaper to install in new facilities, those sources must use the best available demonstrated control technology that aims at zero discharge.[34]

The CWA requires states to establish water quality standards based on the use of the water and the water quality required to support that use and a prohibition against downgrading of water except under unusual circumstances. At a minimum, states must classify their water bodies into one of the following categories:

Class A: primary water-contact recreation

Class B: able to support fish and wildlife

Class C: public water supply

Class D: agricultural and industrial use

Most states have developed more extensive categories and give particular protection to certain waters. These state water quality standards, along with EPA limits on discharges of pollutants from different industrial sources, provide the basis for the permits that establish the specific discharge limits for industries and publicly owned treatment works (POTWs). These POTWs must also have permits before they can discharge effluent, but since they are not equipped to process some industrial wastes, those sources must pretreat their effluents before they are released into the municipal system. These industrial sources are not covered under the National Pollution Discharge Elimination System (NPDES), but POTWs are, and local governments have the incentive to ensure that industrial sources meet their pretreatment requirements so POTWs can comply with their permits. States usually manage their own system, with oversight by the EPA, and can impose more stringent discharge or pretreatment requirements than provided in federal standards. Industrial facilities and local governments must also file for permits to govern their storm water discharges.

States must also identify water bodies that are expected to violate water quality standards because of the presence of toxic chemicals and develop a plan to bring them into compliance within three years. If states fail to act, the EPA must develop its own compliance plan. Major spills of oil and hazardous substances must be reported to the National Response Center. Under section 404 of the CWA, the U.S. Army Corps of Engineers is to issue permits for discharge of dredged and fill material into navigable waters and wetlands or for any other activity that changes the nature of wetlands. The EPA can object to the issuance of such permits if it finds that discharges will have an unacceptable, adverse impact on the environment. Violations of the Clean Water Act are punishable through fines of $10,000/day/violation; for willful or negligent violations, criminal penalties of up to $25,000/day and up to one year in prison are provided and doubled for repeat offenders. Citizen suits are authorized to enforce standards, limitations, permit conditions, and compliance orders and compel nondiscretionary actions required of state or EPA officials. States are to develop plans for nonsource pollutants, and state and local governments have primary responsibility for groundwater quality.

The 104th Congress tried, but failed, to update the Clean Water Act. The House passed in May 1995 a rewrite of the Clean Water Act that would have established a new classification scheme for wetlands: the least valuable lands would no longer be protected by the federal government, and less protection would be given to the remaining wetlands. The bill would have also required government agencies to compensate landowners for any loss in property values of 20 percent or more due to wetlands regulations. A similar bill was introduced in the Senate, minus the provision for compensating landowners.[35] A 1995 National Academy of Sciences report defended the current criteria for identifying wetlands and recommended consolidation of responsibility for wetlands in a single agency. Environmentalists have become increasingly concerned about the loss of wetlands, while farmers, developers, and advocates of private property rights have charged that wetlands restrictions infringe on the rights of landowners. Other issues, such as how to control runoff from melting snow and rainwater, whether or not to tighten controls on discharging toxic chemicals, whether or not to make more stringent enforcement efforts, and expanding the act to include groundwater protection also contributed to congressional failure to reauthorize the act. Moderate Republicans and the Clinton administration opposed the bills, which died when Congress adjourned in 1996. However, Congress did pass the Federal Agriculture Improvement and Reform Act in April 1996, which replaced the traditional price support subsidies to farmers with transitional payments. The act included a Wetland Reserve Program to help landowners contribute to the goal of no net loss of wetlands by permitting farmers to receive payments for allowing part of their land to remain undeveloped as wetlands.[36] But wetlands regulation continued to be controversial, fueled in part by enforcement actions taken against landowners that have become widely publicized and criticized by private property activists. In 1996, a judge in Maryland sentenced James J. Wilson, a prominent developer, to twenty-one months in prison and fined him $1 million and his company $3 million for illegally filling in wetlands. Wilson was convicted of destroying about thirty acres of wetlands from 1989 to 1993 in the planned community of St. Charles. In 1990, another developer, Paul Tudor Jones, was also fined $1 million for damaging wetlands, the largest fines imposed since the law went into effect in 1976.[37]

The Safe Drinking Water Act (SDWA) of 1974, as amended in 1977, 1979, 1980, 1986, 1988, and 1996,[38] authorizes the EPA to issue national primary drinking water standards that set maximum levels of specified contaminants (maximum contaminant levels or MCLs) for substances in drinking water that might be hazardous to human health. Congress identified 83 contaminants to regulate; the EPA has identified some 700 contaminants in drinking water. The act also bans the use of lead in pipes or solder for drinking systems, although existing lead pipes can be left in place. States are responsible for enforcing the law, subject to EPA involvement if states fail to do so. The law requires that consumers be notified when monitoring has not taken place or when contaminant levels exceed standards. States are required to use the "best available technology" to meet the standards. The SDWA also requires states to protect underground water supplies.[39] In 1996, Congress and the White House enacted several pieces of legislation just before the election, including the amendments to the Safe Drinking Water Act. The amendments give more discretion to states and local governments to determine what contaminants pose a threat to human health. The new law emphasizes controlling the greatest risks for the most benefit at the least cost. It requires local water agencies to issue annual reports disclosing the chemicals and bacteria in tap water. The reports must be written in simple, accessible language and sent to residents enclosed with their utility bills. Agencies must notify the public when water contaminants pose a serious threat. The new law also authorizes a $7.6 billion revolving fund to loan money to local water agencies for construction of new facilities. Small water systems can get waivers from compliance with some federal regulations.[40]

THE POLICY DEBATE

Water shortages resulting from droughts in the 1980s and early 1990s, along with projections of future shortages, have heightened concerns about how scarce water resources are allocated.[41] Current patterns of water consumption are unsustainable, and federal budget deficits and the increasing criticisms of pork barrel water projects have dramatically curtailed the development of new projects.[42] Funds to complete the Central Utah Project, for example, were held up for three years as they became intertwined with controversies over efforts to reform Bureau of Reclamation policy and how water from California's Central Valley Project will be distributed among farmers, urban dwellers, and ecosystems.[43]

Despite the water projects in place and planned for the future, there is a growing gap between water supply and use, and addressing these anticipated shortages will be a major policy challenge in states throughout the nation.[44] The figures in the following table provide one estimate of water use in the United States. Agriculture is the single largest user of water; in the West, nearly 85 percent of all water used is in agriculture.[45] Water withdrawal more than doubled between 1950 and 1990 as a result of population growth and increased agricultural and industrial output.[46] Droughts in the late 1980s and early 1990s have greatly increased pressure on existing water resources. High rates of evaporation also contribute to water shortages in the West. Average surface water withdrawal exceeds average streamflow in several areas, particularly the Great Basin, Rio Grande, and Colorado River Basins.[47]

Water Use in the United States[48]

Kind of use	Percent of total
Agriculture	41%
Electric cooling	38
Industry	11
Public*	10

*Includes all other uses

About half the drinking water, 40 percent of the irrigation water, and 23 percent of all freshwater are withdrawn from underground sources; the balance of freshwater for human use comes from rivers, lakes, and reservoirs.[49] In some states, such as Florida, Hawaii, Idaho, Mississippi, Nebraska, and New Mexico, more than 90 percent of their population relies on aquifers for drinking water.[50] But water is being withdrawn from underground aquifers throughout the country at rates much higher than they are recharged; about 25 percent of the ground-water withdrawn is not replenished, and that figure climbs to more than 75 percent in parts of Texas.[51] Depletion also threatens water quality as salt water and groundwater contaminate aquifers.[52] The Ogallala Aquifer, lying under the states of Colorado, Kansas, Nebraska, New Mexico, Oklahoma, South Dakota, Texas, and Wyoming, for example, is used to irrigate one-fifth of all croplands that rely on water sources other than rainfall. The overall withdrawal rate from the aquifer is eight times its natural recharge rate; in some states, including Colorado, New Mexico, Oklahoma, and Texas, the withdrawal rates are as high as one hundred times the recharge rates.[53]

Shortages of water in Arizona, California, Idaho, Nevada, New Mexico, Oregon, Utah, and Wyoming have occurred since 1980; by the year 2000, the rest of the western states and the midwest states are all expected to suffer water shortages. Midwest and western states are also very vulnerable to shortages in water supply that might result if the world's climate becomes warmer, as many scientists have warned will happen.[54] Both water withdrawal and water consumption have dramatically increased in the United States and are expected to continue, as shown in Table 8.1.

Millions of acre-feet of water are used in the western part of the United States to raise crops that are in surplus and must be stored, that are of extremely low value in comparison with other products of water use, and that grow easily in states with adequate rainfall.[55] Federal and state policies encourage wasteful use by failing to ensure that the real costs of producing water are reflected in the price charged users.[56] In some cases, water is not even metered, and the same price is charged regardless of the quantity used.[57] The cost of water to consumer varies across the nation as a result of subsidies as well as a variety of other factors:

Average Monthly Household Use and Cost of Water[58]

	Amount	Cost per 100 gallons
Santa Barbara	4,488 gal.	14.6 cents
Tucson	8,600	13.7
New York City	7,650	12.6
Miami	8,750	10.3-11.9
Chicago	7,480	8.9

Note: Rate varies with season and/or water usage. Rate is averaged between house and apartment use.

Federal water subsidies, subsidies for the development of hydroelectric power, crop subsidies, constraints on the transfer of water rights, and other policies have distorted markets and resulted in inefficient allocation and use of scarce water.[59] Recipients of water generated by reclamation projects in the West have rarely met the reimbursements schedules outlined in federal laws. The U.S. Department of the Interior has identified federal programs that "distort markets, promoting inefficient development and undermining conservation efforts."[60] Table 8.4 provides some examples of projects where the federal government subsidized from 11 to 82 percent of the costs of irrigation projects.

Benefit-cost analysis, now widely used in the federal and state governments, was first used to analyze water resource projects in the 1930s.[61] But critics charge that it has been widely abused and misused in providing justification for wasteful and inefficient projects that are unjustified when realistic projections of costs are compared with the benefits they promise.[62] These criticisms are rooted in analyses initiated in the Ford administration of the costs and benefits of regulation.[63] They continued during the Carter presidency with the formulation of a "hit list" of water projects in many of the western states where the Bureau of Reclamation failed to demonstrate to the satisfaction of White House officials that the benefits of these projects outweighed their costs.[64] Some projects, however, were located in the South and East, including the Tennessee-Tombigbee project in Mississippi and Alabama.[65] Jimmy Carter, running for president in 1976, said that "I personally don't believe that any of these projects ought to be built"; as president, he warned that "the federal government's dam-building era is coming to an end."[66]

The criticisms of these projects continued into the Reagan administration.[67] In 1981, the Reagan administration created the regulatory review process in the Office of Management and Budget (OMB) and the vice president's Task Force on Regulatory Relief.[68] The Bush administration continued these presidential initiatives and created in 1990 the vice president's Council on Competitiveness to ensure that federal projects and regulations satisfied the cost-benefit test.[69] OMB officials continue to be relentless critics of federal agencies for failing to rely on effective cost-benefit analysis.[70]

California provides an interesting case study of the impact of water subsidies. Agriculture consumes about 90 percent of the water used in the state; the metropolitan Los Angeles area, in contrast, uses about 8 percent of the total.[71] One estimate concluded that farmers in California's giant Central Valley irrigation system paid only 5 percent of the total cost of the water provided for them through federal and state projects.[72] The amount of water used for growing crops in the state bears little relationship to the value of those crops. Water for irrigated pastures uses more than 4 million acre-feet of water per year, as much as an urban population of 27 million would require, but the value of that crop is only $93 million in a $480 billion state economy. If Californians were no longer to grow pasture, alfalfa, cotton, and rice, crops that can be grown on rainfall in other states, the state's economy would shrink by only about one-quarter of 1

Table 8.4
Subsidies for Irrigation Projects

Project	Costs Allocated to Irrigation	Costs to be Prepaid by Irrigators	% of Irrigation Costs Subsidized
Central Valley, CA	$ 682,152,000	$ 606,646,000	11.1%
Chief Joseph Dam, WA	11,083,200	6,050,000	45.4
Collbran, CO	6,105,000	1,089,101	82.1
Columbia Basin, WA	745,111,398	135,916,400	81.8
Fryingpan-Arkansas, CO	69,946,000	50,512,300	27.8
Rouge River, OR	18,064,000	9,066,500	49.8
San Angelo, TX	8,853,904	4,000,000	54.8
The Dalles, OR	5,994,000	2,550,000	57.5
Ventura River, CA	18,273,128	10,746,300	41.2
Washita Basin, OK	10,403,011	8,221,000	21.0

Source: Terry L. Anderson, *Water Crisis: Ending the Policy Drought*
(Baltimore: Johns Hopkins University Press, 1983): 5.

percent, but water would be available to accommodate 70 million new Californians.[73] Tables 8.4 and 8.5 provide illustrations of the costs of subsidies and the impact on the kinds of crops that are grown in California.

The prior appropriation system also sometimes serves to discourage the most efficient use of scarce water resources.[74] The first claimant on the water gains a legal right for continued use of the amount withdrawn. Claims for water in prior appropriation systems require a showing of "reasonable and beneficial use," for example, but there is no provision to differentiate uses that are more beneficial than others. During shortages, those who hold senior appropriation rights are entitled to all of their share before junior rights holders can receive theirs, rather than distributing the burden of shortfalls more broadly. Water rights can be lost through forfeiture, if the user intentionally discontinues his or her use of the water, or through forfeiture, if the user does not use part or all of the rights for a period of time defined by law.[75] This discourages conservation, since water not used as a result of conservation efforts is considered abandoned or forfeited unless it can be transferred to other users.[76]

The prior appropriation system also discourages water conservation. Users continue to withdraw the amount allocated to them, even if they do not need it, or their allotment will be reduced.[77] If farmers could sell or lease water they save through conservation, that would create effective incentives to conserve.[78] If investments in new water and storage facilities emphasized conservation and water loss, by lining canals with concrete and covering them to reduce absorption and evaporation, additional savings could be realized.[79] The application of the prior appropriation doctrine may also inhibit efforts to conserve water in other ways; holders of appropriation rights are entitled to the amount of water

Table 8.5
Water Use in California, by Water Used and Crop Value

Crop	Water use in acre-feet/yr	Crop value in $ million
Irrigated pasture	4,192,000	$ 93
Alfalfa Hay	4,092,000	570
Cotton	3,424,000	843
Rice	2,619,000	204
Grapes	1,587,000	1,412
Almonds/Pistachios	1,088,000	633
Tomatoes	651,000	485
Oranges/Lemons	554,000	848

Source: Terry L. Anderson, *Water Crisis: Ending the Policy Drought* (Baltimore: Johns Hopkins University Press, 1983): 31.

that is reasonably needed for the crops they grow; if they make water-saving investments that reduce the amount of water they need, the excess water accrues to other rights holders and may not be sold by the original owners as a reward for conservation investments.[80] Some states have amended their water laws to permit owners who save water to retain legal control over it.[81]

There is increasing concern about the need to reallocate water use toward the maintenance of instream flows to ensure water quality, recreation, and the protection of ecosystems.[82] Courts have given recognition to the public trust doctrine and the subordination of private property rights to a broader public interest in protecting water resources.[83] Just as property rights cannot be used to insulate water rights holders against polluting waters, property rights cannot keep governments from intervening in water systems to protect instream flows and other public purposes.[84]

Most of the water used for irrigation is wasted through evaporation or absorption by the soil. Federal subsidies have made water so inexpensive that farmers have no incentive to invest in conservation. Shortages of freshwater occur throughout the world and are a source of international tension. In the United States, droughts in the West pose a major challenge to water users. Urban areas in the West and Midwest are expected to face water shortages by the year 2000 that will become worse as population grows. If global warming occurs in this area, water shortages will become more acute. Residents of eastern states are expected to have adequate water supplies. They face pollution of water sources and flooding, a problem throughout the country but particularly in the East, as a result of decisions to build communities on floodplains that are inundated by unexpected levels of precipitation, and some loss of vegetation that absorbs rainfall. States and the federal government have made enormous investments to increase the supply of water to the West and to protect eastern communities from flooding. In California, for example, where 75 percent of the population live to the south of Sacramento, but 75 percent of the rain falls to the north, there is an elaborate system of dams, pumps, and aqueducts to send water southward. Southern Californians demand more water, arguing that agriculture produces only 2.5 percent of the state's annual economic gains but uses 82 percent of its water. Northerners insist more water needs to stay to protect rivers, fisheries, wetlands, and salmon spawning habitat and to flush the San Francisco Bay. Water is being pumped from aquifers at levels well beyond recharge rates. Southern Californians could meet their needs if they conserved water or shifted away from crops, like rice, cotton, and alfalfa, that use large quantities of water. They could also pay much more for water than they currently do if they decide to build plants to convert seawater to freshwater, as some communities are considering.[85]

Groundwater provides 23 percent of all freshwater used and about half of all drinking water provided. Aquifers are susceptible to depletion, sinking or subsidence of land when water is withdrawn (resulting in damage to transportation and communication facilities, buildings, and other resources), and contamination by salt water or pollutants. Groundwater is also a major source of water for streams, providing about 40 percent of stream flow. About 25 percent of the groundwater pumped out is not being replenished, particularly in the Ogallala, a fossil aquifer that stretches from South Dakota to Texas. That aquifer is, in reality, almost a nonrenewable resource since it is so slow to recharge and will take thousands of years to recharge. One-fourth of the aquifer is expected to be depleted by the year 2020, and in some areas, where the aquifer is shallow, wells will run dry, and the land will no longer be agriculturally productive. Other areas where groundwater drafts are occurring include California, Arizona, Louisiana, and Mississippi. Salt water that invades aquifers that are drawn down more quickly than they can be recharged threatens the drinking water supplies of Atlantic and Gulf Coast communities.

Water Conservation

As is true for energy, conservation is the solution to problems with the availability of freshwater. One element of the policy response is to end tax and other subsidies that encourage water use, such as permitting farmers and ranchers to deduct the cost of drilling new wells, building large water projects at public expense, and encouraging the planting of thirsty crops in dry lands. Raising water prices to reflect the real costs of developing it is an essential policy reform. Investments in reducing waste through leaks and evaporation, decreasing pollution of surface and groundwater, recycling wastewater from municipalities and industries, more efficient irrigation techniques such as drip irrigation, and more efficient household uses are all technologically feasible and would be economically advantageous if the price of water reflected its true cost.[86]

Conservation, however, is not enough. Other issues related to water use require attention. The Columbia River Basin, for example, is home to the world's largest hydroelectric system, featuring more than one hundred dams mostly built by the federal government in the 1930s to control flooding and produce cheap electricity and electricity prices that are 40 percent below the national average. But the dams have disrupted a major salmon spawning ground and nursery. Salmon runs have declined from 10–16 million a year, before the dams were constructed, to 2.5 million annual runs, a result of dams and reservoirs that blocked spawning runs, logging and mining wastes that have damaged habitat, and overfishing. Efforts to establish salmon ranches to replace the lost production have been plagued by problems of disease and diminution of genetic variability.

Other policy efforts have been similarly problematic. In 1980, Congress enacted the Northwest Power Act to require the development of plans to protect salmon and other fish. The Northwest Power Planning Council was created to bring together federal and state officials and to encourage long-term planning. The council approved a plan from the regional utilities that had formed a consortium, the Washington Public Power Supply System (WPPSS), to build five nuclear power plants. Massive cost overruns, higher than expected interest rates, and lower than expected demand for electricity resulted in WPPSS' defaulting on the bonds it had issued—the largest municipal bond default in American history. More successfully perhaps, although it is much too early to tell, was the council's agreement with the Bonneville Power Administration (BPA), the federal agency responsible for marketing the hydroelectric energy, to try to rehabilitate the region's salmon fisheries. The decades-long project seeks to increase the salmon population, particularly wild salmon, through the construction of new hatcheries, introducing juvenile fish into underpopulated streams, trucking fish around dams during peak downstream migration periods, turning off generators to allow fish to swim over dams, reducing runoff from dirt logging roads near spawning streams, and protecting 40,000 miles of streams from hydropower development. The likely cost is $2 billion in spending on these projects and an annual loss in power revenues of from $30 billion to $60 billion.[87]

Prevention is cheaper than treatment. Congress established in 1986 a $500 million trust fund to clean up leaking underground storage tanks, funded through a tax on motor fuel. But even a partial cleanup of such tanks is estimated to reach $32 billion. Between 1972 and 1993, the federal government spent $75 billion, and industries spent $500 billion on controlling discharges into navigable water. An EPA report estimated that municipal communities will need to spend $400 billion–$500 billion between 1995 and 2015 to comply with clean water standards.[88]

Conservation of water in riparian states is a challenge. The doctrine of reasonable use emphasizes the efficient use of water, but the idea of efficiency has been interpreted to mean serving a useful purpose,[89] rather than some notion of maximum benefit produced from the available resource. Once parties become accustomed to relying on inefficient use of water, and rights are established to use that water, it is difficult to create incentives to conserve. Leaking water may also benefit third parties, complicating efforts to conserve.[90]

A number of options for conservation exists. Water can be rationed, but some users may still have more water than they need, and some apportioning schemes may unfairly penalize users who have invested in conservation measures in the past. More promising are actions that raise the price of water and involve investments in more efficient water appliances and fixtures.[91] The greatest potential for conservation comes from changes in irrigation. Investments can be made to improve dramatically the efficiency of water use in irrigation. Trickle or drip irrigation systems; devices that measure soil moisture levels; computer-controlled systems that set water flow rates, detect leaks, and make adjustments in response to changes in weather and soil conditions; new crops that use less water; and organic farming techniques that produce higher yields with lower water and fertilizer inputs can be developed. Other changes include replacing unlined ditches with pipes, improving the efficiency of furrow irrigation, pumping and reuse of tailwaters that accumulate from furrow irrigation, and low-pressure sprinkler systems.[92] Water savings can be used to protect rivers and streams in national parks and in wildlife refuges so that fragile ecosystems are protected. Irrigated lands suffer from problems of salinity and waterlogging; reduced use through conservation is a key element of protecting soil quality and is much less expensive that constructing drainage systems.[93]

The investments required for conservation, however, will generally not be made until water prices are high enough to generate incentives to conserve. Similarly, industrial and household uses of water can be reduced through investments in recycling and efficiency, but these investments will not be made as long as water prices are artificially low and subsidized through federal water projects.[94] In the western United States, 25 percent of the irrigated land receives water from Bureau of Reclamation projects. Bureau water is provided at greatly subsidized prices, as beneficiaries usually reimburse the government for only a fraction of the total costs of constructing the reclamation facilities. As a result, much of the water is used for relatively low-value crops, such as alfalfa for cattle grazing, while high-value crop farmers cannot find sufficient water.[95]

Some Bureau of Reclamation water subsidies are used to grow crops that the Agriculture Department pays farmers in the East not to grow. In most places, water supplied by federal projects is sold at only a small fraction of its real cost.[96] As prices increase, efficiency and conservation will also. When water is priced more realistically, when governments regulate its use, or when the cost of extracting it goes up, efficiency increases. Farmers in Israel and the Texas High Plains have shown that the irrigation efficiencies can be raised 20 to 30 percent in a matter of years by adopting modern technologies and better management practices.[97] Using lasers to level fields, upgrading sprinklers, recycling used irrigation water, installing water-thrifty drip systems, and irrigating only when crops really need water are just a few of the ways farmer can save.[98]

Economic incentives have become increasingly heralded as the most efficient and effective mechanism for accomplishing natural resource goals. Incentives are championed as being essential to "harnessing the 'base' motive of material self-interest to promote the common good."[99] It is simply not effective to condemn users of resources as immoral or selfish, their advocates argue; what is needed are clear incentives to encourage them to change their behavior, to ensure that they take actions that are consonant with the public good. Incentives are also preferable to more traditional regulatory interventions, because they promote flexibility and freedom of choice and minimize the need for coercion. Natural resource policies that rely on economic incentives include taxes and fees levied on resource extractions and on resulting pollution; tax concessions or direct subsidies for conservation; deposits and refunds on products; and legal liability and associated fines for certain kinds of pollution resulting from extraction of resources. A tax or fee, if it is high enough, can provide a strong incentive for conservation. They can help ensure that the true costs of resource use are included in their price and contribute to a market process that more efficiently allocates scarce resources.[100]

More efficient use of water and conservation are the keys to dealing with water shortages.[101] Water needs to be transferred from existing uses to more productive ones. Water transfers between farmers and metropolitan areas have occurred, but there are significant barriers to efficient exchanges. Some water planners prefer building new dams whenever there are shortages, rather than exploring the possibility of transfers. Some areas lack the infrastructure to shift water from one locality to another. But the biggest barriers are legal provisions that inhibit water transfers. Several states have had some experience with water transfers.[102] Colorado has more experience than any other western state, particularly in developing a water market along the urbanized corridor between Colorado Springs and Fort Collins, including the Denver metropolitan area. The state has also purchased water rights to maintain instream flows.[103] Utah has a long tradition of allowing irrigation companies to exchange water rights. It has allowed water to be transferred across conservancy district boundaries. Some innovative trading of water rights between irrigation and utility users has benefited all parties.[104] Arizona law requires developers in certain areas to demonstrate they have secured a hundred-year supply of water before they can commence construction, leading to the creation of a futures market for water.[105]

Water markets have been slow to develop in California, except in Los Angeles, where groundwater rights are administered as a common pool, and water is sold on a year-by-year basis. The Reno–Sparks area in Nevada has a blossoming water market because it relies on a small aquifer and one modest river for its water.[106] The county in which these cities are located purchased rights from a large ranch in order to ensure a supply for the growing population.[107] Idaho permits banking or leasing of water rights for future use. The more scarce water is, the more likely states have been interested in developing water markets.[108] Other western states with more abundant water have been less involved in markets, although Oregon's water conservation law permits water salvaged from conservation efforts to be transferred. Despite some progress in developing markets, attitudes, practices, and laws have been hard to change, and few states have been able to develop the flexibility that will permit water use to move to its highest use and, in particular, to satisfy concerns about the protection of ecosystems.[109] Some water exchanges are between farmers and municipal water districts; as a result, prices have ranged from $200 per acre-foot in Salt Lake City to $6,000 per acre-foot in Colorado.[110] Other exchanges reduce waste without requiring that any croplands be taken out of cultivation, as has happened in the Metropolitan Water District of southern California.

Water markets have great potential for helping to ensure that scarce water is put to its highest-value economic use and can help prevent environmental damage and economic costs resulting from construction aimed at increasing supply.[111] Transfers and conservation have great economic and ecological benefits. Expensive new dams do not have to be built. Wild rivers can be preserved. Less soil becomes waterlogged. Reduced irrigation return flows mean less pollution of lakes and rivers by pesticides and fertilizer. Agricultural lands can lie fallow, return to native grasslands or wetlands, and provide habitats for wildlife.[112] But markets may threaten rural communities that are unable to meet the higher prices.[113] Instream flows are not necessarily protected but require that investments be made to protect those ecosystems.[114] If not through markets, water conservation will have to take place through other mechanisms. The overarching problem is the failure to recognize how scarce water is and to ensure that prices be realistic reflections of its true value.[115]

Water Quality

Water pollution comes in a great variety of forms. Disease-causing agents such as bacteria and viruses come from human and animal wastes. Oxygen-demanding wastes that include organic material decomposed by aerobic bacteria remove oxygen from the water and threaten aquatic life. Water-soluble inorganic chemicals that include acids, salts, and toxic metals are dangerous to human, animal, and plant life. Inorganic plant nutrients such as nitrates and phosphates generate growth of algae and other plants and deplete oxygen levels. Organic chemicals such as oil, pesticides, detergents, and plastics harm human and aquatic life. Sediment or suspended particles carry dangerous particles, cloud water and disrupt photosynthesis, destroy aquatic food production, damage fish feeding and spawning areas, and fill lakes, rivers, and harbors. Water-soluble radioactive isotopes pass through food chains and cause cancer, birth defects, and other genetic damage. Thermal pollution from water used to cool power

plants and then returned to bodies of water makes aquatic life more susceptible
to disease, parasites, and chemicals. Importation of new species into water bodies may overwhelm native species, reduce biodiversity, and cause other problems. Pollution comes from specific, or point, sources, such as pipes, ditches,
and sewers connected to plants and other facilities, abandoned mines, and the
transportation of oil. Nonpoint sources, not traceable to discrete sources, include
agricultural and storm water runoff. Nonpoint pollution from agricultural sources
such as sediment, inorganic fertilizer, manure, and dissolved salts accounts for
some 64 percent of the volume of pollutants entering streams and 57 percent of
lake pollution. Nonpoint runoff from storm water is responsible for 33 percent
of lake pollution and 10 percent of stream pollution. In the United States, some
44 percent of lakes, 37 percent of rivers, and 32 percent of estuaries that were
tested in 1992 were declared unsafe for fishing and recreational uses like swimming.[116]

Regulating water pollution has had mixed results. Nonpoint sources of pollution have been very difficult to identify and regulate. Flowing streams can
recover naturally from limited levels of some forms of pollution, and depending
on the levels of pollution and the size, flow, temperature, and pH level, regulation may not be needed in a few cases. Federal funding of wastewater facilities
in the United States has stabilized water quality. Some highly polluted rivers,
such as Ohio's Cuyahoga, have been cleaned up. But water quality has not been
tested along 64 percent of the length of U.S. streams. There is an elegantly
simple solution to drinking water pollution: require water users to draw their
water downstream from their discharge points. That would help ensure that
polluters pay the cost of the pollution they produce and create a powerful incentive for polluters to reduce their emissions.[117]

Lake pollution is more difficult to address in some ways, because the stratified
layers of most lakes, the lack of dilution of pollutants from water movement,
and the lack of replenishment of oxygen from water flow cause pollutants to
remain in lakes much longer than in rivers. Some lakes undergo eutrophication
as nutrients accumulate from urban and agricultural runoff, reduce oxygen levels
in the water, and kill fish and other aquatic life. Lake pollution threatens drinking
water supplies, fishing industries, recreational use, and other values. Some 85
percent of the lakes located near metropolitan areas suffer from eutrophication
from sewage treatment plant discharges and runoff from fertilizer, animal
wastes, and nutrient-laden topsoil and from air pollution. Cleaning up lake pollution is usually much more expensive than prevention, but if nutrient levels are
reduced, many lakes can be restored.[118]

Oceans have become the sinks for much of the waste we produce, and much
of the damage is focused on wetlands, estuaries, coral reefs, mangrove swamps,
and other coastal areas. About one-third of the municipal sewage produced in
the United States is untreated and dumped into the ocean. Industrial wastes are
no longer dumped off U.S. coasts, and dumping of sewage sludge from sewage
treatment plants was banned in 1992. Most harbors and bays are highly polluted,

and one-third of the coastal areas of the lower forty-eight states are closed each year to shell fishing because of contaminated waters. Nitrogen and phosphate in agricultural and municipal wastes foster algae growth that depletes the water of oxygen and kills marine life. Air pollutants, particularly nitrogen, also fall into estuaries. Cleanup of the Chesapeake Bay, an area heavily polluted by urban and rural runoff, sewage treatment plants, and air pollution, is expected to cost several billion dollars.[119]

The U.S. Geological Survey reports the percentage of measurements that show a violation of EPA water quality standards. While the violations reported do not necessarily indicate a legal violation, the numbers provide another indicator of the stubbornness of water pollution problems[120]:

Percent of Measurements Exceeding Violation Level

Pollutant	1980	1985	1990	1995
Fecal coliform bacteria	31	28	2	29
Dissolved oxygen	5	3	2	<1
Phosphorus	4	3	3	4

Other water quality reports paint a similar picture: while we have made considerable progress in cleaning up water bodies, some 38 percent of rivers, 44 percent of lake acres, and 32 percent of estuaries are still not suitable for swimming and fishing. Pollution from nonpoint sources continues to be the major problem.[121]

The Environmental Working Group released a report in 1996 analyzing EPA data that concluded that one in six Americans—45 million people—receives water from a utility that has had recent pollution problems, including fecal matter, parasites, disease-causing microbes, radiation, toxic chemicals, and lead. More than 18,500 public water supplies reported at least one violation of a federal drinking water standard in 1994 and 1995. The report urged water providers to provide more information to consumers about water quality. Representatives of the American Water Works Association criticized the study as an exaggeration of sporadic incidents that were unfairly described in the study as chronic problems.[122]

Groundwater contamination by pollution is a growing problem in the United States. Rough estimates conclude that as much as 25 percent of the nation's groundwater is contaminated, and in some areas, the figure is much higher, perhaps 75 percent. Underground storage tanks for gasoline and diesel fuels and toxic chemicals, chemical spills, leaching from hazardous waste sites, industrial storage sites, agricultural runoff, injecting hazardous wastes deep underground, and other sources threaten underground water quality. Once groundwater is contaminated, there is very little that can be done to reverse the damage, except to treat the water after it is pumped. Water can be pumped to the surface, cleaned, and returned to the aquifer, but only at great cost. Prevention is the only feasible way to protect groundwater.[123]

Protecting Wetlands

The Everglades National Park in Florida provides a sobering example of how difficult it is to preserve wetlands and how the failure to understand the ecological functioning of wetlands can have tremendous consequences. Once environmental damage is done, it is very difficult and usually expensive to remedy it. The Everglades is actually a slow-moving river, some fifty miles wide and only about six inches deep, that flows to an estuary at Florida Bay and, in the process, creates the largest freshwater marshland in the world. The Everglades plays a critical role in the Florida panhandle ecosystem in recharging its aquifer and in fostering rainfall and is home to fourteen endangered or threatened species. About half of the Everglades has been lost to development. The Everglades National Park was created in 1947 to protect about 20 percent of the remaining wetlands. Development has caused the Everglades to be the most endangered national park.[124]

Diversion of water from the North is a major threat to the viability of the park. In the 1960s, the Army Corps of Engineers converted the Kissimmee River, a 103-mile-long meandering river, into a 56-mile-long canal, in order to provide flood control. The construction drained water from wetlands, and the land was used for grazing cows. Cow manure flowed down the canal into Lake Okeechobee, where the increased nutrients fueled the growth of algae that depleted the oxygen in the water. Water flowing into the Florida Bay has become warmer and more salty, which, along with the increased nutrients, stimulated the growth of algae blooms in the bay that threaten the diving and fishing industries. Nutrients from sugarcane and vegetable fields also contribute to the damage to the park and bay. As more and more water has been withdrawn from the area to meet Miami's growing water demands, salt water has moved inland to fill the void and has contaminated drinking water supplies. The impact has been dramatic in some areas. Nesting bird populations, for example, have declined by 90 percent in the park during the past sixty years.[125]

State and federal officials and property owners have been slow to remedy these problems. After twenty years of discussion, officials came up with a plan to undo the damage to the Kissimmee, and Congress authorized the Army Corps of Engineers in 1993 to restore fifty-two miles of the river to its natural course, a fifteen-year project that is estimated to cost at least $370 million. In 1993, after a decade of delays from legal challenges launched by industries, sugarcane and vegetable growers agreed to contribute one-third of the initial cleanup costs, estimated to be $700 million, as long as they were immune from the balance of the cost, expected to be at least $1.3 billion over twenty years. Florida taxpayers were required to pay the balance of the costs, but in 1996, voters rejected a referendum that proposed a tax of one cent/pound of sugar to fund the cleanup.[126]

Coordinating Water-Related Policies

Planning and management of surface and groundwater have become increasingly important, given the interaction of water quality and quantity with other environmental concerns, the cutback in federal water projects, increased demands on water bodies for recreational use, and other factors. The growing scarcity of water resources has stimulated increasing demand for planning. The creation of special management districts for water requires some coordination with statewide policies and with a host of other state and municipal water institutions and irrigation companies. Despite the great need for planning, however, such efforts are limited by state agency resources and by vested property rights. Two kinds of planning are needed. The first need is for the development of a long-term plan that indicates the nature of the water resources that are available, what the demand for water will be, and how that demand is to be met, particularly if it exceeds the available supply. These plans are integrated with efforts to prepare for floods and other emergencies. The second kind of planning focuses on specific projects such as a dam or reservoir and how it interacts with other proposed projects and facilities in place.[127]

Water planning is inevitable. It is required by federal projects,[128] by interstate water management compacts,[129] and by a number of federal laws, including the Endangered Species Act (requiring that endangered species living in water bodies be protected),[130] Fish and Game laws (placing limits on the impounding and diverting of water),[131] and the Surface Mining Control and Reclamation Act of 1977 (requiring a surface mine owner to replace water owned by others that is damaged by contamination or diminution).[132] Requirements under the National Environmental Policy Act (NEPA) are particularly important: the law requires the preparation of environmental impact statements (EISs) for all "major Federal actions significantly affecting the quality of the human environment."[133] Construction of dams, reservoirs, and canals, flood control, and other projects involving federal agencies or federal funds require EISs that require comprehensive assessments of water and other elements of the affected ecosystems.[134] Supreme Court cases have also emphasized the importance of water resource planning by states.[135] The Public Trust doctrine was found by the North Dakota Supreme Court to require at least some determination of the consequences of the distribution of water on current supplies and future needs. The development and implementation of some short-and long-term planning capacity are essential to achieve allocation of resources "without detriment to the public interest in the lands and waters remaining."[136]

The requirements of a number of environmental quality laws implicate state planning efforts. The Safe Drinking Water Act imposes planning requirements on state and local governments.[137] The Clean Water Act requires all point sources of discharges into navigable waters to obtain a National Pollution Discharge Elimination System permit.[138] The Resources Conservation and Recovery Act of 1976[139] and the Comprehensive Environmental Response, Compensation, and Liability Act of 1980 both impose requirements on sources of hazardous wastes and provide for their cleanup in order to protect groundwater from contamination. Private and public nuisance laws and court decisions must also be considered in fashioning water policy in states.[140]

Planning and coordination are also difficult because most states regulate water quality through a health or environmental quality agency and regulate quantity through a state engineer's office or natural resources agency. It is important for officials from these two agencies to work together more closely. Merging the two agencies would greatly facilitate the coordination of policy efforts, but such a step is not likely to be politically feasible. One step that can be taken is to ensure that state water codes are consistent with state laws and regulatory programs aimed at protecting water quality. In some state natural resource agencies, planning may also take place in different bureaus than does the allocation of water. Planning for individual projects as well as for meeting long-term water needs is a major function of natural resource agencies.

Elinor Ostrom's study of water basins, irrigation systems, fisheries, and other common pool resources (CPR) in the United States and other nations identified several characteristics of successful efforts:

1. Clearly defined boundaries (individuals or households who have rights to withdraw resource units from the CPR must be clearly defined, as must the boundaries of the CPR itself);

2. Congruence between appropriation and provision rules and local conditions (appropriation rules restricting time, place, technology, and/or quantity of resource units are related to local conditions and to provision rules requiring labor, material, and/or money);

3. Collective-choice arrangements (most individuals affected by the operational rules can participate in modifying them);

4. Monitoring (monitors, who actively audit CPR conditions and appropriations behavior, are accountable to the appropriators or are the appropriators themselves);

5. Graduated sanctions (appropriators who violate operational rules are likely to be assessed graduated sanctions, depending on the seriousness and context of the offense, by other appropriators, by officials accountable to the appropriators, or by both);

6. Conflict-resolution mechanisms (appropriators and their officials have rapid access to low-cost local arenas to resolve conflicts among appropriators or between appropriators and officials);

7. Minimal recognition of rights to organize (the rights of appropriators to devise their own institutions are not challenged by external governmental authorities);

8. For CPRs that are parts of larger systems: nested enterprises (appropriation, provision,

monitoring, enforcement, conflict resolution, and governance activities are organized in multiple layers of nested enterprises).[141]

Private property rights, Ostrom concludes, are insufficient to protect common pool resources, and collective efforts are needed. But regulation by centralized, bureaucratic, governmental solutions may not be effective. A combination of public and private institutions may be the most effective way to protect CPRs. Institutional arrangements are needed that are flexible and adaptive and can change as circumstances do; reduce information and transaction costs; reinforce shared norms and values; create an expectation of harm if agreements are not followed by all parties; assure parties that they are treated fairly, taking into account their circumstances; and encourage trust and reciprocity among parties.[142] According to the old western saying, water runs uphill, toward money. Planning that relies on clear financial incentives holds great promise for managing public lands' most scarce resource.

NOTES

1. Council on Environmental Quality, *Environmental Trends* (Washington, DC: U.S. Government Printing Office, 1989): 21.

2. William Ashworth, *Nor Any Drop to Drink* (New York: Summit Books, 1982): 19–21.

3. G. Tyler Miller Jr., *Living in the Environment* (Belmont, CA: Wadsworth, 1996): 455–57.

4. Marc Reisner and Sarah Bates, *Overtapped Oasis: Reform or Revolution for Western Water* (Washington, D.C.: Island Press, 1990): 55; Zach Willey and Tom Graff, "Federal Water Policy in the United States—An Agenda for Economic and Environmental Reform," *Columbia Journal of Environmental Law* 13 (1988): 325; Terry L. Anderson, *Water Crisis: Ending the Policy Drought* (Baltimore: Johns Hopkins University Press, 1983): 5.

5. Robert E. Beck, ed., *Waters and Water Rights*, vol. 5 (1991): 755; A. Dan Tarlock, *Law of Water Rights and Resources* (St. Paul, MN: West Publishing Company, 1991): sec 3.13.

6. See George Wharton James, *Reclaiming the Arid West: The Story of the United States Reclamation Service* (New York: Dodd, Mead, 1917).

7. For a brief history of water policy, see Jacqueline Switzer with Gary Bryner, *Environmental Politics* (New York: St. Martin's Press, 1998): Chapter 7.

8. Ibid.

9. See Constance Elizabeth Hunt, *Down by the River* (Washington, DC: Island Press, 1988): 11–14.

10. For an in-depth study of this history, see Marc Reissner, *Cadillac Desert* (New York: Penguin Books, 1987).

11. Frank J. Trealise and George A. Gould, *Water Law*, 4th ed. (Charlottesville, VA: Michie Co., 1986): 13.

12. Alaska, Arizona, Colorado, Idaho, Montana, Nevada, New Mexico, Utah, and Wyoming.

13. California, Nebraska, Kansas, Mississippi, North Dakota, Oklahoma, Oregon, South Dakota, Texas, and Washington.

14. Trealise and Gould, *Water Law*: 259.

15. Sec. 850A (1979).

16. *Harris v. Brooks*, 225 Ark. 436, 283 S.W.2d 129 (1955).

17. See, generally, Joseph W. Dellapenna, "Riparian Rights in the West," 43 *Oklahoma Law Review* (1970): 51.

18. Trealise and Gould, *Water Law*: 318.

19. Delaware, Florida, Georgia, Iowa, Kentucky, Maryland, Minnesota, New Jersey, North Carolina, South Carolina, and Wisconsin.

20. Trealise and Gould, *Water Law*: 318.

21. Ibid.: 389–90.

22. Ibid.: 411.

23. Ibid.: 412.

24. Connecticut, Maine, Massachusetts, Mississippi, Rhode Island, Texas, and Vermont. For a discussion of various theories of regulating underground water, see *State v. Michels Pipeline Constr., Inc.*, 63 Wis. 2d 278, 217 N.W.2d 339 (1974).

25. Alabama, Arizona, Illinois, Indiana, Iowa, Kentucky, Maryland, Michigan, Missouri, New Hampshire, New York, North Carolina, Ohio, Pennsylvania, Tennessee, Virginia, West Virginia, and Wisconsin.

26. Arkansas, California, Nebraska, and New Jersey.

27. Delaware, Florida, Georgia, Hawaii, Minnesota, South Carolina, Nebraska, New Jersey, New York, North Carolina, Virginia, and Wisconsin.

28. Alaska, Kansas, Montana, North Dakota, and Utah.

29. Colorado, Idaho, Nevada, New Mexico, Oklahoma, Oregon, South Dakota, Washington, and Wyoming.

30. Reisner and Bates, *Overtapped Oasis*: 64.

31. 33 U.S.C. 1251–1387.

32. 33 U.S.C. 1251–1387.

33. Deborah Hitchcock Jessup, *Guide to State Environmental Programs* (Washington, DC: Bureau of National Affairs, 1988): 6.

34. Ibid.: 9–10.

35. 104th Congress, H.R. 961, S. 851.

36. P.L. 104–127.

37. Todd Shields, "Judge Fines Developers $4 Million," *Washington Post* (June 18, 1996): D1.

38. Safe Drinking Water Amendments of 1977, Safe Drinking Water Act amendments (1979), Safe Drinking Water Act amendments (1980), Safe Drinking Water Act amendments (1986), and Lead Contamination Control Act of 1988.

39. 42 U.S.C. 300f to 300j–26.

40. David Hosansky, "Drinking Water Bill Clears, Clinton Expected to Sign," *Congressional Quarterly Weekly Report* (August 3, 1996): 2179.

41. Miller, *Living in the Environment*: 338–39.

42. Sandra Postel, *Water: Rethinking Management in an Age of Scarcity* (Washington, DC: World Watch Institute, 1984).

43. Lee Davidson, "*Californians Hold Up CUP Funding—Again,*" *Deseret News*, September 10, 1992, at E10; *Reclamation Projects Authorization and Adjustment Act of 1992*, House Report No. 1016, 102d, 2d Sess. (1992).

44. Miller, *Living in the Environment*: 343.

45. Ibid.: 349.

46. U.S. Environmental Protection Agency, *The Potential Effects of Global Climate Change on the United States* (Washington, DC: U.S. E.P.A. 1989): 167.

47. U.S. EPA, *Potential Effects of Global Climate Change*.

48. Miller, *Living in the Environment*: 337.

49. Ibid.: 349.

50. Ibid.

51. Ibid.: 350.

52. Ibid.: 351.

53. Ibid.: 352.

54. Ibid.: 247; World Meteorological Organization/United Nations Environment Programme, Intergovernmental Panel on Climate Change, *Climate Change: The IPCC Scientific Assessment* (Cambridge: Cambridge University Press, 1990): 283–311.

55. Reisner and Bates, *Overtapped Oasis*: 55.

56. Willey and Graff, "Federal Water Policy in the United States."

57. Reisner and Bates, *Overtapped Oasis*: 56–57.

58. World Resources Institute (WRI), *Environmental Almanac* (Washington, DC: WRI, 1991): 105.

59. Anderson, *Water Crisis*: 5.

60. U.S. Office of Management and Budget, *Regulatory Program of the United States Government, April 1, 1990–March 30, 1991* (Washington, DC: U.S. Government Printing Office, 1990): 222.

61. Edith Stokey and Robert Zeckhauser, *A Primer for Policy Analysis* (New York: W. W. Norton, 1978).

62. See Daniel Swartzman, Richard A. Liroff, and Kevin G. Croke, eds., *Cost-Benefit Analysis and Environmental Regulations* (Washington, DC: Conservation Foundation, 1982).

63. See, generally, Lawrence J. White, *Reforming Regulation: Processes and Problems* (Englewood Cliffs, NJ: Prentice-Hall, 1981): 13–26.

64. Randall Ripley, *Congress: Process and Policy*, 3d ed. (New York: W. W. Norton, 1983).

65. See, generally, John Ferejohn, *Pork Barrel Politics* (Stanford, CA: Stanford University Press, 1974).

66. Statement by President Jimmy Carter, at a press conference on March 24, 1977, quoted in Barbara K. Rodes and Rice Odell, *A Dictionary of Environmental Quotations* (New York: Simon and Schuster, 1992): 43. For a discussion of the Carter administration's and other efforts to reform water policy, see Lawrence Mosher, "The Corps Adapts, the Bureau Founders," in The Editors of High Country News, *Western Water Made Simple* (Washington, DC: Island Press, 1987): 15–27.

67. David A. Stockman, *The Triumph of Politics* (New York: Simon and Schuster, 1987).

68. For a review of these efforts, see National Academy of Public Administration (NAPA), *Presidential Management of Rulemaking in Regulatory Agencies* (Washington, DC: NAPA, 1987).

69. White House, Office of the Press Secretary, "The President's Plan for Reducing the Burdens of Regulation through Administrative Action" (January 30, 1992); President's Council on Competitiveness, "Fact Sheet" (n.d.); Jonathan Rauch, "The Regulatory President," *National Journal* (October 30, 1991): 2902–6.

70. Cost-benefit analysis is generally understood to require the quantification of all

costs and benefits and the calculation of their dollar values in a numerical ratio. Calculations of cost-effectiveness in these areas are a means of comparing alternative regulatory strategies or different regulations without requiring explicit calculations of the value of life. A cost-effective standard requires that the goal be achieved at the lowest cost or that the most good be achieved with the resources available. See Stokey and Zeckhauser, *A Primer for Policy Analysis*: 134–38, 153–55. Somewhat differently, cost-benefit analysis requires that the policy goal itself be justified by showing that the projected benefits exceed the anticipated costs. Agencies may select a project with the highest cost-effective ratio and may compare the cost-effectiveness of different regulations in deciding whether to pursue them: Carolyn Goldinger, ed., *Federal Regulatory Directory*, 6th ed. (Washington, DC: CQ Press, 1990): 27–28. Problems with this approach remain, and OMB officials have criticized agencies because regulations vary greatly in their cost-effectiveness. OMB and the federal agencies have also differed over the selection of discount rates for computing the effects of projects over time: Office of Management and Budget, *Regulatory Program*: 40. In many areas, benefits and costs will develop on different time schedules, but their net present values are determined so that alternative actions can be compared; the net present value is dependent on the discount rate selected: Stephen Breyer, *Regulation and Its Reform* (Cambridge: Harvard University Press, 1982): 44–46. OMB officials have preferred a higher rate than do agencies, thus making it more difficult to justify new projects: Office of Management and Budget, *Regulatory Program*: 40.

71. Reisner and Bates, *Overtapped Oasis*: 30.

72. Miller, *Living in the Environment*: 346.

73. Reisner and Bates, *Overtapped Oasis*: 30–33.

74. Nine western states employ a "pure" prior appropriations approach: Alaska, Arizona, Colorado, Idaho, Montana, Nevada, New Mexico, Utah, and Wyoming; nine other states rely on both prior appropriations and riparian rights: California, Oregon, Texas, Washington, Kansas, Nebraska, North Dakota, South Dakota, and Oklahoma.

75. Charles W. Howe, Paul K. Alexander, and Raphael J. Moses, "The Performance of Appropriative Water Rights Systems in the Western United States during Drought," *Natural Resources Journal* 22 (1982): 379.

76. Reisner and Bates, *Overtapped Oasis*: 63–64.

77. Anderson, *Water Crisis*: 8–9.

78. Ibid.: 70–71.

79. Miller, *Living in the Environment*: 343.

80. Anderson, *Water Crisis*: 70–71.

81. California, Oregon, and Montana have amended their laws: Reisner and Bates, *Overtapped Oasis*: 79. The "no harm" or "no injury" rule in transfer cases prevents water users from making changes in existing patterns of withdrawal as a way to protect the interests of each person who enjoys appropriations rights. But it also serves to lock in practices and discourage actions that would improve the value to which water is used. Appropriation rights are usually expressed in flow measures (cubic feet/second) rather than in volume measures (acre-feet), making it difficult for holders to determine how much water they might be able to sell to other users. The "no injury" rule is so vague in many states that virtually any holder of junior appropriation rights can claim an injury and block transfers. Rights holders could be authorized to challenge actions that pose *substantial* injury, required to accept alternative water sources of the same quality, or permitted to sell rights to others. Transfers are time-consuming, requiring permits, ad-

ministrative hearings if parties object (except in Colorado, where disputes are resolved in water courts, and in riparian states), and judicial review. Procedures can be streamlined, and private negotiations encouraged to reduce the barriers to transfers.

82. Joseph L. Sax, "The Limits of Private Rights in Public Waters," *Environmental Law* 19 (1989): 473.

83. *Marks v. Whitney*, 6 Cal. 3rd 251, 491 P.2d 374, 98 Cal. Rptr. 790 (1971); *Morse v. Oregon Div. of State Lands*, 34 Or. App. 853, 581 P.2d 520 (1978); *Kootenai Envtl. Alliance v. Panhandle Yacht Club*, 105 Idaho 622, 671 P.2d 1085 (1983); *National Audobon Soc'y v. Superior Court* (Mono Lake), 33 Cal. 3rd 419, 658 P.2d 709, 189 Cal. Rptr. 346, cert. denied, 464 U.S. 977 (1983).

84. Sax, "Limits for Private Rights."

85. Miller, *Living in the Environment*: 463–64.

86. Ibid.: 471–72.

87. Ibid.: 474.

88. Ibid.: 496.

89. Beck, *Waters and Water Rights*: sec. 2.02.

90. *Erickson v. Queen Valley Ranch Co.*, 22 Cal. App. 3rd 584, 99 Cal. Rptr. 446 (1971) (a delivery ditch from a diversionary dam lost five-sixths of its flow through leakage; the leakage, however, resulted in vegetation that eventually came to support deer and quail in an area of land owned by the U.S. Forest Service through which the ditch passed. The Forest Service refused to allow the plaintiff to replace the leaking ditch with a pipe. The court ordered the parties to work out a solution that would address both parties' concerns.)

91. Beck, *Waters and Water Rights*: sec. 62.01.

92. Reisner and Bates, *Overtapped Oasis*: 116–22.

93. Postel, *Water*: 19.

94. Miller, *Living in the Environment*: 255–57.

95. Ibid.: 343.

96. Anderson, *Water Crisis*: 4.

97. Postel, *Water*: 33.

98. Ibid.: 140–42.

99. Charles L. Schultze, *The Public Use of Private Interest* (Washington, DC: Brookings Institution, 1977).

100. See Timothy E. Wirth and John Heinz, "Project 88 Incentives for Action: Designing Market-Based Environmental Strategies" (Washington, DC: Offices of Senators Wirth and Heinz, 1988).

101. Bonnie G. Colby, "Economic Impact of Water Law—State Law and Water Market Development in the Southwest," *Natural Resources Journal* 28 (1988): 721.

102. See, generally, Charles W. Howe, Carolyn S. Boggs, and Peter Butler, "Transaction Costs as Determinants of Water Transfers," *University of Colorado Law Review* 61 (1990): 393.

103. See Reisner and Bates, *Overtapped Oasis*: 99–100.

104. Ibid.: 100–101.

105. Bonnie G. Colby, Mark A. McGinnis, and Ken Rait, "Procedural Aspects of State Water Law: Transferring Water Rights in the Western States," *Arizona Law Review* 31 (1989): 697.

106. Bonnie G. Colby, Mark A. McGinnis, and Ken Rait, "Mitigating Environmental

Externalities through Voluntary and Involuntary Water Reallocation: Nevada's Truckee–Carson River Basin." *Natural Resources Journal* 31 (1991): 757.

107. Reisner and Bates, *Overtapped Oasis*: 103–5.

108. Ibid.: 106.

109. Ibid.: 106–7.

110. Ibid.: 100–101.

111. George A. Gould, "Transfer of Water Rights," *Natural Resources Journal* 29 (1989): 457.

112. Reisner and Bates, *Overtapped Oasis*: 58.

113. George A. Gould, "Water Rights Transfers and Third Party Effects," *Land and Water Law Review* 23 (1988): 1.

114. Postel, *Water*: 10.

115. Ibid.: 5–6.

116. Miller, *Living in the Environment*: 479–80, 496.

117. Ibid.: 481–82.

118. Ibid.: 484–85.

119. Ibid.: 488–90.

120. U.S. Geological Survey, reported in U.S. Bureau of the Census, *Statistical Abstract of the United States: 1995*, no. 370 (Washington, DC: U.S. Government Printing Office, 1995): 232.

121. EPA, National Water Quality Inventory, *1992 Report to Congress* (March 1994): ES2-23.

122. *U.S. Water News Online* (June 1996).

123. Miller, *Living in the Environment*: 466–67, 493–95.

124. Ibid.: 475–76.

125. Ibid.

126. Robert Pear, "The 1996 Elections: The States—The Initiatives," *New York Times* (November 7, 1887): B7.

127. Beck, *Waters and Water Rights*: 755.

128. See the Reclamation Act of 1902, as amended in 1939, 43 U.S.C. Sec. 485h (1988).

129. See, for example, the Water Resources Planning Act, 79 Stat. 244 (1965).

130. 16 U.S.C. sec 1531 (1988).

131. The Fish and Wildlife Coordination Act of 1958, 16 U.S.C. sec. 661 (1988), and the Anadromous Fish Act of 1965, 16 U.S.C. 1801 (1988).

132. 30 U.S.C. 1201 (1988).

133. 42 U.S.C. sec. 43332(2) (c) (1988).

134. See, generally, Environmental Law Institute, *NEPA Desk Handbook* (Washington, DC: Environmental Law Institute, 1991).

135. *Colorado v. New Mexico*, 467 U.S. 310 (1984).

136. *United Plainsmen Association v. North Dakota State Water Conservation Commission,* 247 N.W. 2d 457, 462 (N.D. 1976).

137. 42 U.S.C. sec. 300g-2.

138. 33 U.S.C. sec. 1252.

139. 42 U.S.C. sec 6901.

140. Tarlock, *Law of Water Rights and Resources*: sec. 3.13.

141. Elinor Ostrom, *Governing the Commons: The Evolution of Institutions for Collective Action* (New York: Cambridge University Press, 1990): 90.

142. Ibid.: 210–14.

9

National Parks and Wilderness

THE POLICY FRAMEWORK

The first European settlers coming to America saw the new continent as wild-lands to be conquered and replaced with orderly farms and towns. The land and its inhabitants were unruly and uncivilized, they thought, and they set themselves to the task of taming the wilderness. This attitude permeated American culture for centuries. The relentless push westward was driven by the search for new lands and new opportunities, but also by a desire to subdue the land and its residents and exploit the tremendous wealth it contained. The preservationists of the nineteenth and twentieth centuries resisted the westward push of development and were occasionally successful in creating pockets of protected lands. But economic growth, the pursuit of riches, and, eventually, demands for outdoor recreation drove public lands decisions. Americans believed that their lands, so richly endowed, were unlimited, that natural resources were inexhaustible. Public policies promoted development, westward expansion, and the conversion of natural resources into money. It took two and a half centuries of growth and expansion before some Americans began to recognize the threat of losing wildlands. Much of the conservationist impulse, from the writings of John Muir in the late 1800s, has been to conserve natural resources so their yields are sustainable.

The first protected lands designated by the federal government were the park-lands established in 1791 for the nation's capital. The National Mall, the White House grounds, and other areas were transferred to the National Park Service in 1933. The Hot Springs, Arkansas, area was set aside in 1832, and a park was created in 1880, becoming a national park in 1921. The federal government gave lands to the state of California in 1864 for a park, and these lands were returned to federal jurisdiction in 1906, when Yosemite National Park was established. The first national park, Yellowstone, was established in 1872. The 1891 Forest Reserve Act gave protection to forests. President Theodore Roosevelt persuaded Congress to create the first wildlife refuge in 1903 at Pelican Island. President Woodrow Wilson signed the National Park Service Act in 1916, giving the Park Service responsibility for the thirty-six national parks that had been established.

Most lands protected within the National Park System (NPS) are designated through an act of Congress. These laws may provide detailed management mandates or may give the NPS broad discretion under the 1916 National Park Service Act. Other designations are made by the president. The designation of preserved lands has not been consistent, primarily because they have been designated by different authorities and during different periods of time. National parks are the flagship of the system. A national park is generally defined as "a large, spectacular natural place having a wide variety of attributes, at times including significant historic assets." Hunting and consumptive activities are not permitted in parks; Congress has created a new classification, national preserves, in order to permit hunting and other activities in areas that have the characteristics of parks. The largest park is Wrangell-St. Elias, a 8.3-million-acre Alaskan park. It was first designated as a national monument in 1978 and was declared a park in 1980. It adjoins a 4.9-million-acre national preserve where hunting is permitted.

National monuments can be established by executive order, under the authority given the president of the United States in the 1906 Antiquities Act. That act empowers the president to "declare by public proclamation historic landmarks, historic and prehistoric structures, and other objects of historic or scientific interest that are situated upon the lands owned or controlled by the Government of the United States to be national monuments." While the act focused on preservation of antiquities, its most common use has been to protect natural areas. The first monument, Devils Tower in Wyoming, was designated in 1906. Other areas, including the lands in Alaska discussed earlier, the Grand Canyon, Zions, and the Channel Islands National Parks, were also first created as monuments. Congress has created several monuments, such as the birthplace of George Washington in 1930 and the Canyon de Chelly in 1931. Monument designation is the catchall classification for lands that do not appear to qualify for other designations. They are also usually smaller than national parks and usually lack the diversity or range of attractions of parks.

National preserves, such as the Big Cypress in Florida and Big Thicket in Texas, might have been established as parks but were otherwise designated to permit hunting, trapping, and oil and gas exploration. Ten preserves are in Alaska, designated under the 1980 Alaska National Interest Lands Conservation Act.

National historic sites are authorized by Congress or the Secretary of the

Interior. They protect a variety of historic sites, including forts, homes of notable Americans, and other structures of historic value. National historic parks were first established in 1933 and usually apply to areas beyond single buildings, such as Independence National Park in Philadelphia or Colonial National Historic Park in Virginia (includes Jamestown and Yorktown). National memorials commemorate a historic person or event. The first monument, the Washington Monument, was designated in 1848. The Lincoln Memorial, the Robert E. Lee Memorial in Virginia, and the Wright Brothers National Memorial in North Carolina are other examples. National battlefields, battlefield parks, sites, and national military parks were first established in 1890, when the Chickamauga and Chattanooga National Military Park was established. In 1958, the Park Service recommended naming all areas national battlefields, but some areas continue to bear the original name. There are within these areas fourteen national cemeteries, including those at Gettysburg and Andersonville, Georgia.

National recreation areas (NRA) typically preserve recreation areas around reservoirs (twelve areas) or near urban areas. The first unit created, the Lake Mead National Recreation Area, was designated in 1936. The Gateway NRA in New York City and the Golden Gate NRA in San Francisco were the first urban NRAs and were both created in 1972. The first national seashore was Cape Hatteras National Seashore in North Carolina, established in 1937. Others have been created along the Atlantic, Gulf, and Pacific Coasts and range from wilderness areas in a primitive state to facilities to accommodate heavy beach use. National lakeshores were first established in 1966 and are all located along the Great Lakes. The first national river was authorized in 1964, the Ozark National Scenic Riverways in Missouri. The 1968 Wild and Scenic Rivers Act added five more rivers. The first national parkway, the George Washington (GW) Memorial Parkway, was created in 1930. The parkways were created to facilitate recreational driving, although the GW Parkway is now a major commuter traffic corridor. The Blue-Ridge, the Natchez Trace, and the John D. Rockefeller Parkways make up the other roads in the system. The first national scenic trail, the 2,100-mile-long Appalachian National Scenic Trail, was designated in the 1962 National Trails System Act. It extends from Maine to Georgia. Other areas are protected by the National Park Service, including the White House and other sites in Washington, D.C.

Public lands legislation that provided for multiple-use and sustained yield on public lands has given federal agencies great discretion in making and implementing policy. But legislation creating parks and other protected areas usually limits agency discretion by providing specific guidelines for what kinds of activities can and cannot take place on these lands. Federal lands that are given special protective status are usually managed by the agencies that had jurisdiction before the new designation, except that national parklands are managed by the Park Service. The BLM, for example, manages 267 million acres, 41 percent of all federal lands, and owns an additional 300 million acres of subsurface minerals. Included in its acreage are 137 wilderness areas that make up 5.1

million acres. The National Park Service has jurisdiction over 77 million acres, 12 percent of all federal lands, including 50.3 million acres in fifty-four national parks and 314 other units (national monuments, lakeshores, seashores, recreation areas, preserves, wild and scenic riverways, and scenic trails). Some 43 percent of NPS lands are wilderness areas. The Fish and Wildlife Service manages 88 million acres in 504 wildlife refuges and thirty-two wetland management districts. Wetlands, islands, and coastal areas make up about half of the total FWS lands, and 84 percent of the lands are located in Alaska. The FWS administers 20.6 million acres of wilderness lands, 22 percent of its total lands.[1]

The National Park Service was established by Congress in the 1916 National Park Service Act. Its mission was ''to conserve the scenery and the natural and historic objects and the wildlife therein and to . . . leave them unimpaired for the enjoyment of future generations.''[2] The 1916 act was amended in 1970 to provide that all units of the system have equal standing and are ''united through inter-related purposes and resources into one national park system as cumulative expressions of a single national heritage; that individually and collectively, these areas derive increased national dignity through their inclusion . . . in one national park system preserved and managed for the benefit and inspiration of all the people.'' Management of individual parks is the responsibility of the superintendent or unit manager. Each park must have a general management plan that outlines how park resources will be preserved and how public use will be accommodated. Parks are divided into four zones—natural, cultural, park development, and special use. Subzones are used to provide greater detail for management of specific lands. As a result, a group of historic buildings will be managed the same way, regardless of whether they are located in a park, monument, or some other designation. Plans are prepared by Park Service employees and are submitted to the public for review and comments. More specific plans are developed for specific problems and challenges, such as back country use or river management.[3] Table 9.1 describes the units of the National Park System.

The Land and Water Conservation Fund, financed by special taxes such as revenue from offshore oil and gas leasing, is used by federal agencies to buy lands for new recreational areas or expansion of existing ones. The fund also provides grants to states for purchase of lands. The fund has been criticized by conservatives as pure pork barrel politics, and less spending usually occurs than is authorized by Congress.[4] The act creating the Land and Water Conservation Fund also provided that land management agencies can charge only nominal fees, or no fees at all, for recreational use of most federal lands, limiting agencies' ability to charge fees reflecting the true costs of recreation.[5]

The Forest Service is required to prepare general management plans for the ''preservation and use of each unit of the National Park System.'' These plans are to include ''measures for the preservation of the area's resources,'' infrastructure, ''visitor carrying capacities'' for all units, and possible modifications of external boundaries.''[6]

The Antiquities Act of 1906 empowers the president to establish national

Table 9.1
The National Park System

Designations	Number of Units
International Historic Site	1
National Battlefields	11
National Battlefield Park	3
National Battlefield Site	1
National Historic Site	69
National Historical Park	31
National Lakeshore	4
National Memorial	26
National Military Park	9
National Monument	78
National Park	50
National Parkway	4
National Preserve	13
National Recreation Area	18
National Reserve	1
National River	5
National Scenic Trail	3
National Wild and Scenic River and Riverway	10
Park (other)	11
Total	358

Source: U.S Department of the Interior, National Park Service, "Parks, etc." (n.d.).

monuments as a way to protect objects of historic, scientific, or scenic value found on federal lands.[7] The 1979 Archaeological Resources Protection Act prohibits removal or sale of archaeological resources from the federal and Native American lands.[8] The Historic Sites Act of 1935 authorized the interior secretary to develop policies to preserve ''historic sites, buildings, and objects of national significance for the inspiration and benefit of the people of the United States'' and includes a requirement that such resources be salvaged if threatened by construction on federal lands or under federal permits or funding.[9] The 1966 National Historic Preservation Act orders the secretary of the interior to establish a National Register of Historic Places and conduct a review of any project that may affect those places.[10]

In 1994, Congress passed the California Desert Protection Act, creating more than 7.5 million acres of federally protected areas in the California desert. This was the largest land withdrawal since the Alaska National Interest Lands Conservation Act of 1980 (ANILCA) and the largest wilderness law in any of the lower forty-eight states. The act included the creation of three national parks, totaling nearly 4 million acres: Joshua Tree, Death Valley, and East Mojave. The first two parks had been managed as wilderness areas by the NPS for more than decade.[11] It protected 3.5 million acres of BLM lands in sixty-nine areas; 2.92 million acres of BLM lands were transferred to the NPS. Congress specified in the law what kinds of activities were permitted: mining and motorized vehicles are prohibited, but grazing can continue in Joshua Tree and Death Valley areas, and hunting is permitted in East Mojave. The navy and marines are authorized to use 1.3 million acres of land in the desert and continue to use low-altitude flight paths. The state can use motorized vehicles to maintain or restore fish and wildlife populations and habitats.

In the final days of the 104th Congress, in September 1996, members passed a 700-page omnibus parks bill that they had been considering for months, which included federal funds to help purchase the Sterling Forest on the border of New Jersey and New York, creation of a trust to preserve the Presidio in San Francisco, creation of a tallgrass prairie reserve in Kansas, a swap of lands in Utah for a ski resort, and dozens of other projects affecting forty-one states.[12]

Private organizations have played a significant role in the creation of national parks and other protected areas. Table 9.2 describes the land acquired by three groups for preservation: the Nature Conservancy, the Conservation Fund, and the Trust for Public Land.

Wilderness

The United States was the first nation to set aside lands as wilderness. Aldo Leopold convinced the Forest Service to set aside, in 1924, 700,000 acres in the Gila National Forest in Arizona, which became the first wilderness area. The U.S. Forest Service began setting aside areas within its jurisdiction in the early twentieth century, and several dozen areas had been established in national forests as wilderness areas by the 1930s. By the 1960s, it had protected some 14.6 million acres.

But administrative designation was only a temporary solution. The growth of highways, motor vehicle transportation, and tourism threatened the preservation of pristine lands. In 1956, Senator Hubert H. Humphrey (D-MN) introduced the first wilderness bill in Congress. Battle lines were quickly drawn between preservationists and champions of economic growth. Eight years later, preservationists won their first major legislative victory when Congress passed by overwhelming margins (374 to 1 in the House and 73 to 12 in the Senate) the Wilderness Act of 1964.

Congress' purpose in enacting the Wilderness Act was to "secure for the American people of present and future generations the benefits of an enduring

Table 9.2
Acreage Involved in the Land Transactions of Three Major Nonprofit Organizations between July 1, 1964, and September 30, 1994

Nonprofit organization	July 1, 1964	July 1,1964, to September 30,1994		September 30,1994
	Acres on hand	Acres acquired	Acres transferred	Acres on hand
The Nature Conservancy	69,424	3,051,730	2,495,366	625,788
The Conservation Fund	0	159,804	85,282	74,522
The Trust for Public Land	0[b]	606,883	585,205	21,678

[a]The Conservation Fund was incorporated on March 8, 1985; it had no acres on hand at that time.
[b]The Trust for Public Land was incorporated on May 5, 1972; it had no acres on hand at that time.
Source: U. S. General Accounting Office, "Land Ownership: Information on the Acreage, Management, and Use of Federal and Other Lands," (Washington, DC: U.S. GAO, March 1996): 7.

resource of wilderness.'' The National Wilderness Preservation System, composed of federally owned wilderness lands, was established to manage lands ''for the use and enjoyment of the American people in such a manner as will leave them unimpaired for future use and enjoyment as wilderness.''[13] The Wilderness Act defines a wilderness land as ''an area where the earth and its community of life are untrammeled by man, where man himself is a visitor who does not remain. An area of wilderness is further defined to mean in this Act an area of undeveloped Federal land retaining its primeval character and influence, without permanent improvements or human habitation, which is protected and managed so as to preserve its natural conditions and which (1) generally appears to have been affected primarily by the forces of nature, with the imprint of man's work substantially unnoticeable; (2) has outstanding opportunities for solitude or a primitive and unconfined type of recreation; (3) has at least five thousand acres of land or is of sufficient size as to make practicable its preservation and use in an unimpaired condition, and (4) may also contain ecological, geological, or other features of scientific, educational, scenic, or historical value.''[14]

The act requires agencies to give priority to ''recreational, scenic, scientific, educational, conservation, and historical use'' and mandates that ''there shall be no commercial enterprise and no permanent road . . . no temporary road, no use of motor vehicles, motorized equipment or motorboats, no landing of aircraft, no other form of mechanized transport, and no structure or installation within any such area.''[15] Motorized vehicles are permitted in wilderness areas if required for administering the areas and for human health and safety emergencies. Mining laws and leases applicable prior to the date of creation of wilderness areas remain in effect, subject to ''reasonable regulations governing ingress and egress . . . consistent with the use of the land for mineral location and development and exploration.'' Transmission, water, and telephone lines and other facilities required for exploration and production are permitted. Once work is completed, the affected lands are to be restored ''as near as practicable.''[16] The president may authorize construction of ''reservoirs, water-conservation works, power projects, transmission lines, and other facilities needed in the public interest.'' [17] Federal lands are not exempt from state water laws under the Wilderness Act.

The 1964 Wilderness Act requires Congress to make the designations as wilderness. Wilderness management can allow some existing uses and limited commercial development. Mining prospecting can continue if ''carried on in a manner compatible with preservation of the wilderness environment.'' Motorized vehicles are permitted only for emergency use and administrative needs. Grazing rights established prior to creation of wilderness areas are honored but subject to ''such reasonable regulations as are deemed necessary.''[18] Logging is not expressly prohibited, but the prohibition against roads and vehicles effectively bans it.

The 1964 act set aside an initial 9.1 million acres of wilderness lands and ordered the secretary of agriculture to review an additional 5.5 million acres of land classified as wilderness areas by the Forest Service for possible inclusion in the wilderness system. The Secretary of Agriculture or the chief of the Forest Service is required within ten years to review lands eligible for wilderness designation and recommend to the president lands to be so designated; establishment of wilderness areas requires an act of Congress. The secretary of the interior is similarly ordered to review all roadless areas of 5,000 acres or more in national parks, monuments, other units of the national park system, and wildlife and game refuges. Before either the agriculture or interior secretary makes a recommendation to the president, he or she is required to "give public notice of the proposed action," "hold a public hearing or hearings at a location or locations convenient to the area affected," and notify the governors and local officials of the proposed action and invite their comments. Modification or adjustments of boundaries of wilderness areas also require public notice and hearings.[19] The Wilderness Act also permitted new mining claims to be filed and patents to be issued on lands in the wilderness system until the end of 1983; beginning in 1984, lands in the wilderness system were withdrawn from further mining consideration unless rights had already been established.

The Forest Service began its Roadless Area Review and Evaluation (RARE) of 56 million acres of Forest Service lands in 1971. Criticisms of the service's failure to include Easter forests, national grasslands, and roadless areas less than 5,000 acres and the failure to conduct an environmental impact assessment of the study caused RARE to be abandoned and a new study, RARE II, to be conducted in 1977. By 1979, RARE II had examined 62 million acres in thirty-eight states and Puerto Rico and proposed 15.4 million acres, 9.9 million of which were in the lower forty-eight states, for wilderness designation; proposed that 10.6 million acres be further studied; and proposed that 36 million acres be made available for logging, mining, and other uses. In 1984, Congress began approving state forest wilderness proposals, often including more land than the Forest Service had recommended. The number of forest wilderness areas grew to 35 million acres, and an additional 6.6 million acres continue to be protected as wilderness study areas. The forest management plans required of all national forests have become the primary mechanism for proposing new wilderness areas.[20]

In 1976, Congress enacted the Federal Land Policy and Management Act, which ordered the Bureau of Land Management to review all roadless areas greater than 5,000 acres within its jurisdiction for possible wilderness designation. The process for designation of wilderness areas is the same—agency inventorying of the lands, presidential recommendation of wilderness creation, and congressional designation of the official areas. The BLM was required to complete its inventory by 1991. By 1980, the BLM had reviewed 174 million acres in the West and classified 24 million acres in 936 areas as wilderness study areas. Congress passed an Arizona wilderness bill in 1990 that created a 1.1 million-acre wilderness area. In 1991, the Interior Department made its final recommendation for BLM wilderness lands: 9.8 million acres in 330 areas. In 1992, the Bush administration recommended the creation of 9.1 million acres of wilderness in 302 parcels in California, Idaho, Nevada, New Mexico, Oregon, Utah, and Wyoming.[21]

By 1996, the wilderness system included 104 million acres, more than half of which are in Alaska. Wilderness areas are managed by the federal agency responsible for the lands before their wilderness designation: the Bureau of Land Management, the Forest Service, the Fish and Wildlife Service, and the National Park Service. Tables 9.3 and 9.4 outline the size and extent of wilderness areas managed by different federal agencies and their distribution across the states. Table 9.5 includes data on all protected areas managed by key public lands agencies. Table 9.6 charts the growth in recreational visits to protected lands.

While the 1964 Wilderness Act provides some criteria for wilderness designation, there has been a vigorous debate over how to define wilderness. Wilderness is protected for a number of reasons: recreation, protection of natural resources, preservation of cultural heritage and national consciousness, creation of refuges and sanctuaries for solitude and contemplation, and recognition of human responsibility to preserve biodiversity. Resource development is usually prohibited in wilderness areas, so the stakes in wilderness designation are often high.

Other legislation was eventually passed to bolster preservationist goals. The National Wild and Scenic Rivers Act protects rivers and their immediate environments that possess one or more "outstandingly remarkable scenic, recreational, geologic, fish and wildlife, historic, cultural, or other similar values." Rivers are to be classified as either wild, defined as "generally inaccessible except by trail, with watershed or shorelines essentially primitive and waters unpolluted . . . represent[ing] vestiges of primitive America"; scenic, where shorelines and watersheds are "still largely primitive and . . . undeveloped, but accessible by road or railroad"; or recreational, "readily accessible by road or railroad," with some development, that "may have undergone some impoundment or diversion in the past."[22] Federal agencies regulate mining and other activities within one-quarter mile of the banks of designated rivers, but the power of agencies to regulate other activities has not been well established.[23]

Only about 4 percent of lands in the United States are protected as wilderness areas, and nearly 75 percent of such lands are in Alaska. The 413 wilderness areas in the lower forty-eight states make up about 1.8 percent of all land and are mainly small parcels of land (only four are larger than 1,500 square miles). The National Wild and Scenic Rivers System protects 0.3 percent of the 3.5 million miles of rivers and streams, in fifteen segments. The National Trails System gives some protection to lands. Only 81 of the 233 distinct ecosystems in the United States are protected in wilderness areas. About 150,000 square miles of public lands could be designated as wilderness areas. Additional wilderness recovery lands could be established by restoring habitat, erasing devel-

Table 9.3
National Wilderness Preservation System

Agency	Units	Federal Acres	(%)
Forest Service, USDA	399	34,676,493	(33.5)
National Park Service, USDI	44	43,007,316	(41.5)
Fish and Wildlife Service, USDI	75	20,685,372	(20.0)
Bureau of Land Management, USDI	136	5,227,063	(5.0)
Grand Total	630	103,596,244	(100)

National Wilderness Preservation System (excluding Alaska):

Agency	Units	Federal Acres	(%)
Forest Service, USDA	380	28,923,594	(62.6)
National Park Service, USDI	36	10,027,946	(21.7)
Fish and Wildlife Service, USDI	54	2,009,052	(4.3)
Bureau of Land Management, USDI	136	5,227,063	(11.3)
Total	582	46,187,655	(100)

National Wilderness Preservation System (Alaska):

Agency	Units	Federal Acres	(%)
Forest Service, USDA	19	5,752,899	(10.0)
National Park Service, USDI	8	32,979,370	(57.4)
Fish and Wildlife Service, USDI	21	18,676,320	(32.5)
Total	48	57,408,589	(100)

Notes: Detailed breakdowns by wilderness within each state and agency jurisdiction can be found in the Annual Wilderness Report to Congress. Some acreage values are estimates, pending final mapping and surveys. Total number of units for all agencies is 630; this is not additive from information above because of overlapping responsibilities.

Source: U.S. Department of the Interior, Bureau of Land Management, personal correspondence, October 15, 1996.

Table 9.4
Designated Wilderness Areas

Bureau of Land Management

State	Total Federal Acres	Total Acres Inholding	Dates of Designation
Arizona	1,405,750	9,590	1984-90
California	3,587,395	0	1978-94
Colorado	51,505	0	1993
Idaho	802	0	1980-84
Montana	6,000	0	1983
New Mexico	128,900	0	1984-87
Nevada	6,458	0	1989
Oregon	6,723	0	1978-84
Utah	26,630	0	1984
Washington	6,900	240	1984
Total	**5,227,063**	**9,830**	**1978-94**

National Park Service

State	Total Federal Acres	Potential Acres	Dates of Designation
Alaska	32,979,370	0	1980
Arkansas	10,529	25,471	1978
Arizona	443,700	1,242	1970-78
California	5,856,450	50,193	1972-94
Colorado	55,647	670	1975-76
Florida	1,296,500	81,900	1978
Georgia	8,840	11,718	1982
Hawaii	142,370	13,350	1976-78
Idaho	43,243	0	1970
Michigan	132,018	138	1976

Table 9.4 continued

State	Total Federal Acres	Potential Acres	Dates of Designation
Mississippi	5,514	479	1978
New Mexico	56,392	320	1976-78
New York	1,363	18	1980
North Dakota	29,920	0	1978
South Carolina	15,010	6,840	1988
South Dakota	64,250	0	1976
Texas	46,850	0	1978
Virginia	79,579	0	1976
Washington	1,739,771	5,604	1988
Total	**43,007,316**	**197,943**	**1970-94**

Fish and Wildlife Service

State	Total Federal Acres	Dates of Designation
Alaska	18,676,320	1970-80
Arkansas	2,144	1976
Arizona	1,343,444	1990
California	9,172	1974-94
Colorado	2,560	1980
Florida	51,253	1970-76
Georgia	362,107	1974-75
Illinois	4,050	1976
Louisiana	8,346	1975-76
Maine	7,392	1970-75
Massachusetts	2,420	1970
Michigan	25,309	1970
Minnesota	6,180	1976
Missouri	7,730	1976
Montana	64,535	1976

Table 9.4 continued

State	Total Federal Acres	Dates of Designation
Nebraska	4,635	1976
New Jersey	10,341	1968-75
New Mexico	39,908	1970-75
North Carolina	8,785	1976
North Dakota	9,732	1975
Ohio	77	1975
Oklahoma	8,570	1970
Oregon	495	1970-78
South Carolina	29,000	1975
Washington	838	1970-76
Wisconsin	29	1970
Total	**20,685,372**	**1968-94**

Forest Service

State	Total Federal Acres	Total Acres Inholding	Dates of Designation
Alaska	5,752,899	35,695	1980-90
Alabama	33,151	80	1975-88
Arkansas	116,560	377	1975-84
Arizona	1,344,970	132	1964-84
California	4,398,919	60,141	1964-94
Colorado	3,147,686	14,695	1964-93
Florida	74,495	4	1975-84
Georgia	113,423	403	1975-91
Idaho	3,961,501	8,256	1964-84
Illinois	25,549	717	1990
Indiana	12,935	18	1982
Kentucky	16,415	1,022	1975-85
Lousiana	8,679	0	1980

Table 9.4 continued

State	Total Federal Acres	Potential Acres	Dates of Designation
Maine	12,000	0	1990
Michigan	91,891	1,594	1987
Minnesota	807,451	279,503	1964-78
Missouri	63,198	429	1976-84
Mississippi	6,046	0	1984
Montana	3,371,770	3,929	1964-83
Nebraska	7,794	0	1986
New Hampshire	102,932	0	1964-84
New Mexico	1,388,063	2,980	1964-84
Nevada	786,067	160	1964-89
North Carolina	102,634	592	1964-84
Oklahoma	14,431	1,537	1988
Oregon	2,079,854	15,111	1964-84
Pennsylvania	8,938	0	1984
South Carolina	16,671	0	1975-80
South Dakota	9,826	0	1980
Tennessee	65,408	40	1975-86
Texas	37,030	1	1984-86
Utah	774,328	192	1978-84
Vermont	59,421	177	1975-84
Virginia	87,255	205	1975-88
Washington	2,572,799	13,783	1964-84
Wisconsin	42,294	2,153	1975-84
West Virginia	80,852	0	1975-90
Wyoming	3,080,358	689	1964-84
Total	**4,676,493**	**44,615**	**1964-94**

Source: U.S. Department of the Interior, Bureau of Land Management, personal correspondence, July 3, 1995.

Table 9.5

Number and Percentage of Acres Managed for Conservation by the Four Federal Agencies, Fiscal Years 1964 and 1994

	Forest Service	Bureau of Land Management	Fish and Wildlife Service	National Park Service	Total
1964					
Total acreage managed	186,274,576	464,346,607	22,650,737	27,493,836	700,765,756
Conservation acreage	16,018,661	628	22,650,737	27,493,836	66,163,862
Percent managed for conservation	8.60	--ᵃ	100.00	100.00	9.44
1994					
Total acreage managed	191,573,857	267,102,376	87,487,290	76,588,003	622,751,526
Conservation acreage	49,893,688	58,165,321	87,487,290	76,588,003	272,134,302
Percent managed for conservation	26.04	21.78	100.00	100.00	43.70

Forest Service Acreage Managed for Conservation
as of September 30, 1994

Conservation category	Acres managed
Wilderness	34,587,437
Wilderness study area	6,638,310
Wild and scenic river	618,283
Research natural area	299,568
National monument	3,404,244
National primitive area	173,762
National recreation area	2,675,274
National game refuge	1,218,953
National scenic-research area	6,630
Other[b]	271,227
Total	**49,893,688**

Bureau of Land Management Acreage Managed for Conservation
as of September 30, 1994

Conservation category	Acres managed
Wilderness	1,653,529
Wilderness study area	26,554,685
Wild, scenic, and recreation river	829,448
Area of critical environmental concern	9,960,843
Research natural area	326,449
National conservation area	14,323,431
National natural or historic landmark	599,042
National recreation area	1,000,000
National scenic-research area	1,365,280
Other[c]	1,552,614
Total[d]	**58,165,321**

[a] Less than 0.005 percent. [b] "Other" includes archaeological, botanical, geological, and national historic areas. [c] "Other" includes national scenic and historic trails, national recreation trails, and national outstanding natural area. [d] Some acres may be counted in more than one conservation category, but the extent of the double counting is unknown.

Source: United States General Accounting Office, "Land Ownership: Information on the Acreage, Management, and Use of Federal and Other Lands" (Washington, DC: U.S. GAO, March 1996): 6, 26.

Table 9.6
Visitation to Federal Recreation Areas, 1980–1994 (in Millions)

Administering Federal Agency	1980	1985	1987	1988	1989	1990	1991	1992	1994
All areas	**6,367**	**6,403**	**7,332**	**7,419**	**7,475**	**7,567**	**7,829**	**7,995**	**(NA)**
Fish and Wildlife Service	17	65	72	81	45	(NA)	(NA)	(NA)	(NA)
Forest Service	2,819	2,705	2,861	2,908	3,030	3,157	3,346	3,452	(NA)
U.S. Army Corps of Engineers[1]	1,926	1,721	2,176	2,290	2,296	2,280	2,306	2,306	(NA)
National Park Service	1,042	1,298	1,394	1,376	1,315	1,322	1,344	1,390	1,338
Bureau of Land Management[2]	68	246	515	461	493	518	540	563	(NA)
Bureau of Reclamation	407	289	306	294	286	280	280	269	(NA)
Tennessee Valley Authority[3]	87	79	8	9	10	10	13	14	(NA)

[1]Beginning 1987, not comparable with previous years. [2]Data not comparable for all years. [3]Beginning in 1989, the TVA discontinued reporting visitation to non-fee-charging area. Data for 1987 and 1988 have been adjusted to reflect this policy.

Source: U.S. Department of Commerce, *Statistical Abstract of the United States, 1996* (Washington, DC: U.S. Government Printing Office, 1996): 250.

opments, and reintroducing native species. But extractive industries lobby strongly to keep these lands open to development.[24]

Congress enacted legislation in 1994 creating nineteen new wilderness areas in Colorado, 611,730 acres on USFS and BLM lands, and 154,940 acres under protective management schemes less restrictive than wilderness. Colorado already has 2.6 million acres of wilderness lands. The new law forbids any assertion of a water right for wilderness in court or administrative proceeding and prohibits development of new water projects in wilderness areas. In 1994, the House passed a bill creating 1.6 million acres of wilderness areas in Montana but the state's two senators could not agree, and the bill died in the Senate. Congress considered but did not pass a number of other wilderness bills in 1995, including one that would have created 1.2 million acres of wilderness in Idaho, a proposal to add 16,674 acres to wilderness areas in New Mexico, the creation of 12,850 acres of wilderness areas in North Carolina, and the Northern Rockies Ecosystem Protection Act, a proposal to set aside 16.5 million acres of wilderness in Wyoming, Montana, Idaho, Oregon, and Washington.

While there is usually great deference paid to legislative initiatives from state delegations concerning issues within their borders, the designation of Alaskan wilderness lands in 1980 is an example of how national interests sometimes override state delegations. In 1979, the House of Representatives voted overwhelmingly (360 to 65) to designate 68 million acres of federal land in Alaska as wilderness. Representative Don Young (R), the lone representative from the state, pushed for a national wildlife refuge designation that would permit oil and gas exploration. The Senate Energy Committee passed a bill that created about 30 million acres of wilderness, as Alaskan senators Ted Stevens (R) and Mike Gravel (D) opposed the designation of wilderness areas in their state and threatened to filibuster. The Senate eventually passed a compromise bill between the House and the Energy Committee versions, creating 56.7 million acres of wilderness, by a 78 to 14 vote. The House agreed to the Senate version on November 12, 1980, after the 1980 election, as wilderness proponents saw that the prospects for a more ambitious bill were greatly reduced by the election of a Republican president. The Alaska National Interest Lands Conservation Act more than tripled the size of the wilderness system.[25] Congress has also considered bills in recent years to designate the 1.5-million-acre Arctic National Wildlife Refuge as a wilderness, but opponents have blocked the measures and hope to be able to release the land for oil exploration.

Proposals for wilderness protection in Utah provide another example of congressional unwillingness to defer to state congressional delegations. Utah has a history of boom-and-bust natural resource development. Once heavily dependent on mining and energy, the state's economy is now much more diverse and includes tourism, electronics, and service industries. The U.S. Forest Service began inventorying lands for possible wilderness designation soon after the Wilderness Act was passed. In 1984, the Utah Wilderness Act passed, creating wilderness areas in twelve mountain regions.[26] Creating wilderness areas in

Utah's red-rock desert has been much more difficult. In the 1970s, various proposals were made for coal development and power plants in Utah, including the Alton strip mine, a coal gasification project, development of tar sands, processing oil shale in the Uintah Basin, building nuclear power plants near the Green River, and constructing a nuclear waste repository near Canyonlands National Park. Several proposals have focused on the estimated 7.9 billion tons of relatively clean-burning coal in the Kaiparowits Plateau, near Escalante, including a power plant, slurry pipeline to ship coal to California, and coal mines. In 1976, utilities proposed a coal mine but canceled their plans just before the Interior Department was to announce whether or not it would approve the new mine. In 1978, the BLM began inventorying roadless lands of at least 5,000 acres for possible wilderness designation and eventually designated 3.2 million acres in eighty-three separate wilderness study areas. Then Governor Scott Matheson created a state committee to work with federal agencies in proposing wilderness legislation.[27]

In 1986, the BLM released its preliminary recommendations and draft EIS that called for 1.9 million acres of wilderness. The 1.9 million acres primarily include Desolation Canyon in the Book Cliffs, Uinta Basin area, the San Juan Anasazi area, and parts of the San Rafael Swell, the Dirty Devil area, the Escalante area, and the Kaiparowits Plateau. Critics complained about several aspects of BLM's inventory of potential lands. The BLM declared ineligible some lands because they did not offer sufficient solitude opportunity and failed to offer a clear rationale for assessing solitude. One area, for example, was excluded because the terrain was too flat for solitude. Other lands were cut because they would be difficult to manage as wilderness lands (primarily the challenge of limiting ORV use). Other areas could have been included if the boundaries had been slightly adjusted. Many of the lands were evaluated by air because of the lack of BLM resources for a more comprehensive assessment. Some BLM officials charged that BLM managers reversed decisions and recommendations from field crews. Some of the assessments are now out of date, since land conditions have changed. The EPA criticized the inventory for overstating the potential value of tar sands, failing to protect biodiversity, and failing to consider impacts on water quality and for its interpretation of wilderness criteria. Other critics argued that the BLM failed to consider how wilderness designation could complement the protection of adjacent lands in national forests and parks. Other areas were rejected because reseeding efforts in the 1950s had produced the wrong kind of vegetation. The BLM also used comparisons to disqualify some lands: some areas were described as less scenic than others, so they were eliminated from the inventory. Some lands were simply excluded because they contained important energy resources. BLM officials provided environmentalists with some opposition, as their comments clearly demonstrated a lack of support for wilderness preservation. Jim Parker, former head of the BLM in Utah, is quoted as having said to the Utah state legislature, "When I'm asked why northern Utah has all the hazardous waste sites and southern Utah has all the wilderness, I reply that northern Utah had first choice.''[28] The Utah Wilderness Coalition, a preservationist group in Utah, prepared its own inventory of eligible lands and published a report, *Wilderness at the Edge*, that called for protecting 5.7 million acres.[29] Earth First! later released its report, which called for the creation of 16 million acres of wilderness lands.[30]

Environmental efforts were countered by the Utah Public Lands Multiple Use Coalition, made up of the Utah Association of Counties, the Utah Cattlemen's Association, the Coastal States Energy Company, the Utah Farm Bureau Federation, the Utah Forest Industry Council, the coalition opposed any further wilderness designation in Utah because of the impact on jobs, mineral and timber extraction, grazing, and some forms of recreation. In 1990, the Utah state legislature created a Wilderness Task Force to hold hearings and visit potential sites, but no hearings or visits took place. In February, the legislature adopted a resolution calling on Congress to designate no more than 1.4 million acres as wilderness, arguing that economic development should be favored over preservation.[31] The proposal focused on lands that were in pristine condition (rather than the Wilderness Act's criteria of land as "an area where the earth and its community of life are untrammeled by man, where man himself is a visitor who does not remain").[32] In October, the National Association of Counties declared Escalante and nine other western communities endangered because of federal land policy.[33] In December, the BLM released its final EIS on Utah wilderness recommendations, designating 1,975,000 acres in sixty-six wilderness units. It added 83,000 acres from the draft proposal and eliminated one large area, in response to 6,200 comments received.[34]

Members of the Utah delegation then introduced competing bills. In March 1991, Representative Wayne Owens (D-UT) introduced a bill calling for 5.4 million acres of wilderness lands[35]; at the same time, Representative Jim Hansen (R-UT) introduced a bill calling for 1.4 million acres.[36] In August, Andalex Resources, Inc., proposed to build an underground coal mine in the Smokey Hollow area of the Kaiparowitz Plateau in eastern Kane County. Andalex had leases on 440 million tons of coal under 7,000 acres of BLM land. The mine would move 2 million tons of coal a year, employ 150–200 workers and become the largest employer in the county, and ship coal in trucks leaving every twelve minutes. Production would not begin until at least 1993. In January 1992, the Utah Division of Oil, Gas and Mining rejected Andalex's initial application for the mine because of numerous deficiencies; the division usually rejects the initial application and asks for more information and analyses.[37] In August, Owens informally proposed the creation of a new Escalante National Park to protect the lands but also encourage tourism; opponents favored a national recreation area where hunting, timber harvests, and other activities could take place.[38] The Coalition for Utah's Future/Project 2000, a citizens group, created a wilderness task force to help break the impasse over wilderness designation. It focused on three issues: grazing in wilderness areas, the impact of wilderness on research conducted in wilderness lands, and impact on school trust lands. Owens ran for the Senate and was defeated in 1992. No member of the Utah delegation favored a 5-million-acre bill; the third representative, Bill Orton (D), proposed his own bill, which created several different designations for the lands but actually created fewer acres of wilderness lands than the Republicans' proposal. Preservationists recruited Representative Maurice Hinchey (D-NY) to sponsor the 5.7-million-acre bill. No action occurred during that session of Congress, as the Utah delegation blocked consideration of any proposal, and Hinchey reintroduced his bill in 1995.[39]

As a result of the Republican takeover of Congress in the 1994 election, Hansen had become chair of the House Resources Committee's Public Lands Subcommittee and introduced his wilderness bill, supported by Enid Waldholtz (R-UT), the other member of the House from the state (Orton continued to work on his own bill). The two Utah senators, Orrin Hatch and Bob Bennett, introduced the delegation's bill in their chamber. H.R. 1745, introduced by Hansen on June 6, 1995, proposed the designation of 1.8 million acres as wilderness in forty-nine separate wilderness areas. Hearings were held, and the bill was reported out by the Resources Committee and was scheduled for a vote in December, when it was suddenly pulled from the House floor schedule just before the bill was to be called up. Proponents of the Hinchey bill said the Hansen bill was pulled because of lack of support; Republicans argued that there was simply not enough time to schedule consideration of the bill.[40]

The Senate bill was reported out of the Energy and Natural Resources Committee in December 1995. The controversies swirled around the size of the protected lands as well as the provisions in the Utahans' bills. Their bill required a "hard release": the lands not included in the 1.8 million acres of wilderness "shall not be managed for the purpose of protecting their suitability for wilderness designation." The Utah bill also required the Interior Department to accept the land picked by the state to swap with the federal government, rather than to negotiate a way to trade for the state lands included in the wilderness area. In March 1996, the Utah delegation added their wilderness bill to an omnibus national parks bill that had garnered a lot of support. By this time, the Utah issue became a national priority for preservationists and leading Democrats in Congress. The Democrats filibustered, forcing the Republicans to peel off the Utah bill, and the package was then passed by the Senate in May. Republicans again tried to add the Utah wilderness bill to the House omnibus package, but determined opposition forced them to remove it, and the parks bill was passed and signed in September 1996, without the Utah wilderness provisions.

The Clinton administration began weighing in on the issue. In an April 1996 House Resource Committee hearing, Interior Secretary Babbitt argued that at least 5 million acres qualify as wilderness areas in Utah; Hansen challenged him to document that figure; Babbitt replied that he accepted that as an invitation to conduct a new BLM inventory. San Juan, Kane, and other county officials started bulldozing roads to reduce the areas the BLM could consider in the new inventory. The state successfully sued the Interior Department to block preparation of a new inventory. On September 18, 1996, President Clinton, looking for opportunities to bolster his environmental record, designated by executive order 1.7 million acres of land in southeastern Utah as the Grand Staircase-Escalante National Monument. He used the Grand Canyon as a backdrop, the area President Theodore Roosevelt had protected under a similar order in 1908. The president's authority for the designation was the Antiquities Act of 1906, which gives the president the power to protect objects of "historic or scientific interest"; Clinton emphasized the protection of the land for current and future generations. In southern Utah, the proposal was met by protests, black balloons released in Kanab, and Clinton and Babbitt hanging in effigy in Escalante. Senator Hatch called the president's order a "war on the west," and virtually every other state official criticized the president for failing to consult him or her about the proposal.[41] The debate continued in 1997 as Rep. Hinchey again introduced his bill, and Senator Richard Durbin (D-IL) introduced a similar bill in the Senate.

THE POLICY DEBATE

National Parks

The National Park Service has been criticized on several fronts. The explosion of forest fires in 1996 that consumed more than 5.7 million acres by the end of the summer was widely cited as examples of mismanagement and confusion over how the parks should be run. The fires in 1996 were a result of decades of fire-suppression efforts and timber-harvesting policy: dead and dying trees accumulated in forests along with a hot, dry summer. The timber industry has urged the Forest Service to increase logging as a way to reduce the risks of fires; environmentalists counter with fears that this will be an excuse to go after old-growth trees. Most foresters agree that some fires are necessary for the overall health of the forests, but the relentless push of construction into forest areas makes it politically impossible to let fires burn.[42]

One of the most difficult issues has been how to define the power of the National Park Service and other federal land management agencies to abate adverse effects on protected lands from external sources such as factories that emit visibility-reducing air pollution or logging and mining activities that pollute rivers. Agencies have no power over activities on adjacent private lands, and Congress has proposed to give, but never given, agencies any legal means of addressing these problems. The great diversity of parks makes a single legislative solution improbable. But Congress, agencies, and the courts have tried to respond to specific threats to parks. The Park Service is authorized to "acquire interests in land from, and to enter into contracts and cooperative efforts with, the owners of land on the periphery of the park and on the watershed tributary to streams within the park."[43] Courts have ordered the Park Service to take reasonable steps to provide as much protection as reasonably possible to protect parks from external threats.[44]

The biggest challenge to the parks is their popularity. Recreation places greater demand on public lands than any other use. The BLM, Forest Service, and National Park Service all have in their mandates providing opportunities for recreation and enjoyment of the lands under their jurisdiction. A number of challenges face the agencies. Different kinds of recreational uses conflict: motorized vehicles intrude on those who seek quiet and solitude, hunters and hikers do not easily mix, and commercial development clashes with preservation of lands in primitive conditions. Concessionaires seek lucrative opportunities for development on public lands, and manufacturers of recreational equipment promote open access to public lands, while others seek to limit access to public lands in order to preserve them for future generations. Public land management agencies continually face choices about what kind of recreation development should be permitted on public lands and how protection should be balanced with access. They face increasingly difficult choices as they move to limit motor vehicle traffic, flights over parks, river trips, backpacking permits, and visits to areas threatened by their popularity.[45] The explosion in the popularity of off-road vehicles is particularly challenging to federal agencies. The vehicles can create severe environmental damage and interfere with more benign recreational pursuits and with ranching on public lands. Regulation and monitoring challenges swamp agency resources, where a handful of officials may be responsible for millions of acres. The lack of regulation in the past has created expectations among ORV users of unrestricted access to public lands. Agency regulations of ORVs have been ad hoc, sporadic, and frequently challenged in court. The process of identifying areas opened or closed to ORVs is time-consuming and burdensome to agencies. A 1972 executive order required agencies to zone federal lands for ORV traffic, and a 1977 order required agencies to ban ORVs where the agency believes they are causing or will result in "considerable adverse effects."[46]

The National Park Service has an impossible mandate, to preserve parklands and accommodate growing numbers of visitors. The number of visitors to parks has increased by 75 million over the past twenty years, but the number of park rangers has remained constant. The annual $2 billion budget has resulted in a backlog of $6 billion in maintenance projects and repairs. The Park Service spends 92 percent of its budget on visitor services, while spending only 7 percent on protecting natural resources and 1 percent on research. Some have called on the Park Service to spend more money and effort to preserve public lands, while others argue that the parks should accommodate more visitors and increase construction and development within the parks. Entrance fees go directly to the federal treasury rather than remain with the Park Service, but those fees represent only about $100 million of the $900 million spent on visitor services. Increased user fees would help ensure that more of the costs of park visits are paid by visitors. Another important source of income for parks could come from increasing the fees paid by park concessionaires. One study found that in 1992, concessionaires paid only 2.6 percent of their gross income as franchise fees, and some companies have contracts requiring they pay less than 1 percent.[47]

National parks are threatened by their popularity and plagued by traffic, pollution, vandalism and crime, and congestion. The introduction of nonnative species threatens native species, including threatened and endangered ones. Logging, mining, grazing, pollution from power plants, diversion of water, and urban development also threaten parks. Air pollution threatens vistas in most national parks most of the time. Other changes that will be part of policy changes to protect national parks include integrating management plans for parks with surrounding federal lands, expanding parks to include surrounding areas that affect park conditions, placing more development outside parks, raising franchise fees for concessionaires, funding the backlog of maintenance needs, raising fees to generate more funds for the parks, restricting traffic and visits in congested areas, increasing the number of park rangers, and increasing research on preserving park biodiversity.[48]

An August 1995 report of the U.S. General Accounting Office focused on twelve of the nation's most popular parks and found them locked in a cycle of increased visits and decaying infrastructure.[49] Critics of expanding the park system question whether growth is warranted when many existing parks are in need of infrastructure improvement and more maintenance and are suffering from personnel shortages. The National Parks and Conservation Association estimates that the parks are already suffering from a $4 billion backlog in maintenance needs. Each summer there are widely publicized accounts of the problems of park overcrowding and needed repairs and upkeep. Parks such as Padre Island in Texas cannot afford to hire lifeguards to patrol beaches. Some thirty-two of the thirty-six buildings at Ellis Island, New York, are in need of repair. Temporary concrete barriers have been erected in Glacier National Park where the road's stone restraining wall has crumbled. Campgrounds, trails, roads, sewer lines, and other park facilities are swamped with growing numbers of users.[50] The Grand Canyon, Zion, and Yosemite National Parks have all developed plans to eliminate automobiles from the most crowded areas of the parks, replacing them with mass transportation systems. The Grand Canyon's general management plan concluded that "the most pressing issue in the park today is the impact created by the annual crush of nearly five million visitors and their private cars on the few developed areas along the canyon rims."[51]

Congress has largely resisted demands to include sites as national parks that do not have sufficient national value to merit such a designation. But a number of groups has identified some parks that should be given other designations. Members of Congress introduced in 1995 the National Park System Reform Act, designed to establish new criteria for the designation of parks and require the Park Service to reassess the existing system. But the proposal was widely attacked by those who feared a major cutback in protection of the nation's priceless national heritage.[52] Members of Congress proposed legislation to change the criteria used by Congress in creating national parks and in reforming the concessions policy, but mistrust of the Republicans' motives and commitment to the parks effectively blocked any real consideration of the proposals.[53] These bills are likely to be reintroduced in the subsequent Congresses.

Wilderness

Preservation of wilderness areas poses difficult choices between pursuit of immediate economic needs and more abstract preservationist impulses. Calls for preservation have largely gone unheeded in the face of the persistent pressure to create wealth and opportunity for the burgeoning population. Writers like Wallace Stegner have warned us that "something will have gone out of us as a people if we ever let the remaining wilderness be destroyed." But these calls have been often dismissed as the rantings of romantics, unaware of the desirability and inevitability of growth, wealth, and human progress. Proponents of wilderness argue that land is itself of value apart from whatever minerals or other resources can be extracted from it. Thoreau wrote that "in wildness is the preservation of the world." Wilderness provides educational and research opportunities to study natural phenomena that are relatively unaffected by human activity. Wilderness experiences provide a variety of remedies to those who seek to escape the pressures and stresses of contemporary life. Wilderness offers profound opportunities for spiritual renewal. Religious traditions are replete with stories of religious figures finding communion with their god in wilderness areas.

Wilderness means different things to different people. For some, it is a harsh, inhospitable environment to be subdued. For others, it is a source of wealth. For some, it is an opportunity for personal introspection and spiritual renewal. For others, it represents a unique opportunity to preserve areas unaffected by human society. Wilderness offers a unique kind of freedom. Wilderness was once feared as inhospitable and threatening to humans. It is now increasingly seen as essential to their survival. Wilderness has helped shape our national identity. It provides a unique way to experience freedom in an otherwise crowded world.

How much wilderness lands should be set aside? One approach is to ensure that at least some of each of the distinct ecosystems are protected. In order to effectively protect lands for biodiversity, the size of some wilderness areas will need to increase. Some have suggested a goal of protecting 10 percent of the world's land in order to protect ecosystems and promote biodiversity. About 6 percent of the land is currently preserved in parks, reserves, and sanctuaries. Some countries have achieved or exceeded the goal of protecting at least 10 percent of their lands. Protected lands require buffer and transition zones to help insulate the lands from external human development.[54]

One of the challenges in designating wilderness areas is the impact on existing water rights. Water rights are typically determined in state courts. Courts have usually held that the creation of a new land designation on federal lands should include sufficient water rights to accomplish the purpose of the designation. Instream use—amount of water needed to nourish the land, without diverting any water—is usually provided for. The problem occurs when a wilderness designation requires additional water. This is more likely to occur on BLM lands than on Forest Service lands that include the headwaters or the beginning of streams and rivers. Requiring a "natural" flow of water to protect wilderness areas is difficult to define and may clash with upstream water users.[55]

About 4 percent of U.S. lands are protected as wilderness; 1.8 percent of the lands in lower forty-eight states is protected. Our present system has wilderness lands in about 80 of our recognized 230 ecosystems. About 100 million acres of wilderness lands remain in the United States. Much of the remaining U.S. wilderness is currently being developed, some rapidly due to perceived threats from wilderness advocates. Many national parks contain substantial wilderness. How much wilderness is required to preserve the level of biodiversity that we currently have? This shift from a state or even a national perspective to a global one is critical. From a global biosphere perspective, we begin with the wilderness lands and habitats that are available and ask how much we should preserve. There is not likely to be any clear, unambiguous answer, but we may have some idea of the magnitude of the landscape required to preserve the existing biodiversity and the biosphere as a whole. Part of the answer rests in what percentage of the photosynthetic product of the world we can safely consume for direct human needs. Part of the answer depends on the carrying capacity of specific ecosystems as well as the biosphere as a whole. Scientists do not appear to know what percentage of the world's remaining old-growth forests should be preserved, in order to ensure an adequate carbon sink, watersheds, and other ecological functions.

How should we proceed in the face of such uncertainty? A cautious, conservative approach is compelling for several reasons. It is conservative and most protective of the survivability of humans and other forms of life dependent on their decisions. It is most sensitive to the rights and interests of future generations who have no direct representation in political decision making. It is reversible: if scientific research tells us we have preserved too much wilderness, we can always develop it later. Pursuing the precautionary principle imposes certain opportunity costs. Timber jobs, corporate profits, and government revenues may fall, although some of that may be offset through value-added industries. These economic losses may also be countered by increased opportunities for recreational uses of lands. As wildlands diminish globally, those that remain will eventually become more valuable.

Protection of public lands is ultimately a public goods question. In this particular case, it may be in the best interests of the global community to have the United States preserve all of its remaining roadless, undeveloped forests, just as it may be in our collective interest to preserve tropical rain forests. The distributional issues are crucial here as in other areas of environmental regulation: the benefits will be dispersed widely—even globally—while, the costs, at least the short-term and transitional ones, will be borne narrowly. One option is to provide transitional assistance to workers and managers who lose their jobs because of preservationist policies and need retraining, relocation, or other aid. Wealthy countries like the United States can redistribute resources to provide that transitional assistance, and given the disproportionate impact their residents have on the global biosphere because of their high levels of consumption, they would be morally obligated to do so. Wealthy countries would also be obligated to provide the resources for the transitional assistance in the less-developed countries, for the same reasons.

NOTES

1. Energy and Environment Study Institute, "Public Lands," *1996 Briefing Book on Environmental and Energy Legislation* (Washington, DC: EESI, 1996): 66–70, at 66.

2. U.S. Department of the Interior, National Park Service, "Parks, etc." (n.d.).

3. Ibid.

4. George Cameron Coggins, Charles F. Wilkinson, and John D. Leshy, *Federal Public Land and Resource Law* (Westbury, NY: Foundation Press, 1993): 890–91.

5. U.S.C. 4601.

6. U.S.C. 1a–7(b).

7. U.S.C. 431–33.

8. U.S.C. 470aa–11.

9. 16 U.S.C. 461–70t, at 461.

10. 16 U.S.C. 470–470w–6.

11. The California Desert Protection Act, P.L. 103–433.

12. John H. Cushman Jr., "Senate Approves Parks Bill after Deal on Alaskan Forest," *New York Times* (October 3, 1996): A1.

13. 78 Stat. 890, Sec. 2(a).

14. 78 Stat. 890, Sec. 2(c).

15. 78 Stat. 890, Sec. 4(c).

16. 78 Stat. 890, Sec. 4(d)(3).

17. 78 Stat. 890, Sec. 4(d)(5).

18. 16 U.S.C. 1133(c-d).

19. 78 Stat. 890, Sec. 3(d)(1).

20. Energy and Environmental Study Institute, "Wilderness," *1996 Briefing Book on Environmental and Energy Legislation* (Washington, DC: EESI, 1996): 93.

21. Ibid.: 93–94.

22. 16 U.S.C. 1271 at 1272(b)(1–3).

23. Coggins, Wilkinson, and Leshy, *Federal Public Land and Resource Law*: 99–100.

24. G. Tyler Miller Jr., *Living in the Environment* (Belmont, CA: Wadsworth, 1996): 631–32.

25. Congressional Quarterly, *Congressional Quarterly Almanac* (Washington, DC: CQ Press, 1980): 575–76; P.L. 96–487.

26. P.L. 98–844.

27. Scott Matheson and James Edwin Kee, *Out of Balance* (Salt Lake City, UT: Peregrine Smith Books, 1986): 138–39.

28. Quoted in Scott Groene, "Watching over Wilderness: Now What?" *Southern Utah Wilderness Alliance Newsletter* (Fall 1996): 3–6, at 4.

29. Utah Wilderness Coalition, *Wilderness at the Edge* (Salt Lake City, UT: Utah Wilderness Coalition, 1990): 34.

30. Lee Davidson, "BLM Wilds Battle Officially Begins," *Deseret News* (March 21, 1991): B10.

31. H.B. 61, 1990 General Session; H.R.C. 13, 199 General Session.

32. 78 Stat. 890, 891.

33. Jerry Spangler, "Escalante Is 1 of 10 Towns in West Facing Extinction," *Deseret News* (October 18, 1990): B1.

34. Joseph Bauman, "BLM Plan for Utah Holds No Surprises," *Deseret News* (December 11, 1990): A15.

35. 102d Congress, H.R. 1500.

36. 102d Congress, H.R. 1508.

37. Joseph M. Bauman, "New Plan Conjures Up Old Ghosts," *Deseret News* (January 31, 1992): A9; Joseph Bauman, "Controversy Heats Up over Kane Coal Deposits," *Deseret News* (August 1, 1991): B1.

38. Lee Davidson, "Owens Proposes Creating National Park in Escalante," *Deseret News* (August 3, 1991): A1.

39. 104th Congress, H.R. 1500 (Hinchey calculated the time at which he introduced the bill in order to keep the same number).

40. Energy and Environmental Study Institute, "Wilderness": 94–95.

41. Alison Mitchell, "President Designates a Monument across Utah," *New York Times*, September 17, 1996: A15; "A New and Needed Monument," *New York Times*, September 18, 1996: A22.

42. Tom Kenworthy, "Burn Now or Burn Later," *Washington Post National Weekly Edition* (September 9–15, 1996): 31.

43. 16 U.S.C. 79a et seq., at 79c(e).

44. Coggins, Wilkinson, and Leshy, *Federal Public Land and Resource Law*: 975–91.

45. Ibid.: 889–90.

46. Ibid.: 932–39.

47. Miller, *Living in the Environment*: 628–29.

48. Ibid.: 629.

49. The report is summarized in Allan Freedman, "Long-Term Solutions Elusive for Stressed Park System," *Congressional Quarterly Weekly Report* (August 24, 1996): 2386–89.

51. Ibid.: 2386–87.

52. Tom Kenworthy, "Shhhhh! Park Ahead," *Washington Post National Weekly Edition* (August 19–25, 1996): 31.

52. Robin W. Winks, "Debating Significance," *National Parks* 69, no. 34 (March–April 1995): 24–25.

53. The National Park System Reform Act, 104th Congress, H.R. 260, reported out of the House Resources Committee in May 1995; National Parks concessions, H.R. 2028, defeated in a House vote in 1995.

54. Miller, *Living in the Environment*: 632.

55. Energy and Environmental Study Institute, "Wilderness": 94.

10

Thinking about Public Lands
and Natural Resources

Public lands and natural resource policy in the United States is permeated by paradoxes. One of the most interesting paradoxes is that government officials, policy analysts, journalists, and others argue that environmental quality has improved dramatically in the United States and that environmental protection is one of the great success stories in American government. Recent reports find that the nation's air and water is cleaner, that national programs are helping implement new international agreements to reduce global environmental threats, threats to children's health posed by lead in the environment have diminished, farmers are reducing soil erosion and pesticide runoff into streams, and that industries are reducing their release of toxic pollutants.[1] On the other hand, criticism of environmental and natural resource policy has been increasingly common in recent years as members of Congress, courts, conservation groups, industry trade associations, scholars, grassroots groups, environmental justice advocates, and others attack the underlying assumptions, basic provisions, and implementation of public lands and natural resource laws. Some progress has been made and some of the criticisms are compelling.

As the chapters above have argued, public land and natural resource policy must ultimately be assessed in terms of its contribution to ecological sustainability. Policies can be explained in terms of political incentives, compared in terms of their cost-effectiveness, and evaluated in terms of their interaction with expectations of personal liberty and private property. But if they do not accomplish the ecological goals at which they are aimed, they must be judged a failure. Policies are a moving target. They are constantly being "reformed," adjusted, and reformulated. Nevertheless, an overall assessment is possible. From an ecological perspective, current public land and natural resource policy is not sustainable.

The 1993 "Warning to Humanity" by some 1,670 scientists from 71 countries, including the majority of the living Nobel Prize winners, cautioned that human beings and the natural world "are on a collision course." Current practices "cannot be continued without the risk that vital global systems will be damaged beyond repair." We have little time to respond: "no more than one or a few decades remain before the chance to avert the threats we now confront will be lost and the prospects for humanity immeasurably diminished." The Warning to Humanity focused on five inextricably linked changes that must simultaneously occur: (1) bring environmentally damaging activities under control, such as moving away from fossil fuels and halting deforestation and loss of farm lands and critical habitats; (2) shift to more efficient use of water, energy, and other resources; (3) stabilize population growth; (4) reduce and eventually eliminate poverty; and (5) ensure sexual equality. Such changes required a "new ethic," a "new attitude towards discharging our responsibility for caring for ourselves and for the earth."[2]

The interconnectedness of elements of the biosphere requires that some areas be protected because of their contribution to overall global ecological health. Preservation of airsheds and watersheds is critical, for example, because human life is directly and immediately dependent on clean air and water for survival. The depletion of underground water sources is a major immediate threat in some areas and a long-term threat in other regions. These sources are, in human lifetime terms, a nonrenewable resource if withdrawal exceeds recharge rates. Similarly, topsoil is a critical element of the biosphere, but large quantities are lost each year through erosion. New topsoil can in some areas take as long as one to ten thousand years per inch of thickness to be produced. Other elements of the biosphere are also critical, particularly in the long-term, although ecological scientists have only a partial understanding of the biosphere.

Preservation of biodiversity is essential. It is possible that some species could be eliminated without posing adverse effects on the biosphere as a whole. Species have become extinct throughout history, but what is different now is the rate of extinction. It is not clear what the ecological consequences of such rapid changes will be, since they are unprecedented in human history. Biodiversity includes genetic diversity, the genetic resources within a species; diversity across species; and ecological diversity, the variability among biological communities that make up ecosystems and eventually, the ecosphere. We are dependent on this biodiversity for our survival and it is the raw material in which we will fashion our adaptation to environmental changes. The healthier and more diverse the biodiversity, the greater the opportunities for successful adaptation.[3] If we destroy the diverse organisms that have lived together in ecological communities for hundreds of thousands of years, we will lose the models from which we can learn about sustainability and preserving the natural systems on which we are dependent.[4]

Forests are also critical elements of a healthy biosphere, because of their role in purifying water, stabilizing climate, and providing habitat. They are renewable resources if carefully managed and cutting occurs at sustainable rates. But all forests are not created equal. Old-growth forests are ecologically much more important than tree farms. Some mistakenly view forests as a renewable resource, but that is only true, in human life terms, for forests as tree farms, where timber production is the most valuable aspect of forests. But the biodiversity represented by old-growth forests takes centuries or longer to develop and once lost, it is irreplaceable.[5] Only small pockets remain and one large area in the Pacific Northwest and Alaska. These forests have been described as "unique ecosystems that developed under climatic and disturbance regimes that may never be duplicated." Their loss will result in the extinction of some species.[6]

Elements of an ecosystem cannot be degraded without running the risk of threatening other ecosystems. The organisms found in the biosphere are genetically, physiologically, and behaviorally adapted to the ecosystems in which they live. Every species has a role to play in the ecological niche it inhabits. The size, growth rate, distribution, and health of species is a function of how it interacts with other species and its environment. Species that survive have developed genetically the characteristics that permit them to adapt and survive within their environment—the principle of natural selection. Species are continually evolving or becoming extinct. Biodiversity results from this evolution within the genetic endowment of species. All forms of life and the environment in which they live—the atmosphere, water, and earth—are continually evolving in response to natural and human-caused changes. Many ecologists believe that there are limits to how much change these systems can tolerate before they become more hostile to the perpetuation of human life. Human existence is inextricably dependent on the health of the ecosphere. Human activity should be shaped in ways that minimize the damage and interruption to natural systems and processes. The first law of human ecology is that everything is ultimately connected to everything else: human actions have consequences that are often difficult to detect, predict, or understand. The key task is to understand which interconnections and relationships are most important for sustaining human life. We only have limited information about that critical question.

We have a fixed natural resource capital base that must be sustained in order for life to continue. Earth capital includes the planet's air, water, soil, forests, wildlife, biodiversity and gene pool, and minerals, and the natural processes of air and water purification, waste removal and detoxification, climate control, recycling of materials, and natural pest and disease control. It includes nonrenewable resources such as fossil fuels and minerals, renewable resources such as wind and solar energy, and potentially renewable resources such as forests, grasslands, soil, wildlife, and water. Earth capital must be maintained by humans so that future generations will have the same life prospects; if Earth capital is diminished, then the prospects for other species and future human beings is jeopardized. This capital is threatened by resource consumption, population growth, and pollution. Exponential growth places tremendous stress on resources; what appears to be initially very modest levels of consumption and resource damage can quickly grow out of control under the relentless pressure of consumption and waste production that doubles in an increasingly short period of time.[7]

The ecological idea of sustainability is built on the idea of carrying capacity. The carrying capacity of an ecosystem is the limit of resource consumption and pollution production that it can maintain without undergoing a significant transformation. If the carrying capacity is exceeded, then life cannot continue unless it adapts to a new level of consumption or receives external resources. Carrying capacity is affected by three main factors: the size of the human population, the per capita consumption of resources, and the pollution and environmental degradation resulting from consumption of each unit of resources. The task of residents is to find what level of resource consumption and pollution production is sustainable. Again, that may not be obvious until it is too late. But there are some intermediate indicators, such as the build up of pollution and an increase in the resultant harms or a decline in a resource as it is depleted faster than it is replenished.

Sustainability simply means the ability to survive for some period of time. It is a socially determined goal that rests on the idea that it would be good for human society to continue indefinitely into the future and that the interests of future generations must be taken into account in determining how current residents live their lives. There is a broad consensus in the world that sustainability is a moral imperative. But it raises a whole set of issues that must be addressed in developing the concept as a guide to environmental policy making. One problem is that it is often difficult to know whether a society is sustainable until it is too late, until after it begins to decline. It is often exceedingly difficult to estimate rates of sustainable yield—the level of use of renewable resources that matches their replenishment rates. Sustainability also requires an understanding of how the resources and opportunities distributed across current and future generations should be compared: what constitutes an equal or fair distribution of resources and opportunities?

Ecosystems are constantly changing and population growth is likely to continue, so there is no way that Earth capital can be preserved in its current state for future earthdwellers. Is there some measure of per capita resource availability that should be guaranteed into the future? What does it mean to seek to guarantee the same level of opportunity for future generations that current ones enjoy? Given the uncertainly about the level of resource consumption and pollution production that is actually sustainable, many scientists support the precautionary principle, that we minimize risks to unsustainability, err on the side of caution, and not assume that technological solutions to our problems are inevitable. Skeptics of the precautionary principle argue that recent trends are more encouraging than discouraging, that faith in technological solutions is not misplaced but should be encouraged: increased population growth will produce new generations of problem solvers, shortages of some goods will stimulate higher prices and subsequently the development of alternatives, and consumption of resources will generate new wealth that can be used by future generations to pursue their own opportunities.[8]

Some optimists believe that "just about every important measure of human welfare shows improvement over the decades and centuries"—life expectancy, price of raw materials, price of food, cleanliness of the environment, population growth, extinction of species, and the quantity of farmland.[9] Some economists argue that we will never run out resources—the earth's air, water, and crust will serve earthdwellers for millions of years to come. The problem is not the existence of these resources, "but whether we are willing to pay the price to extract and use those resources." However, some resources will become increasingly scarce in some localities, and rises in extraction costs will cause consumption of some resources to decline. The failure of markets to incorporate environmental costs, such as pollution, climate modification, and loss of genetic diversity produces "falsely optimistic signals and the market makes choices that put society inefficiently at risk."[10]

The optimists may be right in claiming that human ingenuity can respond to these problems and reverse these troubling trends. While the trends in environmental damage, resource loss, and food production are all negative, they may be reversible. Such changes, however, pose a tremendous challenge to our ingenuity, our governments, and our collective and individual wills. "We may be smart enough to devise environmentally friendly solutions to scarcity," one scholar has written, but we must emphasize "early detection and prevention of scarcity, not adaptation to it." But if we are not as smart and as proactive as optimists claim we are, "we will have burned our bridges: the soils, waters, and forests will be irreversibly damaged, and our societies, especially the poorest ones, will be so riven with discord that even heroic efforts at social renovation will fail."[11] Conservation of lands—setting aside areas for protection or nondevelopment is not enough; human activity is pervasive, and there are only very limited opportunities for establishing wilderness, refuge, and other protected areas. Human's are an integral part of the earth's ecology, and the primary challenge is to find ways of meeting human needs and protecting natural resources.[12]

The case for a conservative, cautious approach to public lands and natural resources is compelling. In the face of uncertainty, we ought to minimize damage to ecological systems that we do not understand well but nevertheless rely on for survival. The incremental reforms are clear. As argued in earlier chapters, the most important reforms are to eliminate subsidies given to encourage resource development; use taxes and other policies to ensure that prices reflect the true costs of production; create economic and other incentives for conservation of water, energy, and other resources; and protect lands, species, and habitats from human encroachment. But all these may not be enough. Just as important as making immediate, incremental reforms, is to engage in a fundamental rethinking of the ideas and assumptions that underlie our current policies and our prevalent economic and social practices.

The stories that Americans have told for two centuries about the West, about its public lands and natural resources, have shaped and formed public policy. The stories told for two centuries about the untamed wilderness, waiting for men to impose their will on it, about untold riches waiting to be harvested, about raw beauty and natural power waiting to be exploited, have all shaped our attitudes and our policies concerning public lands. Susan Griffin, in *A Chorus of Stones*, illustrates the centrality to our lives of the stories we tell:

The telling and the hearing of a story is not a simple act. The one who tells must reach down into deep layers of the self, reviving old feelings, reviewing the past. Whatever is retrieved is reworked into a new form, one that narrates events and gives the listener a path through these events that leads to some fragment of wisdom. The one who hears takes the story in, even to a place not visible or conscious to the mind, yet there. In this inner place a story from another life suffers a subtle change. As it enters the memory of the listener it is augmented by reflection, by other memories, and even the body hearing and responding in the moment of the telling. By such transmissions, consciousness is woven.[13]

The dominant narrative shaping the West was manifest destiny, the obligation Americans had to fulfill God's will that they push their country westward (and other directions as well). Moving westward to propagate the American dream was a religious and political duty. Spoke one senator in the 1840s:

We were a feeble band of pilgrims on Plymouth rock, and a small body of cavaliers on the southern sands. From this small beginning, and in its short time, we have gone on, step by step, multiplying and advancing towards the Pacific, till the aborigines of the country had disappeared before us, like the mists of morning before the sun. . . . Was not the hand of destiny seen in that? He who did not see it must be an infidel, or stone-blind. To the Pacific ocean it is our destiny to go. The hand of Providence pointed us onward. . . . Where shall we find room for all our people, unless we have Oregon? What shall we do with all those little white-headed boys and girls—God bless them!—that cover the Mississippi Valley, as the flowers cover the western prairies?[14]

The Wild West was dominated by miners who told of abundant veins of gold waiting to be tapped and described in vivid terms the fortunes to be won. Drinking, gambling, and brawling were essential elements of the prospectors' lore. Cowboy roundups in the late nineteenth century were a cardinal American experience, etched deeply in the psyche of the West, the long drive through open lands a symbol of the free life. Loggers turned virgin forests into endless trains of thick planks that poured into American cities. Those who settled the vast western lands were models of rugged individualists, dependent only on their mettle and hard work and able to carve a life out of the vast expanses.[15]

Frederick Jackson Turner's 1893 address, "The Significance of the Frontier in American History," gave eloquent voice to that story. Settling the American frontier was the great American enterprise, promoting the virtue and self-reliance of its people and encouraging inventiveness and democracy. By 1893, however, Turner argued, the frontier was gone. One hundred years later, these stories about the West no longer make sense. They are no longer sustainable, as urban sprawl, air pollution, contaminated water, hazardous and nuclear waste, loss of biodiversity, destruction of wildlands, and other consequences of population growth and consumption have come to characterize the West. New stories need to be told that illustrate how the West can cope with growth and preserve the public lands and natural resources that play such a critical role in its ecological sustainability. New ways of thinking about timber, grazing, mining, and energy policies and preservation of wildlands and biodiversity are needed. The previous chapters have described in some detail the ecological imperatives that ought to guide policy making. But what are the underlying values and commitments, the stories, that might guide policy making?

There are other stories about the West and its endless lands. The first residents of these lands told stories that have been largely lost by white America but are increasingly being retold. Native American ideas provide us with an alternative set of stories about public lands, an alternative conceptual framework in which we see the world. For 500 years the Western world has been guided by ideas of growth and progress that have come to represent a threat to our survival. We have come to realize that we can destroy the life-giving qualities of the earth through our incompetence, through our unwillingness or inability to understand nature and respect the way it functions. In the face of possible environmental devastation and even ecosystem collapse, where the tapestry of life may unravel across the globe, we are beginning to recognize the "ineffable and subtle intertwining of living organisms on the Earth," the interdependence of life.[16]

Indigenous peoples have profound knowledge of how ecosystems operate and what is required to sustain them. Examples are plentiful. Forests are protected by tribal peoples who believe certain trees are holy, who rely on forest groves for cultural rituals and protect forests as watersheds. Grasslands are protected through careful control of grazing. Intricate water systems have been developed that recharge groundwater and conserve scarce resources. Rituals protect fisheries from overfishing and prohibit waste.[17] Native peoples throughout the world generally share a strong commitment to their land, and many seek to live in harmony with it. Their relationship goes beyond subsistence living, to intimate spiritual interconnectedness.[18] Their lands are sacred, manifestations of the Great Spirit, and places of profound spiritual importance. Those lands are inextricably intertwined with their identity. They provide the core beliefs of a new paradigm for thinking about the earth and our relationship to it. The authors of *Canada's National Report* prepared for the United Nations Conference on Environment and Development recognized the importance of the wisdom of native peoples:

As people who have lived in harmony with nature and close to the land for centuries, aboriginal peoples of Canada have developed an immensely valuable information base and expertise which can be shared with the rest of Canadian society. As long-standing custodians of this traditional knowledge, they can provide detailed information on the workings of natural ecosystems, and can provide a perspective and information on how environmental systems function over time. There is much to be learned from aboriginal peoples, and they recognize their responsibility to make this knowledge known and accessible.[19]

However, we have done much over the past 500 years to eliminate the knowledge that we now find so compelling. The Spanish invasion of the New World set the tone for what was to follow. The quest for wealth permeated the European settlement of the Western Hemisphere. The relentless westward expansion in the United States and efforts to exterminate Native Americans in the eighteenth and nineteenth centuries were a continuation of the conquest that began in 1492, despite vain attempts at resistance.

The conquest of most of the peoples of North America proceeded almost unheeded for 300 years. The conquest of land went hand in hand. In 1798 Congress declared that the "utmost good faith shall always be observed towards the Indians; their lands and property shall never be taken from them without their consent; and, in their property, rights, and liberty, they shall never be invaded or disturbed, unless in just and lawful wars authorized by Congress." But in 1830 President Andrew Jackson signed legislation providing for the removal of the Cherokee, Creek, Choctaw, Chickasaw, and Seminole tribes from their ancestral homelands in the Southeast. Except for a few small groups that escaped, members of these "Five Civilized Tribes" had all been moved to present-day Oklahoma—part of the Indian Territory—by 1839. Forced marches westward over the "Trail of Tears" left a fourth of the Cherokees—about 4,000—dead of disease, exposure, and starvation.[20]

By 1900, survivors of the Indian wars had been confined to reservations totaling only 4 percent of all the lands within the borders of the United States. Today, Indian reservations constitute only about 2 percent of the contiguous forty-eight states.

The European conquerors of the New World had little understanding of, or interest in, the way in which the natives of the Americas had succeeded and failed in learning to live in balance with their environment. Europeans feared the new land they encountered and sought to conquer it in their arrogance and ignorance. They saw nature as little more than a source of wealth and power. They had little interest in learning how natives tried to live in harmony with the land, how they balanced short-run demands for food with long-run maintenance of hunting grounds. What was lost in the discovery of the New World was a tremendous richness in Native American life. For the Spanish conquerors, "the only wealth they could imagine was what they took."[21] They discovered the material resources but failed to discover the real wealth of the New World, the wisdom, culture, languages, and biodiversity. They never really discovered the Arawak and Lucayo peoples of the Bahamas, the Apalachee, Creek, Chicsaw, Cherokee, Delaware, Susquehanna, Onondaga, Mahican, Huron, Ottawa, Chippewa, Crow, Shoshone; the Salish, Nez Perce, Coeur d'Alene, Yakima, Tillamook, Siuslaw, Coos, Yurok, Pomo, Maidu, Chumash; the Paiute, Havasupai, Papago, Pima, Chiricahua, Apache, Mescalero Apache, Tiwa, Tano, Tewa, Keres, Arapaho, Pawnee, Kansa, Osage, Shawnee, Catawba, Hitchiti, Timucua, Tarahumara—more than a thousand distinct cultures, languages, and ways of thinking, doing, and living, only a fraction of which has survived to today.[22]

The extreme geographical differences of the Americas gave rise to an astounding range of cultures that the Europeans mistakenly lumped under the term "Indian." They ranged from small family groups living at subsistence levels, to small cities of thousands of people in the North American prairie, to the grand civilizations of Mexico and Peru that developed architecture, astronomy, and mathematics to high arts. Various authorities estimate that when Columbus reached the New World, between 6 million and 60 million people, speaking some 550 languages, inhabited the Western Hemisphere. One to eight million, speaking half of these languages, lived north of today's Mexico.[23]

Learning from the indigenous peoples of America is a complex undertaking. Their environmental record is mixed, but illuminating. The Americas were not an idyllic paradise of humankind living in peace and harmony until their pastoral lives were interrupted by the invasion from the east. Torture, warfare, and violence characterized the life of the Mayans and Aztecs of Central America, the natives of the Amazon Basin, and the warring tribes of the American plains. Like their conquerors, many indigenous peoples were quite willing to use power to impose their will on others, their reliance on torture and violence, their lack of respect for individual rights, their militarism and intolerance.[24] Europeans did bring to the New World traditions of religious tolerance, civil liberties, human dignity and rights, equality before the law, and democratic ideals and institutions that could have enriched native traditions of democratic governance and respect for others.

The native peoples of the Americas were likewise not always successful in living in harmony with nature. Ecological damage occurred, threatening some societies and leading to the extinction of others. One of the lessons of reading the thousands of years of history we have of the Western Hemisphere is the importance of living in harmony with the environment. Not all of the people of the Americas recognized this principle. One of the most graphic lessons to be learned from the Mayans, for example, may be the rapid collapse of a society resulting from ecological destruction, from deforestation and unsustainable agricultural practices. The Anasazi people lived on the Mesa Verde in southwest Colorado for some twelve centuries, before depletion of the soil, drought, deforestation, and other problems apparently forced them to abandoned their cliff dwellings at the end of the thirteenth century, leaving their villages intact, to be discovered by white settlers in the late 1800s. The plight of the Anasazi is largely a mystery to archaeologists and anthropologists. The residents left few clear signs of what caused their flight. But the best available evidence indicates that they overconsumed scarce resources and were unable to adapt to a changing environment. Failing to live in harmony with the land has meant the collapse of sophisticated civilizations in the past.[25]

Nevertheless, several ideas characterize the beliefs of Native Americans concerning the environment that are relevant in considering how we might respond to our current predicament. Many believed that everything is connected to everything else, as is reflected in a widely quoted statement attributed, inaccurately, to Chief Seattle:

How can you buy or sell the sky? The land? The idea is strange to us. If we do not own the freshness of the air and the sparkle of the water, how can you buy them? Every part of this earth is sacred to my people. . . . This we know: the earth does not belong to man, man belongs to the earth. All things are connected like the blood that unites us all. Man did not weave the web of life, he is merely a strand in it. Whatever he does to the web, he does to himself.[27]

Many native peoples have a profound commitment to their land and live in harmony with it. Their relationship goes beyond subsistence to intimate spiritual interconnectedness. For Begadi, or Big Thunder, of the Wabanakis Nation, the "great spirit is our father, but the earth is our mother. She nourishes us; that which we put into the ground she returns to us and healing plants she gives us likewise. If we are wounded, we go to our mother and seek to lay the wounded part against her, to be healed."[27] Chief Luther Standing Bear spoke of his view of nature:

We did not think of the great open plains, the beautiful rolling hills, and winding streams with tangled growth as "wild." Only to the white man was nature a "wilderness" and only to him was the land "infested" with "wild" animals and "savage" people. To us it was tame. Earth was bountiful and we were surrounded with the blessings of the Great Mystery. Not until the hairy man from the east came and with brutal frenzy heaped injustices upon us and the families we loved was it "wild" for us. When the very animals of the forest began fleeing from his approach, then it was that the "Wild West" began.

We were lawless people, but we were on pretty good terms with the Great Spirit, creator and ruler of all. You whites assumed we were savages. You didn't understand our prayers. You didn't try to understand. When we sang our praises to the sun or moon or wind, you said we were worshiping idols. Without understanding, you condemned us as lost souls just because our form of worship was different from yours.

We saw the Great Spirit's work in almost everything: sun, moon, trees, wind, and mountains. Sometimes we approached him through these things. Was that so bad? I think we have a true belief in the supreme being, a stronger faith than that of most whites who have called us pagans. . . . Indians living close to nature and nature's ruler are not living in darkness.[28]

One way of thinking about the interconnectedness of the global environment is the idea of Gaia. Gaia is an ancient Greek goddess, the "earthmother who brought forth the world and the human race from the 'gaping void, Chaos.' " Feminists reclaimed her as a symbol for a new earth-based approach to spirituality and ecology. Gaia became the female member of the godhead, giving women equal status with men and a powerful symbol of life.[29] In 1977, British scientist James Lovelock borrowed the term in proposing a theory of the earth as a living organism. His book, *Gaia: A New Look at Life on Earth*, argued that all living matter on earth was part of a single, living, self-regulating entity whose characteristics are greater that simply the sum of its constituent parts.[30] Gaia meant that the earth, as a living organism, could and would make whatever changes and adjustments in its atmosphere were necessary to survive. Feminist spirituality and biological theory became powerfully linked in providing a new image to guide thinking about the environment. Scientific conferences, environmental meetings, music, art, and pop culture all extolled Gaia's virtues as a new way of thinking about, and understanding, the earth.

The idea of Gaia, however, seems to raise as many questions as it answers. Scientists have argued that if Gaia is a self-regulating system, it may correct human-caused problems by gradually eliminating their source. Feminists have raised questions about whether or not Gaia reinforces a deeply held view that men have in Western society that "Mom always comes along and cleans up after them."[31] For some, ecofeminism is a more attractive idea that makes strong connections between women and nature and argues that liberating women and nature are central to environmental preservation. One version, liberal ecofeminism, Carolyn Merchant writes, seeks to "alter human relations with nature from within existing structures of governance through the passage of new laws and regulations." Another version, cultural ecofeminism, "analyzes environmental problems from within its critique of patriarchy and offers alternatives that could liberate both women and nature." Socialist ecofeminism is rooted in an assessment of capitalist patriarchy, focusing on how the "patriarchal relations of reproduction reveal the domination of women by men, and how the capitalist relations of production reveal the domination of nature by men."[32]

Harmony between humans and nature is a powerful theme. Thomas Banyacya, a representative of Hopi Traditional Village Leaders, wrote in a letter to President Nixon in response to a decision by Peabody Coal Co., a subsidiary of the Kennecott Copper Corporation, to strip-mine coal in Hopi and Navajo lands:

The white man, through his insensitivity to the way of Nature, has desecrated the face of Mother Earth. The white man's advanced technological capacity has occurred as a result of his lack of regard for the spiritual path and for the way of all living things. The white man's desire for material possessions and power has blinded him to the pain he has caused Mother Earth by his quest for what he calls natural resources. And the path of the Great Spirit has become difficult to see by almost all men, even by many Indians who have chosen instead to follow the path of the white man. . . .

Today the sacred lands where the Hopi live are being desecrated by men who seek coal and water from our soil that they may create more power for the white man's cities. This must not be allowed to continue, for if it does, Mother Nature will react in such a way that almost all men will suffer the end of life as they now know it. The Great Spirit said not to allow this to happen even as it was prophesied to our ancestors. The Great Spirit said not to take from the Earth—not to destroy living things. The Great Spirit, Massau'u, said that man was to live in Harmony and maintain a good clean land for all children to come. All Hopi People and other Indian Brothers are standing on this religious principle and the Traditional Spiritual Unity Movement today is endeavoring to reawaken the spiritual nature in Indian people throughout this land.[33]

For First Peoples, observing nature, feeling nature, being part of nature were a powerful means of spiritual awakening, because in nature they found manifest the handiwork of God. In the wilderness, the modern, "civilized" world vanishes. For native peoples, wilderness lands are sacred, manifestations of the Great Spirit. As wilderness lands are protected, they maintain their spiritual power. They become "a place in which we know exactly who we are,"[34] providing a sense of where we belong. So has it been for others whose stories are recounted in the sacred writings of Jews, Christians, and other religious peoples. Their wanderings in the wilderness have been essential in pursuing spiritual growth and enlightenment. Wilderness lands can be similarly important to all of us. "Before the vast, wild, inexpressible, subtle beauty of the virgin wilderness," says one writer, "petty human concerns fall away. Faced with the absolute grandeur of nature in solitude, we cannot but stand in reverence before her."[35] Nature can provide an antidote to modern life. Wilderness areas are a "living manifestation of the divine" that can teach us gratitude and reverence toward God and his creations.[36] We can either bow down in reverence before nature or try to consume as much of it as we can in pursuing material wealth and power and listen to voices for commercial interests that argue we have an obligation to extract from nature every possible economic advantage.

Part of what is possible in the West is a sense of connection to the land. Many westerners do not see the land on which they live as purely instrumental. Land provides a sense of place, provides meaning to one's life, provides a sense of belonging and identity. This commitment and connectedness to land are values shared by those who make their living off the land as well as those who call for preservation and wilderness. Perhaps a recognition of the primal nature of land and human connectedness to it can prompt increased empathy and understanding between those whose views seem so conflicting. But perhaps it just demonstrates how high the stakes are and how difficult compromise is. If land were simply an instrumental value, then perhaps proposals to pay workers in extractive industries not to work, and thus preserve the land, may not be promising compromise positions. The value of working the land, being self-sufficient through work, and accepting a traditional role cannot be exchanged for money, even if it might be cheaper for the taxpayer to pay idle workers directly than to pay the subsidies that make extractive industries economically successful.

Aldo Leopold's articulation of a land ethic is helpful. He defines an ethic, in ecological terms, as a "limitation on freedom of action in the struggle for existence."[37] "All ethics," he argues, "rest upon a single premise: that the individual is a member of a community of interdependent parts. His instincts prompt him to compete for his place in the community, but his ethics prompt him also to co-operate (perhaps in order that there may be a place to compete for.) The land ethic simply enlarges the boundaries of the community, to include soils, waters, plants, and animals, or collectively: the land." He goes on: "In short, a land ethic changes the role of Homo sapiens from conqueror of the land-community to plain member and citizen of it. It implies respect for fellow-members, and also respect for the community as such."[38] "The problem, then, is how to bring about a striving for harmony with land among a people many of whom have forgotten there is any such thing as land, among whom education and culture have become almost synonymous with landlessness."[39] Leopold argued that a strong land ethic is required for preservation to occur. As we observe nature, become a part of it, not just live on the land but live by the land and depend on it, we come to treasure it. We also learn to live in community, to recognize our interdependence.

Wallace Stegner has also written with an optimistic voice:

The West . . . is the native home of hope. When it fully learns that cooperation, not rugged individualism, is the pattern that most characterizes and preserves it, then it will have achieved itself and outlined its origins. Then it has a chance to create a society to match its scenery.[40]

We need to protect wildlands, Stegner believed, for social reasons, not just environmental ones: "I want to speak for the wilderness idea as something that has helped form our character and that has certainly shaped our history as a people.

Some believe that we have developed the mechanical and technological power to dominate and control nature. That is a remarkably naive and dangerous idea. It is a sign of our moral laziness, our arrogance to assume that we can indulge ourselves now and then rely on some technological fix in the future.[42] The evidence of our inability to avoid the consequences of our carelessness is significant, from the devastation of natural disasters, to the victims in Utah communities of cancer and other health problems that are rooted in air pollution from local industries, the dumping of hazardous chemicals, and other forms of environmental degradation. It is increasingly clear that we, in our own ways, are just as dependent on nature as the early inhabitants of these lands. We can escape this environmental accounting in the short run; we can avoid the costs resulting from environmental degradation for a time. But sooner or later we run out of lands to despoil; sooner or later we run up against perhaps the chief immorality of pollution, that, so often, those who benefit from industrial and commercial activity are not the ones who bear the burdens of the health effects and risks from exposure to the pollution those activities produce.

The agenda for preserving the biosphere on which all life depends appears overwhelming. Perhaps it is too late to reverse course, and we are destined to eventually render the planet inhabitable for future generations. We can witness the wanton pursuit of wealth that promises to leave to our children a planet that is much less hospitable to them than it has been to us even as we act in small ways to become more careful stewards of the earth in the small part of it on which we reside.

NOTES

1. See, for example, Council on Environmental Quality, *Environmental Quality: 25th Anniversary Report* (Washington, DC: Council on Environmental Quality, n.d.).

2. "World Scientists' Warning to Humanity," distributed by the Union of Concerned Scientists (April 1993).

3. G. Tyler Miller, *Living in the Environment* (Belmont, CA: Wadsworth Publishing Co., 1996): 93–95.

4. Mary Clark, *Ariadne's Thread: The Search for New Modes of Thinking* (New York: St. Martin's Press, 1989): 120.

5. Paul R. Erlich and Anne H. Erlich, *Healing the Planet* (Reading, MA: Addison Wesley, 1991).

6. H. Michael Anderson, "Reforming National-Forest Policy," *Issues in Science and Technology* (Winter 1993–94): 40–47, at 41–42.

7. Miller, *Living in the Environment*, 5–7. See also Lester R. Brown, et al, *The State of the World 1997* (New York: W.W. Norton, 1997).

8. See Julian Simon, *The Ultimate Resource* (Princeton: Princeton University Press, 1981); Simon and Herman Kahn, *The Resourceful Earth* (Cambridge, MA: Basil Blackwell, 1984).

9. Julian Simon, "Pre-Debate Statement," in Norman Myers and Julian L. Simon, *Scarcity or Abundance? A Debate on the Environment* (New York: W.W. Norton, 1994): 5–22.

10. Tom Tietenberg, *Environmental and Natural Resource Economics* (New York: HarperCollins, 1992, 3d. ed.): 356–57.

11. Thomas F. Homer-Dixon, quoted in William K. Stevens, "Feeding a Booming Population Without Destroying the Planet," *New York Times* (April 5, 1994): B5.

12. Anne E. Platt, "It's About More Than Sea Cucumbers," *World Watch* (May/June 1995): 2.

13. Susan Griffin, *A Chorus of Stones* (New York: Anchor Books, 1992): 178.

14. Quoted in Lew Smith, *The American Dream* (Glenview, IL: Scott Foresman, 1977): 145.

15. Kirsten E. A. Borg, ed., *USA Perspectives on our History* (Evanston, IL: McDougal, Littell, 1975): 123–30.

16. Barry Lopez, *The Rediscovery of North America* (Lexington: University Press of Kentucky, 1990): 16.

17. Alan Thein Durning, "Supporting Indigenous Peoples," in Lester Brown et al., *State of the World 1993* (Washington, DC: Worldwatch Institute, 1993): 92.

18. Julian Berger, *The Gaia Atlas of First Peoples* (New York: Anchor, 1990): 15–17.

19. Government of Canada, *Canada's National Report, United Nations Conference on Environment and Development* (August 1991): 84.

20. Robert N. Clinton, Nell Jessup Newton, and Monroe E. Price, *American Indian Law* (Charlottesville, VA: Mitchie, 1991): 145.

21. Lopez, *The Rediscovery of North America*: 18.

22. Ibid.:19–21.

23. National Geographic Society map, "Indians of North America," 1979.

24. Arthur Schlesinger Jr., "Was America a Mistake?" *Atlantic* (September 1992): 22.

25. John Noble Wilford, "What Doomed the Maya? Maybe Warfare Run Amok," *New York Times* (November 19, 1991): B5 David Roberts, "The Decipherment of Ancient Maya," *The Atlantic Monthly* (September 1991):87–100.

26. Quoted in Al Gore, *Earth in the Balance* (Boston: Houghton Mifflin, 1991): 259.

27. McLuhan, *Touch the Earth*: 22.

28. Ibid.: 45.

29. See Charlene Spretnak, *Lost Goddesses of Early Greece: A Collection of Pre-Hellenic Mythology* (Ann Arbor, MI: Moon Books, 1992): 30–31; quoted in Carolyn Merchant, *Earthcare: Women and the Environment* (New York: Routledge, 1995): 3.

30. James Lovelock, *Gaia: A New Look at Life on Earth* (New York: Oxford University Press, 1979).

31. Quoted in Merchant, *Earthcare*: 5.

32. Ibid.: 5–6.

33. McLuhan, *Touch the Earth*: 170–71.

34. Lopez, *Rediscovery of North America*: 37.

35. Versluis, *Sacred Earth*: (Rochester, VT: Inner Traditions International, 1992): 9.

36. Ibid.: 10.

37. Aldo Leopold, *A Sand County Almanac* (New York: Ballantyne Books, 1949): 238.

38. Ibid.: 239–40.

39. Ibid.: 210.

40. Foreword and commentary to Tom Till, *Utah: Magnificent Wilderness* (Englewood, CO: Westcliffe, 1989): 110.

41. Ibid.: 100.

42. Gore, *Earth in the Balance*: 240.

Index

About the Author

GARY C. BRYNER is Director of the Public Policy Program and Professor of Political Science at Brigham Young University.

ISBN 0-313-29688-X

EAN

90000>

HARDCOVER BAR CODE